First to the Party

AMERICAN GOVERNANCE: POLITICS, POLICY, AND PUBLIC LAW

Series Editors: Richard Valelly, Pamela Brandwein, Marie Gottschalk, Christopher Howard

A complete list of books in the series is available from the publisher.

FIRST TO THE PARTY

The Group Origins of Party Transformation

Christopher Baylor

PENN

UNIVERSITY OF PENNSYLVANIA PRESS

PHILADELPHIA

Published by
University of Pennsylvania Press
Philadelphia, Pennsylvania 19104-4112
www.upenn.edu/pennpress

Printed in the United States of America on acid-free paper
10 9 8 7 6 5 4 3 2 1

Library of Congress Cataloging-in-Publication Data

Names: Baylor, Christopher, author.
Title: First to the party: the group origins of party transformation /
    Christopher Baylor.
Other titles: American governance.
Description: 1st edition. | Philadelphia : University of Pennsylvania Press,
    [2017] | Series: American governance : politics, policy, and public law |
    Includes bibliographical references and index.
Identifiers: LCCN 2017012492 | ISBN 9780812249637 (hardcover: alk.
    paper)
Subjects: LCSH: Political parties—United States—History—20th century. |
    Political parties—United States—History—21st century. | Political
    participation—United States—History—20th century. | Political
    participation—United States—History—21st century. | United
    States—Politics and government—20th century. | United States—Politics
    and government—21st century. | Democratic Party (U.S.)—Membership. |
    Republican Party (U.S.: 1854-)—Membership.
Classification: LCC JK2261 .B349 2017 | DDC 324.273—dc23
LC record available at https://lccn.loc.gov/2017012492

To my professors in American politics
and to those voters, past and present,
poorly represented by American political parties

CONTENTS

First to the Party

CHAPTER 1

Building Blocs: Groups and Contested Party Transformations

What do you do if you belong to a small, unpopular group that wants something from the government?

For many political scientists, the answer is obvious: join a political party. Parties are commonly understood as coalitions of groups that, by banding together, can win elections and thereby gain the power to enact the policies they prefer. If a new group—even a small and unpopular one—helps a coalition win an election, it will be rewarded with a share of the policy benefits.

But what if powerful groups in both major parties oppose the group's program? That was the situation faced by African Americans in the 1930s. The Republican Party, their nominal ally, had done little for them in decades. The Democratic Party, though sponsoring the New Deal, was not especially eager to spread its benefits to racial minorities. Its entrenched and powerful southern wing was adamantly opposed to government benefits or civil rights for African Americans. The Democratic Party of Franklin D. Roosevelt was little more promising as a coalition partner than was the Party of Lincoln.

Christian conservatives faced a similar problem in the late 1970s. They believed that abortions were legalized murder but were unable to get either party to take up their cause. The Democratic Party had become home to feminism and Republicans were the party of mainline Protestants, business people, and educated suburbanites, many of whom supported women's right to abortion. As a consequence, GOP officeholders viewed the "Christian Right" as an albatross that would sink the party.

But both African Americans and Christian Conservatives nonetheless found a way to make political parties the solution to their political grievances.

Civil rights organization leaders set aside longstanding grievances with white labor unions, became their allies in the internecine fights of the Democratic Party, and managed to wrest leadership from the party's southern wing. At the 1948 national party convention, delegates passed a civil rights plank that so infuriated southern opponents of civil rights that many of them bolted to form a third party. When Democrats won the presidency without them in that year's election, most Southerners returned to the fold, but their ability to block civil rights reform was much diminished. The party continued on its path to supporting civil rights legislation, culminating with the Civil Rights Act of 1964 and the Voting Rights Act of 1965.

As with the civil rights coalition, the first important step for anti-abortion Christians was to overcome fissiparous tendencies among potential allies. As late as the mid-1970s, the religious denominations that eventually came together as the Religious Right were numerous, independent, and more apt to feud with one another on theological matters than to make common political cause. The Catholic Church was historically opposed to abortion, but its voters were mainly in the prochoice Democratic Party. A handful of Catholic operatives sought to push GOP candidates to toward anti-abortion stances, but lacked connections to voters sharing their position. But by the early 1980s, anti-abortion groups had largely overcome their coordination problems. Focusing first on Republican nominations for president and moving on to state and Congressional nominations, they became regular players in the Republican Party by the 1990s. As one indication of their influence, all but one of the Republican presidential nominees from 1980 to 2016 began their careers prochoice but changed to pro-life as they began nomination campaigns.[1]

These two cases of party transformation illustrate a general process. It starts with individuals and groups unable to accomplish their goals working alone, gains traction with the formation of broader coalitions, and ends with new groups in the core membership of a party coalition. This book follows the path of party transformation from its disorganized beginnings to eventual success, where success is defined by a group's ability to reliably secure the nomination of presidential candidates committed to its goals.

No scholar can understand the dynamics of American politics without understanding the two cases of party transformation described in this book. The cases are paradigmatic examples of how political parties organize neglected political grievances into core voting issues. As important, the cases highlight the role of nonparty groups in using parties to advance their agendas.

To be sure, economic issues remain at the heart of the American party system, as they have since at least the New Deal. But social issues have changed party platforms, demographic bases, and electoral maps. This book explains why and how this happened.

Basic Concepts

More precise definitions are in order. *Political Parties* include officeholders, candidates for office, officeholder employees, and paid party employees (such as party chairs). In V. O. Key's terms, I will study parties as party in government and the party organization, but not the party in the electorate.[2] The groups who seek to influence government through political parties are considered separately from "parties as organizations" and "party in government" because they have different incentives. Following Karol, I define *groups* as "self-aware" collections "of individuals who share intense concerns about a particular policy area."[3] Organizations are groups with formal and legal arrangements. The civil rights movement, the Tea Party, and the National Association for the Advancement of Colored People (NAACP) are groups, but only the NAACP is an organization. Although some organizations are called "interest groups," their interests need not be material. For example, members of Christian conservative groups or the Anti-Saloon League gained little in the way of material benefits. They may take positions on one narrow issue or many major issues of their day.

Party transformation takes many forms, but this book is concerned with what issues a party stands for. Since presidential nominees are the most significant national representatives of the party, I measure transformation by the issue positions of successive presidential nominees. As E. E. Schattschneider wrote, "He who can make the nomination is the owner of the party."[4] Transformations need not be periodic or limited to extraordinary periods in our history, but parties must nominate presidential candidates committed to the new issue line-up for decades; they haven't really changed if they backslide one or two election cycles later.

Eric Schickler has recently shown that other actors in the civil rights transformation, including voters, state parties, and congressional votes, changed before control of presidential nominations changed.[5] But no group is fully integrated into a party until it has a secure role in the selection of party nominees for the country's top office. Using presidential nominations as the measure of when party transformation has occurred, as I do in this book, therefore gives a more valid estimate of when parties change has occurred.

Cultural conservatism refers to government support for traditional or religious moral values. In public opinion surveys, principal components analysis shows that issues like abortion rights, pornography, school prayer, and gay rights are highly correlated with each other and not economic issue positions.[6] On this basis, I treat them as a bundle of related "cultural issues." Cultural liberals either oppose government support for traditional or religious values or promote tolerance for less traditional values.

The Claims

Civil rights and cultural conservatism show how previously marginal groups made their way into a major party coalition and thereby transformed it against the wishes of many party politicians. I offer original, empirical evidence to evaluate how politically effective coalitions form and groups choose the allies they do, and whether party agendas parties are primarily responsive to organized groups or politicians.

The main alternative to group-centered change is the idea that politicians change what their parties stand for. Politicians are responsible for party transformation if they change what parties stand for in response to electoral opportunities or initiate new group alliances that do so. Transformations are not complete in this scenario until voters accept a transformed party's new agenda. In contrast, groups are responsible for party transformation if they persuade reluctant politicians to change or displace holdouts with new candidates committed to their goals. This book shows that group efforts are the most consistent—though not the only—influence on parties in the contested transformations it studies. Groups exercise this influence mainly because they play a disproportionate role in mobilizing voters and delegates during nominations, when most voters are inattentive.[7]

The book shows not just that groups change parties, but why groups make the changes they do. By doing so, it disaggregates parties into their true raw ingredients—the selection of group issue positions and allies. When a group sets out to change a party against other factions in the party, it needs to find allies committed to party change. Since one group is seldom powerful enough to change a party on its own, it needs to maintain good relations with other groups with their own agendas. Usually, this means adopting new issue positions or broadening its focus. Groups evaluate coalition allies and parties not just on common issue positions and ideologies, but the need to grow their membership, raise funds, and compete with other groups for prestige and influence. Once they form a coalition, they tend to support mutually acceptable candidates and platforms.

These points can be digested into three major claims:

1. The critical first step in party change is for groups to form a viable coalition committed to a common agenda they want the party to adopt.
2. Groups, not politicians, are the most important force for transforming parties when other party factions resist change.
3. Groups force parties to change primarily by gaining influence over nominations.

Therefore, party change reflects the groups composing parties and their role in nominations.

This book does not attempt to understand all party transformation—only contested party transformations. In such cases, some party factions oppose the new entrants, if not majority factions. In some transformations, there is little or no disagreement between existing and new party factions. Since both approve the change, there is no telling whether groups or politicians are more responsible. For example, federal attempts to address pollution constituted a new issue in the 1950s, but federal spending and business regulation did not alienate any major Democratic constituency at the time.[8] When transformations are contested, the relative influence of groups and parties come to light.

Claim 1: Party Change Starts with Coalitions of Groups

To help readers identify the relevance of my claims to contemporary debates, let me start by fleshing out the claims. A description and justification of the evidence I use will follow. This book is based on the idea that groups are, in the common phrase, the life of the parties—not only the building blocks of party coalitions, but their most important moving parts. By mobilizing followers and influencing nominating contests, groups pull politicians closer to them than to median voters.

Claim 1 delves deeper than other group-centered theories of parties. In their treatment of parties, Cohen, Karol, Noel, and Zaller admit they examine the activist origins of party change but not where "new activist agendas came from."[9] I argue that party change reflects the agendas groups construct with allies. Using historical evidence, we can trace the positions of parties back to the positions that groups introduce, emphasize, or drop to work in a coalition. Groups stitch together a new agenda with needed allies to defeat their opponents in a party, mostly independent of politicians.

The first step in contested party transformations is for groups to form a viable coalition committed to a common agenda. Nominations are competitive affairs in a large country with only two parties. Even large national organizations like the Congress of Industrial Organizations (CIO) and National Education Association (NEA) can succeed only if they can gain the help of allies. When deciding whom to ally with, groups weigh such factors as issue overlap, the approval of their own members and staff, and the ability to reach new audiences. In viable coalitions, groups broaden their original agenda to accommodate their allies. Whether they succeed in transforming parties depends largely on choosing carefully and making the proper accommodations.

Agreeing on a single nominee for office can be difficult in the best of times. When two or more groups in a party are fighting for the direction of the party, the need for allies is dire. Stalwart incumbents are generally well networked with important groups and party activists that avoid party disruptions. Transformative groups need to defeat not only stalwarts, but politicians hoping for compromise under a big party tent. Even if party change seems inevitable, a politician may hope that a straddle will bring in votes from two inconsistent blocs during the current election cycle. In addition to other considerations, changing the party in the name of a coalition suggests broad demand for change and not simply one "special interest group's" agenda.

Working with allies requires groups to compromise, adapt, or add to their agendas. To earn enough good will, groups must not simply take positions but offer meaningful support such as campaigning, lobbying, and voter mobilization. Naturally, a group will disrupt its own organizations less if it allies with a group that already agrees on one or more issues, even if they agree for different reasons. Schickler calls such issues "common carriers," "policies that a multiplicity of interests support for sometimes dissimilar reasons."[10] Groups in a coalition may bundle common carriers together with their more distinct priorities. If a coalition can present a united front, it shows politicians that they risk losing a broad array of groups unless they adopt the whole bundle.

Groups often choose allies who best complement their strengths and weaknesses. Allies are more desirable if they can message supporters they would not otherwise be able to reach. Political outgroups usually seek to mobilize people who are not motivated by policy concerns alone. One way to expand their base of support is to recruit voters from captive audiences motivated by nonpolitical concerns, like union members and churchgoers. A more socially acceptable group can also lend legitimacy to a less popular group. Some allies make up for a group's deficiencies better than others.

Societal changes beyond a group's control also influence the desirability of allies. Laws protecting the right to unionize made unions a far more formidable partner for civil rights groups than they were for Populists decades earlier. For conservatives in the 1970s, demographic and cultural changes caused the broadcasters and churches they targeted to flourish.[11] Religious broadcasting expanded as television networks changed their rules.

Groups need to worry about whether adopting a new ally or taking a new issue position will alienate members of their own organization. A prospective partner may cause a group to lose donations or members. If a group changes its position or focus to obtain a partner, rival organizations can grow at a group's expense.[12] Rivals for group leadership may also criticize an alliance as a way of competing for power with the current leader.[13] Strolovitch argues that groups on the left betray their ideological commitment to universalism to help their most advantaged subgroups.[14] Less-advantaged groups need the resources of their more-advantaged subgroups, so that, for example, civil rights groups will work hardest on behalf of well-off African Americans, women's groups will do so for heterosexual women, and so on. I found that less-advantaged members could sometimes overcome their disadvantages by compensating with volunteers. In other cases, ideological purists may be crowded out by those willing to compromise to get ahead. In the United Auto Workers (UAW), Walter Reuther changed from a socialist to an anti-communist liberal because socialists and communists blocked his advancement in the union.

Groups must be sensitive to the focus and language of a potential ally. Past conflict or clashing positions may create severe obstacles to working together. In contested transformations, groups need brokers to forge ties with other groups with their own histories and approaches to politics. Brokers are typically familiar with the sensitivities of both camps. Conservative strategists who formed the "New Right" found a broker with conservative Christians in Ed McAteer, a Colgate-Palmolive salesman with an extensive network of evangelical Christians who trusted him. Schlozman (2015) points out that groups need brokers who understand them to forge ties with party insiders. But it might not be in a politician's interest to unite conflicting groups if they have less ability to pressure the politician separately. Groups often need to find brokers other than officeholders to unite them.

Heaney and Rojas point out that when the Democratic Party wanted to shift attention away from the Iraq War to other priorities in 2006, it withdrew brokers and other resources from the antiwar movement, reducing it to a relatively extreme splinter faction.[15] The more a transformative coalition relies on party loyalists as brokers, the less it can muster challenges to its party. As once-disruptive groups become more fully integrated into the party and dependent on its resources, their members may lose leverage.[16] For most participants in the antiwar movement's "party in the street," party identification trumped movement identification. For civil rights activists and cultural conservatives, this was not the case.

Common ideology is seemingly an obvious reason for groups to trust each other. Noel's research on pundit ideology argues that a new consensus among pundits anticipates and constrains new party positions.[17] If we define ideology as a set of issue positions fit together by pundits, it might restrict groups, parties, or both. Alternatively, ideology could be a product of the agenda groups construct, which then constrains both parties and pundits. Three possible formulations are:

1. Ideologies directly constrain parties regardless of groups in the party.
2. Ideologies constrain group positions, and groups constrain party positions.
3. Ideology is the result of groups building coalitions, and ideology constrains party positions.

This book provides evidence against the first position, showing that politicians respond directly to group pressure. Groups could still be influenced in turn by ideology, however.

According to the second position, ideology constrains both candidates and interest groups. By looking at whether groups prioritize ideology over other conflicting considerations, we can weigh their relative importance. I generally find that ideology plays a limited role. Groups can tailor their interpretation of a fluid ideology to their material or social needs.[18] For example, evangelical Christians could downplay biblical exhortations to be stewards of the Earth in order to work effectively in a coalition with opponents of environmentalism. Even if they offer an ideological rationale for opposing environmentalism, it could be an afterthought rather than good-faith deliberation.

The third position holds that ideology is a product of group agreement, assigning a small role for the pundits usually thought to define ideology. In this formulation, pundits rationalize positions that groups had already con-joined instead of being the agents who define ideology. Liberalism might en-tail civil rights and economic liberalism because the NAACP and CIO worked together, largely for nonideological reasons. As Kersch has written, it is only in hindsight that parties appear to be following a linear ideological path toward a natural or logical endpoint.[19] While the third position is consistent with my findings, I do not explore how pundits adopt ideologies. This book merely argues that ideology is not a strict constraint on groups, group leaders, and coalition-building efforts.

Instead, preexisting ideology is one of many influences on a group's choice of allies. Ideological groups, who usually lack captive audiences, can still serve an important role in preserving alliances. The number of voters motivated by ideology alone is small, but groups like Americans for Democratic Action (ADA) and the American Conservative Union (ACU) can offer volunteers and intellectual ammunition to groups with more concrete interests. In doing so, they create an incentive for other groups in a coalition to adhere to an ideology even when group interests change. Over time, they can help con-vince people that some issues naturally fit together. More self-interested allies need to weigh the loss of ideological group support if they change positions for other reasons. Liberal groups, for example, helped ensure that civil rights remained part of the Democratic Party agenda even as rifts emerged between labor unions and civil rights groups in the 1960s.

Looking over past coalitional transformations, I find several reasons to be skeptical of ideology as a primary reason groups work together. First, the inter-ests of two or more groups in working together are often compelling enough that they might have allied without any ideological motivations. We cannot test counterfactual motivations, but group leaders set aside documented ideological commitments when they conflict with their own interests, member interests, or the interest of allies. Second, groups ignore good ideological fits when institu-tions prevent them from capitalizing on them politically or organizationally. Third, purveyors of ideology sometimes attest to the limited impact of their ideology on their readers and practical political groups. This does not mean that it is in a group or party's interest to present their issues as a smorgasbord of disparate issues; ideology can better inspire followers than narrow interests.

Claim 2: Groups, Not Politicians

During contested party transformations, groups enjoy several advantages over vote-maximizing politicians. First, politicians who want to counteract group influence usually need the support other groups or unorganized voters. If they cannot find support among rival groups, voters generally suffer debilitating collective action problems. Second, groups provide a resource for politicians by offering to mobilize their members on their behalf. If politicians accept group issue positions, they can use their own resources elsewhere while groups do considerable work for them. Third, politicians have more to lose than groups by changing the direction of a party.

As Olson realized long ago, intense minorities have incentives to put much more time and effort into working for their public policy agendas than dispersed and less motivated majorities.[20] It takes more work to organize a larger number of people, and activating weakly motivated people is obviously more difficult. Financially, unions have much more at stake than the average voter in labor laws, and Christian school parents have more at stake in tuition tax credits. Olson also pointed out that groups who can mobilize political followers in the process of providing nonpolitical benefits are especially powerful, since they bring votes and volunteers that are otherwise uninterested in political appeals. For example, unions can disseminate political messages while providing job benefits and church groups can do so in the process of providing community services.

Candidates who rely on their own campaigns or formal party organizations need more time and money than competitors who can outsource campaign work to preexisting groups. Such groups coordinate with other groups with shared interests to provide campaign mobilization to the right candidate and withhold it from others. It is therefore in a politician's interest, ceteris paribus, to commit to groups who can provide it. One study finds that the Republican Party developed its own electoral apparatus, the Republican National Committee (RNC), because it lacked the kind of assistance the CIO and its successors provided to the Democrats. The Democratic Party did not develop a worthy counterpart to the RNC until decades later, after unions suffered great attrition.[21] Parties and candidates still develop their own mobilization efforts to target particular groups, but building such an organization is harder than letting existing groups do it.[22]

Politicians may also be less familiar with the norms of groups whose leaders have intimate ties to the communities that they represent.[23] To obtain support, candidates have to demonstrate a reasonable level of congruence with not only the immediate agenda of the group, but that of other groups in their coalition. Opponents to the war in Iraq were able to mobilize rapidly by recruiting from existing networks of groups who respected each others' work.[24]

If groups withhold support from candidates who do not support their allies, candidates have an incentive to adopt the agenda of a group's coalition wholesale.

Finally, groups have less to lose and more to gain by antagonizing incumbent party politicians. In some cases, groups sit out or threaten to sit out an election in order to obtain concessions.[25] It can be a rational strategy for future-minded groups: heads, the politician caves in; tails, the politician ignores them and loses the election. Groups will then have an easier time nominating loyalists in the next election when the party has no incumbent running. They might even raise more money, railing against the opposition party in power or telling donors how they helped defeat half-hearted partisan candidates.

Politicians attempting a transformation need to be more willing to sacrifice near-term electoral prospects than they usually are, since party transformation can divide a coalition during elections. Politician and formal party organization employees hurt their reputations by losing the current election,[26] and threatening an incumbent during a primary season may cost the party during the general election. The media may interpret election losses as a repudiation and ignore the longer game. Any particular party official or officeholder might lose his or her party's esteem before reaping the benefits of party transformation. Politicians tend to refuse a group's advances if it conflicts with other important groups, which is why new groups need to counteract the incentives for inertia.

Hypothetically, politicians might seek new groups to support them to augment their votes, thus transforming their party. But office-seekers will avoid augmenting their base when a new group's goals conflicts with that of existing groups. Stable alliances become more difficult to rearrange as groups become more accustomed to working together. Politicians risk a tense confrontation and the opposing party may pick up the pieces from an alienated partner. Schattschneider realized that a party can have "a vested interest in the old lineup in which it confronts familiar antagonists already well identified in old contests."[27] Even minority party politicians often benefit from maintaining existing alliances when they can obtain a prominent position within the minority.[28] An old saying around Washington, D.C., holds that "the minority leader still rides in a limousine." Vote-maximizing politicians are especially unlikely to risk changing a lineup for a less popular group than the one they wish to displace.

The idea of groups as the fundamental components of parties has a long lineage in political science, but has been neglected for some time. Schattschnei-der called organizations the manifestations of interests and interests and the "raw materials" of politics, but even he did not document the steps on the assembly line, and concludes that the refinery owners (party politicians) rather than the raw materials (groups) dominate the process. For more than a generation, scholars deemphasized groups even farther. Realignment schol-ars, for example, viewed party change primarily as the "reordering of public preferences" by politicians.[29] All the while, sociologists paid close attention to the internal dynamics of social movements and organizations, but seldom studied political parties; only recently has the sociology of parties enjoyed a resurgence.[30]

The main alternative to group-centered transformation has been candidate-centered transformation. In Downs's pioneering theory of politics, politicians maximize votes and aim for nothing more than gaining office. Downs specifies that political parties are the vehicles of politicians and not "agents of specific social groups," implying that politicians transform parties when they need to upgrade their vehicles.[31] A leading contemporary treat-ment of parties, John Aldrich's *Why Parties?* continues to view parties as the electoral tools of ambitious politicians. Although he is aware of the role of "benefit seekers," most of his casework and quantitative evidence stress the role of candidates and politicians.[32] Carmines and Stimson espouse a candidate-centered model of issue "evolution," emphasizing the role of politi-cians in changing partisan voter opinion. Prominent party leaders attempt to increase their vote margins by changing their stance on issues to win new groups. When they win, other politicians follow suit, and voters change their party identification with the politicians.[33] Candidate-centered theories of party transformation are generally voter-centered theories that postulate that politicians take the positions they do in order to win votes.

A new generation of political scientists has conceptualized parties as coa-litions of groups. Bawn, Cohen, Karol, Masket, Noel, and Zaller emphasize that voter ignorance creates "blind-spots" in which parties can satisfy intense party activists because moderate voters usually ignore politics, especially pri-maries.[34] Karol describes party change on civil rights and abortion as party "coalition maintenance" and "coalition incorporation," respectively. As with the others, he argues that politicians are responding to external events or changes in interest group positions, but ascribes a larger role to politicians in coalition maintenance. DiSalvo and Layman, Carsey, Green, Herrera, and Cooperman also view groups as sources of change who extend party conflict to new issues and nominate loyal candidates, but disagree with the group/ party distinction. DiSalvo, for example, writes that Bawn et al. set "up a misleading choice about whether politicians or groups are at the center of a party."[35] However, the distinction is important for deciding where the incentives and strategies for party transformation originate. Without this distinction, it is harder to understand the rotation of party outgroups and ingroups into the proverbial smoke-filled rooms and which groups remain in the room when the decisions are made. Sometimes politicians disagree with the interest groups in a party. While pursuing the Republican nomination in 2016, Texas Senator Ted Cruz gained many endorsements from evangelical leaders, but not national politicians. For the purposes of studying party transformation, we need to know how outgroups can gain influence until they become ingroups, and treating groups separately from politicians adds clarity to the discussion.

Claim 3: Groups Change Parties by Influencing Nominations

Nominations are the primary arena in which groups transform parties. By making sure that parties nominate candidates committed to their agendas, parties are more likely to work for their goals. Whether the nominating system consists of conventions or primaries, voters pay little attention. This provides motivated groups with the opportunity to play an outsized role in who is nominated, since they can provide money, volunteers, and publicity that dispersed and inattentive voters will not provide. Before the McGovern-Fraser reforms required parties to nominate the winners of state primaries and caucuses, starting with the 1972 presidential elections, this mainly consisted of influencing convention delegates; after these reforms, it meant influencing primary elections.

Dispersed majorities are unlikely to research candidates during general elections and even less likely to research them during nominating contests in either system. In presidential elections, primary voters often jump aboard the bandwagon of candidates who won earlier contests.[36] Lacking the party cue to distinguish one candidate from another, they distinguish primarily on the basis of prior victories. Groups who have a major stake in the direction of a party do not usually sit idly and wait for convention delegates or early state primary voters to make up their minds. They contribute volunteers, money, prestige endorsements, and expert advice to candidates who commit to their agenda. Politicians know that pressure groups are more likely to scrutinize and publicize their activities than unorganized voters. They might still refuse a group's advances if it will lose the interest of mainstream voters, but only to the extent that voters would be aware of it. Groups nudge politicians to be as extreme in their commitment as they can be without being noticed by more moderate (but typically inattentive) voters. Politicians backtrack on unpopular commitments in general elections, but on balance, I argue that they are more responsive to groups than median voters. In the general election, median voters can only vote against their party's optimally extreme nominee by supporting an optimally extreme nominee on the other side. This arrangement enables groups to transform a party's agenda in ways against the wishes of more numerous but unorganized voters.

Groups prefer candidates with real commitments in the first place, though recruiting good candidates is usually difficult. Instead of constantly looking over the politicians' shoulder, groups hope to nominate someone who would work for them without supervision. As the CIO PAC founder Sidney Hillman said in 1943,

> the Democratic Party is very open to the proposition of giving our groups a great deal of say right in the party—not merely on policies, but a discussion of the kind of people they are going to nominate before they nominate them. I think if we have real leadership we can work out, especially with the Democratic Party, some satisfactory arrangements so that we do not really have a choice between two evils. After my trip I have seen some of the top leadership of the Democratic Party, and I think there, too, there is a desire to discuss with us before instead of after. You know what happened in New Jersey where, because of the AFL and the CIO and the Brotherhoods working together, we have forced our nominee as the gubernatorial candidate.[37]

Groups scrutinize politicians in office as well as candidates during campaigns, but some important deals, compromises, and lost opportunities may occur in "off the record moments."[38] This explains why Tea Party groups preferred Christine O'Donnell over Mike Castle in the 2010 Republican Primary for an open Senate seat in Delaware. Castle was more likely to win the general election but O'Donnell was more likely to follow the Tea Party's agenda. This does not necessarily mean that ideal nominees will be able to pass a group's policies in office, which depends on circumstances greater than the preferences of an officeholder. But they are more likely to fight for it under a favorable context.[39]

Of course, electability is one factor groups consider. Different groups and politicians value electability more than others. But on a continuum representing the tradeoff between commitment and electability, groups are more likely to choose a place closer to the commitment end; for politicians, it is the electability end. Groups can still have influence in politics even if their preferred party loses a particular election, while a single lost election can damage a politician's career trajectory.

Politicians would have to challenge fellow partisans during nominations to avail themselves of the most opportune moments for party change. Generally speaking, politicians in the same party refuse to do this because they value collegial relationships in small capitol communities. Even when politicians want their party to change, they seldom endorse challengers to their fellow incumbents. Politicians thereby deprive themselves of a powerful tool for party transformation available to groups. In an important exception, President Franklin Roosevelt attempted to purge conservative Democrats in the 1938 midterms, but his effort was an unqualified failure that thwarted his future success in domestic policy. In another rare case in which a sitting politician supported primary challenges to fellow partisans, South Carolina senator Jim DeMint was sharply criticized for raising $7.5 million for the midterm elections of 2010 and using it to support conservative challengers to incumbent Republicans. One congressional aide anonymously reported DeMint was cowed by the party. "If on Nov. 3 there are two or three seats in Democratic control that otherwise would have been Republican victories," he said, "then that anger will come back up to the surface and there will be consequences," without specifying the consequences.[40] Apparently stirred by these criticisms, DeMint only targeted Democrats in 2012.[41]

Nominating the right candidates is the primary mechanism for party transformation, but we need not make the strong claim that it is the exclusive mechanism. Groups may also threaten to withdraw support during a general election, holding their nose for an even worse officeholder in hopes of teaching their party a lesson. In nominating conventions, groups also signal a national direction for a party by passing party platforms reflecting their group agendas. Truman and many other political scientists have dismissed platforms as nonbinding words that appease interest groups without offering them real policies. In fact, platforms offer interest groups a way to vocalize goals that may be too ambitious for the current political climate.[42] Research also indicates that platforms are not mere parchment trophies. Most critically, Pomper and Lederman find that between 1944 and 1978, parties fulfilled platform pledges at a rate between 50 and 100 percent.[43] Another study finds that plat-forms alter the way politicians frame issues and create expectations among issue publics.[44]

My focus on nominations, rather than on general elections, fits squarely with the claims made in Cohen, Karol, Noel, and Zaller's *The Party Decides*. In their account, motivated "intense policy demanders" in one party decide on a nominee that satisfies major party factions before primaries take place, signaling other party members with endorsements. Policy demanders need to find a nominee that can win the general election, but "they cede as little policy to voters as possible."[45] One difference in my account is greater attention to the differences between politicians and other intense policy demanders. Recently, the Tea Party has supported candidates like Ted Cruz, Marco Rubio, and Christine O'Donnell over candidates with more endorsements from politicians. Groups and politicians usually accommodate each other in periods of stability, but sometimes the party's direction is contested. The Tea Party challenges are one example of the need to maintain the distinction even after a party transformation has already taken place.

Critics of the theory like Wayne Steger argue that in many nominating contests, party activists fail to generate a consensus behind one candidate ahead of time.[46] In the transformations covered in this book, groups are intensely active when they are trying to transform a party, but mainly consolidate their gains after the party is on the right trajectory. They still demonstrate their power by vetoing unacceptable candidates even if they do not actively agree on their first choice. President Lyndon Johnson's change on civil rights and President Donald Trump's on abortion rights are just two examples of candidates who flip-flopped to avoid group approbation. One of the coauthors of *The Party Decides*, Karol, emphasizes the role of adaptation rather than displacement. That is, parties mainly change when party politicians change their minds and adapt to new positions in the party, with little need to nominate new candidates. However, one of the reasons they adapt is the risk of primary challenges by groups.

Most recently, Schlozman argues that "anchoring groups" trade independence for "ideological patronage" by providing parties with a reliable stream of money and manpower. Such groups, he says, will not get access to parties if party elites doubt that they provide votes on net.[47] But nominations can force candidates to take losing general election positions, since politicians need to win nominations before they run in general elections. Contemporary Republicans have provoked government shutdowns despite their enormous unpopularity to avoid primary challenges from aggressive conservative groups.[48]

Even if minority factions did not prevent parties from being more responsive to majorities, many majority coalitions are possible, depending on which issues are grouped with which other issues. The United States has scores of independent issues of varying popularity, and no dominant or natural majority exists.[49] The Democratic Party could have been competitive in the 1940s and 1950s either by continuing to rely on the overwhelming support of southern whites and picking up northern votes when conditions were favorable, or by turning to blacks and labor as its core groups. Or it might have bundled support for the New Deal, civil rights, and conciliation with the USSR, as Progressive Party nominee Henry Wallace wanted. Which bundle parties adopt depends on which coalitions gain the most influence over nominations.

Methods

I test the claims with a deep historical investigation of party transformation on two different issues—civil rights and cultural conservatism. History offers the chance to reveal complex processes in which multiple variables—groups, politicians, interests, laws, demographics, and ideologies—are changing at the same time. By conducting a thorough investigation into the interactions between different actors, we can discern who is responding to whom and why. As Truman writes, both parties and groups value unity and the appearance of unity, so "most groups are careful to reveal as little as possible to the outsider concerning such internecine struggle."[50] They are less careful about discussing such struggles in private letters, memos, conference notes, and meeting minutes, which are archived and made available to the public decades later. Removed from the heat of the moment, this evidence reveals different motives than politicians or group leaders admit publicly at the time parties are changing.

Political behavior scholars usually evaluate claims about parties using statistical tests. In testing Claim 2, for example, one might treat party change as a dependent variable and particular cases of candidate-centered change and group-centered change as independent variables. However, each data point of party transformation requires an in-depth investigation to determine who or what is determining the outcome. Party transformation is typically a long process in which politicians, groups, and others are attempting to influence each other. There are simply not enough clear-cut data points—where the outcome was for sure decided by one force or another—for a statistical test. As much has been written about civil rights and cultural conservatism, this book is the first to publish some of the data needed to evaluate the role of groups and parties in party transformations. Given the importance of understanding why parties change, the inability to test the impact of variables through statistical relationships should not prevent us from making inferences from other forms of evidence.[51]

The transformations examined are not simply two case studies but two long processes, each with many data points speaking to the book's claims. For example, Claim 2 implies that the Democratic Party would support a civil rights plank in 1948, because important component groups of the Democratic Party had placed such importance on it. But they also imply that a) Adlai Stevenson would reassure racial liberals that he was a civil rights supporter in 1952, b) the 1956 convention would select Estes Kefauver as the vice presidential nominee, and c) that groups would force John F. Kennedy to distance himself from the South. The nominating contests and separate conflicts within each contest offer plentiful evidence from which to draw inferences.

I chose to focus on civil rights and cultural conservatism because they are the most significant party transformations since the New Deal; parties have maintained the same relative positions on economic and social welfare policies since then. Civil rights and cultural issues, on the other hand, comprise distinct dimensions of issues that changed after the New Deal economic alignment. They are not single issues, but an entire cluster of related issues. While a test of party transformation might conceivably overlook the transformation of the two parties on single issues (tariffs, for example), no theory of party transformation can ignore civil rights and cultural issues. They constitute the major axis upon which parties have turned. For entire decades, one could not predict the position of members of Congress (MCs) on civil rights or cultural issues from their positions on economic issues.[52] Over time, these sets of issues became predictably related; in Poole and Rosenthal's widely used metric of party ideology, second dimension NOMINATE scores were eventually predicted by first dimension NOMINATE scores. Rarely have such orthogonal clusters of issues become straightforward partisan issues.

The civil rights transformation not only bears on the question of how parties transform, but also the current makeup and electoral fortune of America's two major parties. Some historians and political scientists argue that the Democratic Party's New Deal coalition unraveled because of racial issues. Others claim that the civil rights realignment presaged the Republican Party realignment on cultural issues by driving culturally conservative white South-erners away from the Democratic Party. Either way, it was a pivotal change in party history.

However, this transformation took place when party conventions, instead of primary voters, formally selected nominees. Numerous other changes, in-cluding the growth of the mass media and direct mailing, also confound at-tempts to generalize from the civil rights transformation to the modern era. As such, the group-centered transformation might be ascribed to a bygone era of smoke-filled rooms and backroom promises. In order to show that the findings are still relevant in an age of primaries, a more contemporary party transformation is needed. Additionally, Hopkins and Grossman argue that the parties are not symmetrical. While the Democrats are a coalition of groups, the Republican Party is a party of ideology. If true, the group-centered civil rights change of the Democratic Party does not apply to Republicans.[53] An account of change in both parties is needed to examine whether the claims apply to both parties.

The cultural conservative transformation of the Republican Party shows that groups are still the most consistent and powerful agents of change, al-though nominations are legally in the hands of voters. Various religious sects overcame their prejudices toward other sects and also formed partnerships with political conservatives. Resourceful conservatives confronted Republi-can politicians with issues they preferred to avoid or market selectively. Two separate waves of cultural conservative groups were able to complete party transformation with comparatively little help from candidates or the general public by being active in primaries, particularly in important states holding contests early in the season. The cultural conservative transformation differed from the civil rights transformation in some ways that will be highlighted in the relevant chapters and the conclusion. However, these differences do not undermine the fundamental support they provide for the book's theoretical claims.

To demonstrate how my analysis might be applied beyond the focal pair of issues, I investigate nineteenth-century populism and gay rights. Space does not permit me to provide the same rigorous examination that I use for civil rights and cultural conservatism, but the available data suggests consid-erable symmetry. With the Populists, transformative groups failed to trans-form a party because they did not meet the conditions I specify for successful coalition building. Instead, they allowed rifts between farmers and laborers to fester and did little to repair racial divisions. The gay rights transformation, representing one of the most important issues to contemporary liberals, reaffirms that groups are still "first to the party" for Democrats.

I have examined dozens of archives to uncover the actions, attitudes, and motives of the key players in the realignment on civil rights in the 1940s and 1950s. Altogether, I sifted through tens of thousands of documents from ten different states, including records from unions, interest groups, MCs, presidents, and presidential aides. For the realignment on cultural issues, I have looked through the Ronald Reagan and George H. W. Bush presidential libraries and conducted interviews with more than fifty individuals from thirty different organizations. The result is a deeper and more credible account of the dynamics of party change than could be obtained by other means. Some of the findings corroborate existing sources or suspicions, but others offer new insight into the changes taking place. Both major transformations are worthy stories in their own right, only partly told in other accounts.

In searching through the archives, I focused most of my efforts on presidential nominations, relying on secondary sources for congressional and state nominations where possible. Influence over presidential candidates signals a group's influence in a party better than most other measures. Groups need influence over presidential nominees who can fight for lasting policy changes when unified government and public opinion created a favorable context. As we will see, coalitions with transformative ambitions treated national tickets as the cornerstone of their strategy. They thought that a party's national ticket and platforms were more indicative of where a party stands than more localized state and congressional contests. Civil rights groups and cultural conservatives in particular desired policy changes through the judicial system, where presidential appointments played an inordinate role. With congress deadlocked on controversial proposals like discrimination in the military and abortion funding, presidents also signed important executive orders. Frances Lee shows that congressional parties often change their issue positions to match those of a president from their own party and vote more uniformly along party lines..[54]

Party transformation is not so much an explicit coalitional bargain accepted by all groups in a party as much as a shift in which coalition gains the most influence in nominations, often over the continued objections of other groups. If a coalition with a new set of views continuously nominates loyal candidates over the objections of older groups, the party has changed. Parties are large, multifaceted organizations with affiliated politicians in the White House and Congress, and at the state level. Groups may have more influence in one arena than in others, often influencing state parties in sympathetic parts of the country before they influence national leaders. All of these divisions are important to parties in the process of transformation, but presidential nominations are the best single vantage point from which to observe these divisions and who comes out on top.

Historical evidence has its limits, of course. People only know what they witnessed or what they learned secondhand, and seldom know all of the relevant details. They may innocently misremember events. Some political actors prefer not to keep written records (or to dispose of them). Both in written accounts and oral histories, people are apt to exaggerate their own role or distort a course of events to create a narrative that serves their own purposes. When multiple accounts diverge, one can only draw tentative conclusions. For most of the key points in this book, though, multiple pieces of historical evidence confirm the same sequence of events.

The Plan of the Book

The next four chapters delve into the civil rights transformation. African Americans, long neglected by both parties, became part of a coalition that forced the Democratic Party to favor civil rights. Chapter 2 documents the transformation of the prestigious NAACP into a supporter of labor unions and liberal causes more broadly. Internal changes caused the NAACP to accommodate allies who could bring about the party change it wanted. It rejected an alliance with the CIO in the 1930s and changed with its organizational needs in the 1940s. Chapter 3 explains the CIO's interest in working with the NAACP to promote civil rights. The politically ambitious CIO thought black voters could help defeat an opposing party faction—conservative southern Democrats. Both organizations developed constructive ways of improving relations with each other to effect a formidable alliance. Chapter 4 shows that this alliance bore fruit at the 1948 Democratic Convention, which marked the transformation of racial equality from party taboo to a litmus test. The CIO and its allies passed a civil rights plank at the 1948 Democratic Convention against the wishes of most party leaders. As I demonstrate in Chapter 5, Democratic Party nominees did not retreat from the positions taken in 1948. Reflecting the new party equilibrium, serious presidential contenders distanced themselves from whatever ties they had to the southern wing of the party. Future candidates and platforms improved on the civil rights positions of 1948.

A new set of cultural issues confronted parties by the 1970s, including abortion, school prayer, and gay rights. They were slow to grab the attention of the religious conservatives now thought to be a natural constituency for these issues. As Chapter 6 describes, conservative religious sects were neither united nor uniformly culturally conservative. Religious leaders and denominations, like civil rights and labor, were groups that operated according to their own institutional incentives that militated against cooperation. Chapter 7 explains how these sects underwent a transformation themselves before they could bring a cultural conservative transformation to the Republican Party. Conservative critics of the Republican Party formed institutional outlets for their new grievances and helped socialize them into a set of coalition norms. Chapter 8 describes the Christian Right's first attempts to infiltrate the new system of binding primary elections. Republican politicians left to their own devices were about as willing to prioritize cultural conservatism in the 1970s as Democrats were willing to prioritize civil rights in the 1940s. Chapter 9 explains the origins and tactics of a second wave of conservative Christians, which focused on capturing state parties. Since momentum in early states became important for party nominations, state parties in Iowa and South Carolina provided a powerful asset to culturally conservative candidates. Chapter 10 shows that following Reagan's presidency, all viable candidates for the Republican presidential nomination presented themselves as allies of the Christian Right and needed to take them seriously in office.

Chapter 11 looks beyond the two major transformations of the book to investigate party change in other situations. First, it explores the unsuccessful attempts of nineteenth-century Populists to change both the two-party system and then the Democratic Party. The Populist revolt was perhaps the most notable failed transformation in the country's history. Moreover, it casts doubt on the inevitability of a CIO-NAACP alliance by showing that racial solidarity can trump class solidarity in politics. Since the absence of effective coalition formation led to its failure, it strengthens the case for Claim 1. The penultimate chapter also examines the addition of gay rights to the Democratic agenda as an example of contemporary party change in the Democratic Party.

The concluding chapter summarizes the aforementioned transformations and the case for treating them as parallel. As such, we can draw the same conclusion in spite of some interesting differences. I discuss the current state of the parties, including Trump's improbable success in the 2016 Republican primaries and election, in light of the book's evidence. While most of the book considers how parties work, the conclusion evaluates what parties mean for democracy. Parties are often treated as bulwarks of democracy, but the process of party transformation should temper our judgments. Well-organized groups can change parties independently of ideology or politicians, who presumably would cater to voters if unimpeded by groups. Groups continued to do so even after the passage of reforms designed to broaden voter participation in party nominations.

Politicians go hunting where the ducks are, as Barry Goldwater said, but a lot happens before politicians go hunting. Caretakers make some hunting grounds much more appealing to hunters just like some groups can offer more to politicians than other groups—volunteers, money, networks, and expertise. While hunters might focus on the current season just like politicians focus on the current election, caretakers attract prey by minding future hunting seasons. Both natural and manmade climate change alter the desirability of some hunting grounds over time just as new laws and demographic changes affect the appeal of some groups as allies or constituents. And hunting grounds can exclude hunters who drag dirt from other hunting grounds, just like groups in a party can snub politicians who associate too strongly with opposing groups in a party. Deciding where to hunt is only the end of a long process in which some places are, by design and historical accident, more desirable than others.

CHAPTER 2

Overcoming a Troubled History: Civil Rights Groups Seek a Coalition with Labor

President Herbert Hoover hailed from the party of Lincoln, but hoped to build a stronger Republican Party in the South by catering to "lily white" state organizations. In 1930, he nominated North Carolina's John Parker to the Supreme Court. As an appeals court judge, Parker had upheld yellow-dog contracts, which forbid workers from joining unions as a condition for employment. When he ran for governor of North Carolina, he had also said blacks were unfit to vote after state Democrats accused him of supporting political power for the disenfranchised minority. Both the AFL, the largest national labor union, and the NAACP, the nation's most prestigious civil rights organization, campaigned against the Parker nomination, which was ultimately unsuccessful. But they did not work together.[1] After testifying at Parker's hearing, AFL president William Green refrained from exchanging greetings with NAACP executive secretary Walter White, despite having met him several times. Nor had Green raised Parker's poor civil rights record as an issue.[2] This episode demonstrates the dire political straits of African Americans. Their nominal ally, the Republican Party, reached out to their segregationist opponents. Working class groups like the AFL viewed them as a liability and contributed to their isolation. Meanwhile, southern supporters of Jim Crow still had considerable sway over the Democratic Party.

Civil rights groups wanted the benefits of the New Deal without the racial conservatism of southern Democrats. Outnumbered and outgunned, civil rights groups needed an ally of organized labor's stature to counterbalance the forces in the Democratic Party lined up against them. Per Claim 1 in Chapter 1, the critical first step in party change is the formation of a viable coalition of groups committed to seeking change through the party system. The party was ultimately able to dissociate from its southern yoke after a combination of labor, liberal, and civil rights groups gained enormous influence in Democratic nominations.

Since this book traces party transformation from the bottom up, it starts by examining the changes in the groups that came to compose the Democratic Party, rather than the point at which the party changed. Groups need to choose their allies, form issue agendas, and decide to work with one party before they can transform it against the wishes of other influential party factions. The internal group decisions made at the ground level in these groups ultimately change party positions. As Heaney and Rojas write, "microlevel behaviors of individual and organizational actors matter for macrolevel patterns of party and movement dynamics."[3] At the microlevel, we will see that organizational considerations played a bigger role than politicians or ideology in the decision of the NAACP to ally with the CIO.

I turn first to the NAACP. Even though the CIO was a more pivotal organization in the Democratic Party's transformation, the NAACP's support for organized labor enabled a black-blue alliance to flourish. The CIO supported civil rights from the beginning, but emphasized the issue far more when supported by the NAACP. It did not create the Committee to Abolish Racial Discrimination (CARD), its most notable organizational sacrifice in favor of civil rights, until 1942. CARD risked costly confrontations with local affiliates in a way that resolutions and support for antilynching laws did not. Documenting the first steps of coalition building, this chapter shows the policies the NAACP adopted and the gestures it made to earn favor with the CIO. Ample evidence indicates that NAACP leaders previously opposed working with organized labor as a political and economic ally when it appeared to threaten their positions in the organization. They changed when they needed labor to raise funds and membership in competition with rival groups—and after their leadership positions were secure.

The evolution might not have unfolded this way. The NAACP might have prosecuted or otherwise antagonized discriminatory unions. Given the historical tensions between blacks and unions, it could have remained skeptical of the CIO. Unions might have continued to honor merely nominal commitments to civil rights. In hindsight, these counterfactual choices would have hurt both organizations. But, as Chapter 11 shows, with the failure of Populists to build a biracial alliance, many political organizations make bad decisions in hindsight. The motivations of the NAACP and CIO were the coagulants of the alliance, and therefore the primordial ingredients of a racially liberal Democratic Party.

A vast secondary literature exists on the relations between blacks and unions and their representative organizations, but only a small part of it focuses on political coalition building. With different research questions in mind, I searched through tens of thousands of pages of documents from relevant civil rights groups, unions, politicians, and the individual leaders of the relevant organizations. The history of civil rights organizations is much more multifaceted than I can explain in one chapter, so I focus on the NAACP. Several pieces of evidence indicate that it enjoyed broader support among African Americans than any other civil rights group during the 1940s, when the Democratic Party's transformation took place. Politicians and opinion pollsters[4] alike conceded its political clout after World War II, and it is the only African American civil rights organization that is mentioned with any frequency in other groups' primary sources. Most politically active civil rights groups worked in close cooperation with the NAACP.[5] When CIO and Democratic Party records mention civil rights during these transformative decades, they rarely bring up organizations other than the NAACP.

My research leads me to different conclusions than other social scientists. Using early survey data from the 1930s, Schickler and Caughey conclude that African Americans were not opposed to unions at the mass level.[6] But as this chapter will demonstrate, considerable qualitative evidence shows that African Americans in Northern states had difficulty bringing themselves to support unions in the 1930s or the early 1940s. Noel's pundit-driven model of party change shows that the Democratic Party adopted liberal positions on civil rights because an overwhelming consensus of economically liberal pundits came to favor civil rights during the Great Depression. Though both civil rights groups and unions shared similar New Deal ideologies, the timing of NAACP support for labor rights occurred after more particularistic interests became salient. My results diverge from Strolovitch and Paden, who find that minority interest groups tend to represent their most well-off subgroups.[7] Instead, the NAACP reflected its middle-class membership in the 1930s, when it focused mainly on civil rights, but not in the 1940s, when it prioritized labor rights and social welfare. Working-class members and unions began providing resources to the NAACP that the black middle class was not.

Finally, Schickler's outstanding research on the role of labor unions and state parties on racial realignment converges with my findings in many respects.[8] My account differs in its focus on the internal politics of the NAACP, which I argue was a necessary component of party transformation. The internal debates of the NAACP on whether and when to ally with labor suggest that its vigorous support for labor unions and economic liberalism was a historical contingency, not an inevitability. Grappling with the historic discrimination of unions and the uncertain trajectory of race relations in the labor market, the NAACP made a strategic gambit to side with the CIO. I argue that it was an obvious choice in hindsight, but a decision fraught with difficulty at the time, for both the leadership and the membership, leading up to the Second World War. The NAACP had to reconcile itself to labor unions and pursue the correct strategy to prevent race relations from being a wedge issue among the lower classes, as it had been in the past and would become in the future. For such a prestigious organization to antagonize labor unions at a time when the nascent relationship was so fragile, would have altered the trajectory to come.

The first section here details the unresponsive parties that civil rights groups sought to change. Before World War II, neither Democrats nor Republicans offered satisfactory choices, and civil rights groups were unable to transform either party until they formed the alliance with labor. The second section summarizes the complicated relationship between blacks and unions, whose historical discrimination behavior sometimes drove civil rights leaders to oppose them. The NAACP contemplated and decided against working with labor in the 1930s, showing the same distrust as many other black institutions. This history underscores why the NAACP's decision to work with the CIO was such a momentous change. The third section explains the reasons for this change of strategy and contrasts my explanation with others. Fourth, I offer evidence of an alliance forming in 1940, where the NAACP was willing to sacrifice a great deal for a viable partnership. Finally, I show that this alliance benefitted the NAACP substantially, even though it was not inevitable.

Political Parties Before World War II

Any account of party transformation needs to discuss the position of parties before a transformation took place. From the Civil War to the Great Depression, African Americans were nominally represented by the Republicans, the party of Abraham Lincoln. However, African American voters were a small group because most lived in the South, where they were disenfranchised during and after Reconstruction. They constituted only 1.78 percent of the non-southern population in 1900 and 2.5 percent in 1930.⁹ Republican politicians therefore had few electoral incentives to address their problems. Moreover, twentieth-century Republicans hoped in vain that if they paid more attention to white Southerners, they could build a larger voting base in the South.¹⁰

The Great Migration during World War I changed little. African Americans were an unpopular minority and parties feared that any serious efforts on their behalf would make them less popular, as Democrats later feared with gay rights groups and Republicans with evangelical Christians. Warren G. Harding told two NAACP field agents that he supported the NAACP position on the issues of voting rights, antilynching laws, Haiti, and the armed services. Nonetheless, he refused to bring these up during the campaign, candidly admitting that "the injection of the Negro question into the campaign would lose the Republican Party more votes than it would gain."¹¹ In 1923, the Republican-sponsored Dyer antilynching bill met defeat in the Senate, with a vote for cloture split among party lines. NAACP president Moorfield Storey still complained in a private letter that "Republican senators as a rule were not in earnest," noting that Republicans proposed the Dyer bill late in a session, when a filibuster is most likely to succeed.¹²

The Democratic Party, which had institutionalized Jim Crow, was far from a promising alternative. Some civil rights activists had supported the 1912 Democratic candidate, Woodrow Wilson, only out of opposition to Roosevelt and Taft. Just four years later, W. E. B. Du Bois, advised blacks that neither party suited their interests, but the Republican nominee was preferable to Wilson:

> The Negro must expect from [Charles Evan Hughes] . . . the neglect, indifference and misunderstanding that he has had from recent Republican presidents. . . . The Democratic party can maintain its ascendancy only by the help of the Solid South . . . consequently it can never, as a party, effectively bid for the Negro vote.¹³

Democratic indifference continued for the next quarter-century, as its southern wing continued to filibuster Republican attempts to protect basic civil rights. In 1928, the NAACP drafted a statement for Democratic nominee Al Smith to pledge to be a president for all of the people, but Smith never signed the statement.¹⁴ In 1932, Franklin Roosevelt enjoyed only lukewarm support in the North and owed his nomination largely to the South.¹⁵ Roosevelt vacationed in Warm Springs, Georgia, and trumpeted his honorary southern heritage many times during the campaign. He extolled Jefferson Davis and referred to the "war between the states" in speeches to Southerners.[16]

The Democratic Party did not become responsive even when African Americans overwhelmingly voted for Roosevelt in 1936 and subsequent years.[17] The transformation of the party is not a simple story of blacks migrating north and gaining the right to vote, or of Democrats responding to their voters. Roosevelt's press secretary banned black reporters from White House press conferences, while other administration officials told Roosevelt he should not even perform symbolic gestures such as greeting the NAACP convention.[18] Only a small number of Democratic MCs and New Deal officials[19] were concerned that New Deal laws discriminated against African Americans. While the Civilian Conservation Corps withheld funds from states that refused to employ blacks, the Federal Housing Authority (FHA) codified discriminatory housing practices such as "red-lining" into public policy. When civil rights activists complained that the National Recovery Act (NRA) wage rates hurt blacks by pricing them out of the labor market, Roosevelt responded that "It is not the purpose of this administration to impair southern industry by refusing to recognize traditional differentials."[20]

Without enormous pressure on the other side, the president had to remain indifferent because civil rights put his southern support in jeopardy. New Deal legislation could not pass without help from southern MCs, who constituted no less than 41 percent of House Democrats and 44 percent of Senate Democrats at any point of the Roosevelt administration. Southern committee chairs could also serve as bottlenecks for New Deal legislation.[21] During the congressional battle for an antilynching law, South Carolina senator James Byrnes said that the white people in the South "had never voted for a Republican candidate," but only "due to the belief that when problems affecting the Negro and the very soul of the South arose, they could depend upon the Democrats of the North to rally to their support."[22] Florida senator Claude Pepper said that the antilynching bill "is out of harmony with the spirit of that philosophy which has prevailed in the national life of this country since the 4th of March 1933, known under the terminology of the New Deal."[23] In a meeting arranged by the First Lady, Roosevelt lamented to NAACP executive secretary White that "I did not choose the tools with which I must work. . . . If I come out for the anti-lynching bill now, [Southern Democrats] will block every bill I ask Congress to pass to keep America from collapsing."[24] Accordingly, the president refused to support the NAACP when it pressed for an antilynching law in 1934 and again in 1937.[25]

Roosevelt made many efforts to liberalize the Democratic Party on economic issues orthogonal to race. Roosevelt had pushed successfully for the Democratic Party to eliminate the requirement that nominees received two thirds of the convention votes, which gave southern delegates a veto over nominations. He also attempted to purge southern opponents of the New Deal in 1938 midterm elections.[26] It is unclear that civil rights formed a part of Roosevelt's strategy in these matters; each could be viewed as an attempt to make the party into the party of the New Deal rather than the party of the New Deal plus civil rights.

In 1941, Roosevelt signed an executive order for civil rights only because civil rights groups left him without options. Executive order 8802 banned discrimination from wartime industries through a Fair Employment Practices Commission (FEPC). The FEPC was a breakthrough for civil rights groups, who fought for the next two decades to extend its duration and reach to private industry, succeeding in several states. Roosevelt relented not because he worried about losing black votes, but because civil rights groups organized a March on Washington that could lead to violence and embarrass the administration, both domestically and internationally.[27] Brotherhood of Sleeping Car Porters (BSCP) president A. Philip Randolph was able to recruit thousands of blacks behind the March on Washington Movement (MOWM) using union connections. At a meeting with the president and the NAACP, Randolph told President Roosevelt he could mobilize 100,000 African Americans. The president believed that Randolph was exaggerating the number of protestors likely to mobilize until the NAACP bluffed that his figures were accurate.

Of course, presidents and presidential candidates are not the only party leaders capable of assisting underrepresented groups, but qualitative data provide little evidence that other party leaders were helpful. One party boss, Pennsylvania senator Joseph Guffey, believed that the party could recruit blacks on the basis of government programs, and persuaded a reluctant party chairman—James Farley—to create a Democratic Advisory Committee on Negroes in anticipation of the 1936 election.[28] Guffey seems to be an exception. Farley, party chairman from 1933 to 1940, met with labor leaders, Catholic leaders, and Jewish politicians to maintain or augment the Democratic voting base. In 1937, 1938, and 1940, when antilynching laws were proposed, Farley rarely discussed African Americans in his almost-daily notes.[29] New York senator Robert F. Wagner sponsored antilynching bills and attempted to remove the discriminatory provisions of existing government benefits. In the hearings for Supreme Court nominee John Parker, Senator Wagner alone had argued that his opposition to labor rights and civil rights were part of a "single trait of character," a point made to him by Randolph.[30] But neither his letters nor those of his longtime aide, Leon Keyserling, reveal efforts to build a new party coalition. Without such documentation, it is difficult to attribute consensus-building within the Democratic Party to these politicians.

The two parties routinely nominated candidates that were, at best, insensitive to their concerns, and even those blacks who could exercise their right to vote were presented with two unsatisfying choices for public office. Sundquist argues that a new issue is likely to have "greater inherent appeal" to the voters of one of the major parties, but the civil rights question was not among them.[31] The only hope for black voters was to work for long-term change in one or both of the parties, displacing other factions. Luckily, parties can be made more responsive to minorities, and blacks chose to work with a party that ultimately was. Regretfully, it took decades from the time the NAACP was organized in 1909.

Labor Rights Dilemmas for African Americans

A transformation in civil rights groups had to take place before a transformation in the Democratic Party. Civil rights groups needed an ally with organized labor's clout to transform the party, but they were understandably hesitant. This section discusses the historic hostility between blacks and unions, at both elite and mass levels. If this continued, the hopes for a black-blue alliance would have been dashed and along with it, the prospects for party transformation. Black workers were often excluded from unions and employers sometimes hired them as strikebreakers. At least until eve of World War II, black newspapers, churches, and organizations remained deeply suspicious. They also diverged on the importance of focusing on economic issues in addition to purely civil rights concerns.

Hostility to Unions Among African Americans

At the height of Jim Crow, Booker T. Washington was by far the most salient spokesperson for the interests of African Americans. Washington believed that African Americans would obtain political rights gradually as they proved themselves to be skillful members of the workforce. Claiming that unions were impediments to the rise of lower-class blacks into respectability, he wrote, "Before the days of strikes in [West Virginia] . . . I knew miners who had considerable money in the bank, but as soon as the professional labor agitators got control, the savings of even the more thrifty ones began disappearing."[32]

When Washington died in 1915, more than 90 percent of blacks lived in the South, where there were very few unions and even fewer opportunities to vote.[33] His Tuskegee Institute was surrounded by hostile white Southerners and depended largely on northern capitalists and paternalistic Southerners for its funding, prestige, and security.[34] Although we cannot be sure what Washington would have believed in different circumstances, it is clear that he fundamentally accepted capitalism. He even helped to create the National Negro Business League, a black counterpart to the Chamber of Commerce, which would help teach blacks how to succeed in a capitalist economy.[35] Later, he advised the founders of the National Urban League (NUL), which relied more on business philanthropy than the NAACP. Marcus Garvey, an admirer of Washington, gathered a sizeable following in the 1920s.[36] Garvey argued that the "only convenient friend the Negro worker or laborer has in America at the present time is the white capitalist," who would hire blacks to save on labor costs, ultimately leading to a bidding war that would allow black worker wages to approach that of white workers.[37]

Even after the first Great Migration of blacks to the North during World War I, many historical incidents provided reasons to distrust unions. Although blacks constituted 8 percent of nonagricultural labor in 1929, they constituted only 1 percent of unionized workers, and half that number was due to the all-black BSCP.[38] White union members saw unions as social organizations as well as economic organizations, and extending "brotherhood" to African Americans meant recognizing social equality.[39] Generally, AFL affiliates organized separate locals for black workers and often restricted blacks from better-paying positions. In 1929, the AFL said that when blacks learned the appropriate trades, they would be admitted, knowing full well that trade unions refused to apprentice black workers.[40] It declined to hire a black organizer in 1926 even after NUL offered to pay half the salary. (It had earlier promised NUL it would hire black organizers when it had enough money.)[41] In this environment, blacks worked for northern employers that hired them to disrupt white workers on strike and take their place at the workplace. Instead of seeing labor laws as a way of obtaining union jobs, blacks often saw them as a way to lose one of the few jobs available to them— as strikebreakers.

Sophia Lee documents how New Deal labor laws had the potential to exacerbate these tensions. The Railroad Brotherhoods and the Teamsters, among other unions, were able to violently exclude African Americans from work that had previously been dominated by African Americans. Railroads offered some of the few skilled professions available to blacks, but white members of the Fireman's Brotherhood attacked black brakemen and firemen with guns and lead pipes during the Depression. After the Brotherhood gained the legally exclusive right to bargain on behalf of all workers, black and white, it gave away jobs held by blacks to whites with less seniority.[42] Some unions would employ blacks long enough to ensure workplace unionization and then dismiss the black workers.[43] At the U.S. Pipe and Foundry Company in Bessemer, Alabama, blacks lost many of their positions as skilled laborers and sub-foremen after the organization of the plant by U.S. Steelworkers. The number of "one-race" departments in the Pullman-Standard's manufacturing plant in the same location increased after the collective bargaining agreement of 1941.[44]

The emergence of the CIO might have been a game changer. It split from the AFL in 1936 to organize unskilled workers and pursue a full-employment economy. Its constitution was committed to racial equality. But qualitative evidence on the attitudes of black Americans reveals that their distrust of unions continued after the creation of the CIO, partly because the CIO found it difficult to fight discrimination in its own ranks.[45] In 1936, future CIO president Phillip Murray found organizing black steelworkers difficult even with the cooperation of civil rights organizations, and pessimistically concluded "that the organization of the negro steel workers will follow, rather than precede, the organization of the white mill workers."[46] In 1937, African American workers in Detroit mostly declined to participate in sit-down strikes in which many whites took part, and voted against the UAW-CIO's organization of the Ford plant in 1941.[47] Some worried that blacks would be unable to obtain jobs in unionized workplaces dominated by white workers,[48] while others worried that plantwide union seniority rules would weaken the seniority of black workers in departments traditionally set aside for African Americans.[49] These concerns continued for decades.[50]

Northern black churches tended to discourage their congregations from supporting unions both before and after the creation of the CIO. Some of the ministers helped provide local employers with regular members of the congregation. Detroit ministers convinced Henry Ford to adopt a racial quota system in 1921, in which the proportion of blacks in his factories equaled the proportion in the work force, and were represented in every department. Preachers did not want to dislodge the employers' view of blacks as loyal workers, and feared that encouraging unions would do so.[51] One black reverend and community activist in Chicago forbade union organizers from speaking in his congregations and told ministers that they had a duty to warn members about the evils of labor unions.[52] On the eve of the 1941 strike at Henry Ford's Rouge factory another black minister said, if "Ford hires one colored for every ten whites, I am for him first, last, and always."[53]

For a time, black newspapers contributed to black hostility toward unions.

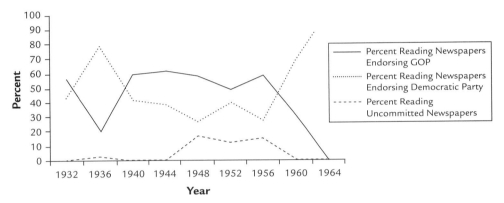

Figure 1. Percent of selected black newspaper readers exposed to partisan endorsements. Newspapers in sample: the *Amsterdam News, Atlanta World, Baltimore Afro American, Chicago Defender, Cleveland Call and Post, Los Angeles Sentinel, Norfolk Journal and Guide, Philadelphia Afro American, Pittsburgh Courier, Washington Afro American.* I determined endorsements with an electronic search for editorial articles with the two candidate's names, or, alternatively, the terms "election," "president," "support," and "endorse." Most circulation figures were either obtained through *N. W. Ayer & Son's Directory of Newspapers and Periodicals* or NAACP A452. The former base their figures on independent audits or statements from the newspaper publishers. Newspapers were not included if their circulation was unavailable. Circulation figures were unavailable for the following newspapers and years: *Atlanta World* (1932, 1936, 1964), *Cleveland Call and Post* (1932), *Los Angeles Sentinel* (1932, 1936, 1940, 1944, 1960), *Philadelphia Afro American* (1932, 1936), *Washington Afro American* (1932, 1936). Endorsements are missing from the following newspapers and years: *Atlanta World* (1964), *Cleveland Call and Post* (1956), and *Pittsburgh Courier* (1960).

A gathering of fifty-two African American newspaper editors in 1914 condemned "all forms of Unionism and economic radicalism."[54] Much of this hostility continued into the 1920s. One prominent black author writing in the *Nation* (later a union supporter) said:

> Capital has never presented as sinister and malevolent a front to the Negro laborer as have the white labor unions . . . Our liberal white "friends" urge us to wait until they can persuade the white unions to see the light. But who can wait when winter has come and there is no coal, no food? . . . In the face of these facts can you give me any good reason for being a socialist or joining with the "organized forces of labor to overthrow a despotic capitalistic regime"? Why shouldn't Negro labor organize to defeat every attempt of white labor to bargain collectively with capital? Why shouldn't we join in this cutthroat game and help capital throttle white labor? This it seems to me is the only way to make white labor see the light. And so I urge all Negro laborers to adopt as their motto: "Hurrah for the Scab and the Open Shop and to Hell with the Unions."[55]

In 1925, the Chicago *Whip* and *Defender* both recommended that African Americans not join the BSCP, which actively supported civil rights, and instead join the company unions.[56] For that matter, most African Americans were reading black newspapers that endorsed mostly antiunion Republicans for president until 1960 (Figure 1).

The most widely read black newspapers in the United States before World War II were the *Pittsburgh Courier* and the *Chicago Defender*. To detect change over time, I surveyed all editorials in several important papers concerning unions in two years—one in the early 1920s and the other in the late 1930s.[57] The *Pittsburgh Courier* supported the entrance of blacks into unions as early as 1911, though it remained a staunchly Republican newspaper until the Great Depression.[58] In the 1930s, editorials condemned discriminatory unions, but praised New Deal laws granting protection to unions, and admonished blacks not to blame unions for not remedying discrimination overnight.[59]

The *Chicago Defender* was skeptical of unions in the 1920s even though it endorsed Democrats before most other black newspapers. Only three of the twelve editorials in the 1920s sample favored unions. While supporting the right to unionize and encouraging blacks to join nondiscriminatory unions, it also favored the right of a worker to not join a workplace union and to serve as a replacement worker. In 1937, twelve of twenty-two editorials were pro-union. Some editorials argued that unions forced blacks to be "scabs," but the *Defender* showed itself to be hopeful about the CIO and its prospects for race relations. In 1947, 90 percent of the thirty-seven editorials about unions were positive. By that time, CIO members had threatened to boycott the paper unless the company accepted a CIO-affiliated union.

Besides the NAACP, the largest civil rights organization in the Great Depression was the NUL, then a harsh critic of unions. It openly opposed the pro-union Wagner Act as written, claiming that "while we deplore the necessity for strikebreaking, we hold that it is the one weapon left to the Negro worker whereby he may break the stranglehold that certain organized labor groups have utilized."[60] Under the Wagner bill, "as strikebreakers [we] have no rights . . . the Negro's position will be made worse as that of other workers is enhanced."[61] Its acting executive secretary even suspected that union leadership encouraged discrimination by the members in order to restrict the labor market for higher pay, writing that "more often such prejudice is nourished and perpetuated by a selfish, entrenched clique of officers who derive material gain from splitting the unity of workers and withholding protection to masses in the labor movement."[62] A future executive secretary called it "the worst piece of legislation ever passed by Congress." Even when the CIO was formed, NUL expressed no preference between the CIO and the AFL.[63]

In short, a number of black institutions made it difficult for civil rights groups and unions to work together. One could regard them as artificial barriers to common economic interests. But partisan, interest group, and governmental institutions have been remarkably successful at keeping groups with common interests apart at many times in history.

The NAACP on Unions and Mission Scope

As the previous section shows, anyone trying to build a coalition of blacks and labor unions faced considerable obstacles. Civil rights groups that formed in opposition to Booker T. Washington superficially showed promise. In particular, the NAACP was founded in 1909 largely by liberals, socialists, and settlement house workers who supported a new direction for civil rights. Like many northern civil rights activists, they took exception to Washington's leadership. Washington exacerbated the conflict by attempting to be the singular national spokesperson for African Americans, spying on rivals and diverting funding from others who might muddy the image he attempted to project for blacks.[64] Some rivals were economically progressive or openly socialist, including the NAACP's in-house pundit, W. E. B. Du Bois. However, neither Du

Bois nor other NAACP leaders believed labor unions would live up to their economic ideals, and the NAACP steadfastly refused to support Du Bois's economic agenda in the 1930s. The NAACP, like other black institutions, had to overcome a troubled history to work with labor.

Du Bois, Washington's most famous rival, consistently opposed capitalism as an economic system, but did not think unions were ready to include black workers. Du Bois's the *Crisis* was arguably the central work of the NAACP until the 1930s. In it, he wrote, "So long as I conduct it," it "is going to be Socialist and Left Wing Socialist."[65] The prickly pundit was nonetheless deeply suspicious of white unions, writing in 1930:

> For years, I have in the *Crisis* and on the platform advocated the trade union movement . . . until the trade union movement stands heartily and unequivocably at the side of the Negro workers, I am through with it. I know that this attitude is a bit unfair to some unions who do admit the Negro, but the attitude of most unions is such that I think I am justified.[66]

By the Great Depression, Du Bois came to believe that both race and class were irreducible categories and prevented working-class solidarity. White workers, including recent immigrants, would sabotage themselves by focusing on upward mobility and refusing to ally with black workers. Du Bois wrote "the lowest and most fatal degree of suffering comes not from capitalists but from fellow white workers."[67] With blacks and whites unable to make common cause, Du Bois urged blacks to form a cooperative enclave where blacks bought, sold, and shared with other blacks until race relations improved.[68]

In the 1920s and 1930s, the NAACP continued to garner much of its support from reformers on the left, including the left-wing Garland Fund.[69] Another early leader, Mary White Ovington, had been a social worker who steered muckrakers away from Washington's agenda at the turn of the century.[70] Arguing that workers of all races gained from labor laws, she voiced her disagreement in academic journals:

> Would the Negro as a workman be better off . . . if there were no labor unions . . . I have heard colored men prominent in industrial school work say that they would be. . . . Caste lines disappear when men are held together by a common interest, and as they feel their dependence one upon another they gain in sympathy and fraternal spirit.[71]

Ovington would often intervene in local NAACP branches dominated by Washington partisans in cases where she believed serious problems would be met with tepid responses.[72]

Despite all this influence from left-leaning leaders, the NAACP restricted its mission to legal equality without focusing on economic issues. Personal economic ideologies were kept personal. In several letters in the 1920s, President Storey discouraged attempts to broaden the NAACP's agenda beyond traditional concerns such as lynching and voting rights. When Ovington suggested that the NAACP consider endorsing a socialist agenda, Storey wrote back "I think the officers of this society and its representatives generally should stick to the particular issue for which this society was formed."[73] Economic progressivism and unionism were peripheral to the NAACP's concerns until the 1940s.

To be sure, there were attempts to broaden the NAACP's agenda or initiate a dialog with unions. The failure of these efforts to take off show that it did not follow an ideological agenda when its leaders thought it would hurt the organization or their own advancement. In the 1930s, the organization hosted heated debates between those who wanted to keep the mission focused on civil rights, and those who wanted to ally with the working class. Du Bois's 1932 annual convention speech, titled "What's Wrong with the NAACP," claimed that many viewed the organization as "highbrow" and funded both by African Americans and by whites who exploited others.[74] At the 1933 Amenia Conference, young intellectuals tended to share Du Bois's view that economic inequality was the source of many racial problems like lynching.[75] One of the "new crowd" argued that the NAACP should look to labor unions to gain more "muscle" in politics.[76] Shortly after the conference, Du Bois's published support for segregated black enclaves was sharply criticized by most NAACP leaders, who prioritized racial integration.[77] When the NAACP board of directors forbade Du Bois from criticizing the NAACP officers or work in the *Crisis*, he resigned.

Executive Secretary White seemed to gain the upper hand in the organization and prevent other members of the "new crowd" from implementing their pro-labor agenda. White specialized in legal action to fight school segregation, and the Amenia Conference strategy would shift responsibility away from him.[78] Du Bois, who had devised reorganization plans for the NAACP transparently designed to remove White and his allies, consolidated White's power by resigning.[79] The "organization man" managed to keep the organization's focus on legal reform by portraying a workers' program as impractical and removing opposition within the organization.[80] Ovington acknowledged that there was not enough support for a workers' program among their members and donors. She called the socialist Harris Report of 1935 a "revolutionary doctrine to which I for one of the Board subscribe, but those who want to bring it to the Negro will do best to bring it through the socialist or communistic organizations." If they used the NAACP for these goals, it would alienate middle-class supporters and "we should run ahead and then [backwards] when dissension came." The NAACP needed to forward a program that commanded a wide consensus.[81] The 1935 annual conference made no commitment to workers' councils, and White vetoed a resolution to support the pro-labor National Negro Congress (NNC), which later received funding from the CIO.[82] Arthur Spingarn, the titular president, complained "When I joined the Association we had . . . a thrilling program . . . Now we have only [legal] cases and lobbying, and every effort I have made . . . has been ignored or thwarted by [Walter White] or the Board."[83] White's critics found themselves without influence.

Not only did the NAACP not ally itself with unions, but it antagonized them in some cases. In the 1920s, Storey had consistently opposed closed-shop unions and eventually supported injunctions against individual strikers.[84] The NAACP recommended that the Garland Fund oppose funding African American unions in 1930, arguing that unions would be a "money sink." In 1932, its annual conference declared "Hitherto the American Labor movement . . . has betrayed the interests of the Negro worker, and the Negro cannot co-operate with this movement until it recognizes him."[85] When the AFL turned down proposals from the NAACP to cease issuing new charters to discriminatory unions and educate its works about discrimination, the NAACP picketed its convention.[86] White wrote privately to a senator that "the Negro is predominantly a worker and his interests are indissolubly linked up with those of the working classes. . . . On the other hand . . . In some instances Negroes have joined the unions, strikes have been called, and when the strikes were ended only white union men were given jobs."[87]

The NAACP (along with NUL) opposed section 7a of the National Industrial Recovery Act, which empowered unions. White told the Federal Emergency Relief Administration supervisor that African Americans had gained better and higher-paying jobs under the open shop.[88] When the AFL forced Senator Wagner to remove a nondiscrimination clause from his landmark Wagner Act, the NAACP plotted to reintroduce it on the floor and take labor unions by surprise. "Trying to get the clause back in the bill now would permit organized labor to line up enough votes in the Senate to prevent its inclusion,"

White wrote. In the *Crisis*, Assistant Secretary Roy Wilkins pointed out "the fact that thousands of Negro workers are barred from membership in American labor unions and therefore, if the closed shop is legalized by this act, Negro workers will be absolutely shut out of employment." Although the NAACP dubiously claimed in 1941 to have always supported the pro-union Wagner Act, written evidence indicates only that it supported an antidiscrimination amendment that failed to pass.[89]

When the CIO emerged as a viable rival to the AFL, Wilkins appeared interested in gauging member interest. The "Young Turks" like Abram Harris and Ralph Bunche were supportive of the CIO from the beginning.[90] One editorial in the *Crisis* said that the CIO's records "give some assurance that they may be depended upon to see that the Negro worker does not receive the usual doublecross."[91] At his prodding, the NAACP held its annual conference in Motor City in 1937 and featured a black union leader on the front cover of the *Crisis*. Many local NAACP leaders, including Detroit's, formed alliances with employers to oppose unions generally and the CIO in particular.[92] The annual conference adopted a resolution backing away from the CIO, citing the lack of attention the UAW-CIO paid to African American employees.[93] Opposition to the CIO was not unique to Detroit. Steelworkers in Birmingham also grew skeptical of the CIO after helping to bring about a local chapter. Despite general enthusiasm for the CIO among southern blacks, Birmingham steelworkers had more difficulty obtaining promotions once a CIO affiliate was in place, and therefore helped replace it with an AFL affiliate in 1940.[94] The National Urban League's Lester Granger, too, warned workers against "jubilantly rushing toward what they assume to be a new day for labor and a new organization to take the place of the AF of L."[95]

Compounding the difficulties of creating a viable alliance with the CIO, the NAACP did little work on behalf of partisan, class, or social welfare issues near and dear to the progressive union.[96] It claimed to be a nonpartisan organization, and when the president openly supported Roosevelt in 1936, he explained that he was only speaking for himself, that other employees supported his Republican challengers. In the 1940 election, White declined invitations to join organized groups for Roosevelt.[97] In the words of one biographer, the NAACP was mainly "non-economically" liberal; the "black man's struggle for full civil and political rights must take precedence over any program of economic advancement, for once color discrimination had been swept away, the black man would be able to compete successfully with his white counterpart in jobs."[98]

There are multiple ways interest groups assemble issue positions to suit their needs. Despite its origins and ideology, the progressive NAACP was not ready to ally with unions or working class whites in the 1930s. Not only was there a diversity of thought among civil rights leaders, but those who supported unions generally thought the organization should pursue a tightly defined civil rights agenda. An organizational rivalry resulted in the triumph of White, who realized that a labor strategy would sink his star. The next section will show that organizational interests changed in the 1940s, leading the NAACP to emphasize some of the causes it steered away from in the 1930s. The organization came to believe that it needed to ally with labor in order to spearhead an effective civil rights program in the 1940s.

Changes in the NAACP

The NAACP changed direction around 1940 not just to build a political coalition, but to recover members and funding it lost in recent years. The CIO offered all of the above. The NAACP encouraged its members to overcome the traditional reservations about unions outlined in previous sections, which enabled the conjunction of labor rights and civil rights in its political coalition. The crucial civil rights coalition in the Democratic Party, then, was brought about largely because of the needs of an interest group to sustain itself. One can interpret the NAACP's earlier reluctance to work with unions as a matter of exploring and discovering their inevitable political allies, rather than evidence that they might have chosen a different course. But it is telling that the change of course took place at the same time NAACP confronted organizational problems. Changes in the raw materials of politics had significant consequences for the Democratic Party.

Internal Considerations

The NAACP changed its positions on labor partly because it needed more money and more members. It appeared that it could obtain both by recruiting black workers and obtaining labor donations, if it were willing to shift its positions and emphasis. Decades later, Wilkins admitted that "memberships are number 1. No matter what successes the NAACP Branches have had in meeting local problems, the general public over the nation will judge the whole NAACP . . . by one question: 'Did the total membership go up or down?'"[99]

In the first half of the 1930s, NAACP revenue was half that of the 1920s, and one study shows that declining middle-class contributions accounted for much of the loss.[100] In 1939, the IRS disallowed tax deductions for donations to the NAACP because of its political "propagandizing" and lobbying, forcing the NAACP to rely less on donations from large donors.[101] The NAACP held discussions about how to maintain member interest and meet mounting financial challenges. Wilkins suggested to White at the time that "a great deal of money seems to be lying around in Left and near-Left circles . . . our cautious conservatism has kept us standing still while a great many persons who were sympathetic with us . . . have become more . . . progressive."[102]

The NAACP also worried about losing members. In March of 1939, Wilkins prodded White to consider new strategies, saying that if the NAACP failed to capitalize on the growth of mainly pro-labor NAACP "youth councils," young people will lose interest.[103] These concerns continued into the 1940s, when White confessed that "some people" believe that the MOWM, an organization that embraced the politics of mass protest wholeheartedly, "should replace the NAACP."[104] With Du Bois out of the picture, White now had to worry about rivalries from outside of the organization.

Perhaps mass public opinion among potential supporters explains the NAACP's change. In contrast to the national organization, the Chicago, Detroit, and Baltimore NAACP branches greatly increased their memberships and revenue by recruiting black laborers.[105] The NAACP could replicate the success of these local chapters by broadening their agenda to include working-class concerns and labor rights. Therefore, its members would not let them pursue a labor strategy in the 1930s, but required them to in the 1940s. Changing attitudes among black laborers and youth councils fit with an ideological explanation of change, but the financial difficulties produced by the Great Depression and the IRS tax classifications were historical contingencies. Without them, middle-class donations might have kept it on its current trajectory. And without the Wagner Act, there might not have been a thriving labor union like the CIO willing to help the NAACP.

Employment Considerations

Additionally, NAACP leaders continued to worry about the danger posed to African Americans by the rising union economy even after it adopted pro-labor positions. Leaders were concerned that continued hostility to unions among black workers would lose them favor among a rising economic superpower. It was clear that a greater percentage of workplaces were being organized by labor unions, as one might expect given the legal protections provided by the Wagner Act. The CIO was even planning a campaign called "Operation Dixie" to organize workplaces in the South, where the majority of African Americans still resided. Many African Americans saw that unions would play a large role in the American economy and saw no point in opposing them.[106]

In 1941, between 1,500 and 2,500 black workers were trapped inside a Ford plant when they refused to join the strike. Both the Chrysler Corporation and Ford Corporation responded to major strikes by organizing "back to work" movements among blacks, raising suspicion among Detroit NAACP leaders that the corporations were dividing workers for their own advantage or even provoking a race riot in order to enlist government aid in repressing the strike.[107] The hitherto anti-union Detroit NAACP president urged African Americans not to serve as replacement workers during the strike, and urged the blacks inside to leave the plant. Detroit's Youth Councils, the most active in the nation, broadcasted the union message using a UAW vehicle with a loudspeaker. The national NAACP quickly became involved. White wrote to the Detroit chapter president that blacks need to be aware of "the new order of things" represented by the union.[108] After securing a pledge from the UAW to reduce discrimination, White sent him a telegram to continue "full cooperation" with the union.[109] White visited the plant with a loudspeaker and urged blacks, some of whom he knew personally, to leave the plant.[110] Since most black Ford employees still voted against the UAW-CIO,[111] the local and national NAACP showed themselves leading, rather than reflecting, mass opinion among blacks.

This episode illustrates that the NAACP believed that black workers had to improve relations with unions given their increasing role in the economy. To a Cleveland attorney, White wrote that some union would organize Ford and "the Negro worker had the grim choice of casting his lot with the union or having its hostility after they organized."[112] He showed considerable awareness of the risky choices he needed to make. Privately, he wrote that "there is really little difference fundamentally between the attitude of employers and of unions toward the Negro."[113] These public and private utterances suggest resignation, not an epiphany about the justice of a union-based economy.

Political Considerations

Neither political party paid much attention to civil rights in the 1930s, but the CIO could provide political "muscle" if the NAACP could enlist its aid. Quite simply, the CIO could obtain political support from large numbers of people who would otherwise not be active in politics. As the Wagner Act offered federal protection for unions, the CIO gained the allegiance of more workers and its clout grew rapidly. The CIO had the ability to issue group appeals to workers, distribute political literature, solicit donations, and recruit canvassers from a captive audience in a given workplace. Long before most politicians used direct mailing to target different constituencies, CIO affiliates had workers' home addresses and could target workers in pivotal precincts.[114] After the CIO PAC was organized in 1943, it published eighty-five million pieces of campaign literature, including some targeted at African Americans.[115] The PAC was also one of the first political organizations to use advanced survey methods previously used by advertising firms.[116]

The CIO appeared to be a major player in Democratic nominating contests. The *New York Times* sensationally reported that the CIO caused Harry Truman to be the vice presidential candidate in 1944. Although the CIO was not present at the meeting where Truman was chosen, Roosevelt did request that the suggestion be "cleared" with CIO PAC founder Sidney Hillman.[117] "Clear it with Sidney" became a popular Republican refrain. President Truman also paid close attention to the CIO. He vetoed the Taft-Hartley Act, which restricted union rights, only because he needed union support for his foreign policy and reelection.[118]

In the 1940s, the NAACP carefully considered how its public positions would affect its rapport with both the CIO and a larger coalition of liberal groups of which it was a part. The NAACP withheld praise from the Republican platforms in 1940 and 1944 even though the Democratic Party platforms were worse on civil rights. As usual, the organization refrained from officially endorsing candidates,[119] but its preferences were still voiced in an oblique manner. Spingarn, echoed by White, said that "the Negro should align himself with all the liberal forces behind the New Deal," and if "we in any way attack President Roosevelt (we have got to be realistic) we are helping to elect Dewey and so are cutting ourselves off from all association with liberal forces."[120] The board considered issuing a statement in 1944 that the Democrats "lost face" with black voters by sponsoring a weak platform and replacing Henry Wallace with Harry Truman. Instead, the NAACP just declared that "neither party platform on the Negro is satisfactory to intelligent Negroes."

The NAACP's deference to the political positions of the CIO, in particular, continued into 1948. It terminated W. E. B. Du Bois's employment a second time when he publicly wrote in favor of Progressive Party candidate Henry

Wallace. Wallace was more supportive of civil rights than Truman, but the CIO PAC and ADA vigorously opposed him as a spoiler candidate with too many ties to the Communist Party. Ostensibly, the rationale for Du Bois's removal was that he violated the organization's policy on endorsements. However, White's support for Roosevelt in 1944 and Truman in 1948 was almost as overt. Firing Du Bois generated considerable embarrassment after the organization went to the trouble of rehiring him to win international support for civil rights.[121]

Ideological Considerations

The NAACP leaders abided by liberal ideological commitments, but not at the expense of the organization's growth or leaders' own position in the organization. NAACP leaders were mostly supportive of federally sponsored social welfare measures at an early time, and surely this facilitated alliances with liberal groups such as the CIO. But those who pushed ahead their own ideas without regard for organizational interest were set aside. Socialist NAACP board members realized that the NAACP's funding and membership would suffer should they conjoin socialism with their civil rights agenda.[122] Despite the hard work being done on behalf of civil rights by communists in the CIO, the NAACP approved of the CIO's communist purge during the postwar Red Scare and even conducted one of its own. If they were not listening to their own in-house pundit, Du Bois, it is unlikely that other writers changed the leaders' minds. Du Bois's writings in the *Crisis* had once been the centerpiece of the NAACP, but he was forced to step aside for the "organization man," Walter White.[123] Ovington was relieved by his departure even though she had been an avid reader for decades, writing that "now we are rid of our octopus, for of late he has been draining our strength."[124] Even after the NAACP sided with the CIO, NAACP leaders privately worried about whether unions were really best for black employment, or just an inevitability they had to accommodate. Ideology was trumped by other considerations in the microlevel decisions of party change.

Initiating the Alliance

The decisions to side with labor on many occasions were important steps in the creation of a black-blue coalition, which needed to happen to change the Democratic Party on race. Groups must actively work on behalf of each other's agenda to earn a place in a coalition. None of the written records of the NAACP provide a "smoking gun" and directly announce a decision to ally with the CIO. Instead, they reveal an unprecedented pattern of generous support. At several junctures, the NAACP demonstrated its sensitivity to the importance of labor as a potential political ally.

The NAACP considered proposing an antidiscrimination amendment to the Wagner Act in 1940, but worried that doing so would alienate labor and set a dangerous precedent for federal harassment of unions.[125] When Senator Howard Smith attempted to make changes to the Wagner Act, the NAACP acknowledged that the Wagner Act was not perfect, but charged that the committee intended to "emasculate" the Wagner Act rather than resolve disputes more fairly. After a meeting with John L. Lewis and several other CIO leaders, the NAACP suggested its own amendment in a strategic move to prevent the Smith committee from using civil rights as an argument.[126] The NAACP even revised its amendment to make it more difficult to prove discrimination. The first draft denied legal benefits to unions that discriminated, but the later draft changed the phrasing to deny benefits to unions that "customarily" or "usually" discriminated. An NAACP memo read:

> These changes leave a certain loophole in the bill. A Union might, for example, take in a few negroes to give lip service to the requirement and refuse admission to others. However, in view of the status of this proposed legislation and of the importance of labor support for it, I personally think it is all right.[127]

In the same year, the NAACP assumed responsibility for a $25,000 debt the International Ladies Garment Workers Union owed to the Garland Fund. The NAACP's publicity director also praised it for retaining a white-only printer's union to publish the *Crisis*, saying that "the NAACP has shown real intelligence in taking this step to show the identity of the interest with that of organized labor."[128]

The NAACP altered its organizational identity to include labor interests, patiently advancing a pro-labor agenda while passing over issues that might highlight tensions between labor and blacks. Although its legal department had considerable success prosecuting labor union discrimination early in the 1940s, Goluboff shows that it soon retreated from litigation against labor unions completely.[129] At the national level, the NAACP donated money to workers on strike and urged local chapters to do the same.[130] The NAACP appointed a "labor secretary" in 1946, acknowledging that black employment was not part of its mission. The secretary, Clarence Mitchell, outlined seven goals. Among them, he wanted to collaborate with labor unions to support labor legislation benefiting both blacks and unions. Mitchell consistently told "working people to join bona fide non-segregated labor organizations, to attend the meetings of such organizations, and to be good members in all respects."[131] From the beginning, Mitchell "perceived the value of coalition-building with organized labor," and later made great use of these contacts when he directed the Washington Bureau.[132] Frymer describes Mitchell's labor department as "vigorous in a multitude of venues, lobbying Congress for greater civil rights protections, asking legislators to pay attention to the consequences of closed union shops, working with local NAACP branches around the country to respond to individual cases of discrimination, and working with both national and local unions to target civil rights abuses."[133] The NAACP removed longstanding officers who did not assimilate to the new, broadened mission.[134] In 1947, the CIO secretary treasurer boasted that "We have tremendous influence in each of the organizations," referring to the NAACP and NUL.[135] For most of the 1950s, the NAACP remained hopeful and enthusiastic about organized labor.[136] Polls showed that African Americans viewed labor unions in an increasingly positive light over the 1950s even as the public as a whole viewed them with increasing suspicion.[137]

NAACP leaders bundled opposition with labor rights with opposition to civil rights. Part of this bundle was attacking the Taft-Hartley Act, right-to-work laws, and Senator Taft himself. The NAACP actively lobbied against Taft-Hartley, writing to AFL president Green in 1947 that they had a "vital and mutual interest" in antilynching bills, FEPC bills, and their "unwholesome twin—the desire to shackle the labor movement with the Taft-Hartley Act."[138] A "labor organization must have some security against the concentrated economic power of management," testified the NAACP representative before Congress.[139] In an address to the CIO's annual convention in 1947, the NAACP stated "there is no difference between the assaults upon the rights of labor and the various forms of discrimination which oppress minorities."[140]

In the wake of Taft-Hartley, the NAACP boasted that it "mobilized its entire resources to crush 'right to work' laws" in individual states. The NAACP sent members to public forums and registered voters in pivotal areas. NAACP publications linked opposition to labor with opposition to civil rights, including a pamphlet entitled "Keep Mississippi Out of California." AFL-CIO president George Meany thanked the NAACP for its work against "right-to-work" laws in 1958 and again in 1964; AFL-CIO analyses found that African American voters were pivotal voters in right-to-work referenda.[141]

Furthermore, the NAACP targeted Robert Taft for intense criticism. Taft was not a leading opponent of civil rights,[142] but he was the Senate's foremost opponent of organized labor. Jack Kroll, CIO PAC director, wrote *A Speaker's Handbook on Robert Alphonso Taft*, and the AFL's Labor League for Political Action solicited two-dollar contributions from nine million members in 1949 to defeat him in 1950.[143] The NAACP's *Crisis* attacked Taft for his position on FEPC and refused to publish a response he submitted.[144] When Taft declared that a high-ranking figure among the NAACP preferred a mere fact-finding FEPC during his reelection campaign in 1950, the NAACP publicized its demand for him to name the official and sent a telegram to the senator four times. White wrote to the CIO that "I am delighted that we have caught him in such a vicious distortion of the truth and you may be sure that we are going to follow it through to the end."[145]

The NAACP joined a broad coalition that assembled liberal economic positions and civil rights into a package deal forced upon the Democratic Party in 1948. In 1944, the NAACP urged both parties to use government programs to secure full employment instead of leaving recovery to private initiative. White—joined by the CIO—called for a Conference of Progressives in 1946. At this conference, White favored universal health care and the continuation of rent and price controls.[146] The CIO took the same position as the NAACP in thirty-eight of the forty-two congressional bills where the NAACP took a stand from 1946 to 1955.[147] In 1950, a member complained that the NAACP was distracted from civil rights, campaigning for rent control and spending five hundred dollars to support primarily white workers on strike.[148] The NAACP acknowledged that "the NAACP has grown in its conception of the scope of our work . . . It is quite true that there are many organizations working in specific fields with regard to some of these matters, but we feel that there should be the utmost cooperation on the part of all organizations committed to a program of bettering human relations."[149]

The NAACP even pursued social welfare legislation favored by labor unions and liberals at the short-term expense of civil rights. It was so committed to economic policies aimed at the working class that it opposed civil rights amendments that threatened the passage of social welfare bills.[150] In the past, the NAACP had opposed social welfare measures such as the National Industrial Recovery Act (section 7a) and Social Security when adequate safeguards were not in place for minority workers. In the future, the NAACP would oppose aid to education that did not exclude segregated schools. For most of the 1940s, however, the NAACP opposed antidiscrimination amendments to social welfare measures, knowing that these amendments would cause the bills to fail.[151]

Benefits of the Alliance

The choices made by the NAACP grew their organization and prestige, further suggesting the importance of group interest in choosing coalition allies. Beginning in 1940, the NAACP received substantial contributions from CIO-affiliated unions.[152] These new contributions were crucial in a time of decreasing donations from the middle class. The NAACP and the CIO collaborated more strongly on fundraising as the 1940s marched on. The CIO readily advised the NAACP on which local unions and individuals were likely to be sympathetic to fundraising drives.[153] The CIO CARD also encouraged local unions to set up committees to run membership drives for the NAACP, not only to help the CIO but to raise awareness of civil rights.[154]

The funding and access to politics provided by the CIO solidified the NAACP's standing as the leading civil rights organization. White was always careful not to let other civil rights groups take a leading role in any visible task. When President Truman created the President's Committee on Civil Rights (PCCR), he tried to dominate the proceedings by providing NAACP information to its members. He wrote to Thurgood Marshall that "We must move fast . . . we must not let anybody else steal the show from us."[155] The NAACP obtained an agreement from the CIO to help maintain its standing, promising not to cooperate with rival organizations such as the NNC, which the CIO originally funded.[156] When a Los Angeles affiliate of the CIO endorsed the NNC, the CIO's national industrial director wrote that "the stated program and agenda of the NNC are largely a duplication of the work of the NAACP" and are "from time to time at variance." The director continued that "the organization with which we work very closely and successful is the NAACP" and warned that the Los Angeles chapter must discontinue its support or be in violation of rules passed by the governing council.[157]

The CIO generally followed the NAACP's lead on civil rights issues and helped shift power away from less supportive civil rights leaders. A. Philip Randolph, who led the National Council for a Permanent FEPC, prioritized the desegregation of the armed forces over the FEPC, and worked with

Senator Taft on both issues. When Randolph was willing to settle for an FEPC without enforcement powers, leaders from the NAACP and CIO contacted other groups in the council and persuaded them to let the NAACP take over the FEPC fight.[158] In 1950, the CIO's position on federal aid to education was to support "progressive equalization of school plant facilities before receiving Federal grants." The NAACP's labor secretary told the CIO that its position was inadequate; it needed to oppose federal aid to education unless the appropriations were barred from segregated schools. Teachers' associations and liberal groups generally opposed the NAACP's position, but the CIO agreed.[159] In 1949, the CIO, NAACP, ADA, and Jewish groups convinced Special Counsel Clark Clifford to drop plans for an omnibus civil rights bill and favored an FEPC by itself, which the coalition believed was more realistic.[160] In matters of legislation, the CIO repeatedly refused to settle for compromise FEPC bills. The CARD argued that it had become a barometer for the progressive position on civil rights and compromising would only lower the bar for ambitious proposals.[161]

For the legal department, the CIO provided essential funding for the *Brown v. Board of Education* decision, which many regard as the most important victory in the NAACP's history. The NAACP ended 1952 with an operating deficit of $34,000 and sought to raise $100,000 in 1953 to prepare for whatever decision the Supreme Court made. It raised $2,500 from the CIO in and $75,000 from the Philip Murray Memorial Foundation (headed by longtime CIO operative James Carey) in 1954.[162]

A useful way to evaluate the internal benefits of the alliance is to consider the counterfactual. Where else would they have raised the money? Business interest groups had not shown the willingness to donate money that would match the contributions of labor unions, and if they had, they lacked the manpower[163] to assist with membership drives, voter registration drives, and workplace integration efforts.[164] Even in the domain of government discrimination against minorities, business was seldom willing to fight vigorously for civil rights.[165] If funded by business, NAACP's agenda may have included its lawsuits against discriminatory unions,[166] but had more difficulty pushing for the FEPC, which outlawed discrimination in employment. Employers would not look fondly at laws that usurped what they viewed as their hiring prerogatives.[167]

That does not mean that the alliance was inevitable. Neither the Great Depression nor the Wagner Act, both of which changed the NAACP's calculations, was inevitable. The NAACP had to endure considerable recalcitrance from the CIO and other unions when it came to in-house discrimination, where less patient organizations might have broken away. African American leaders were not pawns of the CIO; they entered an alliance with eyes wide open to the risks.

Conclusion

This chapter documents the first important steps taken to build a coalition between labor and civil rights groups. In the 1940s, the NAACP changed from a narrow civil rights agenda to collaborating with the CIO on organizational growth as well as political and labor issues. Its new pro-labor agenda was a response to flagging membership, diminishing financial resources, political roadblocks, and realism about the future of black workers. The NAACP followed ideological considerations when they did not interfere with organizational interests, and in Walter White's case, his personal ambitions. Future chapters show that this coalition turned the Democratic Party on civil rights. Had the NAACP raised more money through other sources or challenged labor unions, it would be isolated not only from labor groups but other liberal causes. Next, we turn to the CIO's interest in the alliance. Group coalescence is the first step to party transformation and the CIO's positions on civil rights are the other half of the story.

CHAPTER 3

Labor's Interest in a Civil Rights Coalition

In the last chapter, I explained how and why the NAACP stretched its hand to the CIO. Its overtures to the CIO would not have been politically consequential if the CIO did not have a comparable interest in the alliance. This chapter explores why the CIO's nominal commitment to racial equality translated into political support for civil rights in the 1940s, synthesizing civil rights and labor rights. The alliance between the CIO and NAACP was the most important instance of civil rights groups and labor unions working together. For the CIO, the NAACP could vouch for its civil rights program and persuade black voters and workers to cooperate in elections and at the workplace. It was this cooperation that enabled activists, both in and out of the labor movement, to integrate civil rights into the Democratic Party while keeping backlash from white workers at manageable levels. The alliance was constructed with arduous work and Herculean patience by groups and their leaders, not elected politicians.

In Chapter 1, I claimed we need to understand the motivations of individual groups in a coalition to understand the coalition's positions. Only by investigating the CIO's reasons for supporting civil rights can we understand the genesis of the Democratic Party's transformation. Some scholars argue that the CIO was influenced by the need for black laborers, but it was much more supportive of civil rights in politics than it was at the workplace. The CIO's national political agenda was a way to protect its member interests, and supporting civil rights helped achieve its political goals. Many unskilled workplaces were dominated by whites who resented the inclusion of black workers, so that shop floor civil rights were sometimes an impediment to organizing. In politics, however, there was much to gain and little to lose by supporting civil rights once the NAACP embraced a pro-labor agenda. If the CIO was influenced by ideology such as socialism, one might argue that party transformation comes from ideas. Instead, the hardheaded union leaders showed only a trimming of ideology during important decisions, and were willing to set it aside when it conflicted with member interests.

Conflicts and cooperation between the labor and civil rights movement during this time have been explored in detail by labor historians.[1] The two partners had their differences, and needed to work with each other to maintain a harmonious relationship in spite of the differences. Most agree that the CIO was an overall positive force for civil rights, although its support wavered over time.[2] For our purposes, what matters most is that the NAACP accepted its commitment as sufficient and lent its prestige as the CIO integrated civil rights into the Democratic Party's agenda.

The first section documents the CIO's motivations for participating in coalitions—the first step of party change. In this case, the group's issue agenda in politics is a more credible explanation for its behavior than recruiting members. After exploring the CIO's motivations for supporting civil rights, I describe the steps it took to establish a constructive relationship with the NAACP. I argue that the alliance provided numerous benefits, political and otherwise, to the CIO just as the CIO had for the NAACP. The CIO avoided the poor strategic moves of many working-class organizations before it that had opposed civil rights.

The CIO's Interest in Civil Rights

The early CIO broke away from the AFL in order to organize unskilled labor. The AFL generally organized workers by skill rather than industry, so that practitioners of particular crafts would be organized into separate unions even in an individual plant. A growing movement of "industrial unionists" believed that all of the workers in a plant needed to be organized into a single union in order for less-skilled or unskilled workers to have bargaining power. As the Great Depression threatened union enrollment, unskilled industry leaders in the AFL believed that their survival was at stake, but AFL leaders refused to offer significant support to new industrial unions. The conflict between craft and industrial unions led to a fistfight at the AFL convention between the president of the Carpenter's union, William Hutcheson and the president of the United Mine Workers, John L. Lewis, in 1935. While Lewis relit his cigar and continued speaking at the convention, he later called a number of other union leaders to organize the CIO, formally created in 1936 by eight international unions.

The differences between the CIO and AFL do not stop with the dispute over recruiting unskilled labor. The CIO was a new kind of union that viewed its worker interests as dependent on federal and state policies. It had an ambitious political agenda of supporting government regulations and programs consistent with the New Deal. For unions to survive, they needed to maintain the Wagner Act and the liberal jurisprudence of the New Deal regime. To avoid being laid off, workers also needed the government to adopt countercyclical policies. From the beginning, the CIO sought a package of economic measures designed to promote a full employment.[3] Additionally, as long as the South remained a bastion of low wages and union restrictions, the CIO program was in jeopardy since businesses could simply relocate to the South. In time, the CIO viewed civil rights groups and black voters as important allies in promoting its political agenda. Black voters could help the CIO counteract southern Democrats who wished to keep the region free of unions and federal interference such as minimum wage laws.

From an early date, it was clear that the CIO judged candidates and parties on issues like public spending and not just labor rights. By contrast, the AFL focused mainly on improving wages and working conditions, and only judged candidates by their record on labor.[4] The North Carolina AFL candidly admitted the differences between the organizations when they tried to influence state politics together. The state AFL dissented from the CIO gubernatorial endorsement, telling the governor that fighting for issues other than labor would needlessly create enemies and spread itself thin:

At a recent meeting of the United Political Committee most of the AFL, and R.R. Brotherhood took the position that their membership should not be urged to vote against a candidate unless the record or expressed views of that candidate revealed that he was unfair or antagonistic to the welfare of labor and that your record did not warrant such action . . . We think the CIO view unwise; that it borrows the hazard of defeating and resulting reprisals from other groups, and places labor in the position of attempting to gain political control for special political advantage. We are endeavoring to be realistic.[5]

A CIO activist in the North Carolina coalition complained that other unions, including the AFL, "would not actually do anything progressive unless they were goaded into action."[6]

The Democratic Party was obviously a better vessel than the Republican Party[7] for maintaining and extending the New Deal and labor rights, and the CIO worked exclusively with it. The CIO PAC founder Sidney Hillman boasted that labor groups wielded considerable strength in Democratic Party nominations in 1943, even before he organized the PAC.[8] At the 1944 convention, for example, Roosevelt asked DNC Chair Frank Walker to work with Hillman and ensure a pro-labor delegation at the 1944 Democratic Convention.[9] The CIO had to promise its members' votes as a bloc to the Democratic Party to have the leverage it wanted. During the Republican nomination contest of 1944, Wendell Willkie sought to obtain union support by flanking Roosevelt's left on labor issues in 1944. CIO Executive Board members worried about Willkie dividing their bloc and contemplated making a statement against the candidate, saying "all the work we have done will be damaged, and it will take a terrifically long time to repair it if we don't hit this thing in the head."[10] For the same reason, the CIO dismissed third parties as a means to its ends. Hillman worked to quash third-party movements even though he had previously participated in several of them.[11] He helped unite the Minnesota Farmer-Labor Party and Democratic Party, and sought assurances from other party movements that they would not run challengers to New Deal Democrats.[12]

But the Democratic Party's southern wing, which had a longer history in the party, competed for influence. Southern members of Congress (MCs) began opposing New Deal labor policies before they opposed other liberal economic policies.[13] While southern opposition to labor crystallized in response to the CIO's positions on race, the CIO threatened other pillars of southern electoral politics. It fought for a national minimum wage so that northern businesses would not simply relocate to the South; southern politicians wanted to maintain their region's low-wage advantage. Southern officeholders benefited from elections that excluded working-class voters of both races with poll taxes and a one-party system.[14] Company towns and employers wanted government intervention in strikes and had ample reason to oppose the CIO regardless of civil rights. Other southerners were simply concerned about their place in the party, apart from any policy commitments. As labor's influence increased in the party, the South's influence would decrease.[15]

Thus, the CIO shared a common enemy with civil rights supporters. Politicians who logroll benefit even if they have nothing in common, but if they do have something in common (like a common enemy), the alliance will be stronger.[16] The CIO and civil rights groups not only had a common enemy, but a common interest in civil rights, voting rights, and integrated workplaces and a common enemy in their southern opponents. Before 1948, civil rights referred to federal protection for the freedom of association, and not just the rights of racial minorities.[17] Black and white CIO organizers were both harassed by the police or lynched in the South, as NAACP executive secretary White pointed out to the CIO in a request for funds in 1940.[18] The creation of the civil rights division in the attorney general's office aided CIO organizers in addition to civil rights workers.[19] Laws used to restrict the labor movement's mass protest tactics could be used to restrict civil rights marchers, sit-ins, labor marches, and pickets alike.[20]

National antidiscrimination laws would help the CIO to organize workers all at once rather than meet with the different races separately. Many union leaders found that mandated segregation jeopardized Operation Dixie, an ambitious southern organizing drive. Union organizers struggled to find places in which both white and black workers could meet, since motels frequently refused to let the latter enter the establishment in any capacity.[21] One African American CIO leader reported to the PCCR that CIO officials in the South jeopardized their reputation by voluntarily supporting integration. The wartime FEPC, which outlawed discrimination in defense industries, provided them cover because they could explain that they were just complying with the law. Both the CIO and civil rights groups, therefore, supported a postwar FEPC with great interest.[22]

In addition to common interests in select laws, civil rights were part of a national strategy to help CIO-favored candidates win elections. The CIO PAC hoped to increase turnout among lower-class voters who often failed to vote at all or only voted in presidential years.[23] The CIO needed all the help it could get to dislodge incumbents who, for decades, blocked pro-labor initiatives in committees and forced restrictions on labor unions on Congress as a whole.[24] The CIO believed—perhaps too optimistically—that if they could eliminate poll taxes in some states, persuade workers to pay poll taxes in other states, and register new voters, antilabor southern MCs could be displaced in primaries. African Americans were a large part of the new voters they wanted.[25] Thanks to NAACP litigation, the Supreme Court invalidated white-only primaries in 1944, and the black voting population was increasing in the South.

Between 1947 and 1952, black voter registration jumped from 5 to 20 percent of the voting age population.[26]

Not only could black voters help CIO candidates win elections, but support for civil rights could entice middle-class liberals into joining a broad coalition with unions. The CIO PAC spawned organizations to rally nonunion members to liberal groups that supported labor rights among many other causes. Hillman created the National Citizens PAC in 1944 to provide "an entrée for the CIO into diverse segments of the population not reachable directly through the trade union movement." Of its 142 board members, 22 were African American.[27] The most important fledgling organization, however, was Americans for Democratic Action, which helped to pass the civil rights plank at the 1948 Democratic Convention. ADA was a small, poorly funded organization before the CIO supported it, and it readily admitted it needed labor's support more than labor needed it.[28]

Jack Kroll, CIO PAC director, also worried about pro-union third parties that could cause Democratic candidates to lose, especially Wallace's Progressive Party in 1948. A memo read that broad progressive goals like civil rights would attract nonunion liberals and meet "the demands of those who seek to push us into third party adventures."[29] The CIO PAC could convince union volunteers that it and the Democratic Party were visionary organizations that obviated the need for third parties. Broad ideological groups like ADA and the National Citizens PAC piggybacked off the efforts of large labor unions like the CIO, which "anchored" them with workers tied together for self-interested as well as ideological reasons.[30]

The CIO's commitment to politics did not mean that the CIO prioritized political reform at every turn. Some political goals protected worker interests more than others, and the CIO chose its priorities carefully. Schlozman points out that the CIO's support for universal health care was only general and it was much more vigorous in negotiating its own members' health care benefits. Arguably, this not only showed that it was primarily a member-interest organization, but it undermined efforts to secure universal health coverage through public policy. As more Americans negotiated health care benefits through private contracts, it was harder to make the case for health care through government. Even the most politically conscious unions chose bread and butter over politics when forced to make a choice.[31] This offers evidence against Weyher and others who claim that its civil rights policies were determined by ideology in the face of conflicting organizational interests. Civil rights, unlike health care, were essential to transforming the Democrats into a vessel that served it.[32]

The CIO's pursuit of civil rights in the Democratic Party had a political cost, of course; it helped turn southern Democrats against the rest of the CIO PAC's agenda. They were among the most reliable supporters of the early New Deal.[33] While the South opposed labor rights even before the CIO fought for civil rights, it was receptive to the New Deal until the Democratic Party embraced civil rights. CIO support for civil rights helped extend southern opposition from just labor rights to all parts of the New Deal.[34] Before the President's Commission on Civil Rights report was issued, South Carolina Senator Strom Thurmond declared that "We who believe in a liberal political philosophy . . . will vote for the election of Harry Truman."[35] Milkis and Black and Black argue that many southern Democrats who had supported the national party on issues not related to race relations "angrily revolted against the liberal wing" of the party and "renewed their ties with their most conservative constituents."[36]

Recruitment Drives as an Alternate Explanation

One might argue that the CIO had to favor civil rights because it needed to gain the loyalty of black workers, who constituted a significant portion of industrial workplaces by World War II. At the time it organized, blacks composed 4 percent of auto workers, 15 percent of steelworkers, and 25 percent of Chicago's packinghouse workers.[37] Ten percent of the CIO membership was black in 1945, compared with 3.4 percent of the AFL.[38] Blacks were often an important faction in internal workplace quarrels, and a coterie of loyal workers could help organizers win factional struggles.[39] There are two separate issues that might have affected black worker support: civil rights at the *workplace* and civil rights in *politics*. If a union did not include blacks or treat them fairly, they might vote against unionizing or vote for a competing union.[40] Even if the CIO were to organize a workplace without blacks, they might serve as replacement workers and impede the success of strikes.[41] Black replacement workers could provoke race riots, which could be used as a pretext for state repression of a strike.[42] Supporting civil rights in politics might also attract the support of black workers.[43] Yet, these explanations fall short.

Civil rights at the workplace did not consistently help the CIO grow as a union because it often alienated white workers.[44] The CIO instructed its organizers to improvise based on local needs, generally starting by organizing whites.[45] Operation Dixie bypassed industries where large number of blacks were employed.[46] When steelworkers in Birmingham, Alabama, were accused of bigotry in 1950, CIO president Philip Murray ordered desegregation of all facilities. The southern director of steelworkers reported that white workers signed a petition to quit the union if the order was enforced, and if the AFL learned of their dissatisfaction, it would take over "lock, stock, and barrel." Not only did Murray retreat from the order, but he also cancelled a civil rights conference in Birmingham at the director's suggestion.[47] Many other labor leaders worried not only about takeovers but their own safety. Adding to all of these risks, any gestures toward integration led to police harassment.[48]

Black workers showed on many occasions that they might join a union for job benefits even when it meant belonging to a segregated local or contributing to the racially obtuse AFL.[49] The AFL's success in organizing unskilled workplaces proves that the CIO did more than it needed to do just to organize unskilled labor.[50] The CIO actually considered racial equality in the workplace as a way to obtain the support of black voters in politics, rather than the other way around.[51]

Civil rights in politics were also a liability for recruiting white workers. Much of the rank and file joined for the job security and benefits that a union could provide, not politics. Not surprisingly, the CIO stayed clear of political issues during Operation Dixie. When Secretary Treasurer James Carey was asked whether it would address racial problems, he replied that the director had "a single purpose in mind, that of organization."[52] While other committees in the CIO should deal with discrimination, Operation Dixie organizers should not be "at the present time engaging in a program of publicizing the PAC, anti-poll tax campaign, or any other matter except organizing."[53] A progressive organizer in Mississippi warned that he could persuade his members to overlook everything except for contribution to civil rights causes, which his local paper reported on.[54]

In sum, the CIO had to weigh the need to organize prejudiced workers against the need to organize blacks, and to weigh the effects of politics on both. Both kinds of civil rights were often downplayed or highlighted as local situations dictated. But the need for blacks as political allies remained even civil rights hurt organizing drives.

Ideology as an Alternate Explanation

Some view the CIO's civil rights positions as an outgrowth of ideology.[55] More specifically, many CIO organizers were influenced by various permutations of socialism or liberalism, leading to them to oppose all vestiges of Jim Crow.

Socialists long viewed racial divisions as a way of undermining class solidarity. By extension, a party transformation led by the CIO would mean a transformation rooted in ideology.

Schickler shows that civil rights was not a defining feature of American liberalism until the CIO emerged as a major rival to the AFL. Many liberals criticized the New Deal for failing to achieve economic justice, but few called upon Roosevelt to fight for civil rights. The *Nation* and the *New Republic* brought up civil rights in the mid-1930s only in passing, not as part of the detailed agendas they outlined. Nor did a *New Republic* survey of prominent progressives bring up civil rights as a shortcoming of the New Deal. Social scientists studying liberalism and conservatism in the 1920s and early 1930s almost never included civil rights as a survey instrument.[56] If the CIO embodied a liberal ideology that included civil rights, it was not a preexisting ideology created by pundits but one developed alongside its organization drives, serving its national political ambitions.

Hillman had been a Menshevik before leaving Russia in 1906. UAW president (and future CIO president) Walter Reuther studied socialism and visited the Soviet Union. Reuther defended the Soviet Union to anticommunist New Dealers, paid dues to the Communist Party, and attended the twelfth anniversary of Lenin's death.[57] The CIO's flagship union, the UAW, had an organizing staff of nine whites in 1936, five of whom had been communists. Three of the six black organizers added by the UAW in 1937 were communists.[58] Outside of the CIO, BSCP president A. Philip Randolph had been the editor of the Socialist Party *Messenger*.[59]

Many other CIO leaders were not communist, however. Members of the CIO's CARD frequently referred to communists derisively as "Commies." CARD members saw them as opportunists who sought to draw African Americans away from the CIO to serve as pawns for Moscow.[60] CIO president Lewis (1936–1940) was a Republican and CIO president Murray (1940–1952) attended Catholic mass daily. When Lewis was asked about the role of communists in the union, he replied they were only tools for organizing, asking "Who gets the bird, the *hunter* or the dog?" Murray saw the tripartite war boards of World War II as a model for future economic planning. Business, government, and labor should have input in national economic decisions, and labor should submit to the board's decision so long as it had a genuine role. He opposed full nationalization of industry and did not want the reputation of organized labor tarnished in another Red Scare. While the CIO employed open communists until the late 1940s, Murray often demoted any communists who issued radical statements in the name of the CIO.[61] Murray opposed the anticommunist ADA when he thought it would needlessly split the labor movement, but he turned against the communists when it was politically pragmatic. He funded, encouraged, and helped direct ADA to defeat Wallace's challenge in 1948.[62]

And as with the NAACP, socialist beliefs among organizational leaders did not translate into CIO policies. Even socialists showed themselves willing to subordinate their philosophical positions to advancing the CIO's power, membership, and funding—if not their own personal ambitions. Reuther allied with anticommunist ethnic and religious subgroups in the UAW when the communist wing of the UAW elevated a rival for a leadership position.[63] Hillman believed that the Communist Party (and later, other third parties) "represented a real and present danger to the [Roosevelt] administration and to hopes that Hillman cherished for the CIO," namely, "that it be invited permanently inside the highest policy-making and strategy-making circles of the Democratic Party." Many communists were also allied with Lewis due to his foreign policy isolationism in 1940, when Hillman and Lewis were rivals in a CIO power struggle. Accordingly, Hillman's followers authorized a resolution at the CIO convention in 1941 condemning communism and calling for an expulsion of communists. A biographer characterizes Hillman as a "half intellectual . . . committed first of all to the palpable dynamics of organized power and uninhibited by any prescribed beliefs that might obstruct the pursuit of that power," particularly in his later years when he was involved with the CIO.[64]

Hillman and Reuther showed themselves willing to abandon the fundamental Marxist commitment to democratic organization of the workplace in exchange for contracts giving them more control over the workers. The contracts provided certain benefits to the workers, but also gave unions the responsibility for creating a predictable workforce, disciplining members and preventing wildcat strikes. Subversive behavior was channeled through the grievance procedure. The CIO purged itself of communists during the postwar Red Scare, when they became a severe public relations and legal liability. For the CIO to purge the organizers who helped build their organization suggests that they would have ceased supporting civil rights if it became a net liability to the organization, whatever intellectual commitments they had. As Piven and Cloward write, "Radical ideology is no defense against the imperatives created by organizational maintenance."[65] Hillman and Reuther checked their ideology in at the factory gates when there was an obvious organizational advantage in defying it.

Communism is an antireligious ideology in addition to an antiracist ideology. But union leaders influenced by Marx did not hesitate to invoke religion when it worked in their favor. BSCP president A. Philip Randolph was an atheist, but downplayed his opposition to religion because of its importance to members of the BSCP and later the MOWM. He reminded followers that he was a preacher's son and held BSCP meetings in churches, usually starting with a prayer.[66] Hillman recruited Lucy Randolph Mason as the CIO's southern director of public relations. A patrician southerner with well-known religious convictions, Mason made a sustained effort to assure southerners that the CIO was compatible with religion. She secured statements from most of the major religious denominations that labor unions were at least permissible and possibly commendable.[67]

In summary, many CIO leaders were influenced by different forms of economic liberalism and socialism, but it hardly constrained the union to follow socialist ideas against the union's interests. They adapted their message and their tactics to grow the CIO. Civil rights helped it pursue necessary political goals, but socialism didn't. If the CIO was willing to back away from other ideological commitments for hardheaded realities in the workplace, it would likely back away from civil rights if it conflicted with its interests (as Murray did in Alabama). The CIO would not have played such a prominent role in the civil rights transformation of the Democratic Party had it not been practical for the organization.

Working with the NAACP

In effective coalitions, allies offer vigorous support and not mere lip service. Unlike the southern Populists of the 1890s, who never supported civil rights until election time, the CIO and NAACP worked vigorously on each other's behalf. The decision to support civil rights did not mean that the CIO had to side with the NAACP in particular. But it did. As Chapter 2 showed, the NAACP proved, time and again, that it was willing to compromise for the benefit of its ally. An NAACP endorsement could often decide which union African Americans would support or which inactive union it would revitalize.[68] The CIO also asked the NAACP to recruit members in the South to CIO unions in 1947, even though Operation Dixie steered clear of politics.[69]

In addition, the NAACP was arguably more responsible than any other single organization for quadrupling the number of black voters in the South from 1940 to 1954. In 1944, NAACP litigation led the Supreme Court to reverse a nine-year precedent and invalidate white primaries. The NAACP subsequently offered rewards for local chapters that registered the most voters, and bestowed a fifty-dollar prize for a Louisiana chapter that registered over six hundred black voters in 1947. Historian John Kirk argues that in Arkansas, the NAACP was the most significant factor in increasing black voter registration from 4,000 to 47,000 between 1940 and 1947.[70] Newly registered black voters were important for unseating antilabor members of Congress and holding southern states for Adlai Stevenson in 1952.[71] The NAACP and its local branches were officially nonpartisan, and could not tell new voters who to support. But they helped coordinate (and in some cases, create) independent local groups that registered voters and endorsed liberal candidates sympathetic to civil rights.[72] The NAACP also helped some of these organizations sue election boards that impeded registration efforts.[73]

To satisfy the NAACP's needs for a close working relationship, the CIO needed to at least appear to renovate its own glass house of discriminatory local affiliates. Speaking to the CIO convention of 1953, NAACP Attorney and future Supreme Court Justice Thurgood Marshall declared that political rights were "questions of abstract morality," while rights to work on a fair and equal basis were "burning life and death problems."[74] A thorough examination of the CIO's record on fighting internal discrimination is not possible, but the national organization took several noteworthy steps. It created CARD in 1942. By 1945, one hundred state and local CARD committees existed among CIO unions.[75] In 1950, the CIO directed all locals to disobey state and local laws requiring segregation, since it considered them unconstitutional. Secretary Treasurer Carey told his colleagues on the PCCR that "we had to operate against the patterns of the workers who didn't think it was possible," mixing groups against state laws and getting "away with it to some degree."[76] The national organization also punished affiliates for hate strikes. Clearly, by asserting a civil rights jurisprudence ahead of the courts and Congress, the CIO was exceeding token support for civil rights.[77]

At the workplace level, CARD pushed racial integration through subtle persuasion as the situation permitted. Its director urged CARD operatives to work with discriminatory unions discreetly and through persuasion.[78] Civil rights were integrated into CIO summer school curriculums, although summer schools were typically attended by those already enthusiastic about the national CIO's mission. A CIO conference on civil rights said that integration needed to be "sold" "to the CIO membership in the same manner as wage increases, shorter work week or any other benefit of trade unionism." Some pamphlets emphasized that discrimination was unfair and un-American, but economic benefits were also stressed. A widely distributed pamphlet was entitled "Discrimination Costs You Money."[79] CARD discussed highlighting the role of blacks in World War II and unions to foster interracial solidarity. Their newsletters featured stories about employers approaching black workers offering paid positions as "scabs," and the blacks dutifully turning down the offers.[80] One CIO pamphlet featured a cover with three workers—one black, one Asian, and one white. (A southern employer requested copies of this and used it to defeat a CIO election, arguing the CIO was trying to abolish Jim Crow.[81])

In Detroit, where the NAACP played a role in helping the UAW-CIO organize Ford, the UAW-CIO alone defended blacks in a riot and criticized the city government for police brutality. It also formed a Fair Employment Practices Department, and worked closely with blacks to integrate a housing project and oppose a race-baiting mayoral candidate.[82] The Detroit NAACP gained 20,000 new members during the housing project crisis, when the UAW's support helped keep the housing project open for blacks after the city government attempted to make it a white-only project.[83]

Labor historians question whether CARD and other steps taken by the CIO were adequate. The differences between private and public statements are illustrative of the social realities that limited implementation of the leadership's agenda. Southern public relations director Mason wrote to a friend that

> one of the most interesting sidelines of my adventures down here is on the one hand convincing Negroes that the CIO offers their best opportunity, and on the other influencing white union members and representatives in the direction of a squarer deal for the Negro. Sometimes the latter has to be done by devious methods but I never lose a chance to promote it.[84]

Mason whistled a different tune in public. When a southern newspaper editor asked her about integration, she replied, "It is the business of the unions to organize the workers employed by the manufacturers . . . It organizes the workers just as it finds them. This means that the union may be composed exclusively of white operatives . . . or it may mean that there are white operatives and Negro laborers in the union."[85] CARD also developed model antidiscrimination contracts that were seldom adopted, let alone enforced, by affiliates.[86] Its educational campaigns were, at best, mixed successes.[87]

Whatever the real economic benefits of the CIO's efforts, the NAACP and prominent liberals were satisfied that the CIO was taking reasonable steps to address workplace integration, even as they pressed for more. They did not let resilient union discrimination interfere with their assessment of the CIO as a political ally.[88] After World War II, the NAACP's former in-house pundit, W. E. B. Du Bois, said the greatest "interracial understanding among the working masses" came about through the CIO, echoing the future Nobel Prize winner Gunnar Myrdal.[89] The Rosenwald Fund, created in 1917 by Sears co-founder Julius Rosenwald to promote education for African Americans, also concluded in an annual report that the CIO was more responsible for racial progress in the South than any other institution.[90]

Benefits of the Alliance

The CIO support for civil rights paid off. The NAACP proved to be a useful ally in and out of politics, outweighing the cost of resistant white workers. It registered more potentially useful black voters than any other national civil rights organization. The allies' lobbyists collaborated on many of the same bills and their lawyers filed amicus briefs for the same cases. The NAACP's prestige in civil rights enabled it to cast doubt on the propriety of civil rights proposals that sought to place the burden of integration on unions rather than employers. For example, the NAACP helped the CIO oppose communist proposals to have separate seniority rules for blacks, which would have opened better jobs for African Americans who were only recently allowed into unions.[91]

The CIO recruited thousands of "block workers" to register and encourage people in working-class neighborhoods to vote. Often, they worked with the NAACP and black churches to recruit blacks for this task in African American neighborhoods.[92] A CIO PAC organizational program read:

> We should know and have personal contact with the leaders [of minority groups] in every state and every city (or other area) where the Negroes or Mexican descendants live. We can work closely with the

NAACP, Urban League and the anti-discrimination departments of the different unions. . . . These personal contacts plus, perhaps, some ads might lessen the sellouts during the campaign.[93]

Altogether, block workers registered hundreds of thousands of voters and re-minded them to pay their poll taxes. The CIO would also hire full-time PAC organizers—often black—to recruit black voters.[94] A strategy note declared that if organizers recruited blacks popular with their peers to a citizen's com-mittee, they would have twelve black volunteers within a half hour on the telephone.[95] Both the CIO and the NAACP cooperated with the National Committee to Abolish the Poll Tax to remove state poll taxes, which discour-aged working class voters of all races from voting. In the North, the CIO would organize civil rights conferences to energize opposition to antilabor Republicans. In 1950, an important goal of the CIO conference in Cleveland was "to imbue" black and white groups in attendance "with the idea of defeat-ing [Senator Robert] Taft."[96] One organizer wrote to Roy Wilkins that "a state-ment" against Taft "from prominent Negroes and whites addressed to the voters of Ohio . . . would have a substantial effect" on professional blacks that might vote for Taft.[97]

As with the NAACP, the benefits of the alliance do not prove that the alli-ance was inevitable. Many political organizations have acted against their own interest by acceding to racial division, and CIO workers were not immune to racism. They would have easily been diverted away from civil rights if the most prestigious voice of civil rights in the nation undermined them. In one southern union that attempted to foster racial tolerance among members, an organizer found white members very resistant because of the local African American newspaper's steady opposition to the CIO.[98]

The heyday of cooperation came to an end in the early 1960s, weakening the Democratic coalition.[99] The NAACP eventually used the antidiscrimina-tion section of the Taft-Hartley Act to win a lawsuit against a segregated union, and urged all branches to look out for similar opportunities.[100] One union replied in an op-ed:

If there is anything that Organized Labor in America hates and fears . . . it is the anti-union bias of certain provisions of the Taft-Hartley law. And for the NAACP to urge the NLRB to apply one of the most hatred [sic] provisions of the Taft-Hartley law against Organized

Labor is to make it almost impossible for Organized Labor to continue supporting the programs and the principles of the NAACP.[101]

The NAACP highlighted its new strategy to member branches. It distributed a *New York Times* article describing the case, which deprived discriminatory unions from immunity from raids of other unions. The NAACP solicited complaints and wrote that "We are prepared to spend a major part of our time in assisting employees who desire representation before the Board and in helping them file complaints. Please GIVE THIS PROGRAM PRIORITY."[102]

Thus, it was possible for the NAACP's labor policy to create a wedge in the black-blue alliance, as Frymer shows. By the time the NAACP was willing to publicly clash with the AFL-CIO, the standing of the NAACP among liberal interest groups—and the place of civil rights in Democratic Party politics—was secure. Labor unions even supported a provision in the Civil Rights Act of 1964 outlawing discrimination from unions, going much further than they had in supporting Wagner Act amendments in 1940.[103] It is hard to imagine that the CIO PAC or its liberal allies would have prioritized civil rights in the 1940s if the NAACP were antagonizing organized labor. Relationships can be at their most fragile at their earliest stage. For the CIO to prioritize civil rights with the assent of its members, the NAACP had to support unions without hesitation.

Conclusion

Do underprivileged groups have a common interest in the welfare of other underprivileged groups? Someone observing the Democratic Party today might conclude that the party is a coalition of the "outs," as feminist Gloria Steinem hoped to make it in the early 1970s. During the Great Depression, both blacks and unskilled workers qualified as underprivileged. But the strong alliance between labor organizations and civil rights groups did not exist before World War II. Without this alliance, no force in the Democratic Party was strong enough to change the New Deal balance of northern and southern influence.

The CIO's decision to support civil rights might have been motivated by politics, recruitment drives, ideology, or some combination of all three. I argue that electoral politics, which were necessary to safeguard the policies that kept its members employed, were the most compelling reason. Both the CIO and NAACP shared a common enemy in southern Democrats, and benefitted from civil rights and greater voter turnout. Ideology was mainly useful for motivating some of its organizers and persuading middle-class advocacy groups to support its agenda. As Chapter 3 shows, the CIO spearheaded a liberal/labor/civil rights coalition to unify the Democratic Party behind its agenda and reduce the influence of southern opponents in the party. Building and maintaining a coalition with the NAACP—as documented in this chapter—needed to happen first.

CHAPTER 4

Twisting the Donkey's Tail: How Groups Changed a Reluctant Party

The CIO and NAACP worked tirelessly to merge the agenda of labor rights and civil rights. Through their shared issue positions and mutual assistance, they were well poised to contest longstanding party factions for the direction of the Democratic Party. By carefully selecting delegates to the 1948 convention, the CIO and its allies passed an ambitious civil rights plank against the wishes of a party's incumbent president and congressional leaders. Nearly all the Democratic Party leaders, including the president and congressional leaders, opposed the plank in hopes of keeping Southern Democrats in the party. Only outside groups really wanted them to leave and create room for a new party order. After the platform prompted a walkout of the party's southern delegates, civil rights leaders coaxed the president to ban discrimination in the armed forces. Subsequent party nominees and platforms in the party were at least as liberal on civil rights, and in that sense, the 1948 platform represents a branching point. The platform battle is worth describing in painstaking detail because written evidence documents the precise role of administration officials, interest groups, and the president throughout the affair.

Platforms and nominations do not, of course, bind the "party-in-government" to do anything. But activists nonetheless viewed their convention struggles as meaningful, and correctly so. Extensive behind-the-scenes maneuvers at the 1944 convention led to the vice-presidential nomination of the racially moderate Harry S. Truman, rather than the South Carolina segregationist James Byrnes, as the backup to the visibly moribund Franklin D. Roosevelt. Adoption of a racially liberal platform at the 1948 convention signaled a strengthening commitment to civil rights, which led directly to a walkout by many southern delegates. They grudgingly returned to the party for decades, but the writing was on the wall. Georgia senator Richard Russell's failure to get his presidential nomination off the ground at the 1952 convention was another meaningful signal of the party's direction.

Industrial states with large black and union populations were becoming more important in elections, but electoral pressures were only part of the story. Democrats and Republicans both hedged their bets with African American voters. This chapter provides evidence that groups forced Democratic politicians to change in nominating conventions before they could think about general elections. By forming a united front and working together strategically, pressure groups wielded influence in elections and conventions disproportionate to the number of voters they represented. Additionally, organized groups worked hard to change the kind of policies African Americans supported, forcing party leaders to change with them. Whereas antilynching laws would have gone a long way to satisfy civil rights groups in the 1930s, they were now demanding the FEPC and a variety of social welfare benefits.

Schuman, Steeh, and Bobo emphasize changing racial attitudes as a reason for the changing political fortunes of African Americans. There are some issues that are so unpopular in a given time period that groups have little chance of enacting their agenda, no matter what strategy they employ. Within a range of acceptable opinion, it is less clear that public opinion matters as much, because median voters are often inattentive. During the Truman years, about two thirds of Americans supported poll-tax abolition, but only half favored federal antilynching laws and the desegregation of travel. When Gallup polled nonsoutherners on antidiscrimination laws in 1948, only 33 percent supported them, while 42 percent opposed them. A March poll in 1948 showed that a majority of the public opposed Truman's civil rights proposals as a whole.[1] Parties incorporated ambitious antidiscrimination planks into their platforms just the same.[2] While public support for a new policy may need to rise above a floor for a party to adopt it, group behavior is more relevant once the floor is passed.

Until recently, leading scholarship held that party transformation took place in the 1960s. In particular, Carmines and Stimson argue that the presidential candidates' divergence on civil rights in 1964 caused other important party politicians to follow suit, emphasizing the role of elites in setting the party agenda. Furthermore, they argue that "1948 could not be a critical moment in the partisan evolution of race because both parties were competing for the pro-civil rights pole of the dispute."[3] It is true that Republicans continued to favor some civil rights measures alongside Democrats through Nixon's 1960 campaign, but the earlier change in the Democratic Party's switch on civil rights constitutes a realignment of its own. While the 1964 Civil Rights Act represented the peak of party efforts on behalf of civil rights, the labor-liberal alliance had made these efforts possible through work they began decades earlier.

My work dovetails with Feinstein and Schickler, who show that northern Democrats in Congress were more likely to support civil rights than congressional Republicans in the 1940s.[4] While they credit party change to a network of liberal interest groups, they do not specify nominating contests as the mechanism for change. At party conventions of the 1940s and 1950s, the CIO sought to realign the party by gaining delegate support for nominees and platforms satisfactory to unions, liberals, and civil rights activists. Congressional inaction made the presidency a valuable prize, especially when much of the progress they made came from executive orders and judicial appointments.

Karol highlights the role of business groups in forcing the Republicans to oppose civil rights, rather than the role of the CIO-NAACP alliance in forcing the Democratic Party to support civil rights.[5] Chen et al. also find that California Republicans were more likely to oppose a state FEPC in the same decade due to their antiredistributionist agenda, and Chen finds similar patterns in other states.[6] In my view, the crux of the transformation was not that business groups drove civil rights groups out of the Republican Party, but that the coalition politics described in the last two chapters drew them into the Democratic Party.

Parties and the Second Great Migration

In the 1940s, neither party was going to become the party of civil rights on its own. Instead, both parties simultaneously tried to win black voters and their white southern opponents even though blacks were becoming more important in swing states. As blacks migrated north for job opportunities, they constituted 4.7 percent of the nonsouthern population and an even larger, growing percentage in large cities.[7] *Life* magazine reported that African Americans might decide who the next president was in 1940.[8] This change in electoral incentives was not enough for the parties to enact civil rights legislation. Recognizing the importance of the black vote, politicians in both parties made only cosmetic efforts to recruit African Americans. Existing Democratic officeholders had cordial relationships with opponents of civil rights and were not about to abandon their policy demands for a demographic they had little experience with. This speaks to the importance of group positions over general election considerations for determining party positions.

Republicans

Since the Republican Party had fared poorly in recent presidential elections, it arguably had more of an incentive to recruit black voters. As Carmines and Stimson describe party dynamics, "dissatisfied political losers . . . have an ever-present motive to unseat the governing status quo" by "generating new issue conflicts."[9] The RNC, concerned about the massive black support for Roosevelt in 1936, commissioned Ralph Bunche to investigate why blacks had abandoned the Party of Lincoln and describe how the party might win their votes back. Bunche concluded that the "Republican Party will need to decide whether it prefers to court the dissident white vote of the Democratic South, through continuance of its lily-white program and an obscure Negro policy, or really desires the Negro vote. It cannot seduce both."[10]

Republican politicians were unable to seduce either demographic, although they made an effort. The 1940 Republican nominee, Wendell Willkie, stressed his record in hiring African Americans as a private employer, and described Roosevelt's links to southern opponents of civil rights. Additionally, he called attention to New Deal discrimination.[11] Thomas Dewey, the nominee in 1944, had helped pass an FEPC in New York State and promised a national one. The Republican platform of 1944 supported most of the proposals that civil rights advocates demanded: a permanent national FEPC, an anti-lynching law, desegregation of the armed forces, and a constitutional amendment abolishing the poll tax. In each case, a majority of blacks voted for the Democratic nominee (Figure 2).[12]

The 1944 Republican civil rights plank would have been deeply unacceptable to the Democratic Party, when many southerners were already threatening to bolt the convention over racial issues.[13] The 1944 Democratic platform included only a vague statement that some rights are guaranteed by the Constitution to all citizens. Roosevelt told the only black MC, William L. Dawson, that he would run on his record rather than on specific civil rights pledges, and persuaded him to rally liberals around the vague plank for party unity.[14] Roosevelt, like Harding in 1920, was sympathetic to the demands of black

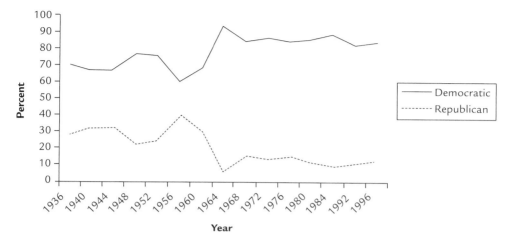

Figure 2. African American presidential vote. David A. Bositis, "Blacks and the 2004 Democratic National Convention," Joint Center for Political and Economic Studies, Table 1, Presidential Vote and Party Identification of Black Americans, 1936–2000, 9. Bositis obtained data from early years from Everett Ladd, Jr. and Charles D. Hadley, *Transformations of the American Party System: Political Coalitions from the New Deal to the 1970s* (New York: Norton, 1975), 60. Ladd and Hadley used surveys from the American Institute of Public Opinion.

voters, but did not want to take risks on their behalf. He hoped Dawson would reassure civil rights supporters privately without drawing attention from their opponents.

Given Roosevelt's unwillingness to deal forthrightly with civil rights, why didn't more African Americans vote Republican?[15] At worst, a split vote would force both parties to bid for the black vote with more concessions. The NAACP did not control who most blacks voted for, but entertained the idea of dividing the black presidential vote. Judge William Hastie said in 1944 that "unless there is some indication that we are willing to take reprisal measures against these people . . . we will be criticized. . . . If we are willing to take the risk of trying to beat the Democrats, both parties will become frightened."[16] However, most NAACP leaders disagreed, holding out for a reformed Democratic Party to maintain their standing with coalition allies.[17]

As it turned out, siding with the Republicans seems unlikely to have won any policy concessions from them. Though Republicans knew that African Americans were an important voter group, they failed to enact their civil rights platform in the postwar Congresses they controlled (1947–1949 and

1953–1955). Republicans prioritized business groups in the party over swing votes. A permanent FEPC was the most unpalatable item on the civil rights agenda to such groups. And during the 1940s, the CIO-NAACP alliance prioritized it over antilynching laws and the abolition of poll taxes.[18] Like many agencies of the New Deal, it placed a burden on employers and implied a federal prerogative to second-guess their business decisions for the public interest.[19] It was designed by progressives such as Sidney Hillman and New York City mayor Fiorello LaGuardia, and it even borrowed personnel from the hated NLRB.[20] Written records offer no evidence that the FEPC was a deliberate attempt of the CIO to drive a wedge between business groups and civil rights groups, but it was an ideal instrument for doing so. House Speaker Joseph Martin acknowledged

> the FEPC plank in the 1944 Republican platform was a bid for the Negro vote, and they did not accept the bid . . . I'll be frank with you: we are not going to pass a FEPC bill, but it has nothing to do with the Negro vote. We are supported by New England and Middle Western industrialists who would stop their contributions if we passed a law that would compel them to stop religious as well as racial discrimination in employment.[21]

During the 80th Congress, conservative leader Robert Taft denied that the 1944 FEPC promise referred to an FEPC with enforcement powers. The furthest Taft would go was to support an FEPC that would investigate and publicize cases of discriminations. Skeptical that Republicans could win the black vote, he wrote privately:

> The Negro situation . . . is a very difficult one. I doubt if we can outbid Mrs. Roosevelt. I don't think we can make much of the issue of forcing a full vote in the South. Just at present the Negroes will be satisfied with nothing except the FEPC Bill. That is something which violates any possible party philosophy we could adopt.[22]

The National Council for a Permanent FEPC approached Taft to cosponsor an FEPC bill, but he only agreed to vote for cloture.[23]

Neither civil rights groups nor black voters supported parties simply because politicians appealed to them. Leading Republican candidates wooed blacks as actively as Democratic leaders, but business groups did not allow them to make good on their promises even though blacks could provide needed votes. The next section shows that parties are not necessarily responsive even if a demographic responds to its appeals.

Democrats

Like their Republican competitors, Democratic nominees knew that black voters were becoming more important, but cared too much about existing party factions to change their policy positions. An unsigned Roosevelt administration memo from 1940 claimed that blacks constituted 4–16 percent of the vote in thirteen swing states.[24] But Democratic politicians could not simply ignore the southern wing of the party; its influence was too entrenched. Nowhere was this more evident than in the selection of a new vice president in 1944. Party insiders knew of Roosevelt's deteriorating health and considered the matter with great care. The existing vice president, Henry Wallace, was widely popular with African Americans and unions, but southerners in particular considered him too radical to be president. Roosevelt and several party bosses considered Byrnes, but worried that he would lose several swing states by alienating African Americans. Byrnes was conservative on both civil and labor rights.

Only the influence of the CIO stopped Byrnes's nomination. Even though he might lose votes in swing states, Democratic leaders nonetheless gave him a "green light" on the eve of the convention. Democrats asked Dawson for input. The Illinois MC, a team player, said that he did not think blacks would leave the party over a running mate. Roosevelt asked Byrnes to "clear" his candidacy with CIO president Murray and CIO PAC founder Hillman. When both offered strenuous objections, the president and several party bosses decided to oppose Byrnes, emphasizing labor's opposition as the foremost reason.[25] While aware of the potential black vote, the Democratic Party very nearly nominated a conservative southerner as the person who would almost certainly be the next president. Labor's objections were the most important reason the United States never had a President Byrnes. Truman, a border state senator, became the compromise candidate.

For a time after Roosevelt's death, it appeared that a group of liberals working for Truman signaled a new direction for the party in order to gain votes. To counter the influence of more conservative advisers, Federal Security Agency administrator Oscar Ewing hosted informal dinners every other Monday evening with other lesser-known administrative officials.[26] Special Counsel Clark Clifford served as this private group's liaison to Truman. In

November of 1947, Clifford presented Truman with a report that Southern Democrats would still vote Democratic even with a civil rights platform, but African Americans might vote Republican without one.[27] Clifford advised that "under the tutelage of Walter White . . . the Negro has become a cynical, hard-boiled trader" that will change parties if the Democrats fail to deliver on civil rights.[28] As for the South, it was "inconceivable that any policies initiated by the Truman Administration, no matter how 'liberal,' could so alienate the South in the next year that it could revolt. As always the South can be considered safely Democratic. And in formulating national policy, it can be safely ignored."[29] The Ewing group anticipated a third-party challenge from Henry Wallace, but not the challenge ultimately formed by southern states with the "Dixiecrats."[30] Additionally, civil rights proposals would gain the president the enthusiastic support of labor groups and liberal groups.[31] Clifford therefore presented the president with an ambitious set of civil rights proposals. Truman began to implement Clifford's advice, issuing a well publicized "special message to Congress" on civil rights on February 2, 1948. He promised he would issue orders to end discrimination in the federal government and the armed forces. His staff reminded him that he was a party leader and he had a responsibility to "make every effort to persuade Southern Representatives and Senators that it is essential that they accept (or at least do not kill by filibuster) a minimal program."[32]

But Truman backpedaled under pressure from Southern Democrats. According to Truman's special assistant on minority problems, "the reaction in Congress to the February 2nd message was such that there was some question in everybody's mind as to whether the President would get the nomination if he didn't back off a little bit."[33] Many Southern Democrats refused to attend the Jefferson-Jackson Day dinner and others discussed bolting the convention. A Southern Governor's Conference warned that "The President must cease attacks on white supremacy or face full-fledged revolt in the South," and each of Alabama's electors pledged to vote for a Democrat other than Truman.[34] Clifford later admitted he seriously erred in his estimate of the South.[35] In May, Truman denied ever supporting the desegregation of federal employees, drawing a distinction between segregation and discrimination. At the 1948 Democratic Convention, Truman instructed his supporters to present a platitudinous civil rights plank similar to that of 1944.[36]

In neither 1944 nor 1948 did the Democratic Party change course due to the growing African American voter base. Democratic officeholders, such as Truman, were unwilling to take that kind of risk to effect party transformation. More surprisingly, even the most transformative of presidential advisors—the Ewing Group—were ultimately unwilling to take it. In fact, they never really aimed at excising the party faction standing in the way of a purely liberal party. As Sundquist describes party leaders, "the normal reaction of the established leaders" to new issues is "defensive. They try to straddle it, to change the subject, to find policy compromises."[37] It fell to external groups to take the risks that politicians would not.

The 1948 Civil Rights Plank: A Branching Point for Democrats

At the 1948 convention, a coalition of labor and liberal groups foisted a strong civil rights plank on the Democratic Party against the wishes of Truman and most congressional leaders in his party. The CIO's ties to the Democratic Party and the New Deal were longstanding, but it did not hesitate to oppose Democrats who stood in its way. It was notably more successful in purging the Democratic Party than President Roosevelt had been in 1938.[38]

The CIO had announced its ambition to exorcise the party eight years earlier. In 1940, future CIO-PAC director Jack Kroll wrote that "the bi-partisan Tory Democratic-Republican bloc must be reckoned with, as through control on the part of the Tory Democrats of key positions in the Congress, they are anything but weak adversaries in spite of the reelection of President Roosevelt."[39] As early as 1944, the CIO was working to campaign against Democratic MCs, if necessary, to bring about this alliance.[40] In 1944, it was widely held responsible for defeating three anti-CIO Democrats in the primary stage, all members of Un-American Activities Committees (which attacked communist influence within the CIO).[41] The CIO would even run challengers where they would lose, hoping it would deprive incumbents of the claim of universal support and "lay the groundwork through education for a campaign that may be successful in later years."[42] Union organizers considered voting for Southern Republicans just to remove antilabor Democrats from their entrenched position of incumbency and fight for pro-labor Democrats in the future.[43] CIO donations in 1944 represented 20 percent of all money donated to the Democratic Party that year.[44]

The 1948 convention provided the CIO and other liberals with the opportunity to herald a new direction for the party and deliver a symbolic blow to the overlapping enemies of labor and civil rights below the Mason-Dixon

Line. When the labor-liberal alliance fought for a stronger platform, a floor
fight ensued. The CIO PAC's 1948 statement of political policy noted that
"progressive factions have existed in the major parties for many years," but
these groups "must now be combined into a unified political party," excluding
"venal and racketeering old-time political machines."[45] In advance of the convention, the CIO distributed the PCCR report, *To Secure These Rights*, to pressure state-level Democratic Parties and the national Democratic Party to
implement its civil rights recommendations. The CIO leaders argued that
failure to implement its recommendations would betray the Democratic president.[46] The CIO knew that Truman might lose, but President Murray explained after the convention that "If the party is defeated," then "opportunity
may be provided for sound reconstruction upon liberal lines."[47] Outside
groups saw opportunity in defeat that officeholders and their advisors did not.

Americans for Democratic Action also planned to make civil rights a central issue. It had little hope that Truman would win reelection, but the plank
would help elect Democrats to Congress and establish the Democratic Party
as the liberal party.[48] Director James Loeb told Franklin Roosevelt, Jr. that
without a strong civil rights plank, "we face, not only a defeat, but a rout of
such proportions as to mean the disintegration of the liberal-labor-
Democratic-Party coalition which represented the support for the New Deal
under your father's leadership."[49] The ADA urged local members to run as
delegates for their precinct in order to constitute a formidable force on the
convention floor. It privately asked Minneapolis's mayor Hubert Humphrey
to sign a statement in favor of civil rights and arranged for a wide variety of
Democratic politicians, including machine politicians, to sign it. The ADA
representatives could then claim a mandate for the outlined civil rights policy
on the convention floor.[50]

Although the ADA was motivated by policy goals, this tactic also saved its
reputation with its donors. The ADA had failed to nominate William O.
Douglas or Dwight D. Eisenhower over the incumbent president, as many
members had wanted. Winning passage for an ambitious platform was the
only way to emerge from the convention with enhanced prestige.[51] Responding to numerous inquiries from donors on the failed nominations, Loeb assured them that the civil rights platform was more important than their
original plans for the convention. The *New York Times*, *Time*, and *Newsweek*
also reported that the platform allowed the ADA to leave the convention with
an enhanced reputation.[52]

Multiple groups created the conditions for the plank's passage. James

Carey, CIO secretary treasurer, proposed the strong plank that was ultimately adopted. According to Carey, the future Democratic Party whip asked him "if we intended to give a fight on the civil rights issue." Carey "told him that there was another substantial group that would join us in that fight—the ADA."[53] Kroll, now CIO PAC director, pushed the late night meeting of the ADA on July 14, urging the ADA to press for this plank on the convention floor.[54] ADA operatives called Truman's compromise "meaningless" and claimed it would only hurt him in the election.[55] Loeb later recalled that the Truman plank "didn't go whole hog and we were frankly looking for a fight."[56] Representative Andrew Biemiller, largely elected by labor forces in his Wisconsin district, introduced the plank on the ADA's behalf.

Transformative groups had to compete not only with southerners but also politicians who wanted to straddle the two sides. Truman and high-ranking Democratic Party officials wanted to augment the party, not trans-form it.[57] They lobbied against the stronger plank late into the night. Truman himself called it a "crackpot amendment" in his diary and wrote that the "crackpots hope the South will bolt."[58] Twenty years later, Ewing confirmed that Truman preferred this plank to the stronger plank that ultimately emerged as a result of the CIO-ADA alliance, recalling that, "Naturally, as the prospective candidate, he wanted a plank that . . . would satisfy both sides of the controversy."[59] Clifford thought the effort was "the wrong time, the wrong place, and the wrong way to further the civil rights case."[60] He later recalled, "I felt that there was no need to mortify the South by pressing for an *extreme* civil rights plank at the convention."[61] Other Democrats were even less receptive. Former DNC chair James Farley said, "This is a terrible thing; it's going to split our party, and we've got to prevent it."[62] The senate party whip reportedly asked of Humphrey, "Who is this pipsqueak who knows more than Franklin Roosevelt knew about Negro rights?" The DNC chair also lobbied for Truman's mild plank.[63] As the ADA portrayed the fight, "we had to fight not only the South but the Administration, which tried to put over a horrible compromise."[64] While Truman and Clifford wanted to support civil rights to reach black voters, they did not want conservative southerners to leave the party.

A stirring speech from Hubert Humphrey, plus intense politicking by ADA and CIO operatives, led convention delegates to adopt the more pro-gressive plank.[65] Humphrey convinced New York party boss Ed Flynn to per-suade the Pennsylvania delegation to support the plank, which provided enough votes to carry the plank.[66] The CIO- and ADA-instigated civil rights plank of 1948 provoked a walkout of several southern delegations and set off a far-reaching set of transformations in the Democratic Party.

For the CIO and ADA, the platform was an intentional effort to displace conservative southerners. After the civil rights plank was adopted, Kroll told a group of workers that the Democratic platform

> will go a long way to separate the sheep from the goats . . . I think that the basis may have been laid for transforming the Democratic party as a whole into a genuine instrument for expressing the will of the vast majority of the people, unencumbered by civil war hangovers, unburdened by the magnolia and mint julep mentality, unhampered by sectional prejudices.[67]

Echoing these sentiments, CIO PAC field director Phillip Weightman told CARD to "read the Dixiecrats out of the party, they have shown their hands. Then we'd be in a better position to run liberal Democrats to oust these cases."[68] Loeb declared that "the strangle hold of the South on the Democratic Party has finally been broken" and told a donor that he was proud that ADA divided the party.[69] Determined to follow through with the plank, the ADA and other liberal groups rallied members around it, eyeing a purge. The National Farm Labor Union, for example, suggested creating a "Southern Democrats for Truman" organization, writing that "if enough people can be gotten together in such a committee and a smart publicity job done, you can drive the rest of the bourbons out and get control of the party machinery in the South into hands of the liberal element. Regardless of what we might think of Truman, a vote down South for him will be counted a vote for civil rights in the end."[70]

Compared with the ADA and the CIO PAC, the NAACP played a small role in the day-to-day events of the 1948 convention. However, they played a much larger role in providing the context needed for the platform to pass. The FEPC, which had done the most to infuriate southern MCs and conservatives, was made possible by the wartime order pushed by the MOWM and NAACP. Throughout the decade, the NAACP and CIO agreed to prioritize the FEPC and defeated Taft's attempt to pass a compromise FEPC with no enforcement powers. Kroll acknowledged that the surge in black voter participation, made possible by the NAACP's legal victories, was necessary for the political realignment sought.[71] And perhaps most importantly, labor unions might not have pushed for a civil rights platform if the NAACP had supported the open shop or otherwise antagonized labor unions in the 1940s.

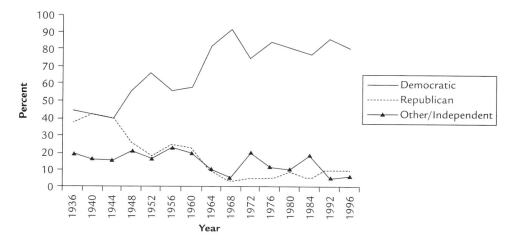

Figure 3. African American party identification. David A. Bositis, "Blacks and the 2004 Democratic National Convention," Joint Center for Political and Economic Studies, Table 1, Presidential Vote and Party Identification of Black Americans, 1936–2000, 9. Bositis obtained early data from Ladd and Hadley, *Transformations of the American Party System*, 112.

The platform represented a branching point for the Democratic Party on civil rights. Insofar as we can conclude party change from black party identification, black identification with the Democratic Party clearly surges ahead of Republican support beginning in 1948 (Figure 3). From 1952 onward, black support for the Democratic Party consistently surpassed working-class white party identification and support for Democratic Party presidential candidates.[72] Black Democratic Party identification was 56 percent at its lowest in 1956 and peaked at 92 percent. By contrast, white Democratic Party identification peaked in the 1950s, never surpassing 50 percent.[73]

The platform also directly affected employment for many African Americans. Truman's executive order to desegregate the armed forces on July 27, 1948, stemmed from the platform battle.[74] When Truman passed the selective service act on June 24 without an antisegregation amendment, civil rights groups threatened marches in several black communities and the Democratic Convention. Shortly after the Democratic Convention and the arrest of thirty draft protestors, Truman issued an order to desegregate the armed forces on July 27.[75] In addition to fearing the bad publicity that might come with protests, Truman no longer saw a point in a soft approach to civil rights.[76] Groups first passed a platform that alienated southerners, which the president did not want. Groups then presented the president with the choice of alienating African Americans in addition to southerners if he did not desegregate the armed forces. President Truman governed in an unfavorable leadership context and accomplished little after the executive order, but the platform set a precedent for future Democratic nominating contests.

Evaluating the Role of Party Politicians

Milkis argues that presidents Roosevelt and Truman had built up an executive branch that increasingly enabled presidents to bypass political parties and work directly with interest groups.[77] However, these presidents mainly worked with civil rights groups because of threat and not opportunity. Even though the southern wing of the Democratic Party was weakened, presidents did not risk losing further support by offering civil rights groups what they wanted. Instead, groups in the party forced a civil rights platform and executive order on the president.

Schlozman views the relationship between the CIO and the Democratic Party as bidirectional. Parties only welcome a group as an "anchoring coalition" with the blessing of party politicians, and groups need to make sacrifices for parties as well.[78] The CIO notably accommodated the Democratic Party by purging members who supported Wallace's third party. However, Democrats did not twist the CIO's tail as the CIO twisted theirs. Third parties not only prevented Democratic allies from winning, but potentially set back the progress made with the 1948 platform. After the 1948 convention, CIO president Murray told the CIO's executive committee

> if we are going to maintain any semblance of constructive liberal representation in the Federal Congress . . . then the best way to do it is by a wholesome endorsement of Truman under those circumstances; you will make more effective and easy the possibility of electing liberals who are running on either the Democratic or Republican tickets . . . Some kind of stratagem has got to be resorted to prevent the continuation of this confusion and division within our own ranks, which will only lead to defeat.[79]

The CIO's opposition to Wallace was not a response to Democratic Party pressure, but simply a calculation that a broad, transformative coalition needs its manpower to support a party it inflicted change upon. Groups can seldom afford to disperse their resources among quixotic third parties. Surely, if

Democratic Party officials had their druthers, the CIO would not have with-held support just from Wallace, but also from liberal Republican MCs. Lead-ers of the CIO and ADA viewed the Wallace campaign as tainted by communist influence. Murray, remembering the 1919 Red Scare's chilling effect on unions, silenced outspoken communists in the CIO well before 1948.[80]

While Truman and his lieutenants opposed the civil rights platform, other politicians, including party bosses, were more supportive. One might view assent of party bosses to the 1948 civil rights plank as evidence that party politicians are gatekeepers, allowing parties to transform with their say-so. As actors of pure political ambition, the bosses would more likely act out of elec-toral calculation than a commitment to civil rights. And Wallace's Progressive Party threatened to help Republicans in swing northern states by attracting African American voters from the Democratic ticket. Yet regional party bosses were surely aware of this possibility before the convention, and offered no discernible support for a strong plank until the CIO and ADA raised it. After the issue was raised, they may have angered black constituents by op-posing it, as a liberal journalist at the time noted.[81] Since most party bosses have not left behind written records,[82] we cannot be sure of their intentions and alternate plans. It is also striking that the party continued on its civil rights trajectory even after the Wallace threat disappeared and party bosses backed away from civil rights.[83]

On the surface, Humphrey's support for civil rights at the 1948 convention illustrates that party leaders can play a decisive role in transforming parties. His support did not reflect mere ambition or constituent service. As a local Works Progress Administration head, he had a reputation for fairness toward African Americans, who formed less than one percent of the population in Minneapolis. However, Humphrey declined to run for public office until the Minneapolis AFL (an unusually liberal chapter) promised financial support for a mayoral campaign. Humphrey's support for a Minneapolis FEPC drew the ADA and UAW to promote his further rise in politics, but its passage was greatly aided by the local AFL, which threatened to oppose alderman who voted against it.[84] At the time, national party politicians rebuffed the local Minnesotan's arguments to move more strongly in the direction of civil rights.[85] Labor groups enabled Humphrey to become an important figure in his party. The ADA spent all night convincing Humphrey to give his civil rights speech at the 1948 convention because he was afraid it would hurt his career; he finally yielded at 5 a.m.[86] This underscores the role of pressure groups, not politicians. Humphrey was later willing to compromise on civil rights when it appeared to hinder his advancement. Seeking to be Stevenson's running mate in 1956, he reached out to potential southern supporters, and joined seventy senators who blocked the introduction of House civil rights legislation to the Senate.[87] Labor leaders then supported Kefauver over Humphrey as vice president. Labor promoted him at times and withheld promotions from him at other times.

The Comparative Contribution of the CIO and ADA

Other scholars present the ADA, not the CIO, as the organization that set the Democratic Party on a path to racial liberalism beginning in the 1948 convention. Not only did the ADA provide the large number of delegates at the convention to support the CIO plank, but it had planned for months to make civil rights a major issue at the convention. If true, ideology would play a stronger role in the transformation than I have allotted for thus far. The ADA was less of a member-interest organization than the CIO needed to be.

Parsing the CIO and ADA before, during, and after the 1948 convention is difficult, but in the end, the ADA depended more on the CIO. The ADA was not a front for the CIO, but the CIO could act as a veto player on the ADA. The Union for Democratic Action (ADA's predecessor) was started by Thomas Amilie in 1942; Amilie went on to work for the CIO PAC in 1944.[88] Both Humphrey and Charles La Follette cleared their ADA presidency candidacies with CIO president Murray. Humphrey admitted to Murray that out of the "progressive influences and forces here in Washington," the "most powerful of these are the forces of labor." Though "labor needs allies . . . independent liberals need labor" and the "organizational experience which the trade unionists have had." [89] Leaders of the ADA complained that declining labor contributions in the 1950s were the most important part of its financial deficit and its declining influence. The liberal organization acknowledged that, as an outside organization, it could not reach rank and file union members.[90] When union leaders supported a political effort alongside ADA, the rank and file would follow; otherwise, it was very difficult for the ADA to raise money from union members.[91] The ADA helped labor win liberal allies that did not belong to unions, but ADA was dependent on labor to be effective.[92]

Conclusion

Presidential candidates speculated that black voters were pivotal voters in several states important to winning the Electoral College. But calculating which voters and which states are pivotal is often a murky undertaking. At first, Truman and his key advisor Clark Clifford thought he could win over black voters without facing serious defections from the South. Then, the southern response was so severe that Truman was forced to reconsider. He was willing to layer new groups on top of the party, contradicting but not displacing older groups. He therefore resisted a strong civil rights platform to the end at the 1948 convention, prioritizing the liberal wing only after a polarizing civil rights plank was passed against his instructions. Group pressure at the convention, rather than general election calculations, forced him to side in favor of civil rights.

Even when electoral calculations are clear, parties are not always in a position to act on them. Republican leaders believed they had no chance of winning the South and wanted to campaign for the votes of African American groups in northern states. Republicans knew that African Americans were important voters, but did not support any civil rights legislation in the 80th Congress. Business organizations aligned with the party limited their ability to do so.

The CIO-NAACP alliance hoped that the Democratic Party would become a vessel for both their economic and civil rights positions, even if this lost votes in the South. In 1948, the party finally announced a progressive position that broke sharply from the party's history of states' rights. National politicians refused to adopt policies that would provoke the South into bolting. It was left up to interest groups to do so. Chapter 5 discusses how Democratic Party leaders were unable to retreat from the standards set in 1948.

CHAPTER 5

Maintaining the Democratic Trajectory on Civil Rights

At the 1960 Democratic Convention, the platform committee wrote the most ambitious civil rights plank to date, supporting *Brown* explicitly and praising the civil disobedience tactics of the growing civil rights movement. The young frontrunner for the nomination, John F. Kennedy, packed the committee with liberals in order to sap the momentum from liberal delegates supporting Adlai Stevenson.[1] Kennedy's southern supporters quietly assured southern delegates that he was a gradualist in civil rights. In the bathroom of senator Lyndon Johnson's office, Kennedy promised Georgia's governor he would never send troops into Georgia to enforce school desegregation.[2] Since 1944, the tables had turned. At that convention, Roosevelt appeased southerners with the party platform while Representative Dawson quietly reassured blacks and liberals. Kennedy appeased the civil rights activists with the party platform while quietly reassuring southerners behind closed doors.

Many view Democratic Party platforms and nominees in the 1950s as a retreat from the ambitious 1948 civil rights plank. Carmines and Stimson, for example, call the 1950s a "return to normalcy," in which the "choice of a presidential nominee" and "changes in the party platform" were an "attempt to steer a more conciliatory course on civil rights after the near disaster of 1948."[3] Schickler writes that the clear position taken in the 1948 platform was "short lived," party leaders adopted "weaker platforms in 1952 and 1956," and nominee "Adlai Stevenson presented a muddled civil rights message."[4] If so, that would undermine my claim that the CIO and its allies created a new benchmark for the national party.

On balance, the transformative groups from 1948 continued to obtain what they wanted from the Democratic Party from 1948 to 1960. Stevenson, though often viewed as a moderate, was the choice of 1960 delegates who thought that Kennedy was not liberal enough. Most of the competitive candidates had civil rights positions that improved on Truman's, whose hand had been forced. The two candidates who did not view civil rights as necessary constituencies, Richard Russell and Estes Kefauver in 1952, learned their lesson. Three competitive candidates—Kefauver, Kennedy, and Johnson—changed their previous views on civil rights in 1956 and 1960 because they recognized how important the black-blue alliance was at conventions. Moreover, their strategy for winning the nomination was group-centered. They either appealed directly to groups or persuaded group activists to work on their behalf in nonbinding primaries that were nonetheless used to gauge candidate strength. Groups were not forced to accept a nominee they did not want, although the nominees selected southern running mates in 1952 and 1960.

While the 1952 and 1956 platforms did not break as much new ground, they did not turn the clock back from the trailblazing 1948 convention. Many of the same Southern Democrats who bolted in 1948 continued to oppose the national party in 1952 and 1956. Democratic candidates were still performing a straddle, but they were straddling a horse of a different color.

Reconsidering Stevenson on Race

Following the contentious 1948 convention, the Democratic nominee in the next two cycles is often viewed as a way of bringing the North and South back together. Illinois governor Adlai Stevenson was a product of the Chicago machine, not known for strident liberalism. Machine politician or not, Stevenson had a better record on civil rights than Truman or most of his rivals for the nomination in 1952. Stevenson supported the civil rights plank that provoked a walkout in 1948. As governor of Illinois, he had desegregated the Illinois National Guard and supported a state FEPC. As a presidential candidate, he favored reforms to remove the filibuster as an obstacle to civil rights legislation. Stevenson's major concession to the South was his preference for FEPCs with enforcement powers at the state level—still a more ambitious stance than Truman's before the 1948 platform. In August 1952, Stevenson finally supported the federal FEPC bill in Congress. That year, he lost support from the same southern politicians that Truman had. At the 1960 Democratic

Convention, liberals chose him as the liberal insurgent against Kennedy and his perceived moderation.

Liberals coordinated to support Stevenson before the 1952 election. Arthur Schlesinger, Jr., Walter Reuther, Eleanor Roosevelt, and the NAACP's future NAACP treasurer each considered Stevenson the liberal standard bearer on civil rights.[5] Conveying the concerns of other Democrats, Schlesinger pleaded with the reluctant candidate to run: "if the President [Truman] runs, it will really tear apart the Democratic party . . . on the other hand, any retreat from the President's platform to appease the southerners would be even more fatal. You appear the only solution."[6] By February 1952, Stevenson won the plurality of support among ADA board members even though many were personal friends of Tennessee senator Estes Kefauver, who was also seeking the nomination. In their view, Kefauver was "doomed first by his bad civil rights record."[7] In March, the Illinois ADA ran a full-page ad for Stevenson in the *Chicago Sun Times*.[8] NAACP executive secretary Roy Wilkins said of Stevenson, "here is a man who understands the whole broad background on civil rights, who needs no kindergarten explanation of philosophy and objectives." While Wilkins offered some praise for Eisenhower's character, he also criticized the Republican nominee for speaking about civil rights only in "general terms" and opposing an FEPC with enforcement powers.[9]

Part of Stevenson's reputation for being a conciliator to the South stemmed from his deft political rhetoric. Stevenson pledged his support for party unity and healing, but also reminded them that he would not change his policy positions on civil rights. In Richmond, he praised the Confederacy for its "political genius" and claimed the Democratic Party had set the "New South" on its feet after the Civil War. In the same speech, he said anti-Southernism and "self-righteousness" were as unjustifiable as racism against blacks and Jews, but remained firm in his support of civil rights.[10] The speech was nonetheless depicted in Southern newspapers as a pitch for civil rights.[11] The notes he wrote to southern politicians were usually brief and promised little. Southern politicians, in turn, generally scolded Stevenson for what they viewed as his uncompromising support of civil rights, comparing him to Humphrey. Stevenson's mail to northern liberals such as Eleanor Roosevelt and Arthur Schlesinger was far more extensive and revealing.

The nominee also helped ensure that southern delegations were seated at the convention. Franklin Roosevelt, Jr., proposed a "loyalty oath" requirement in which delegations had to pledge that their state would place the national ticket on the state ballot. (In the 1948 election, only the southern states without the national ticket on the ballot voted for Dixiecrat Thurmond as a presidential candidate.) A Michigan senator went farther and passed a resolution that no delegate would be seated unless he signed the pledge. Southern delegations, including some Stevenson supporters, viewed the loyalty oath as a gratuitous insult, and complained it was unfair to implement this rule after delegations had already been sent to the convention. Virginia, South Carolina, and Louisiana refused to sign the oath, and were denied seating. Stevenson's intervention allowed them to participate in the convention, but they still needed to commit their state to the ballot.[12] While conciliatory, liberals still obtained the commitment to the national ticket they wanted.

Howard Smith, Harry Byrd, James Byrnes, and other southerners refused to support Stevenson.[13] The mystery is how he managed to keep so many other Southern Democrats in line. Georgia senator Dick Russell argued that Eisenhower's coattails would give Republicans control of Congress. The South's source of power was its committee chairmanships, which could be lost with an Eisenhower landslide, and only a party united behind Stevenson could beat Eisenhower. Furthermore, the other Democratic frontrunners were worse for different reasons. New York's Averill Harriman was even more liberal on civil rights, and Tennessee's Kefauver had angered Southerners by running against the corruption of a popular political machine .[14] Though Southerners usually viewed Stevenson as preferable to Harriman and Kefauver, Stevenson lacked an intense following among them.[15] South Carolina's future governor helped hold South Carolina in line for Stevenson against the "independents" led by Byrnes and only won by about only fifteen thousand votes.[16]

As noteworthy as the nominee's support for civil rights was Russell's failed candidacy. Russell had little hope of winning, but wanted enough delegates to influence the convention. His lackluster campaign in the Midwest failed to garner enough delegates for even this limited goal. At the 1956 convention, Russell told Lyndon Johnson, "don't ever let yourself become a sectional candidate for the presidency. That was what happened to me."[17] Russell showed that nominating a candidate with a conservative position on civil rights was no longer an option.

On Election Day in 1952, Stevenson's support among African Americans was much more remarkable than his support among white Southerners. It was the first presidential election in which black support for a Democratic nominee exceeded working-class white support.[18] Eisenhower performed better in the South than any previous Republican nominee since Reconstruction, winning Texas, Florida, Tennessee, and Virginia.[19] A survey of forty-seven cities by the NAACP showed that the black vote for Stevenson in the South was even higher than that in the nation. The NAACP claimed, based on this survey, that without the black vote the Democrats would have also lost Arkansas, Kentucky, Louisiana, North Carolina, and West Virginia.[20]

Doubling Down in 1956

In 1956, Stevenson and his rivals for the nomination each viewed civil rights as a lynchpin for their strategy. All tried to claim the mantle as the most progressive candidate on civil rights. Their strategy was to adopt new positions and persuade group leaders to vouch for their credentials in primaries that were nonbinding but nonetheless important. Since there are too many voters for candidates to reach on their own, they need core party groups to spread their message on their behalf.

Perhaps learning his lesson from 1952, Kefauver moved to Stevenson's left on civil rights in 1956.[21] In contrast to Stevenson, he supported the "Powell amendment," which withheld federal funding from segregated schools (both the NAACP and the CIO had supported this position since the beginning of the decade). His campaign chose as its chair F. Joseph Donohue, who had a long record as a civil rights supporter and successfully mobilized black voters in Washington, D.C., for Harriman in 1952.[22] This time, Harriman promised to appoint a black activist from the NUL and CIO to his cabinet. Schlesinger speculated, "It looks as if the Harriman strategy will be to push the civil rights issue so that it will split the convention in the expectation that you will end up on the wrong side. In other words, the effort will be to induce a platform fight in a way which will identify you as the southern and conservative candidate and Averell as the northern and liberal candidate."[23] As Schlesinger indicates, the winner of the liberal delegates was more likely to win the convention, so Harriman tried to exaggerate Stevenson's moderation.

In the wake of the *Brown v. Board of Education* decision, liberals urged more moderation on Stevenson.[24] While the frontrunner used the words "moderation," "rationality," and "gradual" in his speeches, his main policy concession to southerners was his opposition to the Powell amendment.[25] He argued that the amendment would deprive schools of much-needed federal aid without having an impact on segregation.[26] Stevenson told Humphrey, who had proposed a compromise amendment, "this is one case in which I don't in the least sympathize with the attitude of the Negro leaders."[27] He wrote to DNC chair Paul Butler that "The philosophy of rule or ruin is no more tolerable among Negroes than whites."[28]

Nevertheless, Stevenson was acutely aware of the need to win the black vote in primaries. Though primaries were not binding at the time, a strong primary performance by Kefauver might be interpreted as evidence that he would be a more competitive nominee. In the summer of 1955, Stevenson asked former NUL treasurer Lloyd Garrison (the great-grandson of the abolitionist) to meet with the NUL board of directors and obtain a list of important blacks to talk to. Garrison urged him not only to meet them, but "bat ideas around" to learn the intricacies of civil rights policy. He advised that "a little of this would go a long way because the educated part of the Negro community is so small the country over and the members of it are pretty well acquainted with each other and news travels like wild fire."[29] Garrison instructed the campaign to hire a Hampton-Sydney Institute professor who was "dark enough to be 'visible' in photographs and therefore would be better than" another black Stevenson aide.[30] Pamphlets of an Eleanor Roosevelt speech for Stevenson in Washington, D.C., were distributed to black leaders, along with some of Stevenson's speeches on race.[31] Stevenson advertised that Kefauver had once called the FEPC "a dangerous step toward regimentation" that "violates the rights of the employers of our Nation."[32]

Stevenson's primary victory in California saved his candidacy after losing Minnesota to Kefauver.[33] Black voters and white civil rights supporters were an important part of each candidate's California strategy.[34] Kefauver and Harriman won the favor of the *Los Angeles Tribune* and *Los Angeles Sentinel* editors, and Kefauver campaigned personally in the black neighborhoods of Los Angeles.[35] Stevenson campaign aides believed the NAACP held considerable sway over white liberals in California, and met with its West Coast representative for campaign advice.[36] Stevenson won over the owner of three Los Angeles weekly black newspapers and ultimately received almost twice as many votes as Kefauver.[37] Butler told Stevenson that the nomination was now within reach.[38]

Though candidates typically backtrack from the more ambitious stances they take when seeking a party nomination, Stevenson supported desegregation more vocally than ever. Convention chairman Sam Rayburn pushed through a platform statement at the 1956 convention rejecting the use of force to implement the *Brown* decision. But Stevenson immediately worked to repair the damage. He urged full implementation in his acceptance speech, and repeated the call in both Harlem and Little Rock. In Harlem, Stevenson criticized Eisenhower for refusing to endorse *Brown* and taking credit for

Democratic Party initiatives on civil rights. To a pro-segregationist crowd in Little Rock, Stevenson said *Brown* was morally correct and that it needed to be enforced.[39] Even governors who had supported Stevenson said it might be impossible to win their states.[40] Stevenson largely retained the same supporters and opponents among officeholders and interest group leaders from 1952. Wilkins and Ralph Bunche privately assured Stevenson of their continued support in the general election.[41] Among prominent black leaders, only Harlem representative Adam Clayton Powell endorsed Eisenhower. Byrnes attempted unsuccessfully to gather support for a third-party alternative to the Democratic Party.[42]

When the general election votes were tallied, Stevenson retained South Carolina and Mississippi, but Eisenhower added Louisiana and Kentucky to the Southern states he won in 1952. Labor analysts fretted that Stevenson lost significant ground among blacks in 1956, but his losses were negligible in northern black areas organized by labor unions.[43] His greatest losses among blacks were in the South, where Democratic opposition to school desegregation was salient. Voting for a Republican president was arguably the only way of protesting Southern Democrats who were unopposed in the general election.

Although the 1956 campaign placed considerable weight on party unity, each candidate ascribed even more importance to black voters. No major candidate thought to provide a challenge to Stevenson by running to his right on racial issues, and the Democratic nominee worked diligently to meet with the nation's black leaders. To the extent that we can measure Stevenson's motives through written correspondence, his true sympathies also lay with the liberals and civil rights activists. In 1948, Democratic candidates thought black voters were a swing constituency in the general election; by 1956, they were a necessary constituency in party nominations.

Kennedy and Johnson Reverse Course for 1960

In 1960, both Johnson and Kennedy scaled back friendly relations with the South in order to obtain the liberal support they needed for the nomination. As in 1956, serious contenders recognized that supporting civil rights was not optional, and hired staff members with extensive ties to black communities. Candidates continued to seek some support from the South, but worked hard to avoid being identified with the region. The Democratic Party had shifted to a new equilibrium in which the risky choice was to cultivate the southern faction.

Johnson, the South's favorite son, had learned from Russell's 1952 campaign and tried not to become a southern factional candidate. Russell refused to campaign for him, saying that "any concerted action that would stamp Lyndon as the Southern candidate" and cause him "a great deal more harm than good."[44] The Senate majority leader persuaded some Southern Democrats to vote for the Civil Rights Act of 1957 so he could solidify his civil rights credentials. As the 1957 Civil Rights Act was taking shape, his advisor told him, "to put it bluntly, if you vote against a civil rights bill, you can forget your presidential ambitions in 1960."[45] Johnson managed to clear the way for the weak civil rights bill, telling southern senators that a worse bill would be introduced if they filibustered this one. Russell refrained from fighting the bill with his normal parliamentary tactics because "he was trying to help Lyndon get elected president."[46] Johnson told his Texas constituents that it was not a civil rights law and he forestalled "a punitive sectional monstrosity," and told liberals that it was a gateway for stronger bills.[47] His record was still not strong enough among northern liberals, who knew that he weakened the bill from Eisenhower's already moderate demands.[48] The ADA published a pamphlet titled *Lyndon Johnson Is Unqualified*, and sent a letter to every delegate labeling him "a conservative, anti-civil rights, gas-and-oil Senator."[49]

Less well known is Massachusetts senator John F. Kennedy's connection to the South. As a presidential candidate in 1960, Kennedy had to shed some of the support he sought when pursuing the vice presidency in 1956. His future southern campaign manager managed to rally Southern delegates in 1956, mainly because they opposed other candidates such as Humphrey and Kefauver.[50] One Mississippi delegate told a reporter he voted for Kennedy because, "Well, we'd be for anybody against that nigger-loving Kefauver of Tennessee."[51] Arkansas governor Orval Faubus later recalled that

the Kennedys at that time were sort of known to us as middle-of-the-road people, they were not extreme liberals, nor extreme conservatives. Kefauver had quite a bit of disfavor in the state because he's from the South and many southerners felt that he had been too liberal on some of the issues which vitally affected the region . . . .Many of the people in the state felt that with the Kennedy background—his father was a free enterprise businessman and a member of the Roosevelt administration—he would not be an extremist on any issue.[52]

Kennedy quipped after the 1956 convention that "I'll be singing Dixie the rest of my life."[53]

In general, white southerners believed that Kennedy was the most sympathetic candidate who could win the liberal vote and therefore the nomination. The *Grenville, South Carolina News* editorialized that "To date, Senator Kennedy's popularity with Southerners is due not nearly so much to his voting record. . . . He has sought the support of the South. In a time when most national politicians seek favor by condemning the South, this can be effective flattery."[54] The other northern candidates were more strongly supportive of civil rights.[55] A former Georgia legislator wrote that "It is my opinion that you are by far the best man for the South . . . you are the only serious contender who would not have to sell the South down the river to get the support of the ultra-liberals."[56] The South's most conservative senators, including James Eastland and Harry Byrd, pledged to support Johnson on the first ballot, but Kennedy on subsequent ballots.[57]

Kennedy's support in the South caused grave concern among NAACP leaders and delegates to their national convention.[58] NAACP activists were also alarmed that Kennedy voted to refer the 1957 Civil Rights Act to the obstructionist Judiciary Committee and allow (white) juries to try civil rights violators. During the Little Rock crisis, he merely issued a statement against mob violence.[59] As he ran for reelection to the Senate in 1958, Roy Wilkins and Clarence Mitchell from the NAACP spoke to black audiences in Massachusetts, emphasizing his votes and southern kinship. When Kennedy defended his record, Wilkins replied that black voters

> know that ordinarily a Democratic candidate must not proceed so far as to destroy all his support in the Southern states; but they view with more than casual distress any events which seems to indicate close identity of the candidate with the well-known views of the Negro's traditional opponents. They swallowed Sparkman in 1952 because they had faith that Stevenson, while welcoming Deep South support, would not go along completely with Deep South sentiment on the Negro. . . . They feel uneasy over this apparent entente cordiale between Kennedy of Massachusetts and Griffin, Timmerman, Talmadge, Eastland, et al., of Dixie.[60]

To repair his standing with black voters, Kennedy recruited a number of civil rights activists, including the president of the Boston chapter of the NAACP and a prominent civil rights lawyer. The latter compiled a list of black community leaders and tried to arrange a personal meeting with them on any occasion in which Kennedy spoke nearby.[61]

After hiring activists from a skeptical community, Kennedy performed well among black voters. Wilkins was apparently persuaded by Kennedy's apology and allies in the NAACP to write a positive letter on his behalf. He now wrote that "Senator Kennedy has one of the best voting records on civil rights and related issues of any Senator in Congress."[62] The letter was leaked to the press and distributed among prominent blacks during the fall of 1958. By the end of October, Kennedy wrote "the NAACP-Roy Wilkins situation has come along rather well."[63]

As the 1960 convention approached, Kennedy seemed far more concerned with the black vote than with the southern vote. In May, Kennedy enlisted law professor Harris Wofford, the first white male graduate of Howard Law School, to help win over black leaders. Campaign manager Robert F. Kennedy told Wofford, "We're really in trouble with Negroes."[64] After offering measured support for civil rights to New York's Liberal Party, a misleading *New York Times* headline read, "Kennedy Assures Liberals He Seeks No Help in the South."[65] With southern support already undermined, Kennedy argued that more subtle forms of segregation needed to be fought outside of the South.[66] At the 1960 convention, Wofford organized a civil rights suite at the hotel that offered breakfast every morning. In the end, Kennedy obtained the votes of 95 percent of the black delegates (Johnson won a few black delegates in Texas).[67]

As in 1956, unions seemed to support the frontrunner with the real danger of a Johnson nomination. Other contenders for the Democratic nomination in 1960, including Humphrey and Stevenson (not a declared candidate), each had significant support among civil rights liberals who viewed Kennedy's civil rights supporters as "cronies."[68] But Humphrey was viewed as an ineffective campaigner. ADA lobbyist Joseph Rauh admitted that Humphrey's campaign "was kind of a useless gesture." Reuther tried to persuade Humphrey to quit, which he did after losing in Wisconsin and West Virginia.[69]

A Kennedy campaign prospectus on the convention ventured that Humphrey's supporters were more strategic than Johnson's supporters. The prospectus argued that Kennedy could obtain 326 votes from southern and border states "if the Johnson candidacy begins to fade," compared with only 198 votes he could acquire from Humphrey. However, a group of liberals led by Eleanor Roosevelt, Eugene McCarthy, and (secretly) Lyndon Johnson tried to gather liberal support for Stevenson. If Stevenson sought the nomination, he could win by augmenting votes from states with loyal governors with Humphrey's votes.[70] Kennedy aides fought back by promising numerous labor and civil rights groups that Kennedy would not nominate Johnson as vice president.[71] Kennedy also packed the platform committee with liberals to sap the momentum of the insurgents.[72]

In the general election, Kennedy not only promoted high-profile events with civil rights, but avoided high-profile events with southerners. Wofford organized a national conference on civil rights in October to discuss how to implement the civil rights platform.[73] More than five hundred of the most prominent civil rights activists in the country were invited, and most attended.[74] The activists chastised the Eisenhower administration for its sluggish enforcement of voting rights, and recommended a series of proposals for Kennedy to implement within the first one hundred days. Orval Faubus agreed to welcome Kennedy to Arkansas during the fall campaign in spite of Kennedy's political liabilities. When Kennedy learned that someone sought a photograph with the governor to distribute in New York, Kennedy left without exchanging planned farewell greetings.[75] In the end, Kennedy won most of the Deep South by a close vote.[76]

The Kennedy campaign's support for civil rights got away from the candidate. Several southern governors warned the campaign that if Kennedy associated too closely with Martin Luther King, Jr., they would support Nixon and Kennedy would lose their states.[77] During the election, King and numerous protestors were placed in jail and threatened with real prison sentences. After a series of miscommunications and withdrawn statements from advisors, Kennedy called King's wife and seemed to arrange for the release of civil rights protestors in Atlanta.[78] When Kennedy won the South anyway, southern politicians were astonished. Since black votes made up for lost white votes, a southern ally said the party "gained a wider margin of freedom on racial issues."[79]

As public opinion created a more favorable legislative climate for civil rights, President Johnson paved the way for the 1964 Civil Rights Act for the same reason that he had to support the 1957 Civil Rights Act. Because of his background and voting record, liberals suspected him of not being committed to their cause. Johnson had to unequivocally support their civil rights agenda in order to secure his own party's support going forward. Fearing a challenge from the left in 1964, perhaps from Robert F. Kennedy, he met with King, the NAACP's Wilkins, and the UAW's Rauh to announce his intention to pass a law. He later told biographer Doris Kearns Goodwin that "I knew that if I didn't get out in front of this issue, they [the liberals] would get me. They'd throw up my background against me . . . I couldn't let that happen. I had to produce a civil rights bill that was even stronger than the one they'd have gotten if Kennedy had lived. Without this, I'd be dead before I could even begin."[80] Presidents need the support of the party's dominant coalition. In 1964, the liberals were the Democratic Party's dominant coalition and civil rights was their flagship issue.

Platforms

Platforms from 1952 and 1956 were at least as liberal as 1948, and the liberal 1960 platform helped derail a liberal challenge to Kennedy. While they were not ambitious enough to provoke a southern walkout, they preserved the commitments made in 1948 and extended support for civil rights into other areas. The 1952 platform was a substantive improvement over 1948 in civil rights. It addressed most of the concerns presented to the party by the Leadership Conference on Civil Rights, an organization of twenty national civil rights and labor groups led by the NAACP. The Leadership Conference focused heavily on the need to change cloture rules, since filibusters had prevented a unified government from legislating any reforms advocated in the 1948 convention.[81] Humphrey met privately with the 1952 vice presidential nominee, Alabama senator John Sparkman, to discuss a platform that would avoid a floor fight. The two agreed to omit inflammatory words like "filibuster," "cloture," "compulsory," or "enforceable."[82] While the platform did not specifically name the FEPC, it supported federal legislation creating the "right to equal opportunity in employment" and using the Justice Department to prosecute civil rights violations. It euphemistically allowed for legislation after "reasonable debate without being blocked by a minority in either house."[83]

The language fooled no one, pleasing most liberals and angering southerners. The NAACP emphasized that the 1952 platform was an improvement over 1948 because it supported cloture reform, while attacking the Republican platform for backing down from the ambitious promises it made in 1944 and 1948. In White's words, it was a "distinct advance over the 1948 plank and is a signal victory for the forces of liberalism. . . . While the plank does not pinpoint the issues in the precise language submitted by the Leadership Conference on Civil Rights, it substantially embodies the recommendations of the 54 national labor, church, minority group and fraternal groups associated in the conference."[84] Byrnes said that the platform was worse than the 1948 platform because it supported federal lawsuits on behalf of civil rights victims.[85] If the platform equivocated, the nominee did not. Stevenson shortly thereafter supported the FEPC bill before Congress by name.

As mentioned earlier, the 1956 Democratic platform fell short of the grand expectations in the wake of the *Brown* decision. It did not call for federal enforcement of *Brown*, so a number of northern delegates considered a roll call vote for the platform. Reuther and Wilkins made plans for three hundred delegates to issue a floor challenge, but Eleanor Roosevelt persuaded them not to on the basis of party unity.[86] The Republican platform arguably had a stronger statement affirming the decision, though claiming that enforcement rested with federal district courts. The NAACP said that the Republican platform was a "shade better" overall, but not without praising the Democratic platform's commitment to filibuster reform and decrying the Republican Party's gradual approach on implementing *Brown*.[87] The Democratic platform did not retreat from any of the pledges it had made in 1948 or 1952, still committed to federal laws outlawing discrimination in voting and at the workplace. While the platform did not move forward as much as the NAACP had hoped, the nominee did. Stevenson committed himself publicly to enforcing the *Brown* decision after the platform was passed.

The 1960 platform not only supported an ambitious civil rights law and federal enforcement of *Brown*, but praised the controversial civil disobedience tactics of the civil rights movement. According to Wofford, the original platform drafted was meant to be ambitious on the assumption that it would be watered down in revisions. Instead, it was passed in full.[88] Wilkins speculated that Johnson's vice-presidential candidacy "helped the Democrats adopt a strong civil rights plank because his followers could not afford to oppose the plank and still hope to recruit votes for Johnson outside the South."[89]

Conclusion

Having examined the nominating contests from 1944 to 1960, let us consider whether, on balance, groups or politicians were responsible for the civil rights trajectory. Stevenson, Kefauver, Kennedy, and Johnson knew that losing the votes of civil rights supporters could cost them the Democratic nomination. With a little bit of pressure from civil rights groups, a Massachusetts moderate distanced himself from carefully cultivated southern politicians. A Texas senator enabled the passage of the first civil rights act since Reconstruction to pass in 1957. Groups changed the electoral calculations these candidates needed to make to win their party's nomination.

African Americans also had different policy demands because of the work of a coalition representing them. Goals that seemed impossible decades earlier were now within reach. Therefore, the Democratic Party continued to move leftward on race even after Wallace's threat disappeared. In 1952, Democrats promised filibuster reform and federal prosecution on top of the anti-discrimination laws promised in 1948. In the next cycle, the black-blue alliance pushed an even more polarizing policy: school desegregation. Although the 1956 platform skirted this issue, the nominee did not. It was no longer possible to appease racial liberals with measures that would maintain the New Deal equilibrium between North and South.

Coalition maintenance was left to groups, not politicians. Thanks to their work, civil rights was a uniting issue among liberals, rather than a divisive issue. Past and future events proved that blacks, liberals, and white union workers could work against each other in politics. The alliance between labor and civil rights brought African Americans into the Democratic Party and eventually necessitated that ambitious Democratic Party politicians support civil rights. The politicians were the last part of the sequence in an alliance between civil rights and labor groups.

The CIO might have bitten off more than it wanted to chew. By elevating the NAACP, the AFL-CIO later found itself unable to back away from civil rights when its interests changed. By the end of the 1950s, the NAACP publicly confronted the AFL-CIO to address discrimination in its own ranks even as it continued to receive funding for its legal and legislative work from unions. Wilkins knew that the AFL-CIO needed to keep supporting the NAACP to maintain its liberal image and role as a leader in the New Deal coalition.[90] The NAACP no longer needed to be a "team player" on all of the issues to remain part of the liberal coalition, although there was a price to be paid for calling out its allies.

As the civil rights movement reached its crescendo in the 1960s, politicians experienced increased pressure to fight for civil rights. Among other organizations, the Southern Christian Leadership Conference, Congress of Racial Equality, and Student Non-Violent Coordinating Committee generated public sympathy for the cause with civil disobedience and public demonstrations. By obtaining media attention, they set the public agenda and contributed to the passage of landmark civil rights laws. Landmark civil rights legislation could not have been passed without the civil rights movement, organized initially through existing societal institutions like black churches and student groups.

But the legislation also could not have been passed if the Democratic Party of James Byrnes and Dick Russell had remained unchanged. The CIO-NAACP alliance had transformed the party decades earlier so that Democratic politicians, attentive to a new set of dominant partisan groups, were prepared to pass civil rights laws when public opinion and favorable conditions on Capitol Hill permitted them. Party change, as with the civil rights movement, had its origins in societal changes below the level of electoral politics.

CHAPTER 6

Conservative Christians Before the Christian Right

Many southern white voters, alienated by the Democratic Party's transformation on civil rights, were no longer firmly attached to it by the 1960s. But like the traditionally Republican African American voters who supported Franklin Roosevelt in the 1930s, southern whites were not attached to a new party either. They were ripe for conversion, but not yet converted. The Republican Party would have to wait for cultural issues and religious mores to congeal into a new social formation, the so-called Christian Right, before it could win the firm loyalties of those left party-less by the civil rights transformation. The formation of the new Christian Right in the 1960s and 1970s is the subject of this chapter and the next. By the 1980s the Republican Party began to appeal to the new Christian Right by endorsing Judeo-Christian values, defining families as nuclear families, and opposing abortion even in exceptional circumstances. By the 1990s, the party's new stance on the issue of the religious right helped make it competitive in congressional elections in most southern states.

As with civil rights organizations, groups who came to transform a party first underwent historically contingent transformations themselves. Before the Christian Right became part of the Republican Party, there first had to be a Christian Right. Theological conservatives became cultural conservatives and formed a coalition capable of changing a party, without the guiding hand of politicians. *Theological conservatives* believed in biblical inerrancy. *Cultural conservatives* fought for the government to uphold traditional values, particularly on the politics of the family. Some cultural conservatives, like Catholics, were never integrated into the Christian Right. Nor did all theological conservatives become cultural conservatives or conservative on other issues. And there is no reason to think that such a transformation was inevitable. In

Canada, theological conservatives from the same sects as their American counterparts adopted culturally conservative views, but never economically conservative views.[1] It is harder for a transformative coalition to challenge a political party when it is divided on a large set of issues. In America, cultural conservatives worked to socialize likeminded activists into economic and foreign policy conservatism.

Cultural conservatism can be traced to the changing gender and sexual norms of the 1960s. Feminists and gay rights groups argued that heterosexual marriage and nuclear families were not better ways of life. They sought to remove public affirmations of traditional lifestyles and lift discrimination against other lifestyle choices. Some fought for a sexual revolution that decoupled sex from marriage and childrearing. Cultural conservatives interpreted their support for no-fault divorce to mean marriage should only be sustained in service of individual preferences rather than religious norms. Evangelical Christians did not initially organize against court rulings on school prayer, Bible-reading, and abortion because they did not view them as part of the public debate over marriage and family values. Abortion, for example, was originally seen as a clash between medical professionals and the Catholic Church. By the late 1970s, evangelical denomination leaders and political groups viewed abortion and secular education as part of a larger "secular humanist" attack on their values, part and parcel of the efforts to redefine families and sexual mores. Leaders converted old organizations and created new ones to persuade rank-and-file evangelical Christians to support a cultural conservative agenda and become active in politics, once thought to be too impure for the religiously devout.

Since I argue that groups are the raw materials of parties, my first chapter on cultural conservatives uncovers the positions of their forbearers before they mobilized for change. Due to numerous obstacles to cooperation, the ingredients for a culturally conservative realignment were simply not ready to be mixed at all until the late 1970s. Most conservative religious denominations had avoided politics and lacked central direction. Small doctrinal differences and competition for followers also interfered with participation in any cross-denominational cause. And as Schäfer demonstrates, religious moderates and liberals were gaining influence in many religious organizations and denominations in the 1960s.[2] A reasonable counterfactual was for today's culturally conservative churches to have followed a more liberal trajectory, at least on economic issues. An even more likely counterfactual was for such churches to remain as they had been—mostly apolitical and decentralized.

Instead, religious broadcasters experimented with politics as a way of reaching larger audiences, and general conservatives helped them form coalitions that welcomed other sects and broadened their agenda.

I differ from recent scholars who view the political turn of theological conservatives as decades in the making.[3] Several authors have demonstrated the well-funded efforts of businessmen and economic interest groups to promote free enterprise through religious broadcasters and institutions (though not all of them were evangelical). Moreton argues that Wal-Mart helped create a Christian free market ideology in the Ozarks, which had been a populist region with a distrust of chain stores.[4] Dochuk shows how many southern evangelists moved to Sunbelt states and forged ties with the business community, institutionalized in colleges such as Pepperdine University.[5] Kruse argues that Americans viewed business interest groups opposing the New Deal with great skepticism, but supporters of the free market found out that Americans trusted religious leaders. As a result, they promoted broadcasters like Billy Graham, who preached against communism and otherwise indirectly promoted capitalism.[6] Bean sees political conservatism among evangelicals as part of a two-step process. First, businessmen convinced evangelicals to meld their piety with patriotism during the 1950s. Over a period of decades, they associated patriotism with economic individualism in a kind of "Christian nationalism."[7]

While these efforts have been amply documented, I argue that they were mostly ineffective by themselves. Both the qualitative and quantitative evidence cast doubt on any kind of a political consensus among religious conservatives. Early efforts may have primed evangelical Christians for Republican politics, but millions more became registered voters when cultural issues were introduced between the late 1970s and the 1990s. Mass-level survey data shows that evangelical Christians were not that distinctive in their economic beliefs even in the 1970s, after decades of efforts like those described above. Activists had to work to convince theological conservatives to become cultural conservatives and cultural conservatives to become economic conservatives.

This chapter shows that religious groups before the 1970s were mostly uneager to join cross-denominational coalitions, let alone conservative coalitions. It only has the space for a brief summary of a large and rich history, focusing on fundamentalists, evangelicals, Baptists, Pentecostals, and Catholics. Though brief, the sketch is enough to show what coalition builders were up against.

Parties Before the Christian Right

Once again, we start our discussion of party transformation by outlining the party alignment before a change took place. Before the 1980 election, neither party reached out to theological conservatives using cultural issues. Cultural liberals like feminists and gay rights groups were gathering momentum in the Democratic Party in the 1970s, even as traditional Catholic and ethnic members of the party protested. Republican politicians considered appealing to disaffected Catholics, but failed to recruit Southern Baptists, Pentecostals, and other conservative sects.

Republicans did not have a history of supporting theological conservatives and theological conservatives did not have a history of supporting Republicans. Mainline Protestants identified as Republicans in a ratio of 3:2 in the 1940s and 1950s, while evangelicals and Catholics leaned Democratic until the 1980s.[8] Evangelicals contributed to the Nixon landslide in 1972, but were divided over Carter's candidacy in 1976. A majority of evangelicals have voted for Republican presidential candidates consistently only since 1980 (Figure 4).[9] One study of the *Almanac of American Politics* finds that very few congressional Republicans espoused culturally conservative messages in 1978. In the 1980s, between 10 and 20 percent did so, followed by a significant increase in the 1990s, peaking in 1998 with 30 percent of Republicans nationwide and 46 percent of those in the South.[10]

Expositions of conservative agendas before Reagan tended to reflect the predominantly mainline Protestant demographic of the Republican Party. In 1938, Republicans held a "Program Committee" to discuss ideas for party reform. The meeting included 8 blacks, 16 Jews, and 30 Catholics among its 273 members. Former president Hoover suggested a proposal to reestablish the "common morals" appropriate "in a Christian country," but it did not pass.[11] The anti-New Deal Liberty League consisted largely of business leaders who opposed Prohibition, the most important cause of cultural conservatives in recent memory. The cosmopolitan Democratic presidential nominee of 1928, Al Smith, was one of its speakers. Even in the 1970s, future Supreme Court Justice Lewis Powell wrote a private memo for the Chamber of Commerce, which is often cited as the strategy that inspired the growth of conservative think tanks.[12] In his list of concerns about the culture, he mainly focused on hostility to free enterprise and only briefly mentions books on "erotic free love" as a concern. (As a Supreme Court justice, Powell also signed

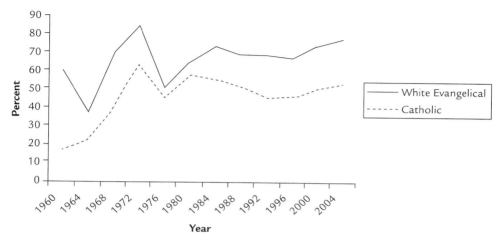

Figure 4. Republican share of two-party presidential voting. Espinosa, *Race, Religion, and the American Presidency*, 15.

on to the *Roe v. Wade* decision.) As the decade came to a close, a group of conservative senators published a "Conservative Manifesto" for the forthcoming decade. Paul Laxalt wrote the chapter on "the family," but it mainly focused on solid childrearing practices and the effects of government programs on families. Laxalt only criticized government funding for abortion, divorce, and legal aid for homosexuals at the end, but not the behaviors themselves.[13] The House Republican Conference, likewise, published a program that covered many issues, but completely omitted cultural issues.[14]

Party platforms in the 1970s did not differ substantially on cultural issues. In 1972, both platforms supported the Equal Rights Amendment (ERA), day care programs, and bars to gender discrimination. Neither one mentioned abortion. Even in 1976, both parties continued to support the ERA, but party nominees had difficulty finessing the abortion issue. Democratic nominee Jimmy Carter favored abortion rights, but angered feminist groups by opposing existing federal funding for abortion. While the Republican platform of 1976 was more antiabortion than the Democratic platform, it stopped short of actually supporting an antiabortion amendment.[15] The 1976 Republican platform enunciated "a continuance of the public dialogue on abortion."[16]

Nor were there signs of cultural conservatism in most state Republican parties. Republican governors signed abortion liberalization laws passed by

Republican legislatures in Colorado in 1967 and New York in 1970. Catholic pressure prevented the New York legislature from passing the same bill when Democrats controlled the legislature. California governor Ronald Reagan signed the most liberal abortion law in the country in 1967, which failed to pass under a unified Democratic state government.[17] Conservative strategist Paul Weyrich tried to persuade Republican leaders to become involved in the school prayer issue and had no success. The Wisconsin state Republican chair told him, "our businesspeople would think that it was strange that we are getting involved in a religious issue." Weyrich vowed, "I'm going to see to it that one day the party will listen to these kinds of issues. And that really became my mission in life."[18]

President Nixon was alert to the potential of both evangelicals and Catholics, but lacked intimate knowledge of the religious sects and the commitment to bring about long-term party transformation. White House tapes reveal Nixon to have had a very rough grasp of evangelical culture. He made several efforts to speak to Southern Baptist gatherings in 1972, but too many pastors complained. Nixon aides even attempted to install his deputy Veteran Affairs administrator as Southern Baptist Convention (SBC) president. Not only did the attempted coup fail, but the SBC instead elected a friend of Jimmy Carter, who supported civil rights and rebuked the Nixon administration after Watergate.[19]

Initially, Nixon opposed abortion rights as part of a "Catholic strategy" in his reelection campaign (he also supported aid to parochial schools, traditionally a Democratic issue). An unnamed aid advised

> the liberal Republican woman in the suburbs who favors abortion won't vote against the President just because he's against it. . . . And the strong pro-abortionists, the women's libbers like Gloria Steinem, they aren't going to vote for him anyhow. But the working class Catholic mother, who thinks abortion is evil, will vote for him just because she's against it.[20]

Nixon dropped the issue when his Democratic opponent, George McGovern, announced he would leave abortion to the states.[21] In his second term, Nixon could have withdrawn federal health care funding for birth control without contradicting his support for federalism, but he never did.[22]

Gerald Ford became the first president to address the SBC convention and Jerry Falwell's independent Baptist congregation. He also told *Christianity*

Today and the president of the National Association of Evangelicals (NAE) that, like Jimmy Carter, he had a "born again" experience and read the Bible daily. Ford lined up many prolife supporters, including leaders of American Citizens Concerned for Life, the National Right to Life Committee, the Christian Action Council, and the Christian Crusade. On the other hand, the First Lady was outspoken in support of the ERA and abortion rights. Ford also refused to let gospel film executive Billy Zeoli (who raised money for Francis Schaeffer's documentaries) write a book about his faith, or lend his name to the Preachers' Committee for Ford.[23] Future nominees worked hard for publicity that Ford eschewed. Strategy notes from Bob Dole's 1976 vice presidential campaign highlighted his pro-life position, though only in the context of Catholic outreach.[24]

Cultural conservatism was not even part of the Goldwater wing of the Republican Party. By winning the 1964 presidential nomination, Barry Goldwater showed that Northeastern moderates held less influence in the party, but he did not push the party in the direction of cultural conservatism. His daughter obtained an abortion with his support.[25] A survey of Goldwater delegates from the South found that they were mostly mainline Protestants, with Southern Baptists constituting only 10 percent. *Christianity Today* reported that only 3.8 percent of Goldwater supporters were fundamentalists.[26] The 1964 convention's keynote speaker was an evangelical Christian, but he had been a delegate for Goldwater's nemesis, Nelson Rockefeller.[27] Goldwater was a conservative leader in the 1960s, but the Republican Party's main divisions at the time concerned civil rights, economic issues, and foreign policy. When Falwell opposed Sandra Day O'Connor's nomination to the Supreme Court in 1981 on the basis of her abortion views, he publicly snapped, "I think every good Christian ought to kick Falwell right in the ass." He later said the party had been taken over by "kooks," referring to the Christian Right.[28]

Ronald Reagan, a Goldwater Republican, brought up abortion in his 1976 challenge to President Ford. Although Reagan had signed the most liberal antiabortion law in the country as governor of California, he claimed to regret the decision because too many women were fabricating reasons to have abortions to protect their health. A South Carolina state Republican activist recalls an impromptu meeting with Senator Jesse Helms as part of the campaign. In an Atlanta hotel lobby, they discussed how the Reagan campaign could use the abortion issue to reach out to the Catholic community—not the evangelical Christian community. The legislator recalled, "I couldn't believe it. It was the first exposure I had to anything like that."[29] Although abortion was discussed in a hotel lobby, neither abortion nor any other cultural issues were brought up in Reagan's strategy notes for the 1976 convention.[30] Don Devine, Reagan's deputy director of political planning and analysis, recalls that many campaign workers in 1976 were afraid that the abortion issue would lose more votes than they gained.[31]

Evangelical churches had to politicize themselves before political campaigns like Reagan's approached them for support. Reagan's 1976 campaign made no effort to reach out to them. Southern campaign director David Keene said that it would have never occurred to him or anyone else to contact southern churches for support, because they had never been politically active. Keene states that "there wasn't some place you could go to do that. Churches weren't that involved. You did not sit down and say 'how do you get the church?'"[32] Devine added that in 1976, churches may have reacted angrily to campaign efforts to politicize their church.[33] As Chapter 7 will show, groups organized themselves into coalitions shortly before the 1980 election. Only then did presidential candidates approach them.

Political Disengagement Among Theological Conservatives

One of the reasons Republicans did not appeal to theological conservatives is that they were not politically active. Religion is no stranger to politics in America; among other causes, churches were highly involved in abolitionism, temperance, and civil rights. Since the Progressive Era, many churches have embraced the "Social Gospel" and attempted to root out sin by fighting social evils, including poverty and political corruption. Both the CIO and civil rights groups used churches to hold meetings, provide information, recruit new voters, and lend moral legitimacy to their cause. Cesar Chavez realized that incorporating Catholic teachings into the Farm Workers of America's mission would both insulate them from red-baiting and attract members of the community not directly involved with the union.[34]

The political activism of theologically conservative Christians, however, is a relatively new feature of postwar politics. Neither their beliefs nor the designs of their institutions lent themselves to political activism of one kind or another. First, let us turn to their beliefs. Theologically conservative churches evolved on a separate trajectory from the more numerous "mainline" Protestant churches, refusing to assimilate secular values absorbed by mainline churches. By the early twentieth century, the religious diversity of America led modernist religious leaders to embrace pluralistic ideals that accommodated multiple religious traditions. Additionally, modernists accommodated traditional religious beliefs to the findings of science.[35] In contrast, theological conservatives believed the miracles of the Bible literally happened. If one were allowed to believe the Bible selectively, followers could form theological doctrines to suit their personal fancies.[36] "Fundamentalist" Protestants, as they often called themselves, gave up debating theology with modernists by the 1920s, acutely aware that the increasingly secular culture scoffed at their beliefs. Modernists made no accommodations for them in institutions such as the Federal Council of Churches. Instead of trying to take over modernist organizations, they kept their own churches and seminaries where they could teach biblical inerrancy unopposed. Despite originating with thinkers from the Northeast, fundamentalism generated a much greater following among southerners.

These different cultural values initially discouraged fundamentalists from politics instead of producing major political cleavage. During the dreary days of the Great Depression, many conservative denominations believed that the end of times was coming. The Bible foretold the return of Jesus Christ, and with Christ's impending return, repairing the material world was comparable to "rearranging deck chairs on the *Titanic*."[37] Many more believed that one went to church to discuss the Bible, sin, and salvation, but not current politics. Such people didn't join liberal political causes, but nor did they join conservative causes.

Theological conservatives believed the church was primarily a way to save individual souls. This, too, set them apart from modernist Christian churches that embraced the "Social Gospel" and supported social reforms. Modernists were more likely to focus on institutions and claim that society was more than the sum of individual acts of sin and salvation. Northern liberals, accustomed to a partnership with churches in the North and West, were frustrated with the lack of involvement from southern churches.[38] These attitudes discouraged political activism even after the Christian Right organized politically. Typical of theological conservatives, one pastor told political scientists that even if political movements had some impact, piety had more: "I suppose my main concern with all the energy put into political issues by many Christians . . . is what would happen if those same dollars and that same energy were put into personal witnessing for Christ and prayer."[39] Individual acts of salvation were the main cause—if not a sufficient cause—of a good society.

Some of the best-known theological conservatives, therefore, had long spoke out against political reform. Charles Fuller, the most popular fundamentalist radio preacher of the 1930s, criticized the political activism of both the liberal Federal Council of Churches and the anti-Semitic radio priest, Father Coughlin.[40] In 1965, when many religious figures considered liberal activism, future Christian Right icon Falwell proclaimed that "Nowhere are we commissioned to reform the externals. We are not told to wage wars against bootleggers, liquor stores, gamblers, murderers, prostitutes, racketeers, prejudiced persons or institutions."[41] In 1967, Harold Lindsell, soon to be editor of the popular evangelical magazine *Christianity Today*, scolded religions for involving "the mantle of the church . . . over democracy, capitalism, the status quo, and opposition to left wing and communistic causes of all kinds." The debate between capitalism and managed economies was not a religious battle.[42] Focus on the Family (FOF), a future leader of culturally conservative groups, blamed social problems on permissive parenting, not government policy, when it was founded in 1977.[43]

Even when theological conservatives later became actively involved in issues like abortion, gay rights, and pornography, many drew a distinction between "moral" and "political" issues. New cultural issues appeared that provided cover for religious leaders to become involved in politics in the name of religion, in a way that older political issues did not. Those eager to involve themselves in political affairs finally had an effective religious rationale. An activist in Iowa's Concerned Woman for America told me, "What you may call politics I would call Biblical principles and I'm thankful that my pastors have always been very good to stand on God's word."[44] James Dobson, FOF founder, said that eliminating the marriage tax penalty was "not a political issue," but a "family issue."[45]

In the 1960s, it was as rare for theological conservatives to weigh in on hot button cultural issues like abortion or school prayer as it was for them to abstain in later decades. Two of the largest theologically conservative organizations, the NAE and SBC, refused to file a brief for *Engel v. Vitale* or *Abington School District v. Schempp*, which prohibited school prayer and the reading of biblical passages in school, respectively.[46] Fundamentalist Carl McIntire declared that the former was a victory for religion because public school prayers tended to be nondenominational "pagan prayers." Despite a clear majority of support for school prayer among the American public, no protestant denomination supported Senator Everett Dirksen's school prayer amendment. The SBC's presidents and legal arms defended these decisions to Southern Baptists and opposed efforts to amend the Constitution.[47] Two theologically conservative magazines, *Eternity* and *Christianity Today*, published articles justifying abortion in some cases.

To the extent that theological conservatives voted before 1980, they tended to be Democrats. Concentrated in the South, fundamentalists in the 1930s were as fond of Franklin Roosevelt as other southerners. Many Alabama Baptist pastors thanked Roosevelt for the New Deal when he solicited information about poverty in their congregations.[48] Theological conservatives could even be pro-union. The SBC passed a resolution supporting organized labor that reads much like a pronouncement from a contemporary liberal church. It said "We recognize the right of labor to organize and to engage in collective bargaining to the end that labor may have a fair and living wage, such as will provide not only for the necessities of life but for recreation, pleasure, and culture." The conservative Southern Methodists similarly praised organized labor.[49] The conservative Pentecostal Holiness Church based in Atlanta banned membership in many kinds of organizations, but declared that the ban "is not intended to prohibit consistent association with a legal effort on the part of labor to prevent oppression and injustice from capitalism."[50] According to the CIO, most religious opposition to labor unions came from independent churches and itinerant preachers, rather than major denominations.[51]

Both Democratic and Republican presidents sought the support of Billy Graham, arguably the most influential postwar evangelist in America. Though Graham was more willing to dabble in politics than other contemporaries, his political opinions were more varied than the contemporary Christian Right. He linked communism with Satan, but supported the War on Poverty and civil rights.[52] In the wake of the Watergate scandal, Graham regretted his association with Nixon and avoided overt political endorsements for the rest of his life.[53]

Sectarianism

Like unions, religious organizations had their own rules and sensitivities, and one needs to understand them in order to understand why conservative denominations took so long to become politically active. For a time, rivalries between theologically conservative denominations and pastors compounded political disengagement as an impediment to political activity. Religious prejudice was an impediment to working with other sects just as racial prejudice was an impediment to a black-blue alliance. The raw materials of parties could not congeal until some of these rivalries were assuaged. Whatever evangelicals thought of politics, their negative views of other Christian denominations often inhibited their cooperation, even after their opinions on cultural political issues began to overlap. Neil Young documents the divisions between evangelicals, Catholics, and Mormons before and after they agreed on a common set of cultural issue positions.[54] Doctrinal disputes, competition for followers, and blatant prejudice militated against any political alliance across theologically conservative churches. The next chapter shows that broadcasters and political interest groups worked hard to smooth over these differences, with only partial success.

A longstanding division exists between "fundamentalists" and "evangelicals." Presbyterian radio preacher Carl McIntire created the American Council of Christian Churches (ACCC) in 1941 as a fundamentalist counterpart to the modernist Federal Council of Churches. More than five hundred stations broadcasted McIntire's show, 45 percent of them in the South. Beginning in the 1940s, many Christian conservatives preferred the word "evangelical" to "fundamentalist" to signal that they were willing to proselytize, but not insist on theological agreement. Evangelicals sought to "evangelize" diverse listeners to support Christian social mores, with biblical inerrancy being only one principle among many.[55] The NAE formed in 1942 to resist the modernization of the church without insisting on complete doctrinal agreement. Like the ACCC, it supported discrimination against Catholics, Jews, and atheists. It drafted a statement supporting civil rights for African Americans in education and housing, but opposed the FEPC because it would outlaw religious discrimination. Though the ACCC and NAE were both fiercely anticommunist and prejudiced against Catholics and Jews, they did not work together. The ACCC condemned NAE for welcoming Pentecostals and other sects seen as heretical.[56] The insistence of fundamentalists like McIntire and the ACCC on doctrinal purity interfered with coalition-building with other theological conservatives.[57]

Holiness churches and Pentecostals, too, were long held in low regard by each other and other sects even though they later provided many of the foot soldiers of the Christian Right. Both were inspired by John Wesley, who believed the Holy Spirit could imbue Christians to attain an outward state of holiness, purging them of original sin. Most of Wesley's followers in Methodist churches believed that the attainment of outward holiness was a gradual process, but Holiness churches claimed that holiness could be attained instantaneously in a born-again experience. Pentecostals believed the Holy Spirit could manifest itself not only in holiness, but in miracles, healing, and "speaking in tongues." Both Holiness and Pentecostal church pastors held that premarital sex and illegal drugs contaminate the body and prevent one from experiencing the Holy Spirit, later lending themselves to culturally conservative politics.[58] While Methodists and other Protestant sects viewed these charismatic sects with disdain, they regarded each other as downright eccentric or sacrilegious, partly because the Pentecostals gained membership at the expense of Holiness churches.[59] Holiness churches criticized Pentecostal services for their "religious frenzy" and "delirium." One theologian derided Pentecostal gatherings for their "pandemoniums . . . worthy of a madhouse or of a collection of howling dervishes."[60]

Fundamentalists predictably remained deeply suspicious of Pentecostals, who focus more on their unique, often ecstatic, experiences rather than any unified body of church doctrine. This focus on religious experience, fundamentalists claim, detracts from attention to the text of the Bible. Many Christians believe that God's revelations to humans were finished with the Bible, leading them to reject Pentecostal revelations just as they reject the revelations of other modern-day prophets, including the Mormons' Joseph Smith.[61] Even after the coagulation of many religious traditions behind the Christian Right, SBC trustees in 1987 forbid anyone from promoting or speaking in tongues from being SBC missionaries or chaplains.[62] Future Christian Right leader Falwell said that speaking in tongues "confuses things . . . God is not the author of confusion."[63] Despite considerable agreement on political issues, Falwell (an independent Baptist) recommended voting against Pat Robertson (a Pentecostal) in the 1988 Republican primary, and Robertson came in last place in Bob Jones University's (BJU) fundamentalist-dominated neighborhoods. Texas broadcaster James Robison was once considered a rising star among Southern Baptists and spoke on Falwell's show occasionally. When Robison claimed an experience with the Holy Spirit and began speaking in tongues in the 1990s, Southern Baptists "turned on him on a dime." He was able to build up a new ministry, but George W. Bush's religious liaisons cautioned against associating with him.[64]

Catholics agreed with theological conservatives in opposing sex before marriage, and over time on a range of political issues like abortion. But fundamentalists and evangelicals had long been blatantly prejudiced against Catholics and, to this day, relations have only been partly repaired. Catholics believed in neither a literal interpretation of the Bible nor "born-again" experiences, and evangelists often viewed the church hierarchy as a conspiracy to corrupt America. Vatican II emphasized the value of ecumenical services, which evangelicals saw as a thinly veiled effort to bring all Christians under the Catholic tent.[65] Fundamentalist Bob Jones, Jr. called the pope the "anti-Christ" and the Catholic Church, a "satanic cult." During the Reagan administration, Jones and the SBC strongly protested the decision to recognize Vatican City.[66] Catholics, in turn, have distrusted evangelicals. President Reagan originally offered Moral Majority director Bob Billings, a fundamentalist, the position of assistant secretary for nonpublic education. On his first day, he learned someone else received the position. Billings reluctantly accepted a different position as "special assistant" to the education secretary. Later he learned Catholic interests had vetoed his original position because they did not want a fundamentalist Protestant overseeing religious schools.[67] Though many Republican presidential candidates have spoken at BJU, they have sometimes paid a price. In 2000, a robocall from John McCain's campaign in Michigan targeted Catholics and tied George W. Bush to BJU's anti-Catholic record.[68]

At first, many sects refused to oppose abortion rights because Catholics opposed them too.[69] Francis Schaeffer, later a cultural conservative icon, initially refused to discuss abortion in a documentary outlining his theological critique of the modern world. While his son eventually convinced him to mention abortion, Schaeffer initially said, "I don't want to be identified with some Catholic Issue . . . I'm not putting my reputation on the line for them!"[70] The SBC's Christian Life Commission head, Foy Valentine, complained that "The Roman Catholic bishops have been pushing very hard with a well organized and well financed campaign to enact their absolutist position about abortion into law in this country."[71] SBC president W. A. Criswell, aligned with the conservative wing of the denomination, stated that "I have always felt that it was only after a child was born and had life separate from its mother, that it became an individual person, and it has always, therefore, seemed to me that what is best for the mother and for the future should be allowed."[72] Mass opinion of Southern Baptists is sparse,[73] but a handful of recollections and surveys shed some light on opinion within the denomination. Before *Roe v. Wade* voided antiabortion laws in forty-six states, a *Baptist Viewpoll* poll from 1970 found that 71 percent of Southern Baptist pastors favored abortion in cases of rape, incest, or danger to the woman's health, while 64 percent favored state laws permitting abortions in the case of deformities.[74]

Prejudice and distrust remained even after prolife positions took hold in evangelical churches. At the state level, prolife Protestants sometimes built their own counterparts to largely Catholic prolife groups. Eric Woolson, a Catholic, has worked on the political campaigns of four evangelical candidates in Iowa: George W. Bush, Mike Huckabee, Michelle Bachmann, and Bob Vander Plaats (a candidate for governor). A prominent evangelical campaign staff member told Huckabee that he should not have a Catholic running the campaign. During Vander Plaats's campaign, an evangelical minister told Woolson that Vander Plaats was not going to defeat ex-governor Terry Branstad in the Republican primary without Catholic votes. The minister said, "You know, some of these Catholics are Christians. If you can figure out which ones are Christians, maybe you can find somebody that can talk to 'em and get them to support us." On presidential candidate Michele Bachmann's campaign in 2012, a staff member suggested attacking rival Rick Santorum's Catholicism as he gained ground in Iowa.[75]

Institutional Design

The decentralized institutional design of most theologically conservative churches also prevented them from being a recruitment tool in politics. Theologically conservative denominations had limited control over their own affiliates and no control over other denominations. Whereas CIO unions all received directions from a powerful national organization, there was no such thing for the Christian Right or even the individual denominations discussed in this chapter. Theologically conservative churches tended to be less centrally directed than mainline churches, which meant that pastors tended to be as politically active or (more often) apathetic as the local congregation prefers. Within and across denominations, preachers hoped to recruit followers from other congregations, leading to personal and commercial jealousies.

To some extent, the apolitical tendencies of conservative churches were a product of this decentralized design. In decentralized churches, pastors simply gained a following or were appointed by a church's board of directors, rather than the church hierarchy. One's intellectual pedigree mattered less at the grassroots level than it did to high-ranking church officials, so theological conservative pastors were less likely to be influenced by the modernist teachings that tended to prevail in elite seminaries. The longer one's education, the more likely one was to adhere to an economic "social justice" agenda and less likely to adhere to a culturally conservative agenda. Moreover, attending a prestigious college or seminary had a large, statistically significant dampening effect on one's orthodoxy, political conservatism, and belief in premillenialism. In one study, only 43 percent of Pentecostal Assemblies of God pastors had college diplomas and only 19 percent had seminary degrees.[76] But even though pastors without prestigious degrees were less likely to be liberal crusaders, they were also unlikely to be conservative crusaders. Politics were frowned upon in the largest conservative denominations.[77]

The diversity of conservative religious sects warns against broad characterizations, but the largest among them—the SBC—provides a telling example of institutional decentralization.[78] Most pastors tended to avoid political controversy at all costs, but the SBC tacitly agreed on a "Grand Compromise."[79] In the wake of the highly publicized Scopes Trial, in which a high school teacher was prosecuted and acquitted for teaching evolution in Tennessee in 1925, the SBC adopted a statement of faith that granted individual churches autonomy in their beliefs, in order to keep as many churches in the fold as possible.[80] The SBC would not define basic doctrines to exclude one tradition or another, or let an ideological faction control the denomination. Not all state chapters condemned the teaching of evolution, for example.[81] The national SBC required that churches send a nominal sum to the denomination and nothing more.[82] Conservatives controlled the publishing houses, but they continued to publish a diversity of views.[83] Southern Baptist Theological Seminary president Al Mohler recalled that issues like homosexuality and abortion were hardly discussed in seminaries at all in the 1970s.[84]

Competition for followers within and across sects also contributed to fragmentation among theological conservatives. While religious broadcasters were able to grow their audiences over time, they also competed with other broadcasters for a similar audience. Some had "gentleman's agreements" not to broadcast in the same media markets, which were by nature difficult to maintain.[85] Across all denominations, the most ambitious pastors expanded their congregations and influence through Sunday schools, private K-12 schools, universities, missions, broadcasts, and even theme parks. Religious operatives competed to expand their reach, sometimes by gaining new converts, sometimes by poaching members of other congregations. For example, Falwell competed with local pastors by creating a "junior church," where he hired fifteen bus drivers to drive around town asking parents whether their children would like to attend Sunday School for free. He hoped this would entice their parents to attend his services.[86] Falwell eventually turned his radio broadcast, titled *Old Time Gospel Hour*, into a television show and started Lynchburg Baptist College in 1971 as a conservative counterpart to liberal seminaries and universities. Now called Liberty University, it boasts over thirteen thousand traditional students, sixty thousand online students, and an endowment of over fifty million dollars. Falwell's business associates pioneered the familiar fundraising techniques later used by PBS, using an eight hundred number for donations, and threatening to cancel the *Gospel Hour* unless viewers donated.

Pundits Before the Christian Right

As mentioned earlier, recent scholarship stresses the vigorous efforts of conservative financiers to link political and theological conservatism in the midtwentieth century. I argue that these efforts were unsuccessful until the introduction of cultural issues to mainstream political debate. Among others, J. Howard Pew of Sunoco worked relentlessly to imbue conservative religion with conservative politics until his death in 1971. Pew said, "Christianity and freedom are inexorably tied together" and "New Dealism, Socialism, and Communism are substantially the same thing—and all of them are the very antithesis of Christianity." Pew believed that practical politics were downstream from the world of ideas, declaring that "For 20 years I have been convinced we never would accomplish anything worth while by merely changing the party in power . . . If we want to save America, we must do it by changing the minds and hearts of our people." He co-created the magazine *Human Events* in 1944 to uphold "Christian principles" and fight despotism and the threat to the "American heritage."[87] Pew also donated to Spiritual Mobilization, which embraced both piety and conservative politics in its publications, and started the magazine *Christianity Today* with Billy Graham and NAE cofounder Carl Henry. Henry favored an inclusive approach and predicted that using politics to unite evangelicals would fail.[88]

There is little evidence that Pew's efforts had an impact outside of a small conservative community. Businessmen feared that donations to Spiritual Mobilization would earn them reputations as propagandists. Religious leaders feared they would be seen as tainted by business influence if they participated in Pew's programs. Among intellectuals, Pew's invocation of religion led some nonreligious conservative intellectuals to merely feign religious sentiment to gain his favor. Conservative writer Russell Kirk noted that Intercollegiate Society of Individualists' president was an atheist, but "now tosses in an occasional condescending reference to God, in the hope of pleasing Mr. J. Howard Pew."[89]

If efforts like this paid dividends, they are not evident in survey data.

Opinion polls have only recently differentiated between mainline and fundamentalist Protestants, but existing polls reveal only modest differences on the economic issues promoted by conservative businessmen through religious outlets. A 1980 Gallup Survey showed that on economic issues, 54 percent of evangelical Christians favored government programs to deal with social problems, compared with 53 percent of all respondents. On cultural issues, they were 1 percent less likely to favor the death penalty, 10 percent more likely to favor banning abortion, 22 percent more likely to favor school prayer, and 16 percent less likely to allow homosexuals to teach in school.[90] As late as 1989, a majority of white evangelicals supported more public funding for schools, AIDS education, civil rights, and increased government spending for social programs. Many were also involved with peace and nuclear freeze movements. Even at the fundamentalist Fuller Seminary, which was committed to biblical inerrancy, a survey in the 1960s showed that nearly half the students thought social justice was more important than evangelism in the 1960s (up from less than 10 percent a decade earlier).[91] Perhaps preachers like Billy Graham were more successful in instilling patriotism to their listeners, which was only later paired with economic conservatism. But correlations between economic and cultural conservatism in evangelical church membership remain relatively weak.[92]

It is also worth noting that much of the intellectual energy among Catholics in the 1960s took place on the left, even though Catholics voters still shifted in a conservative direction in the near future. *National Review* editor William F. Buckley lamented that no conservative Catholic publications existed, but plenty of liberal or radical publications flourished—*Commonweal*, *The Sign*, *Ave Maria*, *The Critic*, *The Catholic World*, *Ramparts*, and *Continuum*.[93]

Conclusion

The Christian Right recruited heavily from theological conservatives between the late 1970s and the 1990s. Before then, most theological conservatives insisted on a literal interpretation of the Bible and paid more attention to spiritual upkeep than current politics. Like civil rights and labor groups, they had plenty to disagree over, even though modern observers might see their common political interests as natural. Viewing each other as heretics, they were unlikely political allies, and the absence of centralized institutional influence over individual congregations made it difficult to unite a single sect behind a single set of political beliefs. This made them unlikely candidates for transforming a political party. Before they can do that, groups in a coalition need to get their own house in order and form a common strategy.

The efforts of businessmen to generate economic conservatism among theological conservatives during and after the New Deal were ineffective. Available survey data from the 1960s and 1970s show that evangelical Protestants did not diverge noticeably from other Americans in their economic views. Nor did they change from Democrats to Republicans until the 1980s and 1990s, and most Republicans did not even try to change them. Turning them into conservative political activists would have to wait until the 1970s, when conservatives persuaded them to broaden their political beliefs and embrace culturally conservative issue positions.

CHAPTER 7

A Christian Right Takes Shape

If Chapter 6 discussed the raw materials of the Christian Right, this chapter shows how they were rendered into a more miscible form as a political coalition, the first step of party transformation. While theological conservatives were obviously invested in their particular ideas about the Bible, their interpretation did not have to encompass the political positions they did. A clear shift to the Republican Party occurred among religiously attentive evangelical Protestants during the 1980s.[1] Without repairing relations with other sects and networking with conservative interest groups, politicians in both parties were unlikely to sacrifice existing party interests for their agenda. Why didn't theological conservatives stay out of politics and focus on religion alone, as they had in the past? Why didn't they combine cultural conservatism with economic liberalism, as the Catholic Church hierarchy continued to?

Some did, but by the end of the 1970s, cultural conservatives controlled important organizational levers of conservative Protestantism. The admittedly messy coalescence of theological conservatives behind a political agenda was no small undertaking. Indeed, there was nothing deserving of so grand a name as Christian Right until this time. In order for theological conservatives to become politically active, religious broadcasters needed to be persuaded that their ministries could continue to flourish with conservative politics. Local churches needed to know that political activism would not cast doubt on their legitimacy. Once cultural conservatives controlled leadership positions in organizations like NAE and SBC, they influenced local leaders in their networks.[2] Broadcasters, religious networks, and individual churches needed political expertise and funding, which they found in the seasoned strategists of the "New Right." This was only the first wave; a second wave, more adept at navigating the differences between religious sects, was brought to life in the early 1990s.

Other accounts of the transformation attribute the conservative coagulation not to groups outside of the Republican Party, but to entrepreneurial politicians or common ideology. Grossman and Hopkins argue that Republican elites and religious leaders worked to integrate the Christian Right into the "larger party organization and ideological movement."[3] Historians and political scientists have focused mainly on the New Right, the conservative strategists credited with recruiting religious broadcasters to conservative causes. However, the implications for party transformation have been overlooked because they treat them as Republican politicians even though they were not officeholders.[4] In fact, they were willing to support Democrats and third parties over Republicans many times. In treating the New Right like politicians, other accounts miss the fundamentally different incentives that officeholders and external groups face. Officeholders have constraints on their ability to oppose candidates from the same party, which limits their ability to affect party transformation. They wish to retain support from as many party factions as possible, when party transformation usually requires traditional factions to be marginalized. If one separates Republican officeholders from activists, the officeholders did not welcome the new recruits. The new recruits had to force their way in.

Noel shows that conservative pundits argued against abortion rights during the 1970s, paying close attention to the *National Review* in particular. Based on the timing, politicians appeared to follow suit.[5] Grossman and Hopkins agree that pundit ideology during the 1950s ultimately defined the Republican Party trajectory.[6] But writers at *NR* readily admitted the limits of their influence and that of their "fusionist" pundit, Frank Meyer. Few claim it was influential among conservative religious denominations. Many more religious conservatives claimed to have been influenced by Francis Schaeffer, who warned of the dangers of secular humanism to all religious sects. Schaeffer's more liberal issue positions were conveniently ignored, suggesting that ideas are both adopted and adapted during coalition-building. Groups in a coalition pick and choose ideas to suit their needs.

The first section below explains why the New Right viewed theological conservatives as "the largest tract of virgin timber on the political landscape," in conservative strategist Morton Blackwell's words. Their ability to reach viewers, listeners, and mailing addresses made them ideal coalition partners if they could be recruited. The second section explains why religious broadcasters were receptive to their approach. Building a coalition with the New Right, conservative across a range of issues, many theologically conservative leaders became conservatives all around. The third section discusses the changes in two large religious organizations, NAE and SBC, on a separate but converging trajectory with New Right organizations. The fourth section evaluates the role of ideas in explaining the alliances that came to fruition in this chapter. Finally, I discuss the ways in which conservatives attempted to solidify all of the groups in their coalition around a common agenda.

The New Right Pursues Theological Conservatives

"The New Right," a coterie of former Goldwater supporters, self-consciously sought to build a new coalition to challenge the complacent status quo in the Republican Party. In time, they recruited evangelicals on the basis of cultural issues. Most of the groups they organized tried to build bridges across different theologically conservative denominations. Some were short-lived, but succeeded in activating new voters and laying the groundwork for future groups like the Christian Coalition.

The New Right began as a group of conservative friends who were infuriated when President Ford chose Nelson Rockefeller, Goldwater's nemesis, as his vice president.[7] Among the New Right leaders were Heritage Foundation cofounder Paul Weyrich, direct mail mogul Richard Viguerie, Conservative Caucus founder Howard Philips, and Morton Blackwell, who later became President Reagan's liaison to conservative groups.[8] By and large, the New Right came from blue collar, religious backgrounds. Weyrich and Viguerie were devout Catholics from blue collar families; Phillips was Jewish but became a born-again Christian. They were experienced in political campaigns, fundraising, and media relations, and learned to mobilize followers by capitalizing on antiestablishment sentiment. None of them were party politicians; Viguerie and Phillips tried running for office and gained no traction, while other members served only in minor positions in Congress and the Nixon White House. Republican Party leaders resented their disruptive influence.

While the New Right had money and expertise, it needed more voters and volunteers. At first, the informal circle tried to create a conservative coalition with George Wallace supporters, disgruntled Democrats who were moderate on economic issues but conservative on race issues.[9] Many believed the post-Watergate Republican Party was declining and tried to replace it with Wallace's American Independent Party. Calling themselves the "Committee for a New Majority" (CFNM), they aspired to bring together a ticket with the socially conservative Democrat Wallace and Republican contender Reagan. The CFNM's commitment to a coalition with the Wallace supporters was strong enough that they would sacrifice economic conservatism to appeal to the union workers and Catholics that supported Wallace. Viguerie stated, "I'm willing to make concessions to come to power. That's what a coalition is. . . . We're going to have to be willing to use the government to stimulate the economy more than I think we should in order to get the votes."[10] Economic conservatives alone, he said, would win only 10 percent of the electorate.[11] The New Right urged the Reagan campaign to be more conservative on cultural issues and less conservative on economic issues. David Keene, the southern regional director for Reagan's 1976 campaign and future head of the American Conservative Union (ACU), complained that "The compromises that we conservatives are being asked to make go right to the core of what we consider conservatism—our dedication to preserving the free-enterprise system . . . We conservatives who have a strong attachment to economic freedoms do so because it is an outgrowth of our attachment to the freedom of the individual— and this is not necessarily shared by some people within the Viguerie group."[12] The CFNM's effort ended in shambles with the American Independent Party nominating neither Wallace nor Reagan, but segregationist Lester Maddox. Perhaps it relied too heavily on candidates to build new coalitions for them, instead of building on the Wallace demographic themselves. But even if the New Right had built up such groups, they would not have had the readymade audiences that unions and churches enjoyed.

Licking its wounds, the New Right began to consider new ways to broaden its transformative coalition. By the late 1970s, they saw theologically conservative churches as a large repository of inactive voters. The New Right viewed them much the way liberal groups viewed unions in the 1940s—a network that could reach out to its captive audience of new voters. If theological conservatives could be enlisted in their political agenda, they could help the New Right nominate conservatives.[13] The new recruits could provide the votes to counteract party moderates, and already shared several overlapping areas of concern. In the wake of the Vietnam War, conservatives increasingly differed from liberals in favoring the aggressive containment of communism worldwide. Evangelical Christians had always opposed communism, which interfered with their missionary work; thousands of evangelical missionaries were forced to flee China alone after its communist takeover. Feminists and gay rights groups were also building a foothold in the Democratic Party as they sought to build on its antidiscrimination laws. Social programs, like government-run day care, competed with those of private churches. Even before theological conservatives opposed abortion rights, they differed with feminists on other important issues like the ERA, gender roles, gay rights, and extramarital sex. And since theological conservatives were concentrated in the South, they were also more likely to oppose liberal groups on civil rights.[14] In short, theological conservatives diverged with rising stars in the Democratic Party on a number of issues.

The time was ripe to reach out to conservative churches generally and religious broadcasters in particular. Like unions in 1940, conservative churches in the 1970s were on the verge of a golden age. Mainline protestant churches have steadily lost members just as more conservative churches were gaining ground. In 1967, the SBC replaced the United Methodist Church as the largest denomination in America.[15] From 1960 to 1993, Assemblies of God grew from .51 million to 2.3 million and the Southern Baptists from 9.7 million to 15.4 million. In 1960, there were 50 percent more Americans regularly attending mainline Protestant churches than evangelical churches; by 1988, the reverse was true. Evangelicals constituted 20 percent of the American public by the 1980s, although not all evangelicals were enthusiastic about political activism or conservatism.[16] Meanwhile, Episcopal Church membership declined from 3.3 million to 2.5 million; United Methodist membership from 10.6 million to 2.7 million; and Presbyterian Church membership from 4.2 million to 2.7 million. Scholars emphasize the adaptability of these churches to changing times, including the use of modern marketing, as well as their function as community centers in rapidly growing neighborhoods in the South and the West.[17]

Fundamentalists and evangelicals took over religious broadcasting on television. Television stations started charging religious programs for air time in the 1970s and mainline churches declined to pay, creating programming space for other broadcasters. Evangelical broadcasters were successful at gaining views—the number of Protestants watching or listening to at least one religious broadcast a month doubled between 1963 and 1981.[18] The emotional services of Pentecostal broadcasters, in particular, made for gripping television. George H. W. Bush's 1988 presidential campaign estimated that about 10 million evangelical Christians watched religious television programming, or 20 percent of the evangelical population.[19] Broadcasters could provide unifying messages to a network of decentralized conservative religious denominations.

Like television and radio broadcasting, religious mailing lists provided enormous potential to reach captive audiences. Many broadcasters asked for donations on their shows, providing them names and addresses. Computerized lists allowed businesses, churches, and political organizations to send mail to thousands of people, growing an organization with small but frequent donations. These lists were highly significant for politics because they were later sold to conservative publications and advocacy groups. Religious leaders depended on their carefully guarded mailing lists to raise money for charity or missions, which often improved their ratings. These lists were literally locked in vaults. When Viguerie obtained access to them, his direct mailing company could mail millions of letters to theological conservatives exhorting them to support culturally conservative and conservative politics more generally. Much of the mail only reached the targeted audience, hiding provocative statements from the broader public.

Politics as Religious Empire Building

The puzzle for the New Right was how to persuade the churches to join their proposed coalition and provide their mailing lists.[20] It was in the interest of religious broadcasters to grow their viewership, whether to spread their version of the Gospels or for their own fortune and fame. Facing competition, they developed their own schools and missions, which added to their ratings, to raise money. Broadcasters contemplated expanding their appeal with patriotism and anticommunism, but preferred to avoid political confrontation.[21] The New Right convinced broadcasters that there was a market for more blatant political activism, which could help them to build not only their audience but their ministries.

Religious empires had already emphasized patriotic themes in order to gain the attention of donors and potential followers. Billy Graham had long incorporated anticommunist politics into his broadcasts. In the 1970s, Florida-based broadcaster D. James Kennedy taught his listeners that the Bible implored people to be active in their community affairs, including voting, and that they should have biblical justifications for their votes. Other religious broadcasters began to urge their followers to become politically involved as well.[22] By 1976, Falwell owed the government $6 million for bonds that the Securities and Exchange Commission said were not issued with enough collateral. Taking a page from D. James Kennedy's playbook, Falwell toured forty-four state capitals with a choir on an "I Love America" campaign to raise money, including a rally in Little Rock where Governor Bill Clinton joined him on the capitol steps.[23] Ignoring his past objection to political activism, Falwell declared that "this idea of 'religion and politics don't mix' was invented by the devil to keep Christians from running their own country."[24]

To emphasize patriotism, anticommunism, and voting was one thing, but participating conservative coalitions or Republican primaries would implicate them in partisan politics. The New Right contacted many pastors who demanded evidence that politics would not alienate their congregations. Weyrich persuaded Lance Torrance and Associates to commission a thirty thousand dollar study to determine whether evangelicals would object to a pastor that became involved in politics. Not surprisingly, the study found that most evangelicals were disappointed that their pastors were not already politically active.[25]

New Right leaders claimed that the Carter administration provided conservative churches with the excuse that they needed to become politically active. During his presidency, the IRS sought to revoke the tax exemption for schools.[26] By 1981, there were an estimated one thousand religious schools starting each year affected by the tax issue, proliferating in the wake of mandated public school desegregation. Though few had explicit policies in favor of segregation, minorities were poorly represented in such religious schools and the IRS threatened to take away their tax exemptions until they could prove they did not discriminate. Fundamentalists had traditionally avoided politics partly because their local communities offered insulation from societal trends they disagreed with. Though parents may have been more racially motivated than religiously motivated, most fundamentalists had publicly distanced themselves from segregation by the late 1960s. The New Right framed the IRS proposal as a federal assault on their religious enclaves, not forced integration. Like the fundamentalists opening the schools, they were more likely to depict the schools as a refuge where prayer and Bible study were allowed in the class.[27] Weyrich and Viguerie said that they were unable to entice religious conservatives in the 1960s but the taxation issue "kicked a sleeping dog."[28] Religious schools did not only run against the federal government, but from increasingly powerful teachers unions in the Democratic Party. The National Education Association (NEA), which has controlled the largest bloc of delegates at Democratic conventions since 1980, had always opposed tax credits for religious schools.[29] Additionally, religious groups had often conflicted with public school teachers by opposing sex education and the right of homosexuals to teach.[30]

The New Right's most visible find among religious broadcasters was Falwell, host of *Old Time Gospel Hour*.[31] Conservative Caucus field director Ed McAteer, a former salesman with extensive ties to religious broadcasters, built the bridge from Falwell to the New Right.[32] The "National Christian Action Coalition," which fought to maintain the tax-exempt status of religious schools, was funded using Falwell's mailing lists. The organization provided evidence that Falwell could create a broader political group using the same lists. Falwell's political arm, the Moral Majority (MM), emerged in 1979 from a meeting at a Holiday Inn with McAteer, Falwell, Phillips, and Weyrich. The MM came to take outspoken positions on a variety of issues, from welfare to foreign policy, and not just cultural issues.

Falwell's political and nonpolitical interests fed into each other. The MM was a means to increase his audience and therefore raise more money for Lynchburg Baptist College. According to one member of the university's board of trustees, Falwell was more interested in growing the school than he was in growing the MM.[33] After his meeting with the New Right, Falwell approached the fundamentalist publisher of *Sword of the Lord* to ask for his mailing list, which contained 200,000 pastors' names and addresses. He implored the publisher to help double Lynchburg Baptist College's size so that there could be a fundamentalist counterpart to the University of Notre Dame, without telling him about his political side project. The publisher let Falwell into the vault of his local bank, and Falwell walked out with giant spools of names and addresses used to grow both Liberty University and the MM.[34] The MM also used the *Old Time Gospel Hour's* mailing list to raise one million dollars in a month. Falwell's donations and church membership flourished. By 1980, MM had 300,000 members, including 70,000 ministers. Falwell's church income doubled by 1990.

The perception of Falwell's influence was greater than the reality. Both the media and President Reagan treated Falwell as if he was the focal point of the Christian Right, and Falwell never disabused either one.[35] Even though he raised more money and grew his audience, he was almost as controversial among evangelicals as he was among other voters.[36] Nonetheless, MM was successful in mobilizing voters, making effective use of captive audiences gathered in church.[37] In addition to the mailing list Falwell obtained from *Sword of the Lord*, he had a list of 100,000 theologically conservative pastors nationwide that he compiled for callers asking for church referrals. He mailed them a voter registration kit and replies indicated that between 25 and 75 percent of congregation memberships were not registered to vote.[38] He told his own viewers that not registering to vote was a sin that one must repent, and said that pastors should not hesitate to endorse candidates "right there in church on Sunday morning." Travelling to many venues across the country, Falwell would proclaim, "everybody stand up. Now the registered voters sit down. The rest of you, we've got an election coming up and I'm going to keep doing this until Election Day."[39] Falwell estimated that he registered six million new voters in 1980. While that number is surely exaggerated, one study finds that there was an evangelical voter registration surge in 1980, showing a 6 percent increase for evangelicals without a corresponding increase for other voters. In the South, 77 percent of evangelicals voted in 1980 compared with 62 percent in 1976, 70 percent in 1984, and 71 percent in 1988.[40] Another study found that more than one-half of Democratic MM supporters voted for Reagan, compared with 24 percent of other white Democratic voters.[41] Between 1980 and 1984, twelve million new voters registered to vote, 28 percent of them identifying as "fundamentalist Protestants" when only 20 percent of the American public identified as such.[42]

Blackwell claims that "other theological conservatives saw what was happening, and probably noticed that lightning didn't strike Jerry Falwell." Shortly after the founding of the MM, other broadcasters became increasingly vocal in national politics. Pentecostal religious broadcaster Pat Robertson cultivated friendships with SBC presidents and worked to bring thousands of Baptists and Charismatics together for a "Washington for Jesus Rally" in 1980. It warned against the evils of homosexuality and abortion. Robertson, James Robison, Campus Crusade for Christ founder Bill Bright, and SBC president Adrian Rogers all used their programs and mailing lists to draw their adherents to the capitol for the rally, which had been the largest gathering in Washington, D.C., to date.[43]

The needs of the New Right and cultural conservatives complemented each other. The New Right needed more people, while cultural conservatives needed money and political expertise. Once persuaded to throw their hat in the ring, cultural conservatives turned to the New Right for leadership. The circle of friends offered several resources that political neophytes could not afford to turn away, including political experience. One White House liaison asserted that politicians felt more threatened by the New Right than evangelical Christian organizations:

From the vantage point of the White House, we were more fearful of someone like Paul Weyrich than we were some-one like Beverly Le-Haye, who had a huge organization, Christian Women of America, with five hundred thousand paid members . . . because Paul Weyrich was savvy, he knew how to work the national media, and he would go to the press . . . [and] get millions of dollars' worth of publicity. And the evangelical leaders didn't know how to do that.[44]

Weyrich recounted that Christian organizations "were so new to politics, they deferred to people like Howard Philips and myself."[45]

Cultural conservatives needed fundraisers with the abilities of the New Right. Viguerie's pioneering direct mailing company was calibrated to the new campaign finance laws of the 1970s. These laws required candidates and interest groups to raise smaller sums of money from a larger number of individuals. Even when recipients of his company's mail did not return a check, they sometimes read conservative arguments for various issues.[46] Viguerie advised several single-issue organizations and mailed appeals on several different issues to the same address. Perhaps this broadened their horizons to new issues, so that the gun rights supporters, for example, became aware of antiabortion arguments. Viguerie could even experiment to determine which appeals worked best with which addresses. Earlier conservatives who attempted to combine economic and religious conservatism, such as J. Howard Pew, lacked Viguerie's technology.[47]

The genesis of the Christian Right, then, was partially the desire of New Right strategists and religious broadcasters to reach more followers, using religious school taxation as the first gateway issue. It was also the result of religious broadcasters attempting to broaden their appeal with politics. Politicizing one's church was not necessarily an optimal strategy for a ministry's growth; plenty of successful religious broadcasters remained apolitical, including the three broadcasters with the highest ratings.[48] It is possible that Falwell miscalculated and that his religious empire would have grown even more without politics. But if ministries thought that they were going to lose ratings with politics, they would not have talked about politics. And if they alienated too many followers, their shows would be canceled and their message unheard. Cultural conservative activism among religious leaders depended on their belief that their religious organizations would remain intact.

From Theological Conservatism
to Cultural Conservatism

Religious denominations and small churches were a separate story. Around
the same time that the New Right recruited broadcasters, politically and theologically conservative activists took control of the highly influential NAE and
SBC. Survey data shows that important changes in political attitudes among
members followed shortly thereafter.

In the 1970s, many religious leaders responded to theologian Francis
Schaeffer's call for a movement against secular humanism and abortion.
Schaeffer was originally a pastor in Carl McIntire's fundamentalist Bible Presbyterian Church, but had a crisis of faith while traveling through Europe, and
came to favor an ecumenical approach to religion. Diverse people—including
leftists and countercultural travelers—visited his home "L'Abri" in the Swiss
Alps for his philosophical insight. Schaeffer criticized modern secular culture
for providing no universal truths, and the effort to find values without religion, dubbed "secular humanism," had already failed. Humans needed religion to provide fixed, transcendent values, derived through reason situated in
faith.[49]

Schaeffer also convinced many evangelical Protestants to oppose abortion. Billy Zeoli, the director of Gospel Films, helped Schaeffer raise money
for documentaries through such politically conservative financiers as
Amway founder Richard DeVos.[50] One of the documentaries, *Whatever
Happened to the Human Race*, featured Schaeffer and future Surgeon General C. Everett Koop discussing the slippery slope from abortion to infanti-
cide and euthanasia. In the motion picture, hundreds of plastic dolls were
placed on a beach to illustrate the number of abortions being performed.
Schaeffer toured the United States in 1979, showing the film to numerous
Christian groups and attempting to broaden the prolife movement beyond
Catholics.[51] Evangelical churches across the United States screened the film,
and the SBC was especially active in promoting it in 1979. Ohio MC John
Ashbrook even read its 1980 resolution in Congress to refute claims that the
prolife movement was a Catholic bishop's plot. "The influence of Catholic
bishops at a Southern Baptist convention is generally agreed to be minimal,"
he said.[52]

Just as groups exploit voter inattention to push forward a more extreme
nominee than most voters would prefer, organizational leaders can exploit

member inattention to change the organization's agenda. In this case, members changed with the organizations. As Bean writes, there was no single "cockpit" from which to control the numerous affiliates of a single denomination, let alone all theologically conservative denominations. But by controlling the leadership positions in organizations like the SBC, both "generals" and "captains" influenced "unspoken customs about how to be a good member in official church settings" and sent strong signals that "real Christians voted Republican."[53]

Secondary literature on NAE and SBC demonstrates that conservatives gained control mostly through superior tactics and maneuvering. Their agenda was also less muddled than that of religious liberals. NAE's Republican cofounder Carl Henry did not intend for it to be a conservative organization of any sort, but a mere alliance of evangelical Christians. He originally worried that NAE's lack of social action would attract too many conservatives to the organization. A politically conservative faction managed to wrest control of NAE from political liberals in the 1970s. In 1976, its Evangelical Social Action Commission (ESAC) drafted a statement listing materialism, war, and economic and racial inequality alongside drugs and abortion as imperative social causes. Liberals in NAE, however, could not agree over whether such statements went far enough. They were also splintered over doctrinal issues such as biblical inerrancy. Members demanded a coherent political and theological message, and cultural conservatives had one. Conservatives used ESAC's implosion to argue that a liberal agenda would be too divisive. Decades after founding the organization, Henry now called for an "orderly vision and coordinated strategy." By the mid-1980s, ESAC reworded resolutions on eradicating hunger so that "solutions to hunger and poverty must be grounded in faith in God," not social legislation. The organization's public affairs newsletter included voter guides and exhortations to vote, and Weyrich offered NAE help in contacting conservative MCs. Office of Public Affairs director Robert Dugan responded to Falwell's call for evangelicals and fundamentalists to work together.[54]

In the SBC, a politically and theologically conservative faction elected their candidate to the presidency in 1979 and has controlled it ever since. Conservatives were increasingly worried about growing liberalism in the denomination in the 1960s and 1970s.[55] The SBC had supported *Brown v. Board of Education* and consulted with experts from the Massachusetts Institute of Technology on how to change member attitudes on race. Other leaders fought against the Vietnam War.[56] Paige Patterson and Judge Paul Pressler masterminded the plan to take—or take back—control of the denomination. A former SBC president advised Pressler:

> If you want to be successful, you must do two things. You must have presidents elected who not only are theologically conservative, but who will use their power as president to appoint other like-minded persons who desire to see changes made. Secondly, you must get to know people throughout the United States so that a president will have a reservoir of people from whom to make appointments in each state.[57]

Patterson and Pressler hoped to elect a sympathetic president who could in turn appoint conservatives to the SBC's Committee on Committees, which in turn could select the Committee on Nominations. Once conservatives gained control of the Committee on Nominations, they could employ likeminded Baptists in important SBC institutions. If they could gain control of the presidency for eleven successive years, they could consolidate power in almost all of them. Pressler and his allies conducted a "get-out-the-vote" campaign in fifteen states prior to the 1979 SBC convention, and their candidate, Megachurch pastor Adrian Rogers, was elected on the first ballot. Other fundamentalists had attempted to elect SBC presidents before, but lacked Rogers's ability to reach out to megachurches and lower-income Baptists.[58] Through the presidency and important agencies, the conservatives controlled funding for Sunday schools and seminaries. While not all seminary professors adhered to biblical inerrantism, few publically opposed it.[59] The SBC managed to deprive institutional pockets of resistance of funding, reversing the Grand Compromise mentioned in the previous chapter and encouraging "doctrinal unity in functional diversity" as its mission.[60]

While the New Right did not instigate these takeovers, it provided the organizational venues for their leaders to be active in politics. Leaders such as Pressler, Rogers, and Dugan participated in the Religious Roundtable, the Eagle Forum, and the Council for National Policy, all created by the New Right. One year after Rogers became president, the SBC passed resolutions denouncing pornography, homosexuality, evolution, and the ERA. Later, it asserted women's roles as homemakers.[61] With national leaders taking such positions, local clergy might have been less worried about violating denominational rules by taking them or participating in political organizations. Survey data indicates important changes over a short period of time. In 1980, only 29 percent of Southern Baptist pastors were Republicans, but by 1984, 66 percent were.[62] Green et al. find that only 21 percent of Baptist clergy approved of protest marches in 1980, but 50 percent did in 1992. They were also more likely to approve of national political organizations and action groups.[63]

Intellectual Coagulants

As many recent books have emphasized, intellectual battles to meld conservative religion and politics have existed since the New Deal. Theological conservatives did not flock to the Republican Party, however, during the New Deal or even the Civil Rights Act of 1964. This would have to wait until after organizations like MM and the Christian Coalition recruited them on the basis of issues like abortion and gay rights. Conservative magazines like *Human Events* and *National Review* did not seem to play a role. When cultural conservatives did follow cues from writers and thinkers, they incorporated ideas that fit well with their coalition partners and abandoned poorly fitting ideas from the same thinkers.

The archival records of longtime *NR* publisher William Rusher and editor William F. Buckley show that they did not believe that *NR* created the Christian Right or facilitated its acceptance. Founded in 1955, *NR* boasted more intellectual heft than J. Howard Pew's *Human Events* and other earlier publications. *National Review* (*NR*) book review editor Frank Meyer articulated "fusionism," as it was later dubbed by others, to bring together traditional values and economic libertarianism. Freedom for the individual and "the knowledge that has emerged over the ages" were both important to Western Civilization. The Judeo Christian ethic was a part of Western values, and one could not have freedom without Western values.[64] Meyer argued that libertarians and traditionalists both needed each other. As much as any other idea, fusionism was the defining ideology at *NR*.[65]

Most of the subjects I interviewed from dozens of organizations, including *NR*-sponsored organizations like ACU and Young Americans for Freedom (YAF), agree that fusionism did not contribute to the ideas of the Christian Right. Grover Norquist, a contemporary conservative movement leader then campaigning for Nixon, quipped "so the magazine was justifying the things we were already doing? That's nice."[66] When I asked former ACU president Mickey Edwards if fusionism was a basis for the Christian Right's beliefs, he said "I think Frank Meyer, if he could, would hurl lightning bolts at you for asking the question."[67] A relative of Meyer's recalls that in 1969, an audience member asked Meyer what his position was on abortion. Frank Meyer indicated that he had not even thought of the issue before then and came up with an answer on the spur of the moment.[68] One early YAF president agreed that cultural conservative values were far less secular than the traditionalist framing of fusionism.[69]

Even in an organization largely created by *NR*, fusionism was not a defining ideology. Buckley helped to create the ACU as a "responsible" conservative counterpart to the John Birch Society. When three ACU leaders proclaimed Meyer the "head of intellectual activities," other members were disgusted. Buckley and his publisher agreed that fusionism did not command enough assent, and acted to repair the damage.[70] Former ACU president Keene recalls that Conservative Political Action Conference (CPAC) attendees in the early 1970s were mostly pro choice,[71] and another observer claims that the ACU annual conference was evenly divided on the abortion issue.[72]

There was a similar split among readers of the highbrow *NR*. Buckley wrote to other *NR* writers that the magazine was attempting to change the views of its readers on abortion as early as 1973. The Catholic editor advised, "We are trying to persuade a lot of our readers on the abortion issue. At least 50 per cent of them don't agree with us."[73] The *NR*'s view on abortion was not shared by its readers any earlier than theologically conservative Christians or Republican politicians. And the fact that *NR*'s signature philosophy was not prominent in its in-house organizations suggests that it could not plausibly link economic and cultural conservatism at the mass level. Perhaps *NR* was more successful in the years after 1973; interoffice communications do not say. But as we saw, other groups were simultaneously remaking old organizations and creating new ones to accomplish their goals in practical politics. When several alleged sources of change are all occurring at once, it is difficult to isolate intellectuals as the cause.

The *NR* might not have been that influential among religious leaders, but theologian Francis Schaeffer was. Three religious leaders of prominent cultural conservative groups—Jerry Falwell, Tim LaHaye, and Pat Robertson—all claimed Schaeffer was one of their favorite authors. On *The 700 Club*, Robertson frequently mentioned *A Christian Manifesto*, which sold twice as many books in 1982 as the bestseller on the *New York Times* list.[74] Falwell distributed sixty-two thousand copies of Schaeffer's book and LaHaye dedicated one of his own books to Schaeffer.[75] The founder of "Operation Rescue," which blockaded abortion clinics in the late 1980s and early 1990s, said that Schaeffer's antiabortion film inspired his activism.[76]

Yet Schaeffer was not consistently conservative on political issues. Early on, he criticized racism and said, "one of the greatest injustices we do to our young people is to ask them to be conservative." Schaeffer's 1970 book *Pollution and the Death of Man* called for Christians to be stewards of God's "pilot plant."[77] Humans should forgo strip mining and mine in more ecologically sensitive ways, even at the expense of profits. For that matter, when *Christianity Today* discussed environmental issues, it favored government regulations to curb pollution.[78] Schaeffer had also criticized the nuclear arms race and excessive greed,[79] and when he visited America in 1981, he cautioned the MM against taking stands on issues where Christians could legitimately disagree, such as gun control or the SALT treaty.[80]

The sketch of conservative intellectuals suggests that, as with the CIO, transformative groups borrowed selectively from intellectual sources. Schaeffer's ideas about secular humanism and abortion ultimately found their way into the conservative movement (and later, the Republican Party), while his antinuclear and environmentalist beliefs did not. These positions would have conflicted with the conservative positions of the New Right and fiercely anticommunist allies. Even when groups in the Republican Party maintained their distinctive positions in the face of aggressive coalition maintenance—such as libertarians on social issues or NAE on government aid to the poor—these positions did not become part of conservative ideology. Likewise, the liberal consensus of Catholic magazines in the 1960s never set the agenda of the church, a political party, or even a major interest group. Conservatism became a dominant ideology after it was institutionalized in an effective political coalition. Had the New Right succeeded in merging conservatives with Wallace supporters, his blend of racial conservatism and economic moderation might have defined modern conservatism instead. But Wallace's dispersed supporters did not complement the New Right's advantages as well as conservative churches.

Coalition Maintenance

Growing numbers of evangelical Christians were ready to fight for traditional moral values, but it was still difficult to work together with other religious sects. Cultural conservatism did not necessarily mean they would assimilate economic and foreign policy conservatism. As with labor and civil rights, groups outside of political parties attempted to socialize cultural conservatives into the agenda of a broader coalition.

Religious Reconciliation

Early efforts to build a Christian Right were only partially successful at over-coming sectarian divisions among different Christian groups with increasingly similar political agendas. They mostly failed to integrate Catholics into their coalition, though Catholics often supported single-issue groups like abortion and the ERA. As the wife of an Illinois legislator complained to Falwell, "We have been trying to get Christians 'out of the Pews and into the Polls' too and we cannot get Fundamentalists to take Republican Ballots in a Primary. . . . The Catholic Church has been super and openly supportive but their people are traditionally Democrats and they too will not take a Republican ballot."[81]

In 1980, Schaeffer developed the doctrine of "co-belligerency" to persuade different kinds of Christians to join forces and oppose the public policies re-sulting from secular humanism. He wrote:

> If I live in a suburb and suddenly the sewer system begins to back up into the water system and all my neighbors are atheists, it does not mean we cannot sign a petition together or go to the city council or the mayor, to say we want our water system fixed. I do not have to wait for them to become Christians to do that. It is the same in the issues we are discussing. We should be glad for every co-belligerent who will stand beside us. It does not mean we will agree with everything he says or that we think he has a sufficient base, or that, over a cup of coffee, we will not try to show him the truth of Christianity. But it does mean that, in these life-and-death issues, we are glad for those who take the right position and we stand with them in the battles that we are fighting.[82]

By implication, cultural conservatives should set aside sectarian differences to fight for common political goals.[83]

Notwithstanding Schaeffer's admonitions, evangelicals found it difficult to work with Mormons and Catholics, among other religious sects. Phyllis Schlafly, a Catholic, recruited Catholics, Mormons, and evangelicals to fight the ERA at the state level. Schlafly's national publications touted STOP ERA's cross-denominational support, but the organization's fliers were tailored to particular sects strong in a particular state. In some cases, fundamentalists and Mormons advised Schlafly that they would not work with Catholics, so two separate anti-ERA organizations were created for fundamentalists and Mormons.[84]

The New Right's tactical advice was to promote abortion as a central issue to appeal to Catholics and link a number of interrelated political issues together. Antiabortion groups could build on a preexisting network of Catholic antiabortion groups.[85] Weyrich said the abortion issue would help split the Catholic vote, and his "Committee for the Survival of a Free Congress" required MCs to oppose abortion in order to gain its support.[86] Viguerie told an interviewer:

> Their convictions against abortion are like the first in a series of falling dominoes. Then we lead them to a concern about sexual ethics and standards among young people. This leads to opposition to secular humanism, then particularly in the schools with a purportedly decadent morality we point out that secular humanism is identified as both the godfather and the royal road to socialism and communism— which points the way to minimally regulated free enterprise at home and to aggressive foreign and military policy.[87]

Yet, the New Right was largely unsuccessful at building cross-denominational coalitions with Catholics. Falwell appeared in public with Catholic priests and attended Catholic prolife events, claiming that "in another context," we "would be shedding blood, but our commitment to the family has brought those of us of differing religious views and backgrounds together to fight a just cause."[88] Despite his rhetoric, forty of forty-five state MM chairmen were Baptists, most of the membership consisted of Baptists, and some of the largest chapters had no Catholic members at all.[89] Catholics complained that evangelicals in prolife organizations tried to convert them and even produced a guide to resist conversion.[90]

Christian denominations had as much difficulty as political operatives in bridging the divide. In 1994, many prominent evangelicals and Catholics produced and signed a document called *Together* to stress the common ground between the two groups. Although the SBC participated, many Southern Baptists criticized *Together* for exaggerating theological similarities. Richard Land, a prominent conservative Baptist, defended the document, since it qualified its agreements by noting serious theological disagreements. When nearly one hundred Hispanic Baptist leaders in Texas opposed it, many of the original signers, including Land, removed their names.[91]

Evangelicals and fundamentalists set aside their differences more easily. Bob Jones and other diehard fundamentalists called evangelicals "soft on liberals" and continued to criticize political coalition-building. He urged Protestants to "turn their back on the MM and seek the soul-satisfying contentment of being a scriptural minority," despite his open political involvement in the past.[92] But others were more open. In 1982, Carl Henry invited Falwell, Schaeffer, and other luminaries of both traditions to his home for a rapprochement. The meeting concluded that evangelicals should be willing to "present Falwell fairly and favorably" and everyone should "cultivate friendship among Evangelical and Fundamentalist leaders. They will promise to be responsible and defend each other."[93] Falwell even boasted that he persuaded Jones to agree to stop attacking him.[94] Though the meeting excluded Charismatic Christians from Pentecostal and Holiness churches, the fundamentalist Fuller Seminary offered a class that included their teachings. One Fuller professor described a trend he coined the "Third Wave" as a movement of traditional evangelical churches to incorporate some of the Charismatic aesthetics and teachings about the Holy Spirit. In another meaningful sign of increased cooperation, Campus Crusade for Christ allowed Charismatic Christians on their staffs. Charismatics, too, made an effort at friendship by hiding their differences. Speaking in tongues was encouraged at Jim and Tammy Bakker's private headquarters but kept off of their popular television show.[95]

While abortion was not quite the Catholic gateway to conservative politics the New Right hoped for, it still helped spur previously indifferent evangelical Protestants to action. Throughout the 1970s, the Christian Action Council emphasized its evangelical credentials as much as its prolife message. Henry mentioned the right-to-life movement as the "one-issue banner under which to learn the public use of political power for registering moral conviction."[96] By 1990, 55 percent of Christian Coalition donors—mostly evangelical— reported in a poll that abortion was the most important issue to them.[97]

Political Reconciliation

To this day, culturally conservative religious groups sometimes oppose other conservative groups on economic issues. The NAE called for government protection for the poor, sick, and disabled through federal spending on education and health care as late as 2004.[98] Conservatives had their hands full acclimating economic conservatives to culturally conservative messages as well. Business groups in the Republican Party have actively avoided cultural issues,[99] and free enterprise organizations like the Cato Institute oppose cultural conservatism as part of their mission. If cultural conservatives did not become general conservatives, as Catholics had not, they may have split their votes and never changed a party.

The New Right tried to build bonds between disparate conservatives. Weyrich's invitation-only "Kingston Group" meetings, beginning in 1972, encouraged economic conservatives, cultural conservatives, and foreign policy conservatives to become interested in each other's projects. Activists who only tried to recruit for their own cause without volunteering to help on other causes, or failed to follow through with their commitment, were asked not to return.[100] The conservative Heritage Foundation, cofounded by Weyrich, purposely finessed the differences between economic libertarians and cultural conservatives by confining cultural conservatism to public forums, without committing much to writing. It did not include family values into its mission statement until the 1990s. Many of its family values polemics consisted of criticizing government welfare programs that impacted marriage rates or funded abortions; fiscal conservatives could agree on these issues.[101] Since 1995, the Heritage Foundation has published *The Insider*, a magazine for policy analysts that emphasizes commonalities among different interest groups on the political right.

These efforts measure input rather than output. However, the New Right's influence on conservative sects is demonstrated by its coalition management on school prayer, long a source of contention among them. The SBC worried that school prayers might not reflect their own interpretation of Christianity and opposed attempts to institute them.[102] The 1982 annual convention happened to be scheduled weeks after Reagan announced his support for a school prayer amendment, and the New Right's bridge builder McAteer wanted the nation's largest Protestant denomination to unite behind it.[103] At the convention, McAteer invited pastors who reframed school prayer as religious liberty, claiming that children were barred from praying aloud in order to accommodate atheists. Other speakers emphasized the secular humanist opposition to the amendment. In the end, the convention supported it by a 3:1 margin, the first time it had ever supported school prayer.[104] Only when issues like the school prayer ban and abortion rights were reframed as part of larger "secular humanist" attacks on their values did theological conservatives actively oppose them.

Conclusion

At one time, both theological differences and religious competition weighed against cooperation among different conservative denominations. But political conservatives encouraged religious leaders to engage in politics to recruit new followers and grow their missions. Conservative congregants became more supportive of political activism shortly after the rise of politicized religious broadcasting, the SBC takeover, and construction of New Right groups. Members of many protestant denominations—though not Catholics—united behind a broad array of political issues and seemed more willing to reach across religious divides.

The groups that change parties come in many shapes and sizes, and the New Right, MM, SBC, and NAE were quite different than the CIO or its allies. The New Right was a small, informal group, not an organization. The circle of friends lacked the manpower of even the smallest organizations that participated in the 1948 convention. However, they knew how to raise money, run campaigns, and gain media attention, making them powerful allies to political newcomers. The various religious organizations and denominations that came to comprise the Christian Right were also different than unions. They were more dispersed, divided, and politically apathetic. While workers needed their jobs in a closed shop, churches had to worry about losing members. A major step in the cultural conservative transformation was convincing churches that they would not. The methods for bringing the mass membership in line differed from the CIO as well, relying on broadcasting, direct mailing, and church groups.

Despite these differences, the first step in party transformation was similar for both civil rights and cultural conservatism. Groups with somewhat overlapping concerns were brought together by brokers outside of formal party organizations, providing political and nonpolitical benefits for the groups involved. Whether it was a crowded field with multiple centers of power (like the Christian Right) or one juggernaut with smaller allies (like the CIO), groups developed a transformative agenda and signaled their members about it. In both coalitions, leading organizations pursued detente to work as partners. Religious groups were once rivals with each other, much like unions and civil rights groups. Both unions and churches could issue political messages in the process of providing nonpolitical benefits—material in the case of unions, and spiritual/social in the case of churches. Partners were persuaded to adopt a broader agenda as part of a political strategy against common enemies, with secular humanists and moderate Republicans as the modern-day counterpart to white southerners.

As with civil rights and labor rights, participants in a coalition showed considerable attention to their organizational needs as well as ideological flexibility. Broadcasters demanded evidence that politics would not cost them market share. Religious schools had a financial incentive in fighting Jimmy Carter and the NEA, which wanted to repeal tax exemptions. Finding partners who work well together and complement each other's' strengths can be difficult, but the New Right and conservative churches found such a match. They were not about to alienate each other by insisting on poorly fitting ideas, like environmentalism and peace. Allies therefore applied intellectual theories to particular issues without embracing the whole intellectual bundle of issues or its underlying reasoning. Modern conservatism would look very different if churches stayed out of politics and the New Right allied instead with, say, George Wallace supporters. Preexisting ideologies are only one factor in a group's choice of allies, and they are often selectively interpreted to fit two or more groups.

CHAPTER 8

The First Wave of Cultural Conservative Politics

In 1983, a number of parents in Nebraska were jailed before Christmas for sending their children to unaccredited Christian schools. Christian School Action, an early Christian Right group built with Jerry Falwell's mailing lists, was unable to reach Ronald Reagan through Attorney General Ed Meese. When Meese did not convey the message, Christian School Action approached Rev. Jesse Jackson, a liberal candidate for the Democratic nomination. Despite the political differences between Jackson and the group, Jackson immediately brought about the release of the parents from jail. White House aides worried that cultural conservatives might support an ordained minister over Reagan in 1984, even a liberal such as Jackson. As soon as Christian School Action held a press conference with Jackson, the White House returned its call.[1]

As this anecdote shows, cultural conservative groups had to threaten wavering politicians in order to obtain representation. Politicians in both parties danced with cultural conservatives and their opponents as they organized in the late 1970s. But, typical of electorally motivated politicians, they did little to implement their promises. They enticed their partners with a slow approach and then rotated to different partners. By the end of the 1970s, Democratic politicians had estranged cultural conservatives, but most of the Republican establishment either failed to see the opportunity or chose to dance in the same old circles. By several indications, the new cultural conservatives were not truly welcome in the party. They were treated like unwanted relatives at a family gathering who were expected to remain quiet. As we will see, they were anything but quiet.

This chapter examines Claims 2 and 3 from Chapter 1 by looking at cultural conservatism in the Republican Party from 1972 through the Reagan administration. Per Claim 2, I examine whether groups transform parties against the wish of politicians; per Claim 3, whether they do so primarily by influencing nominations. As we will see, first-wave cultural conservatives were active in primaries and party conventions, while politicians generally did their best to keep their distance. The Christian Right, as it was dubbed by the press, gained visibility and representation in the party in spite of the party's efforts. When pestered, Reagan promoted their policy agenda, even though he preferred to focus on economic and foreign policy issues.

My account differs from a large scholarly literature on the cultural conservative takeover of the Republican Party. David Karol emphasizes that strategic politicians realized that they could win elections by incorporating opponents of abortion into the party coalition.[2] Before Reagan, such efforts were fleeting as well as clumsy. And while Reagan was broadly responsive to the first wave of cultural conservatism, he was not the source of it. He ignored theological conservatives when he ran for the nomination in 1976, but made veiled use of them afterward when groups organized themselves. He also tried to retain the support of cultural moderates until conservative groups forced him to choose one side. Like Truman, Reagan wanted to keep two incompatible factions in a "big tent." Long after criticizing President Gerald Ford in the 1976 primaries, he proclaimed the eleventh commandment, "Thou shalt not speak ill of any fellow Republican."

The first section shows that Republican politicians and party officials before 1980 showed little or no interest in changing party positions to win the votes of cultural conservatives. They especially frowned upon efforts to change the party direction through primary challenges and attacks on moderate Republicans. The second section discusses the 1980 election, which was arguably a branching point for the party. In that election, cultural conservative groups mobilized voters for Reagan independently of Reagan's campaign. Although Reagan spoke to these groups, he did not help organize them. With a couple of exceptions, his campaign avoided any kind of visible association. Third, Reagan was responsive to their pressure in office. He accomplished almost as much as one could expect given the context of divided government and settled constitutional law.

Republicans Refuse to Challenge their Own

Republican politicians were unwilling to support conservative challenges to their own officeholders, let alone culturally conservative challenges. In the 1976 primary season, few Republican politicians supported Reagan's challenge to incumbent president Ford. Future Vice President and Secretary of Defense Dick Cheney and Donald Rumsfeld, then working in President Ford's cabinet, said that Reagan's wing of the party would be exposed as "really a front for Joseph Coors," who had recently provided essential money to start the conservative Heritage Foundation.[3] Senator Barry Goldwater endorsed Ford against Reagan in the 1976 Republican Primary even though Reagan had delivered what he regarded as the best speech of his campaign.[4] Another conservative activist pointed out that Reagan would not be able to defeat Ford in key states such as Indiana, Illinois, and Ohio, "where party solidarity and organization are constantly stressed" and "the 'pragmatic' nature of the Republican governor and the local Republican machine, and the highly structured party organization all would militate against your victory."[5]

Most Republican politicians steadily rejected any strategy that required them to threaten other Republican politicians. "Old Right" conservatives like Goldwater, John Tower, and Strom Thurmond never coordinated with each other to strengthen their position. Phyllis Schlafly asked Thurmond to withhold southern delegates in 1968 unless Nixon nominated a conservative running mate. Thurmond said that he opposed convention politics of that sort. In 1971, Goldwater defended Nixon to a group of conservatives who approached him to convey a message to the president, arguing that deserting Nixon meant the election of Edward Kennedy or Edmond Muskie.[6]

Officeholders viewed cultural issues in particular as losing issues. The Senate Republican leader did not see the potential for gay rights as a wedge issue, saying "it has a high quotient of emotionalism but does not deeply divide this country."[7] When Weyrich first advised RNC chair Bill Brock to reach out to evangelicals and fundamentalists, "he didn't understand what I was talking about . . . it was so foreign to him that it didn't make any sense." Brock told the press:

> You can't build a party around these emotional cultural issues and I'm not sure government can solve them. The New Right groups . . . draw attention in Congress from the broad issues of tax reduction, job

creation, health care, housing—the American Dream issues. We can only become a majority party by bringing people around those issues.[8]

The chairman announced that he was receptive to working with the New Right, but he had earlier appointed a prochoice feminist, Mary Dent Crisp, as his co-chair in 1977. As is often the case, party leaders wanted to straddle controversial issues.[9]

The RNC's "Operation Switch," a sustained effort to convert southern Democrats to Republicans, drew fire from Republicans anticipating that an influx of new voters would generate challenges down the road.[10] These efforts were resisted by the small number of existing Republican politicians from southern and western states, who had more control when state parties were small.[11] David Keene, who worked on Operation Switch for Vice President Spiro Agnew, recalls that a Florida MC "screamed" at him for twenty minutes, claiming that "we don't want these people in the party. He went on and on about how they were no good, they were lowlifes. . . . And then he said that if they come into the party, next thing you know there are going to be primaries." In the 1980 election, the same MC lost a primary contest to a Democrat who had defected.[12] But the party's southern strategy was not yet an evangelical strategy. As Chapter 10 shows, even George H. W. Bush's southern strategy in 1988 was not an evangelical strategy until Pat Robertson posed a threat.

New Right strategists—who largely came from modest backgrounds—portrayed the moderation of Republican leaders in the face of overwhelming electoral incentives as a product of their social class. The difference reflected social and economic differences as well as beliefs. Reagan's public liaison said that, "To take a position that is opposed by the Washington establishment has lots of implications for one's future life: You don't get invited to the right parties, you don't get invited to sit on the corporate boards, you don't get certain clients . . . if you try to practice law. There are all kinds of future financial implications."[13]

Political sophisticates know it pays politically to portray oneself as an excluded outsider. However, several pieces of evidence, then and later, suggest that Republicans disdained cultural conservatives. More than 10 percent of contributors to Republican presidential candidates in 1988 rated religious broadcaster Robertson zero degrees on a feeling thermometer, and nearly one third of the donors to George Bush, Bob Dole, and Pete Du Pont rated Rev. Jesse Jackson more highly than Robertson.[14] In private, George H. W. Bush referred to Christian conservatives as "temple burners."[15] Bush's son Neil called Robertson's 1988 primary supporters "cockroaches issuing out from underneath the baseboard of the South." Bush's secretary of state referred to cultural conservatives as "the full-moon bayers of the Republican Right."[16] For their part, traditional Republicans believed cultural conservatives wanted to exclude them. A political brief written for Reagan in the fall of 1980 read, "There have . . . been some problems with the movement of Christian fundamentalists into the Party ranks. Some fundamentalists have rubbed party regulars the wrong way with statements that they will soon be 'taking over' the party."[17]

Only groups outside of the Republican Party were bold enough to challenge incumbent Republicans to change the party. The New Right had proven, again and again, that it was willing to spoil elections for Republicans as well as elect conservative Democrats. In 1976, the New Right's National Conservative PAC (NCPAC) sponsored twenty to thirty Democrats, and its founder retrospectively thought they should have supported even more.[18] It also challenged "Rockefeller" Republicans in Texas, New Jersey, Illinois, and Massachusetts.[19] Weyrich campaigned for conservative Democrat Kent Hance against future president George W. Bush, who Weyrich viewed as a product of the "Eastern Establishment."[20] Hance's law partner mailed a "Dear Fellow Christian" letter to four thousand members of the Church of Christ, attacking Bush's eastern education and profligate campaign spending. According to Hance, Bush vowed "he wasn't going to be out-Christianed or out-good-old-boyed again" after losing with 47 percent of the vote.[21]

As one might expect, Republican officeholders were unhappy that anyone was purging their fellow partisans. Brock was furious with efforts to unseat liberal Republicans. He asked NCPAC, "How can we defeat Democrats by attacking Republicans? . . . The more fundamental matter at hand . . . [is] the replacement of this Administration and its advocates in Congress." As an employee of the RNC, Republican seats lost during his tenure could be reported as a failure by the press. The New Right publicly criticized Brock and the RNC as part of the problem. By having conservative luminaries sign liberal fundraising letters, the RNC diverted money from their organizations, and then dispersed it to liberal, moderate, and conservative Republicans.[22] Replying to *National Review* publisher William Rusher, Brock said that it is "illustrative of the ilk, that neither you, nor [NCPAC] have taken the trouble to spend even five minutes discussing with me your concerns . . . other than by the obvious pleasure you gain in telling each other what demons we are."[23]

Evaluating Reagan's Role in Party Transformation

The election of 1980 was a branching point in that all subsequent platforms and nominees received at least a passing grade from cultural conservatives. Groups, rather than candidates, were responsible for any party transformation that took place during Reagan's election. When the campaign directly communicated with cultural conservatives, it did so through networks of groups set up by external conservative activists before the campaign began. Reagan did not campaign for the then-unorganized voters when he ran in 1976 and did not organize them in the meantime. Even in 1980, he deliberately outsourced mobilization efforts in order to keep an unpopular group at arm's length. Whether Reagan was sincere or not, he was responsive in office, and his success helped publicize and legitimize their existence. Reagan may have won the Republican nomination without them—his endorsements and perceived electability were probably more decisive.[24] But future Republican nominees soon regarded these groups as essential for winning the nomination.

Campaign Outreach

The Reagan campaign tried to connect with cultural conservatives within the public's blind spot, turning to movement experts to understand the unfamiliar market.[25] Reagan asked Third Century Publishers cofounder John Conlan to obtain the support of one hundred of the most important evangelical ministers in the country, and write a detailed strategy on winning the evangelical vote.[26] Conlan advised the campaign not to advertise its religious credentials to the general public, which could lead to a competition with Jimmy Carter. "We should not provoke an endorsement battle," he said, "as the liberal media could step in and confuse lay voters by spreading confusion as to 'who are the real' Christian leaders. By 1984 the Christian leadership network will be in-place and tightly organized. But right now it isn't quite monolithic and disciplined." Reagan instead narrowcast his appeals by attending evangelical events, including the SBC and NRB annual conventions.[27] There, he cited a verse from the Gospel of John.[28] He could obtain many important endorsements just by sharing his faith with theological conservatives without discussing issues.

If left up to the campaign, the 1980 election would not have increased the visibility of cultural conservatives at all. Most senior staffers viewed cultural conservatives with grave reservations.[29] One emphasized, "there is a very thin line to tread between getting the support of the fundamentalists . . . and people who need to know how strongly RR is opposed to bigotry [against homosexuals], on the other. The latter, in my opinion, are much more potent politically and in terms of swaying the opinions of others."[30] Most strategy meeting minutes and memos on how to win the culturally conservative South do not mention cultural issues. One senior strategist wrote that "All messages have got to be tied back to leadership and the economy. These are two crucial areas to keep in mind about the South."[31] Senior campaign adviser Mike Deaver, who scheduled Reagan's campaign appearances, asserted that the campaign developed no infrastructure for various culturally conservative groups.[32] Conlan was ultimately disappointed at the mishandling of the "Christian voter marketplace" and the campaign's limited outreach. A liaison replied to Conlan that "in a national campaign . . . we must often compromise with differing views."[33]

The campaign did include a "Voter Groups" division, including a "religious groups" subsection to reach evangelicals. Elizabeth Dole, who would become Reagan's director of the Office of Public Liaison, oversaw a range of specialists who reached out to targeted populations, including Hispanics, African Americans, Catholics, ethnic voters, and evangelical Christians. The budget allocated for the evangelical Christians group (titled "religious groups") was not especially high (Figure 5). One reason was that many evangelical publications and media outlets did not accept political advertising, and of those that did, many were not in the states in which Reagan most needed their support. But another reason was that external organizations were already registering evangelicals to vote and mobilizing them on behalf of conservative causes.[34] Conlan, for example, had been able to raise a half million dollars from Christian businesses for a nonprofit that registered new voters.[35] The campaign firmly refused to develop an in-house Christian Voter Registration Program suggested by a senior adviser. A campaign aide warned, "If this is to be done at all, it would have to be done by the Christian movement itself—on their own. I want to make absolutely certain that you fully understand that this is our position."[36]

As the aide's reservations indicate, the campaign fretted over the appearance of a major outreach to an unpopular constituency. Dole said that "We feel a need to operate" the evangelical Christian section "on a very low key, even questioning whether an announcement should be made."[37] The campaign hired Bob Billings, the first executive of MM, with glowing recommendations from a pantheon of prominent cultural conservatives.[38] The Reagan campaign, however, carefully controlled his speaking schedule to a limited

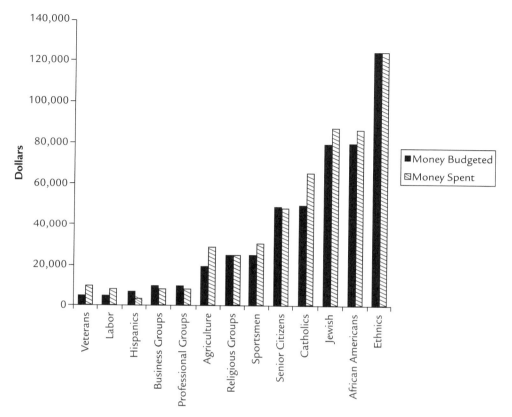

Figure 5. Budget allocation by group, Reagan campaign voter groups division (1980). Budget allocations varied with incoming donations and budgets from different dates use somewhat different figures. This figure uses the totals from the last dated budget. The campaign also spent over $100,000 on the Hispanic Voter Group section, but using mostly RNC funds.

number of states. An internal memo read that "Bob should not talk to the secular press unless specifically authorized by you, and you shouldn't authorize."[39] After Billings spoke to a secular newspaper, one counsel complained, "I thought we had him under wraps." When Billings notified that campaign of his plans to speak to Dutch television, the counsel wrote "NO" in bold red letters. The campaign stopped the interview from taking place.[40]

Only a small number of advertisements were developed for evangelicals, and they emphasized foreign policy and the economy. They were the same commercials created for other voter blocs, but aired at a time when evangelical Christians would see them—Sunday morning between 9 a.m. and noon, before and after church services.[41] The campaign's evangelical mailer avoided controversial issues, only declaring that "America has a need beyond the realm of the political. . . . The time has come to turn to God and reassert our trust in Him for our nation's healing." It emphasized the problems inflation and unemployment brought upon families, and only briefly mentioned school prayer and the "vendetta launched by Jimmy Carter's IRS."[42] Campaign posters for evangelical Christians focused on the economy, national defense, strong families, and tuition tax credits without discussing more pointed cultural issues.

The 1980 convention showed far greater sensitivity to cultural conservatism than the 1976 convention, but this sensitivity was arguably an attempt to avoid publicized debate on cultural issues. Hundreds of delegates belonged to the MM.[43] Brock reported that many Republicans went along with the antiabortion platform because fighting cultural conservatives would attract far more attention, saying, "A lot more people would have seen the fight on the floor than would ever read the platform. And that's just about what it came down to."[44] In fact, only 21 percent of the public were aware of Reagan's support for a prolife amendment.[45] Cultural conservatives used their own negative publicity as a tactic, threatening to call more public attention to their association with the candidate unless the campaign yielded. While the conservative platform might be viewed as a campaign-led effort to transform the party, it was paradoxically an effort to retain the median voter.

The platform supported an antiabortion amendment, a ban on federal abortion funding, and the appointment of antiabortion judges. The committee even voted down motions to recognize the right to differ on abortion by a vote of 75 to 18. For the first time since 1940, it opposed the ERA (by a vote of 90 to 9). Crisp, a supporter of abortion rights and the ERA, was forced out of her position as RNC co-chair.[46] Paralleling the Democratic platform's pledge to make "federal programs more sensitive to the needs of the family, in all its diverse forms," the Republican platform reaffirmed its "belief in the traditional role and values of the family in our society." It continued, "The importance of support of the mother and homemaker in maintaining the values of this country cannot be over-emphasized." Falwell said the 1980 platform as a whole was "identical to what we asked for a year ago and hoped we might get half."[47]

Reagan arguably avoided advertising his ties to cultural conservatives in office, as well. Every year on the anniversary of *Roe v. Wade*, prolife activists

assemble on the Washington Mall for a "March for Life." Reagan always invited their leaders to the cabinet room and then addressed the March for Life
by a telephone call from the White House, visible behind the White House
windows from the speakers. He never spoke in person. In another potentially
telling move, Reagan declined to call the Christian Broadcasting Network
(CBN) on the day it opened a West Coast facility in 1982. Robertson asked
Reagan to call in, but a White House memo suggested sending a telegram
instead. The question, "Should this go as telegram only and on July 8 (one day
ahead) to minimize impact?" was asked on the memo, with a space for several
different White House aides to offer their input. All checked off the answer
"yes."[48] One biographer concludes that the Christian Right needed Reagan
more than he needed them.[49] On the other hand, Reagan still appeared on
CBN's *700 Club* for an interview three times as president.

Perhaps it is too much to expect politicians to highlight controversial issue
positions. But Reagan's support for cultural conservatism, intended to be narrowcast, is hardly the stuff from which new party coalitions are built. Instead,
it was capitalizing on organizational channels already built by activists outside
of the party, as described in the previous chapter.

External Groups in 1980

Culturally conservative groups worked tirelessly to choose the right candidate
and use the election to publicize their views. Before the 1980 primaries began,
cultural conservatives coordinated to find a Republican nominee loyal to their
agenda, mainly choosing between Reagan and John Connally. Connally, the
formerly Democratic governor of Texas financed by Texas oil companies,
seemed like a promising candidate to mobilize voters in the Bible Belt. He had
failed to convince evangelical Christians of his fealty, however. At a meeting
with prominent leaders, Florida megachurch pastor D. James Kennedy posed
a question that he often used to determine if someone met his test for a true
Christian. He asked what Connally would say if God asked him why he should
be given eternal life. Connally answered, "Well, my mother was a Methodist,
my pappy was a Methodist, my grandmother was a Methodist, and I'd just tell
him I ain't any worse than any of the other people that want to get into heaven."
The gathering was not impressed; evangelicals believe that salvation came
from Jesus.[50] On another occasion, conservatives asked Connally for his opinion about "secular humanism" and he said, "well, I don't know much about it,
but it sounds good to me!"[51] Conlan arranged a similar gathering similar for
Reagan. When Kennedy asked his signature question, Reagan answered, "I

wouldn't give God any reason for letting me in. I'd just ask for mercy, because of what Jesus Christ did for me." According to Conlan, the participants were all convinced of Reagan's religious sincerity.[52]

As Chapter 7 demonstrated, New Right groups were highly active in registering evangelical Christians in the 1980 election. They also arranged Reagan's most visible appearance and told him what to say. Shortly after the Republican Convention, fifteen thousand evangelical Christians and cultural conservatives attended a "National Affairs Briefing" in Dallas, organized by the New Right's McAteer and his "The Religious Roundtable." In an unusual move, Reagan addressed the audience, using a line Texas religious broadcaster James Robison suggested on the ride from the airport: "I know you can't endorse me, but I want you to know that I endorse you and what you are doing." Reagan's campaign advisors cringed at his appearance with the lineup of controversial speakers, especially Robison, who had been removed from Texas radio stations for his stridently antigay statements. Although the event was officially nonpartisan, Falwell told attendees to vote for the "Reagan of their choice."[53]

Cultural conservatives also counteracted Reagan's ambidextrous appeal to a group of Republican feminists at the 1980 convention. Republican feminists were satisfied with his assurances to enforce antidiscrimination laws and appoint women to high office, including the Supreme Court.[54] Reagan was also careful to say that he supported women's equality, but merely opposed the ERA as a means of achieving it. In the fall, Reagan worried about the "gender gap" in his support and appointed a "Women's Policy Board" to give him policy advice on women's issue. He appointed mostly ERA supporters to the board and advertised it in a press release.[55] STOP ERA founder Schlafly then instructed her readers to refrain from working on Reagan's campaign to protest the Women's Policy Board.[56] Reagan created a separate "Board on Family Policy," which espoused traditional gender roles, only after Schlafly issued the ultimatum. A presidential campaign became more conservative only because external groups threatened it; by itself, the campaign wanted to keep the moderates happy.

While the Reagan campaign attempted to keep its outreach to evangelical Christians "low-key," cultural conservatives capitalized on Reagan's popularity. Perhaps Reagan's most significant contribution to their groups was to win the election of 1980. Despite his campaign's best efforts to conceal his association, cultural conservatives advertised it, and his perceived landslide gave them the appearance of electoral relevance. It was not until the election that the media paid significant attention to cultural conservatives. The *Reader's Guide to Periodical Literature* had two articles on "religion in politics" from March 1979 through February 1980, compared with sixty-eight for the following year. The *New York Times*, likewise, had no political articles for its "religion and churches" subheading in 1979, but had eighteen in 1980.[57] The press treatment of the MM, and Falwell in particular, was reminiscent of the CIO PAC after Roosevelt's admonition to "clear it with Sidney." Pollster Lou Harris declared, probably incorrectly, that "Reagan would have lost the election by one percentage point without the help of the MM." The media looked for a spokesperson for the new "Christian Right" and often turned to Falwell. Liberal groups such as People for the American Way also exaggerated Falwell's influence in order to raise money for their own groups as a counterforce. In the 1984 election, the Democratic ticket painted Falwell as a powerful force in the White House. In the second presidential debate, Walter Mondale said that when "Jerry Falwell announced that that means they get at least two justices of the Supreme Court—I think that's an abuse of faith in our country."[58]

To the extent that events like the National Affairs Briefing were transformative, groups were responsible. Reagan's campaign made no comparable efforts to recruit evangelical Christians in 1976 because conservative groups had provided no comparable forum.[59] Even when the forum existed, Reagan's campaign often shied away from it. Reagan didn't build the cultural coalition, groups built it—even if Reagan inadvertently legitimized it. The New Right and the theological conservatives it recruited provided the organizational megaphone and the coded language through which Reagan could appeal to evangelical Christians.

Reagan accomplished little in two terms, but about as much as one could expect given public opinion, constitutional law, and divided government. He was no more able to change public opinion on cultural issues than he was on supporting anticommunist rebels in Nicaragua.[60] And the only way to promote school prayer or abortion restrictions was to change the makeup of the Supreme Court or pass constitutional amendments, both difficult to obtain even under the best of circumstances. Reagan's Supreme Court appointments allowed states more freedom in restricting abortions, and had the Senate approved either Robert Bork or Douglas Ginsberg, *Roe v. Wade* would have almost surely been overturned. When the MM's vice president warned that cultural conservatives would not vote in the 1982 midterm elections without an antiabortion amendment, Reagan announced his support within weeks[61] and provided tactical support in Congress. He leaned on Thurmond to persuade Utah senator Orrin Hatch to withdraw a competing prolife amendment.[62] Reagan also announced support for a less controversial school prayer amendment in the rose garden, a public spectacle that led supporters to inundate MCs with an unmanageable volume of phone calls.[63] An Oklahoma senator said that Reagan personally called him to muster support for the amendment and estimated Reagan worked 75 to 90 percent as hard as he had for his policy toward the Nicaraguan contras.[64]

Mostly obstructed by constitutional law, the divided congress was able to pass marginal reforms with the administration's support. Senator Jesse Helms introduced one bill in 1982 to prevent the National Institutes of Health from experimenting on aborted fetuses, and another to end health insurance coverage for abortions for federal employees. Reagan helped find votes to end the Senate filibusters for these votes.[65] The president's executive orders had also discontinued government funding for abortion and prevented Legal Aid organizations from fighting for gay rights. Reagan fought successfully for the passage of the Equal Access Act, which provided student religious groups the same access to school facilities as other student groups. One exception was tuition tax credits, which he ignored partly because it would strain the already-ballooning deficit. He might have passed a tax credit with the help of ethnic Democrats on the House Ways and Means committee. Cultural issues may have taken a backseat to foreign and economic policy in the Reagan administration, but for the most part, the president did not let them fizzle without a fight.

Conclusion

The Republican Party experienced a transformation of sorts during Reagan's election and presidency. External organizations and strategists like the New Right opposed moderate incumbents against the wishes of party leadership. They provided candidates with the speaking platform and the network to reach cultural conservatives. As we will see, all subsequent nominees hired insiders from cultural conservative organizations to reach out to the new market. Prochoice Republicans like Mary Dent Crisp and Barry Goldwater were no longer party leaders. Platforms from 1980 onward broke with earlier platforms in their unequivocal opposition to abortion rights and the ERA. In office, the Reagan White House offered measured support for most of the cultural conservative agenda, which seemed to have little impact on Reagan's popularity. Reagan capitalized on a new current, but did not necessarily work to strengthen it. Instead, his victory gave it visibility and prestige in spite of the campaign's efforts to avoid a public association. Conservatism by the 1980s "braided"[66] cultural and economic conservatism just as liberalism braided economic liberalism and civil rights in the 1940s.

CHAPTER 9

Eating the Elephant, One Bite at a Time: Influencing a National Party Through State Politics

The first wave of cultural conservatism had lost momentum in the late 1980s. Had it been the final wave, the Republican Party may have veered from its culturally conservative trajectory. In the 1990s, a second wave of cultural conservatives organized its members and displaced state party leaders. Like others we have considered, its success followed an active role in party nominations and persistent efforts to manage the tensions in its own ranks and with allies. The mechanism for influencing nominations was different from the civil rights transformation, however. In the 1940s, the CIO and ADA wielded enormous influence over nominations by electing delegates to the national convention. In the 1990s, cultural conservatives found ways to influence nominations by influencing primary voters. By capturing strategic state Republican parties, the second wave not only influenced state politics but used their network to help likeminded presidential nominees in primaries. Since presidential candidates need momentum from victories in early states, networking with state cultural conservative leaders has been crucial to candidates.

The largest organization in the second wave, the Christian Coalition (CC), was able to help chosen candidates with state party officials. It continued where Pat Robertson's presidential campaign in 1988 left off, urging previously inactive Christians to run for unpaid state, county, and local Republican positions. In this capacity, the CC provided likeminded Republicans at all levels of government with endorsements and access to its supporters.

Presidential candidates use such endorsements to convey the sense of momentum necessary to win primary elections. Like other groups that have brought about party transformations, the CC exploited preexisting religious networks that were often developed for nonpolitical purposes, and capitalized on intense beliefs that their more moderate opponents lacked. It was also more successful in building a cross-denominational alliance than first-wave organizations.

Part of the reason second-wave organizations stressed state and local party positions was to address state and local concerns, such as obscenity laws, sex education, homeschooling, and textbook selection.[1] But they also hoped to play a large role in congressional and presidential nominations. Conservative state activists had to be involved in national politics because Supreme Court decisions circumscribed state laws on abortion, education, prayer, and gay rights policies. A CC pamphlet read, "There is an old expression that goes 'How do you eat an elephant? One bite at a time.'"[2] Although the pamphlet referred to changing American politics, it is also an apt analogy for taking over the Republican Party, starting with the local level. State and local control gave them enormous influence in party primaries and caucuses.

I conducted extensive interviews among party and interest group activists in Iowa and South Carolina due to their strategic timing in presidential primaries. The McGovern-Fraser reforms created a series of binding primaries to determine a party's nominee, but some primaries turned out to be more important than others. Soon after the advent of binding primaries, it became apparent that primary voters tended to support the winners of earlier primaries. Since most voters knew too little to differentiate between candidates in the same party, they tended to join the bandwagons of candidates who performed well in early contests.[3] In most primary seasons since 1988, candidates have emerged as de facto nominees after Super Tuesday, a largely southern slate of state primaries. Those candidates who win earlier contests, such as Iowa and South Carolina, are well-positioned to win Super Tuesday. A presumptive nominee has usually emerged after this regional primary.

The Christian Coalition at the National Level

First-wave organizations did not continue to play an active role in nominations after the 1980 election, instead hoping to appeal to its audience through moral suasion. In 1989, the MM dissolved without much of a track record since the 1980 election, failing to oppose Republicans that fell short. Weyrich argued:

> What we needed to do is set up an operation that is strong enough that we go into somebody's district or somebody's state and say, "Okay, Senator X, we want your vote on this, and here are ten thousand people in your state that have signed up for their effort." And when Senator X says no, we go out to defeat Senator X. [Falwell] didn't grasp it . . . His whole concept was just to rally people.[4]

Hence, the MM failed to perform the ground-level organizing that helped in the 1980 election, or extend it to Congress. One employee noted that its DC lobbyist was "spread thin" and "it did not have its impressive mailing list coded by congressional district."[5] Falwell himself had overextended his religious empire and found himself in mountainous debt. This is not to say that political activism had not worked to Falwell's advantage; he raised far more money in the 1980s than before, but managed it poorly. In addition to MM's collapse, Robertson lost his bid for the presidency in 1988, and many voters associated cultural conservatives with disgraced televangelists. Some commentators thought the Christian Right was over.[6]

However, a new organization emerged and improved upon the coalition maintenance of the first wave and played an active role in nominations. Robertson filled the vacuum left behind by the MM with the CC, which better bridged divides between different kinds of conservatives and different religious sects. Headed by his young campaign operative Ralph Reed, the CC was able to mobilize networks of Robertson's voters along with theologically conservative churches, broadcasters, and bookstores. Robertson exploited preexisting networks just as the New Right had. After the 1980 election, Robertson formed the "Freedom Council" to have a self-directed counterpart to the cultural conservative organizations founded by the New Right. It began energizing Christians and conservative voters in anticipation of Robertson's 1988 campaign.[7] Most of its financial support came from the Christian Broadcasting Network (CBN), which became a source of legal trouble when it was apparent that it supported Robertson's candidacy. The campaign would gather names from church directories and *700 Club* mailing lists and immediately ask people to gather signatures for Robertson, turning them into "instant volunteers."[8] Though Freedom Council precinct leaders acted locally, they thought nationally; all of the precinct leaders received their instructions from a national headquarters. Robertson was also able to stitch together religious supporters by being financially generous with them. For example, he purchased Oral Roberts University's law school and thereby helped Roberts avoid deep financial trouble.[9] All in all, he reached thousands of evangelical Christians that traditional Republicans, as well as the first wave of cultural conservatives, did not.[10]

Though Robertson's electoral ambitions were a precursor to the CC, they were the precursor and not the group itself. Furthermore, Robertson was a group leader in addition to a candidate, and he might have run for office to advance his ministry rather than with a real hope of winning. Though he was unable to spend much time on his broadcasting during the election, running for president drew more media attention to him, solidifying his role as a spokesperson for the movement. His candidacy enabled him to augment his mailing list, which could be used in the future for both political and religious projects in Robertson's name.[11]

Overcoming Sectarian and Political Divides

Second-wave groups were more effective at uniting multiple religious sects behind a common agenda than first-wave organizations, as the name "Christian Coalition" suggests. Robertson was well-positioned to build bridges across many conservative groups. He was born a Southern Baptist, but became a Pentecostal minister. He also had solid ties to the New Right; Holly Coors, whose husband had helped to create the Heritage Foundation, sat on the board of Robertson's CBN University.[12] As the first wave of cultural conservatism congealed, Robertson participated in McAteer's Religious Roundtable and helped organize the well-attended "Washington for Jesus" rally, a political event thinly disguised as a religious event.

During Robertson's election bid, his green shock troops were not always effective. They appalled some observers with their tendency to behave the same way in politics as they do in their religious meetings. An Iowa Christian bookseller describes some of the people participating in politics for the first time. Some said, "repent and vote for Pat Robertson or be judged by God. Some people could not tell the difference between a tent revival meeting and a political caucus. There were many of those. . . . We tried our best to inform those people that this is a little different. This is not a church meeting. This is not an evangelical crusade. This is politics. There were many others who worked for Crane and Reagan who understood that you can't just preach a gospel and transform a political party."[13]

The CC worked hard to cultivate political grace among its enthusiastic followers. For starters, it recruited leaders who were capable of working with diverse sects. While most of the MM's county chairs were pastors, only 15 percent of CC chairs were. Pastors might have been viewed as competitors by other pastors who would otherwise become involved. Instead, the CC recruited housewives, retirees, and professionals through church networks. Executive director Reed was careful to exclude "extremists" from leadership positions, and it was comparatively successful at recruiting conservative Catholics and mainline Protestants.[14] The Iowa CC, for example, worked heavily with Catholics in that heavily Catholic state.[15]

The CC's ten-year plan emphasized the importance of recruiting Catholics and Orthodox Christians. Falwell himself, though usually dismissive of Pentecostals, was present at Robertson's founding meeting. He warned others, "Do not let this project become a strictly Evangelical Protestant effort with limited Catholic involvement." At its peak, 16 percent of the CC's 1.7 million members were Catholic, a much greater number than most similar organizations.[16] Marlene Elwell, a Catholic political organizer, said the MM made her feel unwelcome because of her religious beliefs, which was "just the opposite of what I experienced with Pat Robertson."[17]

Reed continued New Right efforts to socialize cultural conservatives into other conservative issue positions, supporting economic conservatism almost as vigorously as the NAACP had supported economic liberalism in the 1940s. These efforts were an important part of its strategy for avoiding opposition from other kinds of conservatives. As Miller and Schofield explain, marriages of convenience, such as between cultural and fiscal conservatives, tend to dissolve if parties to the marriage do not share an entire agenda.[18] Layman et al. write that parties cannot add a new dimension of issues to their repertoire "unless activists are willing to accommodate one another's most important policy preferences by including them in the party agenda."[19] Some survey data indicates that Robertson voters and donors, who provided the first influx of CC activists, were moderate on economic and tax issues.[20]

As an example of the CC's coalition maintenance, it played an active role in promoting free markets to accommodate other kinds of conservatives. Reed explained:

> We decided that as long as there were gonna be tensions between the economic conservatives, who were socially libertarian, and the social conservatives, that these two companion elements of the coalition had

to find a way to agree more than they disagreed. They had to agree that there were some things that they didn't agree on, and having settled that, then move on to work together on things that united 'em.[21]

During the Bill Clinton presidency, the CC lobbied against Clinton's health care proposal. In anticipation of the Congress elected in 1994, the CC announced in a press conference that its priority was to fight for a tax cut for middle-class families with children. Reed asserted:

> The pro-family movement has limited its effectiveness by concentrating disproportionately on issues such as abortion and homosexuality. These are vital moral issues, and must remain an important part of the message. To win at the ballot box and in the court of public opinion, however, the pro-family movement must speak to the concerns of average voters in the areas of taxes, crime, government waste, health care, and financial security.[22]

One of the former South Carolina CC directors admitted that she often had to "coach" new members on issues other than the cultural issues when she presided over the South Carolina chapter.[23] The CC garnered respect from moderate Republicans and libertarians because of its strategic decisions to broaden its issue agenda.[24] Reed held the group together even though donors cared more about noneconomic issues.[25]

The CC even reframed culturally conservative issues in a way that sounded more compatible with libertarian or liberal values. The MM and Christian Voice used phrases such as "putting God back in the schools" and "stopping murder of the unborn." CC leaders were taught to emphasize "parental rights" over school curriculums and the Internet, "student rights" to voluntarily pray or form religious organizations, and "no special rights" for homosexuals. Abortion was reframed as a civil rights issue involving equality for the unborn.[26]

Like the CIO PAC and MM, the nominally nonpartisan CC concentrated its resources on one party—the Republicans. It supplied voter guides that listed candidate issue positions on relevant issues in church foyers and districts in Republican-leaning districts. In one case, the CC voter guide rated an incumbent Republican senator at 20 percent when he faced a more conservative primary challenger, but 100 percent during the general election against a Democrat.[27] Leaders would inform members of who to support in local, county, state, and national elections through emails, conference calls, and word of mouth.

The CC sometimes promoted moderate Republicans to incur goodwill for its agenda from Republican partisans. It supported conservative challengers to more secular candidates in Republican primaries when they could win, but it also helped elect prochoice Republicans such as Paul Coverdell and Kay Bailey Hutchison when more conservative Republicans were unelectable. Newt Gingrich's nationally orchestrated congressional takeover, the "Contract with America," barely mentioned cultural issues, but Reed agreed with Gingrich that Republicans would win more seats that way.[28] As House Speaker, Gingrich acknowledged the important role the CC played in his takeover of Congress in May of 1995, promising to act on restriction of pornography on cable television and the Internet, art funding, and a five hundred dollar tax credit per child. Sure enough, the tacit commitment was honored. Republican Congress passed the tax credit in 1995 and a "Communications Decency Act" in 1996, which was subsequently overturned by the Supreme Court for being overly broad. A late-term abortion ban passed Congress but was vetoed by Clinton.

Influencing Nominations Through State Parties

An examination of the national CC will only take us so far in understanding the tactics that helped cultural conservatives succeed in influencing nominations. State organizations and CC state chapters familiarized themselves with local party politics to gain influence in state parties, also conscious of their ability to influence national politics in the long term. As explained earlier, Iowa and South Carolina are arguably the most important cultural conservative states due to their early place in a sequence of primaries.

State-level cultural conservatives, most notably CC chapters, used preexisting networks to find volunteers and candidates in Iowa and South Carolina. Newly organized cultural conservatives familiarized themselves with the rules for electing state party officers and delegates and won elections. Their less fiery peers lacked the patience and intensity to learn tedious party rules and organize against them for unpaid positions. Once in place, they screened candidates for beliefs and helped likeminded candidates with media attention and access to their networks.

The Iowa Springboard

In Iowa, cultural conservatives took over a competitive Republican Party and used their party positions to advance presidential candidacies in caucuses. Although Iowa delegates are not technically bound by caucus results, the victors receive valuable media publicity heading into New Hampshire, required by state law to hold the first primary in the nation. Increased press coverage from Iowa correlates to performance in New Hampshire, which predicts vote share over the course of a nomination.[29]

Two background features of the Iowa caucuses help explain the relative influence cultural conservatives have had since 1988. First, the caucuses require participants to do more than pull a lever or punch a hole in a ballot. Participants must attend a local meeting that lasts hours, often held during one of the coldest months of the year. Typically, only the most motivated voters are willing to attend. Candidates with small groups of highly motivated followers, such as Pat Robertson or Ron Paul, can defeat candidates with moderately enthusiastic followers, who are more likely to stay home.[30] Around 100,000 voters attend the Iowa caucuses, spread out over 1,400 precincts. Many caucuses are attended by thirty people or less. One of Mike Huckabee's campaign officials in 2008 exclaimed that he had "hit the jackpot" when a neophyte county chair turned out sixty-five people to his local caucus.[31]

Second, state and local party officials are unpaid volunteers, except for the state chair. Even Iowa state legislators are only paid part-time salaries of twenty-five thousand dollars per year. Compared with other states, state and local party officials resemble amateur activists more than they do professional politicians. As such, they are likely to be issue-motivated rather than career-motivated. My interviews revealed them to be more willing than other state party activists to endorse statewide and federal candidates, enabling like-minded Republicans to build on each others' success.[32] Twice in the last decade, Republican state conventions considered resolutions to prevent state committee members from endorsing candidates, and they were defeated overwhelmingly both times. Motivated activists can help each other obtain party positions and take over the party machinery, although some party officials frown upon it. Once they do so, they are an important source of signaling for legislators, voters, and candidates.

The activist-driven Republican Party enables Iowa party officials to influence state party nominations more easily than those of some other states. Most candidates for public office submit themselves to state central committee interviews, hoping committee members will recommend them to other activists and voters. An Iowa state representative and former Republican Central Committee official insists,

> they have a bigger role than most people in the electorate realize . . . If you really want to effect change in the party, you need to get elected at the county level or central committee level. . . . Nobody wants to give up their Tuesday nights . . . but the hardcore activists understand that this is where a lot of things happen.

He describes prospective candidates, "When they're talking to us, they know they are talking to over 100 people in the district."[33] While it would be inappropriate to use committee time to promote a candidacy, state committee members are free to work on behalf of candidates in other settings.

Presidential candidates often hire current and former party officials as campaign consultants to help them win caucuses.[34] In the high-turnout 2008 presidential caucuses, state party officials constituted 25 percent of the participants,[35] but they arguably account for a larger percent of the results because of the role they play in networking and signaling. Eric Woolson, a veteran of the George W. Bush and Mike Huckabee campaigns, divulged that Huckabee's campaign worked hard to gain the endorsements of party central committee members, who knew critical contacts. Woolson would ask them, "do you know anyone in your district who likes Mike Huckabee that I'm not talking to? Who should we be working with in your district?" The campaign attempted to have a chair in each of Iowa's ninety-nine counties. Bob Vander Plaats, a former Republican gubernatorial candidate associated with the Christian Right, led Huckabee through the state's sixty-nine Pizza Ranch restaurants and advised him on how to talk to voters. Despite offering free pizza, many of the stops had fewer than ten people, but Vander Plaats quipped "seven people can swing a county."[36]

In addition to social networking, party officials provide media attention. Press coverage predicts outcomes in Iowa more than fund-raising, polls, and time spent in the state.[37] Local media outlets often announce when a major candidate receives an endorsement from party officials, preferring to quote people with titles to other voters. In the 2012 election cycle, Woolson recalls that

> when I went with Pawlenty, it was probably 36 point, 40 point headline story, "Woolson picks Pawlenty." My folks were like, "really? You're

that big of a deal?" I went to 9:00am mass on Ash Wednesday . . . I came out of there and I had about 75 calls that day from the media and 20 of them by the time I got out of mass. . . . Coverage is so over-wrought that you have a central committee person like Wes [Enos] who goes from a guy I hired to "one of the architects of Huckabee's victory in 2008."[38]

Candidates also issue press releases of endorsements to convey the impression of momentum.

Presidential campaigns sometimes network directly with interest groups without the mediation of state party officials, of course. Huckabee's experience with homeschoolers in 2008 is instructive. As governor of Arkansas, Hucka-bee had appointed homeschoolers to the state board of education. In 2007, he was endorsed by the Home School Legal Defense Association. With a home-schooler on his paid staff, the Huckabee campaign contacted the tightly knit Iowa homeschool community. In rural Hardin County, one homeschooler spoke to friends in church foyers and grocery stores, and emailed fifty home-schooler families on the eve of the Ames Straw Poll vote.[39] Though Mitt Rom-ney had finished first place in the poll, Huckabee's unexpected performance helped catapult him to victory in the caucuses. Kansas governor Sam Brown-back, who competed for similar voters, decided to drop out of the race after a dismal performance.[40]

Even with a favorable context for amateur activists over professional pol-iticians, cultural conservatives took years to take over the state party. Moder-ate Republicans were historically competitive in Iowa and may have remained so without the second wave of cultural conservatism. In parties where some outgroups become ingroups and others never join a winning coalition, the eternal riddle of parties is how outgroups can become ingroups. Cultural con-servatives overpowered moderates with group-orchestrated party meeting participation. They made use of a preexisting network, built a base, played an active role in the party, and enforced litmus tests once in power.

Moderates had traditionally elected the Republican leadership. The Repub-lican governor of Iowa from 1969 to 1983 obstructed socially conservative plat-form planks.[41] Another prominent Iowa Republican, Mary Louise Smith, served as Republican National Committeewoman from 1964 to 1984, and became national chairwoman from 1974 to 1977. In her lengthy career, she supported Planned Parenthood and fought for federal subsidized day care at Republican platforms. Iowa politicians confronted a different demographic than Bible Belt states. A majority of the state's Protestant population is evangelical, but 23 percent of the state's population identifies as Catholic. Baptists constitute only 5 percent of the population, and an even smaller share affiliates with the SBC.[42]

Cultural conservatives scored their first statewide victory in 1978. That year, Iowans for Life, a mainly Catholic prolife group, led a successful effort to unseat a liberal senator. Church volunteers placed antiabortion literature on cars at Catholic mass services on the Sunday before the general election.[43] Another victory was led by evangelicals at the state convention of 1986, when the state party platform opposed abortion for the first time. After the antiabortion plank was passed in 1986, it was contested each year until the early 1990s. Every state party chairman has been openly opposed to abortion since the early 1990s. One of the activists present each year recalls that "Every year there would be people who wanted to strip prolife from the platform . . . until it got to a point where the people who were fighting over it just disappeared."[44] Another remembers that "there was some open shouting at the conventions and disorderly turns at speaking . . . I guess what's being thought of today as the discomfort over Ron Paul libertarians coming into the party is almost mild compared to what I saw back then."[45]

The 1986 victory was engineered using preexisting church networks and voter blind spots. Since 1986 was an off-year convention, it was poorly attended and most voters were not paying attention. Among the strategists behind the 1986 antiabortion platform was Steve Scheffler, then working for Robertson's Freedom Council. Scheffler, characterized as a "party boss" by the *Washington Post*, had been involved in state politics for more than a decade. He was able to pass an antiabortion plank at the 1986 midterm convention, conventions that are typically poorly attended. At county conventions, Christian organizers from churches like the First Assembly of God and First Federated Church distributed flyers titled "How to Participate in a Political Party." The flyer read,

> to a degree, keep your position on issues to yourself . . . Come across as being interested in economic issues . . . Give the impression that you are there to work for the party, not to push an ideology . . . Hide your strength . . . Try not to let on that a close group of friends are becoming active in the party together . . . Don't flaunt your Christianity, this is predominantly friendship evangelicalism.[46]

Their numbers were concealed so that party regulars would be unaware of a long-term effort to take over the party. Steve Roberts, a Republican state central committeeman, recalls that on average, fifteen people attended his precinct caucuses. In 1986, forty conservative church people suddenly attended. Roberts was targeted, he claims, because he belonged to the mainline Presbyterian Church (USA). He had heard through an informant that they said conservative church members said he was not a "true Christian."[47] In Polk County, Mary Louise Smith was elected only after five ballots to the county convention with a 3-3 split in a precinct caucus of six people. Overall, evangelicals elected half of the delegates to the Polk County convention and 40 percent in neighboring Dallas County.[48] At the state convention, Scheffler distributed slates to his followers explaining who to support. These slates were so effective that in 1988, Scheffler lost the vote to become an alternate delegate to the national convention when another party member stole the slates.[49]

Iowa Right to Life president Marlys Popma also brought in new activists to influence the state party during and after the 1986 convention. Popma had been raised in the Christian Reformed Church, but found that Iowa Protestants had not been active on the abortion issue. After giving several well-received presentations among church groups in the early 1980s, she was soon invited to give more presentations than she had time for. Popma started and presided over Iowa Right to Life to address abortion issues statewide. Iowa Right to Life was a Protestant counterpart to the older Iowans for Life group, with the groups apparently unable to consolidate into a single organization.

After cultural conservatives passed an antiabortion platform, the Freedom Council tried to use Robertson's presidential campaign as a means to change the state party. Other campaign officials seemed to care as much about bringing new Republicans into the party as winning Iowa for Robertson. Robertson's field director advised campaign volunteers to go forward with a campaign activity only if it satisfied an "acid test." First, "Will this get Robertson people to their local caucus," and second, "Will this bring them permanently into the Republican Party, if at all possible?"[50] When Robertson's director worked to recruit voters for the Bush ticket in the general election, he wrote to the state party chair, "I truly hope these new Republicans will make the winning difference for a great victory in Iowa for Bush/Quayle. This victory will help us all to fully adopt these newest Republicans into the 'Family'!"[51] The second wave of cultural conservatism had taken hold in Iowa. The state that supported Bush's moderate candidacy in 1980 was beginning to become the state that supported the consistently culturally conservative candidacies of Huckabee in 2008, Santorum in 2012, and Cruz in 2016.

By the 1990s, state Republicans paid a price for cultural moderation. Even state party officials worked to defeat moderates in primaries. One former Republican state political director admitted "getting involved" in campaigns "at the state level is a little dicey, but that's what we did in 1996." The director assisted in steering party funds to six culturally conservative Republican candidates against the wishes of the culturally liberal senate minority leader. When the Republicans gained control that year, the leader was voted out of his position.[52] The state party transformation was so complete that the party selected the state's CC director as a delegate to the 1996 Republican Convention and relegated Dole's state campaign chair as an alternate.[53] In 2008, state legislators proposed an amendment to outlaw gay marriage, which had been legalized by a court decision. The four Republicans who voted to block the bill did not survive—two retired, one was defeated in a primary, and one ran for the House of Representatives and lost.[54]

Moderates lacked several advantages in their struggle to maintain a place in the state Republican Party. Some interest groups, like Scheffler's Iowa Faith and Freedom Coalition, have full-time, paid employees that can spend time at work promoting their issues, and indirectly, their candidates. No moderate Republican group in Iowa has paid employees. Roberts adds that there is no obvious network of moderates. The mainline churches are more heterogeneous, consisting of Democrats, independents, and liberals, as well as moderate Republicans.[55] Former lieutenant governor Joy Corning, an abortion rights supporter, said that moderates stayed home from weeknight meetings when cultural conservatives began attending. Alienated by what they perceived as a shrill tone, they would exclaim, "we don't have to listen to this."[56] Huckabee's communications director corroborated Corning's explanation, saying that Christian conservatives were "the people that understood the rules, that knew what it was gonna take to get their people on to the central committee and state chair . . . They stuck with it long enough to make that happen. The other people stayed home and said 'to Hell with it.'"

The South Carolina Firewall

South Carolina has an influence on presidential primaries even more disproportionate than Iowa relative to its voting population. Traditionally first in the South, it consistently moves its primary earlier to compete with other states vying to be kingmakers. It has held the first primary in the South in every year since 1980 except for 1992. Four of the Republican candidates in 1988 came closer to violating spending limits in South Carolina than any of the Super

Tuesday states.[57] And it is understandable that they did. From 1980 to 2008, every South Carolina victor became the Republican nominee.

The Palmetto State's primary has been strategically situated just before Super Tuesday since 1988.[58] In 2012, the national party penalized South Carolina for changing its primary date by reducing its delegates and assigning the remaining delegates to a hotel forty-five minutes away from the convention. Longtime party activist Drew McKissick claims that the state executive committee would unanimously vote to be the first primary in the South even if the RNC deprived the state of all of its delegates.[59] Voters in New Hampshire, the first primary in the nation, sometimes show an independent streak and support more moderate candidates. McCain's victory in New Hampshire in 2000 provided him with a 19 percent increase in press coverage.[60] But the South Carolina primary, which immediately precedes Super Tuesday, can serve as a firewall for slowing the momentum of any candidates using New Hampshire as a springboard.

South Carolina's transformation differed from Iowa's. Where Iowa already had a viable two-party system, South Carolina was historically a Democratic state and its Republican Party desperately needed more voters and volunteers. Even so, some Republican leaders did not welcome them. As with Iowa, state activists in South Carolina consciously used the Robertson campaign to electrify theological conservatives into politically conservative activists and displace moderates. The state party's fortune changed dramatically just as cultural conservatives hitched their wagons to the party. Counties that were solidly Democratic in the 1980s became solidly Republican in the 1990s.

Fundamentalists had held a foothold in Spartanburg County, the home of BJU, since the 1970s. Prior to Watergate, the county Republican Party had been led by Goldwater Republicans more focused on business than on family values. After Nixon resigned, BJU pastor Al Janney preached that the country was in a period of moral decay and Christians had to become involved in politics. Elmer Rumminger, who hosted a radio show at BJU's station, also told local fundamentalists how to become involved in politics. BJU students brought six hundred people to the county convention, seizing the county party from its leaders, who then continued to meet as the "Piedmont Republican Club." The county party was so divided it lost seats in the legislature. However, in the 1980 election, an accommodation was made between the two factions, and Republicans have held a strong grip on the county ever since.[61] Ronald Reagan, Bob Dole, Pat Buchanan, and George W. Bush each spoke at BJU during at least one of their presidential campaigns. Representing the theological conservatives who never really worked with other sects, BJU Fundamentalists were completely unreceptive to a bid from Pat Robertson, a Pentecostal, in 1988.

But Robertson still hoped to win the 1988 primary by stealth. He realized that he could not win the primary, but his dedicated followers might win in a setting more akin to the Iowa caucuses. The campaign strategy was to overwhelm the Republican Party's county conventions, where his followers would vote to eliminate the Republican Party primary and return to the older nominating system, in which a state convention awarded delegates to the Republican National Convention. A Baptist minister who had worked for future vice president Dan Quayle during his election to the Senate in Indiana was charged with implementing the strategy by quietly speaking to pastors and devout Christians. At one point, he had to duck out of a restaurant when Republican Party officials were eating at another table, fearing that he would have to explain why he returned to the state. The Robertson campaign put on skits titled "How to Take Over a Party," emblazoned in bold letters at campaign rallies. The skits explained to new voters how to go to precinct meetings and run for local and county party positions, defying unfriendly establishment party leaders. The grassroots, unaware of the grand strategy to implement a convention system, were to attend county conventions, watch Robertson supporters with colored hats, and vote according to their "thumbs up" or "thumbs down" signals.

Needless to say, other Republican Party officials resisted the takeover. A state senator attended one of Robertson's campaign meetings, comparing it to a Nazi rally. George Shissias, the prochoice Republican campaign manager who recruited Bush campaign manager Lee Atwater, orchestrated a legal challenge to many Robertson delegates at the county convention. Since Robertson delegates had not registered to vote in their precinct by the deadline, the judge disqualified just enough of them to prevent them from having a majority at the state convention.[62] Existing party officials also found subtle ways to obstruct early CC activists. Some viewed party offices as a "garden club" where they could gather with their own friends. Others believed that CC activists had not been involved in state politics long enough and needed to "wait their turn." According to a CC field director, "they tried to keep information away from you, like who is running for delegate. . . . They wouldn't let you know the list of who had been elected from each county so you could go and pick out the people ahead of time. They would keep that to themselves."[63]

Robertson's defeat was arguably the last hurrah of the traditional South

Carolina Republicans. Unlike Iowa, the tiny state party needed the cultural conservatives to fill unpaid positions to be competitive. Though Robertson lost the South Carolina primary, his followers continued to be active in state politics. A former South Carolina CC director recalls that "We had a master-plan. Precinct-by-precinct, statewide. And the county chairmen were involved in that, and they would turn people out to the meetings . . . each county had so many goals, how many delegates we wanted to get, how many delegates we needed."[64] McKissick said:

> All of that stuff would shake out in a cycle or two and people under-stand who is actually doing work and will work and bring something to the table . . . This is about addition, not subtraction or division . . . Your average county chairman of the party . . . [is] looking around for someone who can do a, b, c, and d. . . . pretty soon you couldn't get choosy about who you ask [to volunteer] because it's so hard to find anybody . . . Half the time you can't get anybody to do anything. Even-tually the guy who shows up and shows up and shows up and shows up gets asked to do something. And next thing you know he's running something. People who ask me, how do we end up with so many idiots elected? Usually . . . it's just the guy who always came to the meetings. Eventually everybody gets promoted.[65]

Ultimately, the CC was able to overwhelm the ranks of state party officials by the early 1990s. In a state of 3.5 million, only about seven thousand voters typically attended precinct or county party meetings, and the CC registered far more people to vote than that.[66]

The CC exercised fairly effective control over state government in the 1990s. It was able to displace party officials supported by BJU, just as BJU-supported officials had displaced Goldwater Republicans in 1976.[67] Many del-egates to state conventions allowed the state CC to pick their proxies, including Strom Thurmond. One state party chair's office leaked confidential documents to the state CC. Governor Carroll Campbell even withdrew his support from one candidate after the CC backed a different candidate.[68] Another governor, David Beasley, held monthly conference calls with CC county chairs and pur-sued a cultural conservative agenda with gusto, outlawing the well-funded video poker industry at the end of his first term. Moderates attempted to take back the Republican Party, now as the outsiders cultural conservatives had been in the 1980s. Shissias and allied state legislators formed a competing

"Republican Leadership Council," but Shissias has not regained an official party position.[69] As the next chapter will show, South Carolina's established network of party officials and cultural conservatives held the state in line for George H. W. Bush, Bob Dole, and George W. Bush at pivotal moments.

Conclusion

A second wave of cultural conservatives effectively captured state parties that were well-situated to influence presidential nominations. The CC in particular consolidated and extended the influence the first wave had gained in the Republican Party. It was more successful at building bridges across religious divides and more tactful in its relations with other kinds of conservatives. But where it was possible to displace existing party leaders with dedicated cultural conservatives, the CC chapters did so.

Since the CC had a state-by-state strategy, this chapter zeroed in on two of the most important states for Republican presidential nominations, Iowa and South Carolina. In contemporary nominations, presidential candidates need to coordinate with state party members to gain endorsements and recruit volunteers/caucus voters. These positions represented low-hanging fruit in states with sparsely populated Republican parties, like South Carolina. With more effort, they also managed to take over a competitive party in states such as Iowa. Culturally moderate Republicans in these states now find themselves without a party. The cultural conservatives that have been in control for decades provide valuable resources for likeminded presidential candidates.

CHAPTER 10

Conversions: Republican
Nominations After Reagan

It has become increasingly common for political candidates to share their "testimony," an account of their born-again experience, with evangelical Christians. Leading up to the 2000 election, George W. Bush claimed that he experienced his conversion (avoiding the phrase "born-again") while walking on a beach with Billy Graham near his family's vacation home in Kennebunkport, Maine. Traveling preacher Arthur Blessit blogged that Bush's testimony greatly resembled a conversation he had with him in 1984. Even though Graham did not confirm the story at first, people quickly dismissed Blessit's claims, and Bush mentioned him neither on the campaign trail nor in his autobiography.[1] Evangelical Christians respected Blessit, but also considered him eccentric. Before his conversion, he had participated in the counterculture and used hallucinogenic drugs, and now carries a twelve-foot cross everywhere he travels. He often held ceremonies where former drug users would flush their drugs down the toilet in his presence. Bush had supervised his father's efforts to win over evangelical Christians in 1988. When he looked over a list of his father's one thousand evangelical targets, Blessit was on the list, and Bush asked the campaign's religious adviser an inordinate number of questions about him. Graham, of course, was ranked most influential on that list.[2]

It takes more than Ronald Reagan's presidency to show that cultural conservatives transformed the Republican Party. A party transformation entails a series of nominations committed to a new agenda. This chapter examines cultural Republican nominations from 1988 onward to determine whether cultural conservatives continued to circumscribe the issue positions of Republican presidential candidates. While individual organizations came and went, cultural conservatives were there to stay. Nearly all of the Republican nominees from 1980 to 2016 changed their positions on abortion rights. Like Estes Kefauver, John F. Kennedy, and Lyndon Johnson, Republican candidates adapted to new groups in the party. While I do not show that Republican presidential candidates would have failed without cultural conservative support, I do show that successful nominees treated cultural conservatives as if they were a necessary constituency. Like the 1956 Democratic presidential contenders courting the African American vote, Republicans no longer viewed the cultural conservative constituency as optional. The one frontrunner who did not change his prochoice position, Rudy Giuliani, failed to win a single state in 2008 despite leading in the polls before the Iowa caucuses.

The main change since 1956 was that convention delegates were no longer autonomous agents, but bound to the primary or caucus results from their precinct. Candidate-centered campaigns might have relied on commercials, retail politics, and rallies to win over uncoordinated voters in primaries. While candidates used these tactics, they also networked extensively with culturally conservative groups. And it is understandable that they did. With fifty states to win, even the best-funded campaigns needed volunteers and networking that groups could provide. They wooed Iowa's state party activists and South Carolina's interest groups, largely constituted by cultural conservatives. Groups supported different candidates for different reasons, but none so far have been forced to choose a candidate or even a running mate that did not pass their litmus tests.

An alternative explanation is candidate-centered politics. After all, presidential campaigns largely replaced convention politics with media politics. However, candidates were not eager to highlight their cultural positions in the mass media. Candidate outreach to unpopular constituencies usually takes place behind closed doors. Thanks to previously unpublished primary sources from both Bush campaigns, we gain a glimpse into a normally opaque process. This chapter shows how campaigns viewed cultural conservatives and plotted to recruit conflicting religious groups without gaining unwanted publicity. Other sources show what cultural conservatives demanded from candidates and how they pushed back.

George H. W. Bush and the Struggle for Credibility

The Republican Party could no more turn back the clock in 1988 than the Democratic Party could in 1952. Most candidates realized that targeting un-organized primary voters was no substitute for the well-organized networks of cultural conservatives. Vice President George H. W. Bush originally be-lieved that officeholder support would be enough, but changed strategies after Robertson threw his hat in the ring. For a time, Bush convinced evangelical Christians that he was one of them. By seeming to share their faith, he ob-tained their support while giving himself more freedom on controversial is-sues during the campaign. This helped him win early states in the primary season and emerge as the presumptive nominee after Super Tuesday. When he did not provide the kind of public policies they wanted as president, they rebelled. To regain their trust in the 1992 election, Bush decided to advertise his cultural conservatism more openly.

Cultural Conservatives and the 1988 Nomination

Several features of the 1988 Republican Primary conform to the expectations of the claims outlined in Chapter 1. Competitive Republicans and their advi-sors believed they needed the support of a set of activists with different views than the mass public—in this case, cultural conservatives. To obtain their support, they leaned on advisors with deep knowledge of the movement and portrayed themselves as religious brothers-in-arms. At the same time, candi-dates avoided appearing so connected that it would cost them votes in the general electorate. Organized activists forced them to go further in order to obtain their support.

Four leading Republican candidates in 1988 had detailed strategies to win the cultural conservative vote: religious broadcaster Pat Robertson, New York representative Jack Kemp, Kansas senator Bob Dole, and Vice President George H. W. Bush. Robertson forced candidates to move ahead their timeta-ble and recruit key evangelical leaders, but his own campaign failed. Activists may value policy commitment over electability, but seldom support unelect-able candidates. By and large, the American public had a negative view of religious broadcasters like Robertson, derided as "televangelists." Public ap-proval sank even lower as the media published news of Jimmy Swaggart's sex scandal and Jim Bakker's financial scandal. Not only did general election vot-ers dislike televangelists, but many cultural conservatives thought it was inappropriate or tactless for one to run for president. Some thought religious officials should not seek political office, which inevitably sullies a person's behavior. Furthermore, a sectarian pastor such as Robertson undermined their efforts to offer nonreligious justifications for their issue positions. An aide to senator Jesse Helms explained that critics would accuse Robertson of basing public policy on his religious beliefs. As a Pentecostal, the candidate could not base his policy on any other grounds without losing his fans' support.[3] Sectarian divisions also turned other cultural conservatives against the Pentecostal broadcaster. Falwell, a commercial rival, said that Robertson's candidacy could divide the evangelical cause.[4] In South Carolina, Robertson was evaluated poorly among most religious denominations, particularly Catholics and Fundamentalists.[5] Going forward, Southern Baptists comprised 20 percent of the voters in Super Tuesday states, while Pentecostals comprised only 2 percent.[6]

Other candidates had an easier time committing to cultural conservatives without appearing too extreme to the public. Kemp had attended a seminar at L'Abri with Francis Schaeffer. His campaign published a tract on his testimony in 1985, and Kemp himself appeared on Jim and Tammy Bakker's "Praise the Lord" show and the Trinity Broadcasting Network.[7] In candidate debates, Kemp dropped the name of FOF founder Dobson, then relatively unknown to the public but well known to cultural conservatives.

A campaign plan developed for Bob Dole in May of 1987 emphasized the importance of recruiting fundamentalist and prolife groups in states with early primaries. The plan highlighted that their "good organizational strength and skills at the local level" were important to the campaign.[8] Dole recruited volunteers from Right-to-Life Conventions. Bob Billings, the first executive of MM, chaired "Evangelicals for Dole" and persuaded Southside Baptist Fellowship president William Pennell to write a letter to seven thousand preachers. Dole's wife Elizabeth, an evangelical Christian, spoke at evangelical gatherings such as the National Prayer Breakfast. Dole also purchased radio ads on Christian radio in urban areas.[9] In Iowa, Dole's victory was driven more by regional appeal than his evangelical strategy, and it was eclipsed by the unexpected second-place finish of Robertson. The Dole campaign also found that Bush had already won over cultural conservatives in the South.

At first glance, George H. W. Bush's nomination in 1988 does not seem to illustrate that cultural conservatives had a proverbial seat at the Republican table. Reagan named Bush as his running mate in 1980 to appeal to moderates, although Bush agreed to drop his prochoice position. As an upper-class

Episcopalian with an Ivy League education, Bush was part of the "Eastern Establishment" that the New Right looked upon with contempt. Bush had even earned the nickname "Rubbers" for his support for federally funded birth control in Congress from 1967 to 1970. Sensing the future of the party, Bush said he would allow the states more leeway to regulate abortion in the 1980 presidential primaries. Still, he called Reagan's opposition to the ERA "unwise."[10]

The mainline Protestant patrician appeared uncomfortable with more conservative religious denominations. In 1979, then a candidate for president, Bush met with a group of evangelical Christian leaders as a presidential candidate. When they asked if he had undergone a "born-again" experience, he answered with a curt "no."[11] After meeting with lesser-known Pentecostal leaders in 1985, an evangelical working on Bush's campaign reported that "[Bush] really smoked a 'grass root' on this trip. . . . While no one can divine the mind of the Vice President, I can't help but feel that he was at once fascinated and repelled by what he encountered. I just hope he was not sufficiently 'turned off' to retard the process of cultivating this important constituency."[12]

Cultural conservatism was not even part of Bush's original strategy to win the Bible Belt in 1988. Campaign manager Lee Atwater began crafting strategies to win southern primaries years before the election. As Bush later told his ghostwriter, "Let me tell you something. It's all going to be over on Super Tuesday."[13] But Atwater and Bush largely ignored the Christian Right. Inspired by Clark Clifford's memo on the 1948 election, Atwater wrote a forty-page memorandum to Vice President Bush in 1984. Atwater's strategy was to line up Republican officeholders in South Carolina and the southern states as a "fortress" for Bush. First, he arranged for the South Carolina primary to be held immediately before Super Tuesday. Second, Atwater gathered together three hundred prominent Southern supporters to meet at the Buckhead Ritz-Carlton in June of 1987. His former clients included the popular Republican governor and former state chair.[14] Atwater's memorandum did not anticipate the importance of evangelicals in the campaign and most campaign workers lacked basic information common to evangelical Christians. Often, they misspelled religious terms and did not know who authored well-known passages in the Bible.[15] Bush's special projects coordinator said that "this was a different breed of cat from that which [Atwater] was used to dealing with . . . Lee didn't think the way the religious right thought; he didn't operate the way they did. And so, [their importance in the election] might have surprised him somewhat."[16]

Bush demonstrated how much nominees needed cultural conservatives when he suddenly decided that Atwater's secular strategy was inadequate. Once Robertson emerged as a serious rival in Michigan, which held an unusual contest in 1986, Bush's campaign bent over backwards to win evangelical support before it was too late. Fortunately, the campaign had a movement insider who had written elaborate evangelical strategy memos, which were largely ignored before the Robertson threat.[17] Spy novelist Doug Wead prepared these lengthy memos in 1985. Wead said that at the grassroots level, evangelical Christians were more numerous and better organized than they had been in 1980 or 1984. A religious broadcaster such as Falwell or Robertson was likely to run, if for no other reason than to promote his ministry and augment his mailing list by using political appeals to transcend theological distinctions. Bush and his staffers regarded Wead as a seer after Robertson demonstrated surprising strength in Michigan in 1986.[18] And they were right to worry about Robertson, who raised nearly thirty-three million dollars by Super Tuesday, compared with Bush's twenty-seven million and Dole's twenty-three million.[19] Press secretary Marlin Fitzwater wrote that "I wish I had read your memos as closely as I read your spy novels. You were right on the mark about Pat Robertson. I have gone back and reread some of 'the best of Doug Wead' and it's clear we should have acted on more of your advice."[20] Bush's special projects coordinator acknowledged that "once [Atwater] grasped" the potential of the evangelical vote, "he acted very quickly on it.[21]

The Episcopalian vice president tried to learn a new language of cultural conservative keywords and ideas to show kinship with the new target group. Wead provided Bush with important books by C. S. Lewis and Francis Schaeffer and advised him to refer to them in meetings with evangelicals. If Bush admitted to a born-again experience, evangelicals would wonder why it was revealed only recently.[22] Wead suggested telling them that "I have accepted Jesus as my personal savior," but admit that he had not had a dramatic, life-changing event. Since many evangelical Christians had children who had not undergone a life-changing experience, they were all too willing to view it as an honorary born-again experience. If asked why he answered differently in 1979, Bush should say he misunderstood the question and thought it required an instant conversion. In audiences with evangelical leaders, Bush used the answer effectively even though it said nothing specific about Christian theology. The answer did not address the divinity of Christ or whether Christ was the only route to salvation. Few people probed deeper and McAteer happily informed his network of what he heard.[23]

Bush ran a group-centered campaign because concentrated minorities mattered even in a system that formally turned nominations over to millions of primary voters. At first, he thought officeholder endorsements would be enough to win the South, triggering such voters to follow their lead. Then he sought the support of religious leaders who could spread their message among networks of followers. Religious leaders would influence other pastors and hold their followers in line against Robertson. Wead generated a list of one thousand "targets," based on influence in the evangelical movement, influence on the public, influence in denomination, and importance in early primary/caucus states. At the top of the list was Billy Graham, with 315 "points," followed by Robert Schuller with 237, Jerry Falwell with 236, and Jim Bakker with 232.[24] Bush met with most of Wead's targets in the two years following Robertson's Michigan victory.

The mechanism for winning primaries was winning important groups, and the mechanism for winning important groups was to win over the right opinion leaders in private. Influential religious leaders served as the first domino that would unleash a chain of other falling dominoes. For example, SBC president Dr. Charles Stanley (ranked seventh on the list) was "the key to building relationships with the 7 or 8 pastors of the largest SBC churches."[25] Bush could win over an important Michigan pastor with Billy Zeoli, a spiritual advisor to President Ford. "Billy Zeoli should be there to whisper in DeHaan's ear the whole time. Billy can deliver him with a boost like this," Wead wrote.[26] Sometimes, group leaders extended help on their own. Former SBC president Adrian Rogers offered to arrange a meeting between Bush and other Baptist leaders to offer advice on the general election in June of 1988.[27] Robertson's campaign manager in South Carolina acknowledged that Bush's religious endorsements kept many evangelicals in line.[28]

As outlined in Chapter 7, conservative religious denominations were still prone to sectarianism. The Wead memos stressed that Bush could not appear partial to any one sect. He could do this by building a diverse portfolio of evangelical Christians, including Southern Baptists and Pentecostals.[29] Broadcasting the religious message too loudly could make him "suspect to Catholics, Jews and other constituencies which are now open to him."[30] Although Graham did not provide an explicit endorsement, Bush made a widely applauded appearance on a televised special with Graham, and another on Schuller's uncontroversial "Hour of Power."[31] Jimmy Swaggart's anti-Catholic remarks made him a controversial choice, but if he endorsed Bush together with many other evangelicals, "they give the appearance of a spontaneous support from all evangelicals in general."[32]

The campaign could not appear to be captive, but nor could it appear to be opportunistic. It had to be willing to sacrifice public approval for evangelical approval from time to time. Bush embraced Falwell's endorsement despite his low public approval. Bush met with the television show host in 1986 and declared that he represents a "moral vision" that "America is in crying need of." Moderates complained and predicted that Bush would lose the moderate support and the 1988 Republican primaries.[33] But Falwell's support was the lynchpin for the support of several others. Wead wrote:

> In conversations with Schuller and Bakker, it has already been very useful for me to point out how loyal the VP is to Jerry, even though polls show him to be a liability. It says to them that this man is more than a politician. . . . It holds out the promise that they are not going to get "dumped" after their usefulness has ended.[34]

Falwell endorsed Bush publicly, declaring that of the remaining Republican candidates, Kemp lacked Bush's experience and Dole was "lukewarm on social issues."[35]

One technique to minimize the damage was to cultivate relationships early, before most voters were not paying attention. Doing so in advance of primaries would also avoid the appearance of a last-minute change-of-heart. By appearing to be one of their own, Bush might be able to soften controversial policy positions, making up for them with religious sincerity. Most of the meetings were also private. For example, he met with faculty of the controversial BJU, but not on campus, as his son later did.[36] His evangelical mailers avoided red meat appeals, not even mentioning abortion.[37] Additionally, evangelical Christians would receive the signal if he appeared with evangelical musicians and athletes, who were unlikely to offend other voters.[38]

After Bush lost in Iowa to Dole and Robertson, Atwater thought it was essential to create an evangelical firewall in the South, not just a firewall of officeholder endorsements.[39] Wead identified the South's 215 largest evangelical churches and sent delegates to report on Robertson's support in the congregations. If any of the churches advertised support for Robertson, the Bush campaign asked Bush supporters in the congregation to appeal to the pastor, which usually neutralized in-house appeals to Robertson.[40] The Bush campaign also hired people to serve as Robertson delegates, and then switch to Bush at a strategic time with a carefully constructed announcement.[41]

Bush had many advantages in the 1988 primaries, but the campaign treated the evangelical constituency as if it was one he had to win. He enabled disparate theological conservatives to support someone they perceived as their own without being perceived as a threat to any particular sect or religious empire. Likewise, his association with this unpopular constituency did not appear to dampen his support among the general voting population.

Who Led Whom?

Bush's evangelical appeals might be viewed as a successful "bait-and-switch," evidence of a candidate's skills rather than the ability of religious groups to influence candidates. Instead, the bait only worked because Bush assured cultural conservatives of his commitment at an early stage, which forced him into a corner once in office. By stopping short of their demands, he was forced to offer visible support during the 1992 campaign. His perceived moderation in office backfired on him by forcing him to repair relations in full public view.

Evangelical Christians realized Bush was inauthentic before the election. Though it did not cost him their endorsement, it would later cost him their trust. After lining up evangelical endorsements, he invited several leaders to his house in 1986. D. James Kennedy asked Bush the question he used to screen Reagan and John Connally: what he would answer if God asked why he should be given eternal life? Bush said he "had been a good person, that I had tried my best to be kind to others, to be fair and truthful." Kennedy "blinked in amazement" and "the color drained from the face of Jerry Falwell," who announced two weeks later at a press conference that he was leaving politics. Evangelicals believe that Jesus died for mankind's sins and one gains salvation through his sacrifice, so long as one accepts Jesus by faith. When pressed, Bush replied, "You can't tell me that a good Muslim or Hindu who is sincerely trying to do his best is going to be rejected just because he doesn't believe in Jesus Christ?" While the attendees realized they misjudged Bush, they had already publicized their support, and were unwilling to lose face with their followers.[42]

The campaign scaled back its evangelical outreach after Super Tuesday was over. Asked whether Bush should appear on the Trinity Broadcasting Network in April of that year, Wead unequivocally advised the campaign that "Super Tuesday is over. It is not necessary to risk association with these controversial ministries at this time."[43] Bush even dismissed the New Right's bridge builder, McAteer, from the campaign after Robertson dropped out.[44] As part of the effort to avoid losing public support, evangelical leaders were excluded from the convention television cameras. Wead warned that "One

Jesus bumper sticker on an attaché case is hardly noticed on the floor of fifteen thousand people in a Coliseum, but an NBC television camera with a zoom lens will show it to millions of people around the country." Falwell and other broadcasters were invited to the convention and expected to attend numerous private meetings so that they had no free time in their schedules. This kept them from drawing attention to themselves and their support for Bush in press interviews.[45]

If Bush had misled religious conservatives, he had misled their opponents even more. Most prominent Republican moderates and feminists supported Bush,[46] whom they remembered as the moderate from 1980. They hoped the Republican Party would revert to its pre-Reagan positions, but had no success in 1988 or future conventions. When abortion rights were debated, Bush workers told delegates that voting for an antiabortion platform was a test of delegate loyalty to the nominee.[47] The platform read that the "unborn child has a fundamental individual right to life which cannot be infringed," which suggested that no exceptions would be made even for the health of the mother. A feminist delegate proposed removing the last four words, noting that Bush favored such exceptions, but it was defeated 55 to 32. Former RNC chair Mary Louise Smith and a few other feminists also fought successfully for a child care program in the platform, but it was conjoined with a more conservative statement on Judeo-Christian family values.[48] Bush offered nothing comparable to Reagan's Women's Task Force and promised appointments.[49] A dwindling moderate Republican faction, like the Dixiecrats, failed to restore the party's past positions.

President Bush paid a price for falling short of cultural conservative expectations. Like Reagan, he faced a Democratic Congress that was unlikely to support their agenda. Presidential scholar George Edwards argues that due to large Democratic majorities in both houses of Congress, Bush had "perhaps the worse strategic position" to pass legislation "of any president in the twentieth century."[50] However, as the private meetings with Kennedy suggest, cultural conservatives believed Reagan's commitment was more genuine. Bush's inauthenticity deprived him of the trust he needed to argue that he was doing what was possible. A better rapport with groups provides presidents with more room to disappoint them.

Bush was more interested in containing the influence of the Christian Right than repairing relationships among its diverse groups. Rather than facilitating alliances across cultural conservative groups, he sought a balance of power to prevent any one from becoming too powerful. The president would have more bargaining power if the Christian Right were divided into smaller subunits. In late 1988, NRB presumptuously published that Bush would attend its annual convention without asking the president-elect. Wead reminded Bush that presidents bestow power on organizations by attending their conventions, and the president should not do so for organizations that are already too powerful. However, President Carter's religious liaison and Missouri governor Ashcroft advised that he had to go if he wanted to be reelected. Bearing in mind that no other event draws as many powerful conservative leaders in one place, Bush attended.[51] Bush also spoke via a loudspeaker to the March for Life in 1989, even though the organization was not helpful to him during the 1988 campaign, while other antiabortion organizations were.[52] He preferred coalition containment to coalition maintenance, but was forced to pursue the latter anyway.

At the time, Bush's judicial nominations were received enthusiastically by cultural conservative groups.[53] On the other hand, the president did not consult family values groups for most administrative positions and his FCC appointments showed no inclination to fight risqué broadcasting.[54] Worst of all, Bush refused to dismiss the National Endowment for the Arts chairman after the media revealed that the agency funded sexually explicit and religiously provocative art.[55]

Bush's failure to live up to the commitments he made to cultural conservatives provided room for insurgent candidate Pat Buchanan in the 1992 Republican primaries. As soon as Buchanan criticized the president for publicly funded art, Bush fired the National Endowment for the Arts chairman. Bush's communications director said, "There was a real concern about the right . . . [The firing of] Frohnmayer was a symbolic gesture to the right that needed to be done."[56] His campaign mailed a letter from Robertson endorsing Bush to voters in the Georgia primary, the first contest in the South that year, to weaken Buchanan's momentum after the New Hampshire primary. The CC's support for the wavering president was a way to indenture the party to them. Director Ralph Reed explained, "If Bush wins, the evangelical vote will have made the difference. If George Bush loses, the evangelicals will step into the vacuum created by his defeat." Reed's words parallel those of CIO president Murray four decades earlier. Murray pointed out that if Truman lost in 1948, the "opportunity may be provided for sound reconstruction upon liberal lines."[57]

In the end, Bush appeared to be more of a servant than a master. The president felt forced to cater to Christian conservatives at the 1992 convention in order to regain their trust, conceding much more than the platform to them.[58] A survey of delegates revealed that 52 percent were either members of or sympathetic to the "Christian Right."[59] Of the 2,209 delegates to the Republican Convention, three hundred were CC members; on the platform committee, 20 of the 107 platform committee members belonged to the CC.[60] Buchanan, who had pugnaciously criticized Bush during the primaries, was invited to give an unedited convention speech if he endorsed Bush. In the speech, he linked the 1992 election to the "religious war going on in our country." Robertson said that Governor Clinton had a "radical" plan to destroy the American family.[61] The Bush campaign thought he needed to shore up conservative support somehow, even if these statements went too far.[62]

The Bush campaign offered no resistance to a platform more conservative than the last. While earlier platforms ignored gay rights, the 1992 platform committee adopted a number of planks against same-sex partner rights and affirmed the Boy Scouts, who refused to employ homosexuals as scout leaders. Criticism from the SBC and NAE then seemed to subside. An effort to make an exception to the antiabortion plank for rape or incest was defeated by voice vote.[63] The platform supported limited legal protection for home schooling and "Operation Rescue," which blockaded abortion clinics. School prayer planks that had previously supported "rich religious pluralism" were reworded to read "our Judeo-Christian heritage." The CC commented that "nobody thought we could do better than 1988 but this platform is more precise."[64] Christian Action Network's president claims that his group had approached the campaign about gay rights early in 1992 and was told changing the platform would be difficult. By the summer, he passed antigay amendments without a fight.[65]

Christian Coalition director Reed speculated that the campaign focused on "family values" because it could no longer campaign on the economy or win over economic conservatives. Because cultural conservatives never believed that Bush shared their values, the campaign had to exaggerate the message:

> [After President Bush approved a tax increase and a civil rights bill], the only card . . . the Bush campaign had left to play was the social-conservative moral issue, "family values" card. And they played it very well. But the problem was . . . with people who don't really believe it on their own, you have to say it louder than you might otherwise say so. If . . . you've been neglecting your spouse for the last decade, you

might feel it necessary to shower her with or him with four dozen roses. But if you've been a faithful and loving husband or wife forever, a simple "I love you" will do. Well, the Bush campaign found it necessary because of a real problem with conservatives in its own Party to send the equivalent of four dozen roses, and that became known as the Houston Convention.[66]

Journalists asked Bush if the platform went beyond his own views. Caught between a rock and a hard place, he replied, "Well, I'll have to wait and read the platform, which I confess I've not done . . . Never mind. I'll be compatible with the platform on many other things."[67]

Reagan's heir expected that he would be able to manage cultural conservatives after gaining their loyalty in 1988. Instead, he had to accumulate more political liabilities securing them in 1992 than he would have with either policy victories or a genuine commitment. Where Bush had avoided public appearances with controversial cultural conservatives during the 1988 election, he spoke at the CC convention in October of 1992 and at Falwell's Liberty University close to Election Day.[68] The overtures were more costly during a general election. If Bush manipulated cultural conservatives in 1988, he had little to show for it in 1992. His son, George W. Bush, had to convince cultural conservatives that he was not his father's son. His centrist policies were political miscalculations, not evidence that politicians overpower external groups.

National Elections after the Second Wave

By the 1996 election, cultural conservatives were well-organized in many states with early nominating contests, such as Iowa, South Carolina, and Super Tuesday states.[69] Furthermore, they were poised to provide the campaign with the specialists and unpaid volunteers necessary to any presidential campaign. Republican presidential candidates who were not personally inclined toward cultural conservatism adapted their campaigns and issue positions to fit the new realities of the party's makeup.

The successful candidates were able to tailor a message to cultural conservatives without attracting too much attention from median voters. But candidates had to learn how to speak the language of evangelical Christians and forgo the support of moderate and prochoice Republicans. Dole found himself unable to control the 1996 platform and George W. Bush had to oppose gay marriage more aggressively than he wished. As with civil rights leaders of the 1950s, cultural conservatives did not always support the candidate most aligned with their issues, such as Robertson in 1988, Buchanan in 1996, and Gary Bauer in 2000. They realized they could not win an election for long-shot and no-shot candidates. Instead, they supported the strongest conventional candidate before that candidate had actually sewed up the nomination. By putting the strongest candidate over the top, they sought to incur a debt that would later be repaid in policies they cared about. They were quick to threaten candidates who strayed too far, forcing them to fall back in line.

Bob Dole as an Unlikely Savior

The 1996 nomination showed the continued importance of cultural conservatism in the party. In that year, groups and Republican officeholders both supported the same candidate, Senate Majority Leader Bob Dole. While Dole was not an ideal candidate, he was arguably better than the other candidates. With no inspiring choice in the presidential race, cultural conservatives chose the candidate who was least likely to undo their gains at the congressional level.

Dole and the other Republican candidates each sought the support of the CC. All the major candidates—Lamar Alexander, Pat Buchanan, Richard Lugar, Bob Dole, and Phil Gramm—spoke to their convention.[70] None of them were perfect. Dole was the only Republican nominee from 1980 to 2016 who had been prolife since *Roe v. Wade*, but he wanted a "tolerance" statement in the platform to welcome different views in the Republican Party. His wife was an evangelical Christian, but the couple attended a liberal church in Georgetown until the pastor publicly criticized her husband.[71] Buchanan was an outspoken cultural warrior, but his anti-Zionist position was troubling to Pentecostals who saw Israel as a sign of the second coming of Christ.[72] Alexander had been prochoice until recently. Gramm positioned himself as the conservative heir to Reagan, but when FOF's Dobson interviewed Gramm about his faith, Gramm snapped, "I'm not running for preacher. I'm running for president. I just don't feel comfortable going around telling other people how to live their lives." Dobson told Reed, "I walked into that meeting fully expecting to support Phil Gramm for president. Now I don't think I would vote for him if he was the last man standing."[73]

The best the CC could do was to consolidate its gains in Congress. In 1994, Republicans took control of both houses for the first time since 1952. MCs mentioned cultural issues in campaigns more than ever before.[74] The CC pointed out that as a nominee, Buchanan would not only lose to Clinton but jeopardize Republican control of Congress with his coattails.[75] Reed did not want the CC to be labeled as "extremist" for supporting Buchanan, and performed a "delicate dance" to encourage the "activism and energy" in the Buchanan campaign. He told cultural conservatives that they "must do more than 'send a message' . . . They must win elections. They must govern."[76]

Cultural conservatives in early states once again figured prominently in the victor's strategy. The Iowa springboard and South Carolina firewall minimized the cost of Buchanan's challenge. Dole employed Iowa CC director Scheffler as his coalitions coordinator. After Buchanan won the New Hampshire primary, the South Carolina CC helped keep the state in line for Dole. Robertson and governor David Beasley, both CC icons, endorsed the presumptive nominee. Although the CC itself could not endorse Dole, the state director's husband did. And while the state CC offered advice to any candidate that asked, it only offered its mailing list to the Dole campaign.[77]

One might repeat Schattschneider's claim that interest groups have no choice but to support a suboptimal nominee, when the alternative is an even worse candidate from the other party.[78] In the absence of better candidates, Dole may have been a pragmatic choice, but it was in no way forced upon the CC. Making a pragmatic choice had its cost, lowering evangelical turnout by 6 percent compared with 1992, but still maintaining Republican control of Congress.

"The Most Overtly Evangelical White House in History"

In 2000, Republican officeholders and cultural conservative groups again agreed on the same candidate, Texas governor George W. Bush. Bush carefully courted the same religious conservatives that his father did. Having undergone a born-again experience himself, he was able to convince them that he would not be a disappointment like his father. While he was genuinely committed to prayer and prolife policies, he was also someone who could resonate with ordinary voters. Pundits said that voters would prefer having a beer with Bush to having one with his Democratic rival, even though Bush had stopped drinking after his conversion.

Bush's primary tactic was to project himself as a frontrunner,[79] but he also sought group endorsements with gusto. He knew that antitax groups and cultural conservatives, in particular, needed reassurance due to his father's policies. The governor read *The One Year Bible*, which presented the Bible in a format accessible to readers who wanted to learn essential points over the course of a year. Wead coached Bush for hours well before he was a declared candidate, instructing him in "code words and names that can transcend the media and liberal critics."[80] Perhaps Bush's biggest selling point was that he was a born-again Christian, not a mainline Protestant like the rest of his family. Drinking problems risked his career and marriage until his conversion on the beaches of Kennebunkport in 1984. Privately, Bush met with evangelical Christian leaders in small group settings and shared his testimony, claiming it took place with Billy Graham. Upon hearing that the governor was a born-again Christian, D. James Kennedy said that "this changes everything."[81]

The way to win over cultural conservative groups was to persuade group leaders to win friends and followers to his side. As with his father, Bush realized that group endorsements could lead to a chain reaction. Wead delivered the endorsement of Amway founder DeVos, who could tell numerous leaders like Robertson, Bauer, Falwell, and Dobson to stay out of public view, since he donated to all of them. He could even stop Schlafly from criticizing Bush's Texas education policies on her "Eagle Forum."[82] Bush also needed Falwell, even though he was not a "subtle weapon." If "you veer too far away from the evangelicals and need to send a signal of reassurance," Wead wrote, "a public association with Falwell can do that in an instant."[83] Most of the "major SBC hitters," including takeover-architect Paige Patterson, endorsed Bush by 1999.[84] Bush met with the New Right's Council for National Policy in October of that year and solidified his conservative credentials on cultural issues.[85] The governor invited Missouri's Pentecostal governor John Ashcroft, then running for the nomination, to the governor's mansion. Bush told Ashcroft, "I'm glad you're in the race" and "I hope you stay in the race" because "it's strategically important for me."[86] Ashcroft conversed with FOF's Dobson weekly and could "bring Dobson into line."[87]

Some of candidates for the Republican nomination in 2000, including Alan Keyes and Gary Bauer, were more culturally conservative. However, the only candidate capable of competing with the comparatively secular John McCain, let alone winning the general election, appeared to be Bush. Senator McCain became a favorite with independent voters and the media partly by distancing himself from the same cultural conservatives that Bush was enticing. McCain compared Christian conservative leaders to union bosses. He called them "agents of intolerance," and singled out Falwell and Robertson as an "evil influence" on the party.[88]

Once again, South Carolina repaired the damage from McCain's victory in secular New Hampshire. The Bush campaign treated the Palmetto state as if the entire nomination hinged on it.[89] Robertson recorded a phone message that was forwarded to many Republicans during the primary, arguing that Bush had stronger prolife credentials than McCain.[90] The CC's state director introduced Bush to religious leaders around the state, who were eager to hear his testimony and stance on the issues.[91] This support may or may not have been decisive; Bush's well-funded campaign also used negative advertising to counteract McCain's free publicity after New Hampshire.[92] While I cannot prove that one tactic was more effective, I can prove that the Bush campaign treated old-fashioned networking as if it was necessary to winning. He ultimately won South Carolina, going on to win all the Super Tuesday states outside New England.

Cultural conservatives managed to bend Bush's will to their gay marriage position during his reelection campaign in 2004. The Bush campaign developed a highly effective get-out-the-vote (GOTV) organization for cultural conservatives, but even the best candidate-driven outreach could not negate Bush's need for group leader support. In 1998, Governor Bush observed other candidates getting applause with their opposition to gay rights and told Wead, "I think it's bad for Republicans to be kicking gays." In a phone transcript, he said, "this is an issue I've been trying to downplay," though he opposed granting "special rights" to homosexuals (the exact frame used by the CC).[93] In attempting to court Ashcroft, Bush lamented, "he's not going to like my homosexual stand. I think he wants me to attack homosexuals." Wead replied "Yeah, a lot of 'em will," and Bush in turn replied, "I can't do that."[94] Leading up to 2004, Bush supported the right of states to recognize civil unions.

A small group of cultural conservatives still persuaded Bush to support a federal amendment banning gay marriage. Several prominent evangelical leaders, including Dobson, formed the "Arlington Group" to unite cultural conservatives behind a common agenda. In 2003, the Massachusetts Supreme Court declared marriage a right, regardless of sexual orientation. Dobson said a federal marriage amendment defining marriage as heterosexual was "our D-Day, our Gettysburg, our Stalingrad."[95] In January 2004, the Arlington Group presented Bush's strategist Karl Rove with an ultimatum to support the Federal Marriage Amendment in the State of the Union address. Dobson said millions of evangelical Christians would abstain from voting otherwise.[96] Bush criticized judges practicing judicial activism on the marriage issue, but that didn't go far enough. After renewed pressure, Bush announced that he supported the amendment. Dobson broke with his custom of not publically endorsing candidates and megachurch pastors mobilized their congregations behind the amendment.[97] While the president contacted MCs to support the amendment in 2004, he did not in 2006, no longer worried about reelection. Groups in the Republican coalition forced Bush to act contrary to his revealed preferences.[98]

Historian Daniel Williams writes that all things considered, the second Bush administration was the "most overtly evangelical in American history." His attorney general, national security adviser, education secretary, and health and human services secretary had strong ties to the evangelical Christian community. Bush prayed frequently and 40 percent of his staff attended weekly Bible studies or prayer meetings.[99] Twenty years earlier, devotion to prayer was considered eccentric at the Reagan White House.[100] Notwithstanding Bush's reluctance to support a federal marriage amendment, his prayers and appointments did not seem to be empty gestures to the Christian Right, either. The Bush administration proscribed government funding of stem cell research and late term abortions. His Supreme Court appointments (and most of his circuit court appointments) voted against extending marriage rights to homosexuals in landmark decisions over the next decade.

Groups and Parties Diverge

Reagan, Dole, and the two presidents Bush gathered sizeable endorsements from both cultural conservative groups and Republican officeholders. Groups and parties disagreed on the best nominee thereafter. Perhaps cultural conservatives were so disappointed by the policies of Reagan and Bush that they no longer trusted candidates endorsed by party politicians, as the book title *We Won't Get Fooled Again* suggests.[101] While many groups supported Santorum in 2012 and Cruz in 2016, the lion's share of officeholder endorsements went to Romney and Jeb Bush (later, Marco Rubio). Cultural conservatives failed to coalesce with other groups behind an ideal candidate, but their litmus tests remained in place. Nominees continued to reverse previous positions to gain their approval and groups continued to veto popular candidates.

McCain, who had alienated some cultural conservatives in 2000, waged a much more vigorous effort to recruit cultural conservatives in 2008. He hired Iowa Right to Life founder Marlys Popma to meet with religious conservatives throughout the country. The Palmetto Family Council arranged a private meeting between McCain and some of his most outspoken evangelical critics in South Carolina. McCain talked about his version of faith and how it helped him survive his experience as a prisoner of war in Vietnam. While the meeting may not have impressed anyone, those present avoided publicly criticizing him.[102] At Liberty University, McCain declared that the Christian Right, whom he once compared to union bosses, has "a right to be a part of our party."[103]

Cultural conservatives were divided between Huckabee, Romney, and Thompson. Huckabee, an ordained Baptist minister, may have still won the nomination but for happenstance. The former Arkansas governor beat expectations in the Iowa straw poll with the help of homeschoolers and perennial gubernatorial candidate Vander Plaats. The popular radio host Steve Deace also promoted Huckabee's candidacy and repeatedly broadcast old prochoice statements from Romney, who invested significant funding in Iowa.[104] Huckabee won the caucuses with ten percentage points over Romney, the second place winner, with far less money. McCain was once again boosted by New Hampshire, but this time, South Carolina worked in his favor. Former Tennessee senator Fred Thompson, with tepid support from the Arlington Group,[105] spent much of his effort there. McCain narrowly defeated Huckabee—33 percent to 30 percent—while Thompson garnered 16 percent. Exit polls in South Carolina showed that Thompson took more votes away from Huckabee.[106] Huckabee still won five states on Super Tuesday, but McCain won nine of the remaining nineteen states. Had Huckabee won in South Carolina, he would have at least prolonged the nominating contest.

The 2008 nominating contest is perhaps more revealing in what did not happen. Throughout the spring of 2008, McCain planned to nominate Joe Lieberman, a Democrat-turned-independent senator who supported abortion rights. When the news leaked, conservative radio host Rush Limbaugh proclaimed that the McCain campaign "will have effectively destroyed the Republican Party and put the conservative movement in the bleachers." McCain's advisers said that the campaign would have to spend September repairing the party instead of attacking the Democratic nominee, and searched for a running mate who met the standards of the Christian Right.[107] At the last minute, McCain accepted Alaska governor Sarah Palin, who supported abortion restrictions and intelligent design. A Council for National Policy meeting burst in applause over her nomination, and Dobson told one activist, "I've never been so excited about a ticket in my life."[108] Dobson had earlier said he could never support McCain.[109] The vice presidential nomination revealed the culturally conservative boundaries of Republican politics.

Though cultural conservatives failed to unite behind Huckabee, they united effectively against the only cultural liberal to win the invisible primary since 1980. Former New York City mayor Giuliani led opinion polls throughout 2007, and raised more money than any Republican besides Romney. Even Giuliani wanted to reverse his positions on gay rights and abortion despite his favorable position. The cosmopolitan mayor told Falwell's son that "if I were president you'd have an open door. Let's be honest, I can't pull a Romney and flip-flop. That would kill me."[110] He managed to obtain an endorsement from Robertson due to his hawkish pro-Israel views, but that was not enough. In an unusual strategic move, Giuliani ceased campaigning in Iowa and New Hampshire and focused his efforts in Florida, hoping to win and gather momentum before Super Tuesday. Giuliani did not ignore the necessities of front-loaded primaries out of ignorance, but because he could not win Iowa or New Hampshire. He made dozens of visits to both states but failed to build up an adequate ground organization without the volunteers that conservative groups could provide. Florida was the only realistic state left before Super Tuesday. As Cohen et al. conclude, "A party saying no to its most popular candidate does not fit candidate-centered politics."[111]

The 2012 nominating contest confounds both conventional and group-centered theories of nominations. Former Pennsylvania senator Santorum, perhaps the most culturally conservative candidate, managed to gain traction in Iowa on a shoestring budget. Although Santorum was the actual winner of the Iowa caucuses, the results were close and the media inaccurately reported Romney as the winner. An attempt to coalesce was made after the Iowa caucuses, but it was too late. A furniture store entrepreneur from South Dakota organized a gathering at Judge Pressler's Texas home. The attendees hoped to hold several ballots until a frontrunner emerged, and thereby enable cultural conservatives to issue a unified public statement in favor of the winner.[112] Santorum prevailed with 75 percent support only on the third ballot, after many had left.[113] Several participants publicly criticized the meeting as "rigged" in Santorum's favor, casting doubt on its legitimacy.[114] Christian Right kingmakers were slow to agree on the ideal candidate, but most of the candidates were in agreement on their core issues. All of the candidates besides Ron Paul and Jon Huntsman signed the National Organization for Marriage's pledge to oppose judges who favor gay marriage and support the federal marriage amendment and the Defense of Marriage Act. Rick Perry and Michele Bachmann had to backtrack from earlier positions leaving the matter up to the states.[115]

The 2012 election should not obscure the overall trajectory of the Republican Party and the role of organized groups in maintaining that trajectory. Reagan, McCain, Romney, Trump, and the two presidents Bush had *all* changed from prochoice to prolife positions in advance of their candidacies. All of them recruited insiders from cultural conservative organizations to network with potential sources of support, including pivotal figures described in the last chapter. Efforts to soften the Republican platform have also failed. Every platform since 1980 opposed abortion without exceptions for rape, incest, and the mother's health, despite support for these exceptions from a supermajority of the public. By 2012, a majority of the American public supported full gay marriage rights, but the Republican platform would not even support civil unions.

Conclusion

Some political scientists have argued that post McGovern-Fraser campaigns have been candidate-centered contests where successful nominees win by directly appealing to voters through the mass media. The past three chapters show that Republican nominees also network extensively with important cultural conservative powerbrokers much as candidates networked with party bosses under the old system. Where pre-reform Democrats networked with Sidney Hillman, Walter Reuther, and Roy Wilkins, recent Republicans have privately networked with Jerry Falwell, Ed McAteer, D. James Kennedy, Pat Robertson, and Paul Pressler. And once in office, Republicans made concessions to such powerbrokers, supporting policies they privately opposed and platforms unpopular with the mass public. Candidates performed a balancing act as they sought to be responsive to cultural conservatives without appearing captive to them. George H. W. Bush hoped to keep cultural conservatives at a manageable level of influence but ultimately kowtowed to them.

CHAPTER 11

Other Evidence: Populism and Gay Rights

A similar process unfolded in the two most important contested party transformations of the twentieth century. Groups formed effective coalitions on
their own and influenced party nominations, leading parties to change positions. What about other issues? Future researchers might look into the
economic transformation of the Democratic Party during the New Deal or
the still-unfolding role of the Tea Party. For now, I will briefly examine two
other attempts at party transformations to suggest that the processes documented in this book are not exceptional. I cannot devote the same space and
time I did to civil rights and cultural conservatism, and the evidence is not
as conclusive. But the available evidence points decidedly in favor of my
claims.

First, I will look at the late nineteenth-century Populists, where groups
failed to form a viable electoral coalition. Unlike the other party transformations I described, Populists sidestepped effective coalition-building and relied
on a political party to unite workers and farmers behind free silver. Later, they
supported a major party nominee, but failed to extend the party's commitment to future contests. Populists identified potential allies, but failed to win
their trust or emphasize common interests. The absence of coalition-building
was coupled with a failure to either build a viable party or transform a major
party, providing evidence for Claim 1. Second, I will look at the recent case of
gay rights to suggest that change in the contemporary Democratic Party, like
the Republican Party, is group-driven. Gay rights groups obtained the blessing
of other Democratic Party groups and threatened politicians with unwanted
attention. For both transformations, I rely heavily on secondary sources, but
fewer sources are available on gay rights. Therefore, I combine existing accounts with primary sources from the National Organization for Women

(NOW), the National Gay and Lesbian Task Force (NGLTF),[1] National Gay Rights Lobby (NGRL), and the Human Rights Campaign (HRC).

The Populist Revolt

In the late nineteenth century, farmers tried to obtain a series of ambitious reforms through interest groups, third parties, and eventually the major party candidacy of William Jennings Bryan. Suffering from large debts, unfair railroad rates, and low food prices, they supported various state and federal regulations, but the most insistent demand over time was currency inflation. Paper money or silver coinage could reduce their debts and raise the price of farm goods. The two major parties did not respond to their demands, instead prioritizing the support of big business on the Republican side and laissez-faire "Goldbugs" on the Democratic side. Excluded from both parties, agrarian rebels ultimately created the Populist Party challenge in 1892, which endorsed the Democratic nominee in 1896 before dissipating into irrelevancy.

Like civil rights groups and cultural conservatives, the farmers committed themselves to party politics and identified potential allies. Schlozman has recently looked at the Populists as an instructive example of failed transformations, but does not trace the cause back to the absence of coalition-building by groups. Unlike civil rights groups and cultural conservatives, the Populists did not obtain lasting commitments from prospective allies. Hastily planted with shallow roots, the Populist coalition failed to weather the many storms coming their way. Farmers wanted higher food prices, without offering enough to compensate urban workers for their near-term losses. Additionally, racial divisions among southern farmers were often insurmountable.[2] Transformative groups need to form more resilient alliances than the Populists did.

A brief overview of their vigorous efforts and electoral failures will help us to identify missteps in the process. Farmers fought existing parties from the Civil War to the end of the century. At first, many turned to third-party options such as the Greenback or Populist Party. In some cases, they tried to form fusion parties with Democrats or Republicans, most of them short-lived. Populists obtained the nominee they wanted in the Democratic Party with Bryan in 1896, 1900, and 1908. However, Bryan emphasized one of their demands, silver inflation, far more often than others, and only in 1896 at that. President Wilson passed some of their policies, including an income tax amendment, a strengthened antitrust law, and a federal lending system. However, Wilson was not responding to enfeebled rural reformers but to progressive Republicans, who differed substantively from both Populists and more traditional Democrats.[3]

Bryan's limited support of the agrarian rebels did not change the trajectory of his party. In other conventions, Democrats nominated much more economically conservative candidates. In 1904, the party nominated Judge Alton Parker, who often struck down government economic regulations, while the party softened its antitrust and pro-labor planks. Parker's running mate was a coal and lumber industry leader who supported the gold standard and fought labor unions. In 1924, the Democratic Party was hopelessly split between the cosmopolitan New York governor Al Smith and the southern favorite, William McAdoo. As a compromise, the party chose John Davis, a corporate lawyer who called the income tax an assault on human liberty. Smith, the 1928 nominee, mediated labor disputes and supported public works programs as governor of New York, but later joined the Liberty League and attacked New Deal programs as unconstitutional.[4]

Populists failed to launch the Democratic Party on a long-term trajectory because they failed to undertake the kind of coalition maintenance other groups in this book undertook so carefully. Civil rights groups in the 1940s were willing to back down from civil rights amendments that would sink legislation supported by their allies, while labor groups defended controversial proposals like integrated housing projects and antidiscrimination laws. Populists prioritized free silver, their toughest selling point for labor, and sometimes criticized worker strikes. Other potential allies, such as prohibitionists, risked dividing the ethnic workers they hoped to win over.

Farmers and Workers

The Populist Party was formed by the Farmers' Alliance shortly before the 1892 election. Farmers formed the organization in 1875 to address low prices for farm goods and high prices for shipping, arguing that states should nationalize the railroads and buy or store grain surpluses. Supportive lecturers and newspapers spread their message around the country. Though the Alliance had national goals, it was divided between "Northern," "Southern," and "Colored" chapters. The Southern Alliance boasted more than a million members and was able to win control of eight state legislatures; alliance-backed candidates were elected governor in four states.[5]

Both the Farmers' Alliance and Populist Party were influenced by the

Greenback Party and Knights of Labor (KOL), which adopted impressively broad agendas. The Greenback Party supported not only paper money to raise farm prices, but also union rights and shorter workdays. The KOL, like the CIO, grafted an ambitious policy agenda on top of labor organizing, even encouraging women and blacks to organize alongside white workers. In many cases, KOL leaders played prominent roles in the Greenback Party. KOL leader Terrence Powderly, for example, had won an election to mayor in Scranton, Pennsylvania, on a Greenback ticket.

Populists did not suffer from a lack of ideology. Groups like the Farmers' Alliance, the Grangers, and followers of Henry George and Edward Bellamy disseminated their ideas to the public for decades.

The Farmers' Alliance hastily constructed the People's Party, commonly known as the Populist Party, hoping to win both worker and farmer support. Alliance men from around the country met in 1891 to discuss forming a third party. The Populists nominated James B. Weaver, a veteran of many Greenback campaigns and the Union army. The nominee won five states—Kansas, Colorado, Idaho, Nevada, and North Dakota—but obtained little support from the South and Northeast.

Though the Populists recognized the need for broader support, they had not built sturdy bridges between farmers and laborers. The circumstances leading to an alliance between the CIO and NAACP in the 1940s were far more auspicious than a farmer-labor alliance in the 1880s. While the CIO was growing rapidly with the help of labor legislation, the KOL peaked and declined in the 1880s with no legal protection to speak of. A much smaller percentage of workers joined unions compared with the 1940s and the KOL never recovered from being associated with the violent chicago Haymarket Riot in 1886. Furthermore, the KOL never held much strength in the Northeast and barely contained racial prejudice in its own ranks in the South.[6] And where the CIO took great interest in the issues of its allies, farmers publicly disagreed with the KOL and other unions. In Texas, the state Farmers' Alliance pointed out that higher wages for railroad workers meant higher freight rates. It also opposed proposals from a miner's union to raise property taxes for new prisons.[7]

The Populist Party formally adopted many of labor's concerns without receiving significant support from labor during the general election. Although the platform supported a shorter workday, abolition of strikebreakers, and nationalized railroads, Populist leaders were not versed in worker sensibilities. The convention reluctantly agreed to endorse a KOL boycott only after a speech by one of the party's best orators. Weaver did not have a history of supporting labor rights. In the past, he only supported the right to strike as a last resort, and simplistically attributed worker-management problems to bad monetary policy alone.[8] The nominee and other Populist leaders also threaded their rhetoric with evangelical Protestant themes that alienated immigrant laborers. The KOL was in a weak position to make up for their shortcomings with its own appeals, and AFL founder Samuel Gompers refused to support them.[9] In the absence of countervailing signals from labor leaders, it is not surprising that workers ignored a party that wanted to raise food prices.

Populists might have joined with prohibitionists and suffragists, stitched together in Frances Willard's Women's Christian Temperance Union. As a leader of the Prohibition Party, Willard could have brought about a fusion between the two third parties. Willard invited most of the major leaders of the Populist Party and Prohibition Party to Chicago to discuss a merger, but Populists were divided on the prohibition issue along ethnic and religious lines. They also believed southerners would be alienated by female suffrage beyond the municipal level. Ultimately, the Populist Party decided to leave prohibition and women's suffrage out of the platform. Willard, eager to sow seeds for a broader coalition, swallowed her pride and supported the Populists anyway. But without receiving anything in return, her followers were annoyed at her decision. The Prohibition Party convention renounced all parties not supporting temperance in their platform.[10] Whereas the CIO-NAACP alliance and cultural conservatives socialized their members across the full range of issues, populists had to avoid issues like Prohibition.

Even though the Populists worked hard to maintain southern support, they did not win a single southern state. Originally, National Farm Alliance president Leonidas Polk was favored to win the party's nomination, but he died. The aging southern Whig might have added southern states to the Populist Party column. Weaver had been a brigadier general for the Union and naively underestimated how threatened southern voters would feel about a biracial party. Southern audiences were often downright hostile to Weaver. Despite being booed and even assaulted, he was too proud to cancel southern speaking engagements or seek support instead in the Northeast or Midwest.[11] The "Lodge Force Bill," a bill to authorize the federal government to ensure fair elections, magnified the troublesome racial issue for Populists. In 1892, Democratic vice presidential nominee Adlai Stevenson convinced audiences in the upper South that Democrats were the best chance for blocking the bill. A stronger showing in the South, which might have happened with a Polk nomination, could have spoiled the election for the Democrats and weakened the Goldbug wing of the party. Alternatively, a strong performance in 1892 might have made the case for displacing the Democrats with the Populist Party as a new major party.

Separately from the Farmers' Alliance, a small group of mine owners in Nevada and Idaho formed the American Bimetallic League (ABL) in 1889. While its wealthy founders remained discreet, the league formed a network of silver clubs and sponsored nationwide lectures. The ABL opposed the Populist Party and created a half-hearted Silver Party to preempt its broader agenda. A strategy developed in 1895 hoped to "wean the Populists away from their other doctrines and commit them to support a program in which silver should be the only item of consequence." The ABL didn't even really support the inflationary goals of farmers, hoping only to restore silver's previous value. It targeted the Democratic Party, fully aware that "free silver" did not threaten Jim Crow as other Populist Party positions did. A Kansas state senator admitted silver inflation was not the most important issue to the people, but "the only question that the great majority of the people are really interested in."[12]

Nebraska MC Bryan capitalized on both the ABL and Populists. He toured the country promoting free silver in fiery speeches leading up to the 1896 Democratic Convention, also meeting Populists in backrooms to convince them to join forces. Weaver, having participated in several failed third-party ventures, gave his blessing to Bryan. Perhaps more importantly, the Bimetallic Democratic National Committee put together western Democrats and fusionists at a conference in Memphis in 1895. According to Bryan, "it was largely through the efforts of these men that the silver Democrats gained control of the national convention." State conventions adopted pro-silver platforms and bound their delegates. Bryan convinced the Populists to hold their convention after the two major parties to pick up dissatisfied silver advocates in both parties. Deprived of their most salient issue, the Populists had little choice but to nominate Bryan after the Democrats nominated him.[13] Some believed a fusion with Democrats would detract from issues other than silver, but many more viewed silver as a gateway to other demands.[14] While the Democratic platform of 1896 incorporated many concerns of farmers and workers, silver inflation and tariffs became the election issues.[15] Again, had the Populists formed a more robust alliance of workers and farmers, they might have pressured state Democratic delegations to support more than free silver. Other Populist demands, however, ran afoul of laissez-faire Bourbon-dominated Democratic Parties in the South, which were more amenable to ABL.

While Bryan won the solid South, he had the same trouble with urban laborers as other supporters of free silver before him. The ABL cultivated worker support in mining states, the only ones to vote Democratic in 1896.[16] Corporations warned their employees that Bryan's election would mean lay-offs and bankruptcy. To support higher food prices, the party needed to offer some countervailing enticement or powerful argument that it furthered their long-term political interests. Of the major union leaders, only Eugene Debs endorsed Bryan.[17] Otherwise, there were no intermediary groups between parties and workers willing to deliver workers as a bloc, placing the onus on Bryan to persuade a dispersed demographic. Historian Michael Kazin writes that Bryan's "hope that urban wage earners would unite with his agrarian supporters depended almost entirely on his ability to persuade them to vote their ideals and their consciences rather than their fears and their wallets."[18] Ethnic differences again made it difficult to consolidate workers behind one political agenda, and only the most radical workers ignored them.[19] Irish wards in Massachusetts supported Bryan, but without much enthusiasm. Substantively they were antimonopoly without being pro-silver, and stylistically they were alienated by self-righteous Protestant rhetoric.[20] Adding to these difficulties, the economy was improving and people were less desperate for radical solutions. In 1900, McKinley's campaign manager Mark Hanna even persuaded employers to settle a coal strike to subvert Bryan's appeals.[21]

After 1896, Populists split their loyalties between Democrats, Republicans, and Socialists, with none receiving a majority.[22] The remnant of the Populist Party split over whether to endorse Bryan in 1900, and Midwestern states (including Bryan's home state) voted Republican in the end. Over the next few decades, the Democratic Party tried to win majority support with various issue amalgamations, the Populist synthesis often absent. Bryan won the nomination but lost the general election again in 1900 and 1908, with free silver barely a campaign issue in 1900 and even less in 1908.[23] As long as groups had not reconciled ethnic and worker-farmer differences, perhaps no candidate could do better. Groups like the CIO lobbied their members to vote as a bloc for one party even when Republicans like Wendell Willkie courted the union vote. No Populist leader had this kind of sway—not even Bryan. Combined with Bryan's defeats, Populists gave Democrats little incentive to focus on their agenda.

State Farmer Groups

In the South, state Farmers' Alliances and Populists failed to unite black and white farmers to pass economic agendas they both wanted. Many white

Populists recognized their common economic interests and argued that they could overturn the Democratic Party monopoly only with the help of black voters. Both black and white farmers faced a common enemy in southern "Bourbons," who supported Grover Cleveland, Jim Crow, and the Gold Standard. It was common for black voters to be forced or bribed to support particular candidates, or to stuff ballot boxes with the fraudulent votes in the name of black voters. Nonetheless, more blacks cast legitimate votes than often thought in the 1880s and 1890s—voter suppression laws crystallized after Populists emerged.[24] While white Populists recognized the usefulness of black votes, they never demonstrated a longstanding commitment that could survive race-baiting. Bourbons are often to blame for depriving Populists of black votes, but Populists failed to avail themselves of existing opportunities too.

Populist support for civil rights varied over location and time, but many party pronouncements on civil rights bear striking similarities to those later made by the CIO. Tom Watson, a newspaper editor and Georgia MC, was among the most farsighted advocates of a biracial alliance in the South. He told audiences of both races that

> you are kept apart that you may be separately fleeced of your earnings. You are made to hate each other because upon that hatred is rested the keystone of the arch of financial despotism which enslaves you both. You are deceived and blinded that you may not see how this race antagonism perpetuates a monetary system which beggars both.[25]

Furthermore, Watson was optimistic that common economic interests were compelling enough to bring about an alliance, declaring "Self interest always controls." At their best, state efforts to reach across the racial barrier were scattered and short-lived.[26] At their worst, white Populists joined others in fighting to restrict black rights. In a transformation symbolic of the shifting alliances of the era, Watson became an embittered race baiter in his later career.

Populists did not breach the racial divide partly because the Farmers' Alliances composing them did not breach it. The Northern and Southern Farmers' Alliance diverged sharply on civil rights. While the Northern Alliance stressed agitation and voting rights for black members, the Southern Alliance merely argued that their economic policies would also help blacks.[27] All Southern Alliance charters specified that their organizations were for whites only. One activist insisted that "it is better for both white and black to keep their orders separate." Otherwise, "Mr. Negro will soon play second fiddle with only one string to it."[28] The Southern Alliance opposed the Lodge Force Bill and deftly told blacks that "that equal facilities, educational, commercial, and political, be demanded for colored and white Alliance men alike, competency considered, and that a free ballot and a fair count be insisted upon and had for colored and white alike." The "competency considered" clause provided a loophole by which they might support restrictions on the black vote.[29] Though the Southern Alliance offered qualified support for Jim Crow, it recognized the necessity of black votes to defeat Democratic opponents. Colored Farmers' Alliances were therefore organized by white members of the Southern Alliance in some states. Exemplifying Schickler's "common carriers," black farmers often had different reasons for favoring the same inflationary policies; white farmers generally prioritized higher food prices, while black farmers prioritized debt reduction.[30]

In some cases, alliance-controlled legislatures actively curtailed rights for African Americans. In Georgia, an Alliance-controlled legislature segregated railroads, reinstated the whipping post in chain gangs, and prevented black and white prisoners from being chained together.[31] In Texas, the state Farmers' Alliance campaigned to nationalize the railroads, explaining that this would allow the state to segregate them more easily. In Alabama, Farmers' Alliance supporters in the legislature mandated segregation in 1891, and only reluctantly supported the "but equal" qualification to "separate but equal."[32]

When biracial coalitions did congeal for brief moments, their opponents easily split them apart. In 1890, the Florida's Farmers' Alliance boldly met the Colored Alliance in their own hotel and then passed a resolution for voting rights and equal facilities. Shortly thereafter, black cotton pickers loosely associated with the Colored Alliance launched a controversial strike in 1891 that ended in violence. In a similar situation in the 1940s, the CIO might have worked to defuse the tension, perhaps distributing its literature on "discrimination costs you money" or warning that racial division is a shell game for suckers. Perhaps the Florida Alliance could have stayed silent or explained that many Colored Alliance leaders opposed the strike. Instead, the Florida Alliance immediately condemned it.[33] As one historian concluded, "black laborers were welcome as long as they promoted or enhanced the interests of their white mentors."[34]

Populist parties were no more opposed to civil rights than Democrats, but not racially liberal enough to win black voters. To protect themselves from charges that they would overturn white supremacy, populists defensively asserted the social inequality of blacks as soon as they discussed legal rights.[35] Virginia and South Carolina Populists quickly viewed civil rights as a net liability and supported Jim Crow. In other states, Populist politicians had opposed civil rights in the past, and black voters did not trust their recent change of heart. Had Farmers' Alliances mended relations between black and white farmers more carefully and over a longer period of time, perhaps they could have nominated candidates acceptable to both races.

Where Populist outreach was effective, state Democratic Parties often competed for black votes or fought back with fraud and force. In Texas, Governor "Big Jim" Hogg promised black voters he would fight lynching and honored his promise by offering cash rewards for lynch mob members.[36] In Alabama, Democrats manipulated the votes in black counties. In Louisiana, a Democratic Party boss called on white mobs to riot against populists before Election Day, claiming they would incite blacks to fight for their rights.[37] In states where Democrats manipulated black votes, Populists were happy to support vote suppression, because black votes were being used against them.[38]

Populists formed fragile fusion parties with Republicans in North Carolina, Alabama, Tennessee, and Texas. Only in North Carolina, where they controlled the governorship from 1894 to 1898, did they control a state government for any length of time. Coming to power briefly during a Democratic administration's depression, the fusion party raised taxes on business and increased spending on public services. North Carolina Populists allied with Republicans locally and Bryan's Democratic ticket nationally. Shifting between the local and regional parties tested the partisan loyalties of its Democratic and Republican supporters alike.[39]

While southern Republican Parties were generally more supportive of civil rights, North Carolina Republicans promoted fusion with Populists to prevent their party from nominating black candidates. The state party was divided between the eastern "lily white" and western "black and tan" divisions. As the state's black and tan faction gained strength, lily white Republicans joined with the Populists.[40] Black turnout was lower for the fusion ticket than it was in normal contests between Democrats and Republicans. The fusion party alienated black Republicans by excluding them,[41] while simultaneously alienating many pro-silver Democrats just for being Republican. In 1896, the fusion party nominated an open white supremacist, but that did not stop Democrats from reminding voters that Republicans were the party of Reconstruction. For the final touch, Franklin Roosevelt's future secretary of the navy instigated a riot in North Carolina to discredit the fusion ticket in 1898.[42] The

Democrats' white supremacy campaign led them back to power in 1898 and
1900, when they disenfranchised black voters.

The Populists performed little of the painstaking work done by the labor-
civil rights alliance in the 1940s. To be fair, Populists faced many institutional
pitfalls even apart from third-party politics. The KOL barely survived the
Haymarket Square Riot and the AFL refused to involve itself in party politics.
Where blacks and union workers could unite behind the FEPC in the civil
rights transformation, there was no comparable institution that could unite
workers and farmers in the 1890s. For workers, silver inflation was the Populist's most harmful proposal, but it was the issue favored by Bryan's best-
organized and best-funded supporters. Southern Populists ultimately had the
worst of all worlds. They failed to build an alliance with black farmers as Republicans, but being Republican made it hard to influence the national Democratic Party's agenda in 1896. In hindsight, they could have made common
cause with pro-silver Democrats, but there was no predicting Bryan's rise to
prominence until it was too late.

In contrast, Minnesota farmers and workers formed a successful third
party, the Farmer-Labor Party, decades later. An alliance of farmers called the
Nonpartisan League joined together with the Minnesota Federation of Labor
in 1918. The league's founder had tears in his eyes as he watched "the impossible in American politics" come to pass, having witnessed ethnic division and
inflation sink farmer-worker alliances so often before. Farmer-Labor Party
politicians, however, focused on public works programs, labor rights, and
farm foreclosures—not raising prices. In the 1920s, the party still had difficulty bridging ethnic gaps between Irish and German Catholics and Scandi-
navian Lutherans, but the Great Depression's severity submerged these
differences in the following decade.[43]

Gay Rights

Gay rights groups were once ostracized by both major parties and eventually
became a celebrated part of Democratic Party politics. Unlike African Americans or cultural conservatives, gay rights activists were never concentrated in
the opposite party. As Karol has asked, the question was if and how they could
persuade one party—the Democrats—to represent them. Although the expectations of gay rights groups have changed over time, support of basic gay
rights became a litmus test for Democratic nominees by the 1990s. Delegates

at the 2008 Democratic convention settled for a ticket that defined marriage as heterosexual, but it seems certain they never will again.

Several features of the gay rights transformation fit the patterns of the other cases. National politicians paid little or no attention to gay rights until after gay people organized themselves into political interest groups. Initially, gay activists obtained some concessions by threatening politicians with unwanted publicity. This was frustrating for gay rights groups, who were trying to acquire symbolic support from public figures. Like other groups I have investigated, gay rights groups focused heavily on coalition-building with more mainstream groups, such as labor, civil rights, and feminist groups. More than other groups in this book, gay rights ones were seeking acceptance and legitimacy as a precursor to policy victories. Finally, Democratic politicians supported gay rights mainly in the "blind spot" of the public articulated in *The Party Decides*. Politicians could avoid the taint of being associated with unpopular gay groups by focusing on AIDS funding and hate crimes, which were not seen as gay issues by voters who otherwise thought gay rights signaled an extreme agenda. I do not have enough evidence to show that gay rights groups and their allies collaborated on nominations, but I can show that gay rights groups worked hard to build alliances and that allied interest groups demanded that presidential candidates commit themselves to gay rights. Unlike Farmers' Alliances, they were highly sensitive to the interests of prospective allies.

Tina Fetner argues that antigay ballot propositions and the New Right contributed to gay rights by creating awareness of gay issues, which the media had been neglecting. Conservative policies on gay rights forced the public to confront the issue for the first time.[44] But public opinion, by itself, does not explain the Democratic Party's change. Karol shows that party affiliation explains congressional voting much better than public opinion.[45] Furthermore, President Barack Obama was reluctant to prioritize gay rights even as they gained majority support due to opinion in swing states. It was not public opinion in those states that changed his mind, but the consensus of fellow partisan elites following decades of coalition pressure.

First, I will summarize the relationship between gay rights activists and Democratic candidates up to 1980, when the party first included gay rights in the platform. Second, I document the construction of a gay rights coalition. Two important gay rights groups, NGLTF and NGRL, worked to persuade other kinds of interest groups to openly support gay rights. Other important groups had common enemies and separate but converging issue agendas.

Feminists and teachers unions, who played a growing role in Democratic Party politics, were committed to gay rights, sometimes for different reasons. Third, I examine the effects of AIDS on the politics of gay rights. Finally, I sketch party nominations in the wake of this coalition-building.

Gay Rights in the 1970s

The Democratic Party was a better fit for gay rights activists even before the first wave of cultural conservatives congealed in the late 1970s. Part of the gay rights agenda was civil libertarian; participants wanted to be left alone to experience gay relationships, raise children, and marry who they wanted. But gay rights groups also wanted public services such as specialized health clinics, since many homosexuals felt uncomfortable with traditional health care providers.[46] Later, gay rights groups sought government funding for AIDS research and treatment, setting them in opposition to Republican budget hawks. Not surprisingly, 91 percent of HRC contributions have gone to Democratic candidates since 1991, and other groups have criticized HRC for donating to Republicans at all.[47]

Democrats in the 1970s were far more likely to support the kind of jurisprudence that would protect minority rights, if not gay rights in particular. Gay rights groups were not only seeking legal equality but also used laws to promote a dialog and cultural acceptance. One NGLTF leader said, "compared with [other] groups, far more importance has been attached to using legislation to overcome the long standing media-blackout on gays, and to provide a forum for carrying out our education program. We believe that a large portion of our movement's successful public educational campaign has related to forcing the media to deal with us through debate over our demands (and reaction against this) for legislative and administrative protections."[48] Symbolic support from candidates was important enough that gay rights groups sometimes considered it more important than winning elections. Consultants to a gay rights group in 1988 advised that groups may care more about the legitimacy a politician's support might signal than putting forward an agenda:

> Again, all agreed that gay organizations must decide their goal: is it to elect sympathetic candidates to office or is it to empower or legitimize themselves through the association of candidates and campaigns. Sometimes the two may be consistent goals, but at other times the need for visibility may be inconsistent with the campaign's view of its own best interests. It is much more difficult to build a "movement"

organization when much of your community chooses not to be visible. Being an acknowledged part of a campaign is therefore much more important to the organizational agenda of gay groups [than mainstream interest groups].[49]

Needless to say, Republicans were even less likely to use government to signal social equality for gays than to enforce legal equality.

Though gay rights groups wanted to work with Democrats, national Democrats did not want to reciprocate. Gay rights activists threatened George McGovern's campaign with protest in 1972 to achieve minimal recognition. At one point, the campaign endorsed a "seven point plan" gay rights groups wanted, but later attributed the support to a lone staffer. A group of gay rights activists in New York chained themselves to the furniture to McGovern's headquarters until the McGovern campaign made a positive statement about gay rights. The campaign relented and made the statement, but McGovern's campaign sent an unsigned note on unofficial stationery until the activists demanded official campaign stationery.[50] A gay rights speaker was allowed to address the convention, but only at 2:00 a.m. and after a speaker that linked homosexuality to pedophilia. The platform did not address gay rights. Even Democratic representatives from New York City, which had a sizeable gay population, supported gay rights with considerable trepidation. Bella Abzug and Edward Koch introduced the first gay rights bill proposed in Congress in 1974, but refrained from campaigning for the bill. Abzug called gay rights a "dangerous" issue and even tried to stop gay activist Jean O'Leary from serving as a delegate to the Democratic convention in 1976.[51]

Jimmy Carter, an evangelical Christian, was eager to avoid cultural issues that might divide his winning coalition in 1976. In his campaign, he refused to be photographed with Troy Perry, who ran a church for the gay community in Los Angeles. Carter nonetheless left Perry with the impression that he would sign an executive order against gay discrimination in the civil service.[52] At the convention, gays had at best a nominal presence. Carter's issues coordinator literally locked two lesbian activists out of a regional platform hearing. The party created a gay and lesbian caucus at the convention, but only two delegates attended.[53] One activist optimistically said, "It was in 1940 that the first black person took part in a Democratic Convention. It wasn't until 24 years later that the civil rights act was passed . . . The Democratic Party is not hostile. We've got to work within it."[54] The NGLTF made a presentation to the platform committee, but even sympathetic delegates responded that "it's bad politics to make promises which are obviously impossible to deliver on."[55] The issues coordinator told his future coalitions director, "Midge [Costanza], let's do what we have to do for the gay rights movement—but let's do it after we get to the White House. For God's sakes, don't let us carry this albatross going into the campaign. We have to win this election."[56]

The Carter administration accomplished more for gay rights more than any previous presidential administration,[57] but deliberately kept the issue out of the public spotlight. This was especially vexing to gay rights groups hoping for a public dialog. Carter was the first president in history to accept a gay delegation to the White House, but Costanza had arranged the meeting without Carter's knowledge.[58] In a carefully considered bill to address civil service discrimination, Carter rejected an explicit provision to bar discrimination against gays. Such discrimination was already illegal according to court decisions, so it would have been a merely symbolic concession at high political cost.[59] When asked his opinion about whether gays should be allowed to adopt children or teach in schools, Carter answered, "That's something I'd rather not answer. Look, this is a subject I don't particularly want to involve myself in. I've got enough problems without taking on another." (He eventually opposed California's Briggs Initiative, which barred teachers from being gay or supporting gay rights, in public. Reagan's opposition to the initiative probably helped provide cover.)[60] During the campaign, Carter promised a "White House Conference on Families," but he soon realized that his supporters among the feminist and gay rights communities would confront supporters of more traditional family values. His staffers delayed the conference until the year before reelection and tried to downplay any association with abortion rights or gay rights.[61] Carter resisted appointing O'Leary to the National Commission on International Women's Year and asked, "Does she have to use her title?" as NGLTF coexecutive director.[62]

At this point, gay rights groups were unpopular enough that they could use the threat of protest as a bargaining chip, much like the antiabortion groups who threatened the RNC with a floor fight that year. Thanks in part to the "National Convention Project" with a forty-thousand-dollar budget, eighty openly gay activists attended the convention, most of them in support of Ted Kennedy's challenge to Carter. The project highlighted the potential of the platform to activate and organize gay people in politics and argued that "gay rights would never get anywhere in the Congress until at least one of the major parties put gay rights on its agenda in the form of a platform plank."[63] President Carter's supporters refused to concede until a group of gay rights delegates pointed to committed Ted Kennedy delegates and said, "See those guys with the clipboards? We have the support to make this go. You can give it to us now in the basement of the Mayflower Hotel without the TV cameras, or you can watch us fight it out on the floor of the convention in New York." With reluctant support from the Carter delegates, the party rules were amended to prohibit discrimination against homosexuals in party affairs. At the convention itself, the Democratic platform included sexual orientation in its antidiscrimination plank for the first time.[64] Just as public opinion of homosexuality kept many gay people in the closet, it kept Democratic political ties to gay rights groups in the closet. In both the 1972 and 1980 campaigns, gay rights groups gained recognition by threatening to "out" these ties.

Building a Gay Rights Coalition

Gay rights groups were not going to obtain the kind of party representation they wanted without help. Two of the oldest politically active gay rights groups were NGLTF and GRNL. Repeatedly, they made the case that other groups should support them because of their common enemies. NGRL said to remind civil rights and feminist groups that "anti-gay efforts were once leading opponents of civil rights of Blacks and Women and/or were prominently involved in 'unrespectable' campaigns."[65] Gay rights were not simply seeking to win elections, but to learn from political insiders and gain legitimacy by association.[66] A GRNL leader argued that "It is clear that we must gain official support from various aspects of mainstream America before passage of federal gay civil rights legislation will be achieved. Support from organized labor is essential in this process."[67]

One early ally that helped provide legitimacy before unions offered support was the National Organization for Women (NOW). The NGLTF encouraged its staff and members to adopt a feminist outlook and support the ERA. Records from gay rights groups mention NOW far more often than the reverse. In one letter to its members, it claimed that "the future of gay civil rights legislation rests heavily with the" ERA. Just as "gay civil rights is truly a feminist issue, so too, is the ERA a genuine gay concern." Using a familiar frame, the letter stressed that the opponents of the ERA and gay rights were one and the same.[68] Reviewing a gay male resource book, NGLTF insisted on adopting feminist frames:

> The commitment of NGLTF to feminism should be clearly reflected throughout the book. Some were offended by the way the "Working

with Women" section was written, i.e., "how to attract women to your group" A theme of feminism should be found throughout, perhaps the concept of coalition building between women and men in gay/lesbian groups could replace the thought of attracting women. A feminist theme might also deal with drag, male privilege, competition, etc.

Moreover, the resource book should concede that gay males "are socialized to be sexist . . . despite our realization of how we are oppressed as gay males."[69] Other gay rights organizations, like NGLTF, tend to endorse abortion rights and affirmative action. The Gay and Lesbian Victory Fund, which helps to elect openly gay and lesbian officials, mandates that endorsed candidates be strongly prochoice. At several junctures in the 1970s, feminist groups like NOW offered tangible support for gay rights. When gay rights legislation was introduced in Congress in 1974, NGTLF's met with NOW's director, who was persuaded to appear at the bill's press conference, lobby Congress, and rally national support.[70] NOW delegates even helped gather signatures for gay vice presidential candidate Mel Boozer at the 1980 Democratic convention.[71]

Here and there, gay rights groups persuaded traditional labor unions, still an important Democratic Party bulwark, to support their cause in the 1980s. The GRNL pointed out that unions had been essential to earlier civil rights legislation.[72] By lining up several locals to submit a resolution in favor of gay rights at the American Association for Municipal, State, and County Employees, HRC persuaded the national union to endorse gay rights in 1982. The AFL-CIO first condemned discrimination on the basis of sexual orientation in 1983.[73] New York governor Mario Cuomo agreed to support a domestic partner benefit bill if a major union would support the measure. Ginny Apuzzo, now working for Cuomo, met with the corrections officers' union leader and recognized "common carriers." Since they were required to move to different locations for work, their divorce rates (and therefore their rate of unmarried partnerships) were high. Once the corrections officer union supported the bill, other unions fell in line and Cuomo supported the bill.[74]

Perhaps most importantly at the national level, teachers' unions generally supported gay rights. The National Education Association (NEA) could point to many instances where it was ahead of the class on gay rights, and was recognized as such by NGLTF.[75] The NEA supported gay teachers at an early stage and eventually recommended antidiscrimination contacts to local branches.[76] A growing presence in Democratic Party politics, NEA had an average of four thousand high-turnout voters in every congressional district, and constituted the largest labor organization represented at the Democratic Convention.[77] The NEA offered important resources to its allies. In 1981, for example, it hosted meetings of gay rights and civil liberties groups (including NOW, NGLTF, ACLU, and NAACP) to strategize against the New Right's Family Protection Act. The NEA produced a policy paper on the bill and offered to host future meetings to oppose it.[78] Like civil rights groups and unions, teachers' unions and gay rights groups shared a common enemy. The New Right worked to curtail what many teachers considered their control over curriculum, including sex education, and privacy after school hours, including sexual orientation.[79] The second largest teacher's association in America, the American Federation of Teachers (AFT), also fought antigay initiatives as the gateway to a New Right agenda that threatened many of the union's positions.[80]

The Implication of AIDS for Party Politics

AIDS was a game-changer for gay rights groups in politics. First, it provided gay people with much more media presence. Second, many gay people were unable to legally make end-of-life decisions for their partners and therefore had new reasons to become open about their sexuality. Once out of the closet, they were more invested in protecting their rights.[81] Third, gay rights groups became more integrated into liberal coalitions for health and human services, including public health advocates. The NGLTF even decided to prioritize AIDS funding over gay rights legislation.[82] A former executive director recalls that government services had been "much lower on the agenda. You didn't see gay organizations advocating around Medicaid. You didn't see them advocating around Medicare. You didn't see them advocating around social security. And suddenly those were very big issues in our lives." Exit polls in 1992 revealed that gay respondents were more concerned with health care than any other issue.[83]

The NGLTF helped to legitimize gay rights by gaining support from mainstream organizations on AIDS, including the U.S. Conference of Mayors. In 1984, NGLTF lobbied the conference to endorse gay and lesbian protection and secure the first federal funds for AIDS education at the local level.[84] The conference supported these proposals unanimously. Internal documents of the NGLTF read that "The open support of a fellow governor or mayor will have far more impact on the thinking of these politicians than our making the very same arguments."[85]

The Triangle Institute published a strategy paper in 1988 arguing that

AIDS also provided a "dog whistle" for politicians who wanted to support gay rights. At the time, support for gay rights could brand politicians as extreme liberals or lead to rumors about their orientation, but support for AIDS funding would not. The euphemism of "human rights" did not work for gay rights groups, but "all agreed that AIDS allows candidates to address an issue of concern to the gay and lesbian community in a way that is acceptable to the larger community—scientific, public health, education, parental."[86] The Ryan White Act of 1990, which created the largest federal AIDS program, provided further camouflage for politicians to signal support. While AIDS was often regarded as a homosexual disease, the public face of the law was Ryan White, a young teenager who was infected with HIV during hemophilia treatment.

By the 1980s, gay rights groups were strongly integrated with a broad liberal coalition. Many echoed AFT in calling antigay policies the first in a string of attacks on American liberalism. AIDS added public health groups to feminists and teachers' unions as reliable coalition allies. Investing in other Democratic Party policies arguably softened their criticism of Democratic politicians who pursued different priorities. As the next section shows, perhaps criticism was necessary to spur Democrats into action.

Gaining Party Recognition

Unlike other issue transformations, I lack documentation showing that gay rights groups coordinated with their allies during Democratic primaries, or that prominent endorsements had a domino effect on likeminded activists. However, evidence shows that allied interest groups insisted that nominees support gay rights.

Feminist groups prioritized gay rights as a criterion for their endorsement in 1984. After soliciting the views of state and local chapters, NOW used gay rights as a litmus test on its questionnaire and in-person interviews. While California senator Alan Cranston was the best candidate on both feminist and gay rights issues, many members thought that Mondale was the best of the "electable" candidates.[87] NOW complained that Mondale's main rival, Colorado senator Gary Hart, had not endorsed the gay rights bill (he finally did in April of 1984) and evaded their questions. The feminist organization's president endorsed Mondale in February of 1984, highlighting his commitment to "millions of lesbians and gay men who will no longer tolerate second class citizenship. Mondale has a long history of support for civil rights for everyone. His support for an end to discrimination against lesbians and gay men was an important factor in our endorsement, and we are pleased that he has joined us in supporting" a gay rights bill. NOW boasted that it had worked with the Mondale campaign ahead of time to ensure that gays would be represented at the convention.[88] Another feminist group, the National Women's Political Caucus, dubbed the ERA and gay rights "our issues" at a strategy meeting for the 1984 platform.[89]

The election of 1984 broke new ground as Democratic candidates espoused gay rights to stay on good terms with the party coalition. The nominee, Walter Mondale, became the first to have spoken at a gay rights group meeting (an HRC fundraiser in 1982), though he veered from the script to omit any use of the word "gay," not even to say Gay Rights National Lobby.[90] He became the first Democratic presidential candidate to hire a consultant for gay issues and voters.[91] Among the other Democratic contenders in 1984, only John Glenn offered any opposition to gay rights, saying that civil rights should not cover "areas of personal behavior." In response, his New York campaign manager quit.[92] In 1992, a number of Democratic presidential candidates in 1992 openly discussed gay rights.[93]

Gay rights groups would have to wait before Democratic presidential candidates called attention to their issues during and after the general election. Activists complained that Obama was elusive in the presidential campaign of 2008. Sensing evangelical dissatisfaction with McCain, Obama met with megachurch pastor Rick Warren and defined marriage as between a man and a woman.[94] As California voters considered "Proposition 8" to repeal the state supreme court's decision in favor of gay marriage, a robocall quoted what Obama told Warren.[95] Obama's longtime political strategist David Axelrod claimed that Obama had always supported full marriage, but opposed it for political reasons with his counseling, writing that "opposition to gay marriage was particularly strong in the black church, and as he ran for higher office, he grudgingly accepted the counsel of more pragmatic folks like me."[96]

Militant gay rights activists were upset with Obama's perceived lethargy. Public approval of gay marriage increased substantially while Obama was president. By 2012, two-thirds of Democratic voters and a majority of independent voters supported gay marriage before the president publicized any support. The president, at best, moved with the public but not ahead of it. A hate crimes bill was passed in 2009, the first federal legislation specifically designed to protect homosexuals. The same year, Obama held the first gay pride celebration at the White House. But repeal of "Don't Ask, Don't Tell" (DADT) was passed only after enormous pressure from militant gay rights groups. Defense Secretary Robert Gates had advised Obama to wait until a study on the matter was released in December 2010. Waiting that long pro-vided the Democratic Congress little time before an incoming Republican Congress would block repeal. To press for immediate action, activists dis-rupted several public appearances and fundraisers. More than 150,000 activ-ists converged on the White House lawn in 2009, even though HRC and openly gay Massachusetts representative Barney Frank told activists to call it off. [97] Members of "GetEqual" received a lot of attention as they were arrested or dragged out of a fundraiser Obama held for California senator Barbara Boxer. A twenty-four-hour cycle of bloggers instantly responding to the news posed new challenges for elected leaders. Gay blogs disseminated stories of protest like this, often leading mainstream sources to publish the stories. The DADT legislation was introduced in May and passed by the House, ultimately passing the Senate before the next session.

One writer argues that Obama's subsequent decision not to enforce the Defense of Marriage Act (DOMA) would have been untenable without the repeal of DADT, because the policy implied that the government had a ratio-nal basis for antigay discrimination.[98] Pressure also mounted for Obama to endorse gay marriage as more states began to legalize gay marriage. At an HRC appearance in 2009, he promised to end DADT, but refused to endorse gay marriage in referendums in Maine and North Carolina. The inner circle of Obama's campaign knew that supporting gay marriage would help with young voters and donations, but hurt in several swing states, including Iowa, Ohio, North Carolina, and Virginia.[99]

Obama announced his support for gay marriage not because opinion changed in these states, but because of growing support in his own party. An outside organization took the first step by recruiting prominent officeholders to support gay marriage in the party platform. "Freedom to Marry" almost immediately obtained support from the convention chair, House speaker, and twenty-two senators. Obama repeatedly told reporters that his ideas on gay marriage were evolving, but that he refused to make history at any par-ticular interview. Privately, he said he did not want to go against his party on the issue.[100] His timeline was forcefully truncated when his unprepared vice president revealed his position on *Meet the Press* in May. After the interview, Axelrod dubiously claimed that this had been the administration's position all along. Journalistic accounts show that Obama did not want to defy the leading party members who pledged themselves to Freedom to Marry's platform.[101]

Even after public opinion turned a corner on gay marriage, the issue was ultimately resolved in the courts with judges appointed by Democrats. Democratic presidents were able to appoint sympathetic justices on the Court of Appeals and Supreme Court with little public fanfare. All Clinton and Obama appointments to the Supreme Court voted to uphold gay rights in anti-sodomy law, DOMA, and gay marriage cases. Of seven Supreme Court justices appointed by Republicans since 1980, only three (O'Connor, Kennedy, and Souter) sometimes supported gay rights. After DOMA was struck down in 2013, circuit courts struck down state gay marriage bans in three out of four cases, convincing the Supreme Court that the country was ready to overturn all statewide bans in 2015. Combining the twelve justices in these four circuit court cases, all six Democratic appointments supported gay marriage, while only two of six Republican appointments did so. Judicial appointments demonstrate that the Democratic presidents honored their commitments to gay rights groups when they could push rights along in the public's blind spot.

In summary, gay rights groups gained some support from the Democratic Party on their own with donations, campaign support, and protest. But Democratic candidates tried not to call attention to their position. In fact, Carter and Mondale avoided using the word "gay" at all. In time, gay rights became a merit badge rather than an albatross. During the years in between, gay rights groups spent much of their time nurturing strong relationships with reliable party groups. Obama's historic announcement to support gay marriage was prompted not just by changing public opinion, but by a growing consensus of elites in his party, nudged along for decades by the party's component groups.

This chapter reaffirms that the book's central arguments apply to contemporary as well as historical cases of party transformation. Both Populists and gay rights groups realized that political parties were valuable tools for pursuing a policy agenda. Populists, however, took a shortcut and created a political party before potentially supportive groups forged lasting ties. They didn't build a coalition that might have kept the Democratic Party on Bryan's trajectory. Gay rights groups, in contrast, realized that they were unlikely to succeed in politics until they first gained recognition from groups with more legitimacy, like unions and feminists. In viable coalitions, groups portray a common enemy's victory over an ally as a slippery slope, where they can only end at the bottom. In fragile coalitions, like that of farmers and the unions in the 1890s, groups do not experience an attack on another group in the coalition as a threat to themselves. Without that sense of unity, they find that they cannot change parties on their own.

Conclusion

In a country with two major parties, it helps a lot to have one of them committed to your goals. Party change is not the only route to change, but it is a good way to get it, if you can. Among other advantages, parties can disseminate talking points to the general public and limit voter choice in the general election between two package deals, one of which contains your agenda. This book argues that the first step for groups is to unite their members behind a common set of goals as well as those of a broader coalition. The second is to put their members to work nominating candidates in the party it chooses. Let us review the evidence for each step in turn.

Coalition-Building

One of the most dramatic and well-studied shifts in party transformations is the Democratic Party's support for civil rights. Before World War II, both parties were composed of groups that impeded the pursuit of civil rights. Naturally, civil rights interest groups wanted to change the configuration of groups in the parties. Before they could change a party, they needed to be part of a larger coalition, and to be part of that coalition, they needed to change themselves. Due to a history of discrimination, African Americans were reluctant to ally themselves politically with white labor unions, and without their support, they were isolated in the Democratic Party. The nation's foremost civil rights group, the NAACP, had rejected a labor-based strategy in the 1930s, but reversed its organizational decline by pursuing one in the 1940s. The CIO was able to use workers gathered for nonpolitical reasons to pursue political objectives, providing blacks with the most potent ally they had since Reconstruction. The politically ambitious CIO, despite racism in its own ranks, thought black voters could help defeat an opposing party faction—

conservative southern Democrats. Both organizations developed constructive ways of improving relations with each other in pursuit of an alliance. When they were active in party nominations, they were able to shift the balance of power.

Cultural conservatives, as with civil rights supporters, had to invite themselves into a political party before it took up their concerns. But before they could compel change in the Republican Party, they needed to rise above sectarianism and organizational rivalries. Religious leaders and denominations, like civil rights and labor, were groups that operated according to their own institutional incentives that militated against cooperation. Upset by the cultural changes of the 1960s, many important religious groups took steps to reduce their historical animosities and began speaking with a relatively unified voice. They also shed their aversion to politics and began working with political operatives who shared their religious attitudes, the informal network known as the "New Right." Like civil rights groups, the New Right wanted to transform their party, and found an ally with an extensive network of people and resources drawn together largely for nonpolitical reasons.

Gay rights groups also pursued the right alliances. They persuaded other minority groups like feminists and civil rights groups to support their cause, which helped them frame their issue as a civil rights issue. With the emergence of AIDS, they formed new partnerships with city governments and public health groups who wanted the government to take stronger steps to address the disease. One might also say they were dealt a more favorable hand when teachers' associations organized PACs and began collective bargaining. By the 1980s teachers' unions surpassed other unions in influence at Democratic conventions, and viewed New Right attacks on gay rights as a long-term threat to their members.

A similar process preceded each successful transformation. Groups found other groups with common issue concerns and complementary strategic advantages. Each of the successful transformations capitalized on existing groups that were able to reach nonpolitical as well as political audiences. Unions and churches both had door-to-door canvassing and phone trees of people networked for nonpolitical reasons. While both the CIO and NAACP were broadly supportive of the New Deal, they were also able to help each other where it counted. The NAACP could help the CIO unionize workers, register black voters, and legitimize its civil rights program. The CIO could reverse NAACP's flagging membership and funding, and provide the NAACP with the "political muscle" it needed. Theological conservatives provided the volunteers and voters that the New Right was lacking, while the New Right knew how to start political organizations and garner media attention. Political causes also helped to raise money for the ministries of religious leaders like Jerry Falwell and Pat Robertson. Teachers' unions had an interest in working with gay rights groups to fight a common enemy. They opposed the New Right's attempts to dismiss gay teachers, control school curriculums, or provide tax credits to religious schools.

Populists, through their failure, demonstrated the need to form viable coalitions. While they faded for numerous reasons, most accounts agree that they did not find committed allies. Rural reformers and urban workers had no longstanding relationship and Farmers' Alliances quixotically hoped that a political party could bridge the divide in a short time. Silver inflation was the most publicized and best-funded issue in their agenda, but also the least likely to resonate with workers. State-level Populist candidates mimed support for civil rights in the South, but black farmers did not believe most of them because they had no history of working as allies. In contrast, the CIO and NAACP developed significant organizational infrastructure to improve relations years before their goals were combined in a party platform.

The NAACP, the New Right, and gay rights groups also struck alliances when the iron was hot. The CIO, evangelical churches, and teachers' unions were gaining new members and resources just as the alliances were taking shape. In contrast, the unsuccessful Populists had no iron to strike other than disgruntled farmers and silver miners. Unions did not yet have protective labor laws and recently suffered severe setbacks. Southern politicians manipulated or disenfranchised blacks just as soon as Populists made common cause with them. Even the hot iron of angry farmers cooled down in 1896 when the economy recovered.

We should not let the similarities blind us to the complexity of history. Each coalition faced different preexisting political configurations, institutional constraints, and technological opportunities. Unions and civil rights groups, unlike cultural conservatives, had the dangerous task of fighting just for the right to vote in some states. Civil Rights groups wanted to join a party partly that, until recently, had been dominated by their fiercest opponents; cultural conservatives and gay rights groups confronted a party that merely hid their association or straddled their demands. The Christian Right was not a dominant national organization like the CIO, but a cluster of likeminded organizations. Post McGovern-Fraser groups also had new technology for reaching a broader audience. These differences do not undermine the fundamental process at work—groups formed coalitions that were capable of transforming parties, mostly without the help of politicians, and adapting their positions to these coalitions.

One might imagine that politicians have a vested interest in making sure that two supportive groups work well together. Occasionally, we have evidence of politicians serving as brokers. California senator Cranston, for example, invited both gay rights groups and civil rights groups to his office to discuss strategies to defeat conservatives. Michigan senator Phil Hart helped form an interest group to maintain good relations between environmentalists and labor unions—although the organization did not last long. But more often than not, groups were forging ties long before politicians. Neither Franklin Roosevelt nor the assorted conservative politicians of the 1970s put in the time to construct the new coalitions on the horizon. One might also imagine groups choosing their allies based on the prevailing ideology existing before the alliance. Most of the groups in this book incorporated ideology selectively, seemingly changing with their allies rather than changing with the pundits. For example, the NAACP changed its position on labor issues while conservative religious denominations changed their positions on working with other denominations, both at the moment when it was most likely to facilitate their growth.

Riker argues that given that there is no natural equilibrium for party positions, "Outcomes are the consequences . . . of those who manipulate agenda, formulate and reformulate questions, generate 'false' issues, etc., in order to exploit the disequilibrium of tastes for their own advantage. And just what combination of institutions, tastes, and artistry will appear in any given political system is, it seems to me, as unpredictable as poetry."[1] Although parties are shaped by multiple trajectories that are difficult to sort, the prevailing equilibrium is more predictable than poetry. Civil rights groups and cultural conservatives were able to succeed because their groups had symbiotic interests with other groups that were becoming more powerful, thanks to recent historical changes. These common interests were identified by far-seeing observers as they were happening and to others only in hindsight.

Influencing Nominations

The second step in party transformation is for coalitions of groups to change parties by nominating candidates. Democratic officeholders did not support civil rights simply because they had African American constituents, as is often thought. Officeholders deferred to southern Democrats even though southern states were becoming less important in national elections. Nor were white working-class Democrats natural supporters of civil rights. Rather, the change in the Democratic Party began with changes in the interests of groups composing the party. The black-blue alliance quickly became a force at Democratic Party conventions, pushing for civil rights platforms and presidential nominees. The alliance bore fruit at the 1948 Democratic Convention, which marked the transformation of racial equality from political taboo to a litmus test. In the years after 1948, labor unions and their liberal allies would not let nominees retreat from the positions taken that year. Reflecting the new party equilibrium, serious presidential contenders distanced themselves from the southern wing of the party. Ambitious politicians, notably John Kennedy and Lyndon Johnson, did not lead this change; rather, they evolved their positions on civil rights as necessary to gain the support of powerful groups within the party. Their counterparts in the 1980s committed themselves to gay rights in meetings with important groups like NOW and the National Women's Political Caucus.

Republican Party change on cultural issues follows the same outline. Groups with their own dynamic—religious organizations—developed grievances and a political agenda independently of party politicians. The Republican Party suited their culturally conservative agenda better, but Republicans did not often welcome cultural conservatives with open arms. In fact, party politicians mostly obstructed their rise to prominence in both the national party and state parties. Even Reagan did not approach conservative churches for support until church leaders organized into political groups, and straddled some of their demands at the 1980 convention. Many party politicians were skeptical or dismissive of the votes they could provide. Cultural conservatives transformed the party instead by threatening politicians and populating party meetings that no one else wanted to attend. Both presidential nominees and congressional leaders switched positions on key cultural issues to meet with the approval of the new powers in the party. All but one of the leading contestants for the Republican nomination from Ronald Reagan to Donald Trump changed their position on abortion at some point before seeking the nomination.

The differences between civil rights and cultural conservatism was more one of technique than one of substance. In successful party transformations, politicians had to privately build trust with group leaders years before elections. Stevenson met with the NAACP, Mondale met with NOW, and both presidents Bush met with the prominent evangelicals on Doug Wead's list. Each group inquired about the candidates' views on their litmus test issues, including civil rights, gay rights, and their faith. In the 1940s and 1950s, the CIO and ADA made sure to elect delegates to the national convention. In the 1980s and beyond, the New Right and cultural conservatives ran primary challenges to their opponents under the post-McGovern-Fraser system of nominations. Cultural conservatives took over state parties and provided loyal but electable candidates with momentum in early primary states. They also added direct mail, electronic broadcasting, and eventually online communication to their political arsenal. The one Republican to lead the invisible primary without taking culturally conservative positions on abortion and gay rights, Rudy Giuliani, failed to gain a following in such states.

Once again, the Populist calamity sheds light on the success of other groups. They failed to control the election of 1896, which might have been a turning point in the Democratic Party. In the years following the 1892 election, state populist groups diverged on whether to run fusion tickets with Republicans in the South. If they ran as Democrats, they risked losing the support of black farmers, and might not have been able to displace Bourbon opponents in the party. But by allying with Republicans, they reduced their ability to influence national nominations. At the national level, Republicans were the principal opponents of their agenda and unlikely to listen to southern party delegates. Meanwhile, the ABL was able to exert strong influence on the national Democratic Party by controlling southern Democratic delegations to support free silver, but not other Populist positions. After Bryan's nomination, a third-party challenge could not hope to differentiate itself. As the third party faded, Populists might have worked to maintain and broaden Bryan's trajectory in the Democratic Party, incorporating both rural and urban concerns. Instead, their members dispersed between Democrats, Republicans, and Socialists, not exercising controlling influence in any one of them.

General election calculations were not the most compelling reason for parties to change on civil rights or cultural issues, though here and there, groups effectively threatened to sit out an election. In the civil rights transformation, white Southerners had been a longstanding Democratic constituency and provided the party with reliable strength in Congress and the Electoral College. Democrats could not be sure how many votes they would obtain from the largely disenfranchised African American population. As President

Johnson allegedly lamented, the Civil Rights Act of 1964 would sink the party's fortunes in the South for a generation. Nationally, Republicans clearly needed more votes in the 1970s, but party insiders resisted finding them in the controversial Christian Right. In Iowa and some other states, the Republican Party was competitive statewide before cultural conservatives played a role in state parties. In those states, cultural moderation made as much sense for winning elections as cultural conservatism. But only cultural conservatism would do once cultural conservatives gained control of the state parties.

For much of the twentieth century, Americans chose between parties that were liberal on some issues and conservative on others, according to current understandings of those terms. The Democratic Party of the Great Depression consisted of liberal Northerners who favored both civil rights and New Deal economics, as well as Southerners who opposed civil rights at every turn. The Republicans were led by economic conservatives and moderates who still hoped to regain the allegiance of African Americans. Today, the parties have sorted on all counts. Nearly everyone recognizes the Democratic Party supports liberal economic policies, civil rights, abortion rights, and gay rights. Meanwhile, the Republican Party is no longer just the party of business, but the party of cultural conservatives and white Southerners. Entrenched politicians did not make these changes because they independently decided this would gain their party more votes. In fact, they resisted these changes, and fell in line because new groups made it excessively costly to oppose them, mostly during nominating contests. Voters elect a party nominee in the general election, but external groups dominate the process by which parties select these nominees. The average voter fails to observe, let alone fight against, the lurking organizations shaping party nominations.

The Role of Ideology in Party Transformation

An ambitious task for future research is to further explore the relationship between groups and ideology. The familiar objection is that people have ideas about their interests, so parsing the two is difficult. I argue that ideology is not a strict constraint on group coalitions, but that group coalitions are a strict constraint on party transformation. Ideology might be one factor in a group's choice to work with other groups, but so are money, membership, comparative advantages, and personality conflicts.

To review, consider the civil rights transformation. The most powerful group examined, the CIO, was both ideological and self-interested. Its ideas of a full-employment economy, economic justice, and racial equality inspired many of the members, recruiters, and groups allied with it. At the same time, the CIO nurtured its own interests as it sought to unionize more workplaces, facing stiff competition from other unions. Its private negotiations for health care arguably undermined public support for universal health care, as Schlozman points out.[2] Much of the rank and file worked for the CIO for higher pay, benefits, and job security, and cared little for ideology. They simply contributed to its political goals in the process of protecting their jobs. The NAACP was consistently motivated by the issue of racial equality, but its decision to expand beyond purely racial issues into working-class issues was motivated largely by the need to be a competitive interest group. The *National Review* (*NR*) and affiliated groups were the first to admit the limits of "fusionism." If fusionism did not dominate *NR* organizations, it is even less plausible that it dominated religious organizations for whom scripture came first. There is little evidence that fusionism anticipated the Christian Right or even the prolife position of the conservative movement. In the case of cultural conservatives, politics became a strategy for broadcasters to expand their audience.

Ideology could influence parties in many different ways. It is possible that interest group employees rise to the top of the organization because their beliefs happen to synchronize with group interests. Groups then influence parties. In this case, the story would be "groups adopt ideologies that suit their interests" rather than "ideology changes groups." It is also possible that intellectuals persuaded group leaders to adopt their intellectual positions, but the biographical accounts of Walter White, Walter Reuther, Sidney Hillman, and Phil Murray show them to be highly malleable. Still another possibility is that ideological pundits unify the mass public behind their constellation of issue positions or rationale for those positions. Interest group leaders then have to follow them to avoid splitting their natural base of support. There is some evidence that the NAACP was attuned to the pro-labor ideology of its "Youth Councils," but looking at their broader membership, NAACP leaders were more pro-labor than its followers. Survey data on theological conservatives before the Christian Right is sparse, but they appear as liberal on economic issues as the general public and only slightly more conservative on cultural issues.

Although this book shows that groups tie issues together for reasons other than ideology, it does not show that groups create pundit ideologies or that pundits base their ideologies on group alliances. Existing pundits might stitch issues together by observing what issues could bind a winning party coalition. Alternatively, pundits might rise in prominence when their ideology fits the new party order, without bringing that order about. Perhaps future research will explore these questions.

I think of ideology as a bundle of issue positions on a shelf. Groups seem to privilege a particular bundle as they advance the interests of group leaders and members, ignoring the philosophical rationale when inconvenient. Many intellectually compelling bundles of ideas stay on the shelf if they do not also fit the interests of coalitions that gain control of party nominations. Ideologies without parties are forgotten by most people, but a new coalition might take an old bundle off the shelf or construct a new one.

Looking Ahead

It was not inevitable that each group would end up in the party they support today; it was the result of moving parts reacting to each other in the face of historical contingencies. Are moving parts in the works right now? In the Republican Party, many party leaders have tried to reduce the influence of cultural conservatives and, more recently, the Tea Party. Most admit they have not had much success. Former New Jersey governor Whitman has formed "It's My Party, Too" (IMP-PAC) to support Republicans who are moderate on issues such as abortion rights, the environment, and gay rights. She has not made much progress because moderates are less apt to become activists on most issues. "We need extreme moderates" and "radical centrists," she said. Unfortunately for her, there are few preexisting networks to draw upon.[3] Without them, cultural conservatives will add momentum to their preferred candidates in Republican presidential primaries.

Likewise, Republicans have had mixed success in fighting Tea Party efforts to nominate pure conservatives over "establishment Republicans" or RINOs (Republicans in Name Only). Former House Speaker Boehner openly complained that Tea Partiers were preventing the party from winning. At the 2012 Republican National Convention in Tampa, Republicans made several attempts to roll back Tea Party influence. Romney strategist Arthur Ginsberg proposed shifting control of convention committee selection to the nominee's campaign, which would have restricted the ability of grassroots activists to vote on the party platform and convention rules as delegates. Conservative delegates believed that Republican leaders were paving the way for platforms that reflect the nominee's (more moderate) strategy, rather than what state party activists want. This reform might have passed but for a hurricane in

Tampa that weekend, which gave state-level activists a chance to organize against the proposal. South Carolina delegate McKissick forwarded the proposal to other party activists and 2008 vice presidential nominee Sarah Palin posted it to her Facebook page. Other delegates were inundated with complaints by phone and email. Supporters of Ginsberg's proposal, concerned about Romney's favorability among grassroots GOP activists, backed down.[4]

The 2016 nominating contest provides conflicting evidence on the role of groups in the party. On the Democratic side, Hillary Clinton towered over Vermont senator Bernie Sanders in endorsements from both party politicians and interest groups, including NEA, HRC, NOW, Emily's List, and the National Women's Political Caucus.[5] And while Sanders generated a surprisingly successful grassroots movement, Clinton ultimately won more popular votes and delegates, even without the superdelegates who pledged their support before the contest. The Democratic nomination was a straightforward test between a candidate with group and party support, and a candidate who bypasses both to appeal directly to voters. The candidate with group and party support won.

The Republican nominating contest, however, was far more complicated. It confounds conventional theories of frontloaded primaries as well as theories of group-centered parties. In 2015, no candidate had enough endorsements to indicate widespread support among coalitions in the Republican Party. Even by 2016, groups differed with politicians on who to support. In the language of Cohen et al., the Republican Party didn't decide.[6] Marco Rubio received more endorsements from current officeholders, but Ted Cruz won the support of many of the cultural conservative leaders discussed in this book, including James Dobson, Steve Deace, and Bob Vander Plaats. Meanwhile, casino mogul Trump appealed directly to the voters through the media with little support from groups or parties. Among evangelical Christians, he performed far better among irregular churchgoers, who are less culturally conservative, and only held a slight lead over Cruz among weekly attendees. Trump won the nomination despite his unconventional views on foreign policy and economics.[7] As party scholar Seth Masket has argued, many Republican politicians refused to endorse Trump even after he won numerous primaries and even the nomination.[8] His comments on race and religion severely undermined the hopes of party leaders that wanted to broaden the party's appeals after 2012.

Trump's rise is so dramatic that both pundits and political scientists are discussing the possibility of Republican Party realignment. Based on my findings, I would not count on it anytime soon. Primaries are low-information contests where groups can usually exploit voter inattention to nominate a candidate acceptable to their coalition. Normally, organized groups rush in to message their supporters about their favored candidates. Cultural conservatives have had the opportunity to create early frontrunners in Iowa, South Carolina, and the states voting on Super Tuesday. Trump's dominance of the news media meant that he could provide that message himself, but that doesn't meant that future candidates can replicate his success. He depends on a combination of personality, celebrity, and willingness to embrace controversy that is rare in politics. Voters not normally invested in primaries have followed his sensational media persona. Candidates whose positions contravene party orthodoxy most often fade away. See, for example, Giuliani, a prochoice candidate in an antiabortion party.

Trump's nomination does not undermine the claim that cultural conservatives changed the direction of the Republican Party. Trump conforms to the party transformation fought for by cultural conservatives decades earlier; he opposed gay marriage and reversed his earlier support for abortion rights. He even received an early endorsement from Jerry Falwell, Jr in the primaries. Most of the other Republicans running in 2016 adhered to the cultural conservative transformation as well. Out of seventeen candidates, only George Pataki's nonstarter candidacy was prochoice. Most also opposed gay rights, though some (not Trump) said that gay marriage is settled law. Rubio's campaign needlessly antagonized born-again Christians with an email quoting Russell Moore, declaring, "I would say that Ted Cruz is leading in the 'Jerry Falwell' wing, Marco Rubio is leading the 'Billy Graham' wing and Trump is leading the Jimmy Swaggart wing."[9] Rubio's campaign was faulted for pigeonholing Charismatics—a majority of born-again Christians by some counts[10]—and tying them to Swaggart, the disgraced religious broadcaster. In the general election, many cultural conservative leaders, including Dobson and Ralph Reed, stood by Trump even after a controversial lewd video was released, citing his power to appoint sympathetic judges.[11]

It is not clear what groups would carry Trump's distinctive economic and foreign policy agenda into the future. Which interest groups aligned with the Republicans would advocate for protectionism or withdrawal from world affairs? Maybe new groups will emerge, but in past transformations, groups spent years building influence with their allies until their impact on the party became real. Candidates might adopt Trump's more strident rhetoric against Islamic terrorists, since it does not antagonize existing groups in the party. Adopting

Trump's position in immigration is trickier, as it divides business and free-market groups against many anti-immigrant Tea Party groups. But Trump's positions on immigration and terrorism amount to differences in degree, not differences in kind. It is much harder to adopt his truly heterodox positions. In 1994, the House Republicans' "Contract with America" could adopt H. Ross Perot's concern for balanced budgets, but not his protectionism.

To use another historical example, Trump supporters resemble the profile the New Right ascribed to supporters of George Wallace, who they were unable to harness for their own party agenda. In a paper discussing a coalition between conservatives and Wallace supporters, CFNM wrote they were:

> [Less concerned with] unrestrained free market economics [and] more concerned with retaining social structures that maintain social cohesion. . . . Social conservatives have a basic animosity against social control by the upper classes in general, which includes the economic conservatives. . . . Their talk is rougher and many racist statements they make in their bars and homes reflect the rhetoric of a frustrated and unrepresented voting block that is not more capable of a more articulate vocalization.[12]

Like Trump supporters, Wallace's supporters were economically moderate and socially conservative. The hostility of both to what is now called political correctness, along with their contempt for protestors on the left, show strong parallels. But CFNM's failure to merge conservatives and Wallace supporters might confront any would-be Trumps of the future. There were no groups that organized Wallace supporters and maintained their interest over time.

Without organized groups, it is difficult to sustain a transformation, even with a sitting president trying to leave behind a legacy. One of the most effective presidents of the twentieth century, Franklin Roosevelt, was unable to purge his own party of MCs that opposed the New Deal. It seems unlikely that President Trump could succeed where Roosevelt failed, when protectionism and isolationism have less support in the party than had the New Deal. Two decades later, Eisenhower encouraged the development of modern Republicans who made peace with the New Deal, only to see the party drift in the direction of the Goldwater wing of the party.[13]

If future Republican nominees forego group support to increase votes from unorganized voters, then Trump can claim credit for party transformation. But it is far too early to claim what future Republican presidential nominations will hold. Noel points out that the Internet, social media, and numerous presidential debates before Iowa might have changed the nature of presidential primaries.[14] It would not be the first time groups were confounded by new electoral processes; in 1972 and 1976, they had not yet found a way to win nominations in the wake of the McGovern-Fraser reforms. But by 1980, they knew how the system worked and adopted strategies that effectively "beat reform."[15] If new electoral strategies are changing how nominations work, it seems likely that the most organized groups in politics will master these strategies in due time, as they did with the McGovern-Fraser reforms.

Implications for Democracy

Many readers will be interested not only in how parties changed but whether they should have changed in that manner. Parties are a powerful asset for accomplishing policy objectives, so how parties respond to competing demands for their attention is a central problem in the study of American democracy. Most twentieth-century accounts of political parties treat them as bulwarks of democracy. Schattschneider claimed long ago that democracy is "unthinkable," save in terms of parties. Only parties can mobilize the majority will against interest groups with proper regard for the rights of minorities.[16] More recently, Burnham concurred that only parties can "generate countervailing collective power on behalf of the many individually powerless against the relatively few who are individually—or organizationally—powerful."[17] And Hershey's textbook on political parties claims that "the party has been the form of political organization most available to citizens who lack the resources to influence public decisions using other means."[18] Assorted political luminaries in the mid-twentieth century, echoed by the American Political Science Association, called for ideological parties. Only by having clear differences between parties would voters grasp the choices at the ballot box.[19]

In the preceding chapters, groups without party representation were shown to obtain policies they wanted by transforming a party. Did this bring America closer to the ideal of universal representation? They accomplished change through superior organization and coalition building, not by persuading the median voter. No one was keeping voters away from the polls, but intense activists exploited other voters' inattention to politics. Political candidates, the public face of parties and trustees of the people, were not the agents of party transformation and the resulting policy changes.

   Although the representation of political minorities is normally celebrated by supporters of democracy, their entry into the parties are accompanied by a shift in party positions away from the median voter. Some democratic theorists might be willing to provide intense minorities with more representation than indifferent majorities, weighing passionate voters' preferences more heavily than a pure one-person, one-vote system.[20] Their vision was, in fact, realized by civil rights groups and cultural conservatives, though it took years or even decades. But for other democratic theorists, my research suggests an opaque political system that belies pretensions to pure representation. As Olson lamented, democracy in practice is not a one-person, one-vote system because not all individuals have the same incentive to organize.[21] Narrow, intense groups have most other groups at a disadvantage.

   Let's call the issue positions that are grouped together party agenda "bundles." To repeat Arrow's profound but frequently overlooked point, many different majority coalitions are possible, so that more than one bundle of issue positions could win elections for a party.[22] Party leaders are often content with their existing bundle even if a newer one might obtain more votes. New party bundles are formed in part by the kind of transformations discussed in this book, with groups fitting together separately from politicians, sometimes at the expense of general election votes.

   In general elections, voters have little choice but to choose between nominees that reflect the bundles of some voters and groups better than others. Some people are forced to vote for one or more cherished issues along with a larger bundle they may not agree with. If the bundles are an outcome of a fair nominating process where everyone gets her turn, it is hard to complain. And nominations have been formally in the hands of primary voters since the McGovern-Fraser reforms first put in practice in 1972. One might assume that politicians are forced to take positions that enable them to win primary votes before the nomination and then general election voters in November. It's a sanguine view of democracy in that politicians and parties need to be responsive to voters in order to win elections.

   If this book is correct, however, unrepresentative groups can force parties to change by nominating candidates that are less responsive to voters. Party bundles are less a response to general electoral pressures than the influence of organizations in nominations and elections. While power would be technically in the hands of the voters, organized groups have ways to win nominations for candidates more responsive to them. *In this case, parties offer bundles in the general election that most voters had no say in constructing.* Therefore, which groups gain access to parties gets to the heart of representation, because parties delimit who voters can choose in the general election. If unpopular minorities can force parties to cater to their preferences, extreme groups can gain representation at the expense of median voters as well.

Take the tradeoffs the Catholic Church has to make as an example. By happenstance, Boston's bishop Bernard Law sat down next to Doug Wead on a flight in 1986. Wead, Vice President Bush's liaison to evangelical Christians, had a long conversation with the future cardinal about politics. He reported back to the campaign that Law was uncomfortable "with the fact that his emphasis on prolife issues played into the hands of Reagan-Bush." The Catholic Church's support for antiabortion legislation and government antipoverty programs forces Catholic purists to choose between the Democratic Party, whose issue bundle opposes the church's cultural agenda, and the Republican Party, whose issue bundle opposes its economic agenda.[23] In the end, a personal meeting with Bush persuaded Law not only to vote for the vice president, but to help the campaign win over Catholic voters.[24]

Many Catholics experience the same sort of cross-pressures when deciding which party to support. How does one weigh these moral imperatives against each other? Cardinal Law was convinced to set aside his economic reservations about Bush. Another Catholic bishop during the Reagan administration had declared in opposition to the arms race that, "On right to life you called us right-wing and I am sure on this [nuclear arms] you will call us left-wing. We like to see ourselves as thoroughly consistent in both instances."[25] Still more voters set aside their cultural issue positions and vote on the basis of economic issues.[26] Ahler and Broockman demonstrate that many voters are idiosyncratic, holding relatively extreme views on different issues that do not fit a pattern.[27] Many Americans have difficulty making choices in the general election because parties bundle issues together in a different way than these voters would. Moderates, idiosyncratic voters, and Catholic purists have to make a choice between two bundles that liberals and conservatives find easier to make.

Of course, no party alignment could satisfy everyone—one reflecting moderates or Catholic bishops would constrain the vote choice of pure liberals and conservatives. But for the "outgroups" represented by neither party, political parties in a two-party system constrain their choice in the general election to package deals that are distasteful to their dear beliefs. In committing parties to a new bundle of issue positions, other ways of combining issues in a party platform were lost. The outgroups presented in this book were able to become ingroups, but other outgroups never will. They either lack the ability to organize and gain resources, or may time their strategies poorly and hitch their fate to an ally in decline. In most successful party transformations, outgroups or their allies had captive, nonpolitical audiences that could be exhorted to political activism. Not every outgroup has one.

Given that parties have already adopted binding primaries, I am not sure that it is possible to give voters more say in party positions. Even if we disregard financial differences, some voters are highly motivated by politics and others are uninterested or unable to devote time to political groups. As long as this is the case, some peoples' positions will always be better represented by a party than others. Although jettisoning political parties would make it easier for candidates to bundle issues in new ways, this has to be weighed against the information shortcuts voters would lack without parties.

Instead, my point about parties and democracy is that we should be realistic about how well parties can represent people. As Shapiro comments on legislatures, "we should not delude ourselves that what is at work here is a 'pluralism of dispersed preferences' where everyone gets her turn." The same applies to parties. Relatively small groups can change a party's trajectory, so party rule can be minority rule. Shapiro appropriately sounds an optimistic note in that at least in a democracy, a "dominant coalition with their ill-gotten gains will from time to time be displaced."[28] But groups are still the fundamental building blocs. They invite themselves into the party coalition, creating lasting effects on party nominations and public policy.

N O T E S

Chapter 1

1. Bob Dole was the only consistently antiabortion nominee from *Roe v. Wade* to his nomination in 1996.

2. V. O. Key, *Politics, Parties, and Pressure Groups* (New York: Crowell, 1950).

3. David Karol, *Party Position Change in American Politics: Coalition Management* (Cambridge: Cambridge University Press, 2009), 9.

4. E. E. Schattschneider, *Party Government* (New York: Holt, Rinehart and Winston, 1942), 64.

5. Eric Schickler, *Racial Realignment* (Princeton, N.J.: Princeton University Press, 2016).

6. Christopher Baylor, "Big Red and Deep Purple: The Dealignment of Highly Cross-Pressured Voters in an Era of Cultural Issues," paper presented at the annual meeting of the Midwest Political Science Association, Chicago, 2010.

7. I sometimes provide evidence of groups working in lobbying coalitions to pressure politicians in office, but mainly as evidence that groups are working together, and not because lobbying is the primary means of controlling party agendas.

8. Environmentalism was arguably an extension of existing policies of business regulation on behalf of workers and the middle class, more than a transformation of the existing Democratic Party stance. Later, conservatives would attempt to drive a wedge between laborers and environmentalists, but the party's position on environmentalism was established well before then. On a series of votes on pollution control from 1956 through 1995, I found a negative correlation coefficient between first dimension NOMINATE scores (a measure of economic liberalism) and supporting more government pollution control, indicating that economic liberals consistently support more pollution control. A 1960 vote on amending the Water Pollution Control Act, for example, had a -.23 − correlation with first dimension scores. In future decades, conservatives argued to union workers, mostly without success, that environmental regulations cost jobs.

9. Marty Cohen, David Karol, Hans Noel, and John Zaller, *The Party Decides: Presidential Nominations Before and After Reform* (Chicago: University of Chicago Press, 2008), 146.

10. Defined by Daniel Schlozman, *When Movements Anchor Parties: Electoral Alignments in American History* (Princeton, N.J.: Princeton University Press, 2015), 31.

11. Bethany Moreton, *To Serve God and Wal-Mart: The Making of Christian Free Enterprise* (Cambridge, Mass.: Harvard University Press, 2009).

12. Robert Salisbury, *Interests and Institutions: Substance and Structure in American Politics* (Pittsburgh: University of Pittsburgh Press, 1992), 19.

13. Salisbury, *Interests and Institutions*, 30.

14. Dara Z. Strolovitch, *Affirmative Advocacy: Race, Class, and Gender in Interest Group Politics* (Chicago: University of Chicago Press, 2007).

15. Michael T. Heaney and Fabio Rojas, *Party in the Street: The Antiwar Movement and the Democratic Party After 9/11* (Cambridge: Cambridge University Press 2015).

16. Paul Frymer, *Uneasy Alliances: Race and Party Competition in America* (Princeton, N.J.: Princeton University Press, 2010).

17. Hans Noel, "The Coalition Merchants: The Ideological Roots of the Civil Rights Realignment," *Journal of Politics* 74, no. 1 (January 2012): 156–73, and *Political Ideologies and Political Parties in America* (New York: Cambridge University Press, 2014).

18. Social scientists attribute organizational behavior to many causes and have long debated the extent to which organizations can separate ideology from interest. In an important study of the YMCA, Zald and Denton argue that "as the environments of organizations change, as the needs or demands of clientele change, organizations must, if they are to persist, be able to adapt goals, structure, and services." Mayer N. Zald and Patricia Denton, "From Evangelism to General Service: The Transformation of the YMCA," *Administrative Science Quarterly* 8, no. 2 (1963): 214). The YMCA—an organization financed mainly by membership—transformed from a Christian evangelist social movement focused on character to a service organization offering sports and physical exercise to all. Other sociologists have gathered considerable evidence that organizations are not purely rational and that "less efficient organizational forms" persist in spite of any "natural selection" processes that punish inefficiency. Paul J. Dimaggio and Walter W. Powell, "The Iron Cage Revisited: Institutional Isomorphism and Collective Rationality in Organizational Fields," *American Sociological Review* 48, no. 2 (1983): 147). Of course, decision-makers may misjudge their own or group interests. V. O. Key writes, "Even if pure self-interest motivated political action, pressure groups would often be in a quandary about what position to take, for the determination of the direction in which one's interest lies is often fraught with difficulty. In fact . . . many groups often pursue courses of action directly opposite to their most selfish interest, so remarkable is the capacity for self-delusion" (Key, *Politics, Parties, and Pressure Groups*). For the purposes of this book, it is enough to know that group leaders change previously held ideologies when they appear to contradict a group's interest. Again, the first case study on unions illustrates this point. Reuther and Hillman reversed themselves on domestic communists, shop floor democracy, and third parties as their interests changed.

19. Kenneth Kersch, *Constructing Civil Liberties: Discontinuities in the Development of American Constitutional Law* (Cambridge: Cambridge University Press, 2004).

20. Mancur Olson, *The Logic of Collective Action* (Cambridge MA: Harvard University Press, 1965).

21. Daniel Galvin, *Presidential Party Building: Dwight D. Eisenhower to George W. Bush* (Princeton, N.J.: Princeton University Press, 2010).

22. In the 2012 presidential election, Mitt Romney benefited from an organization called "Evangelicals for Mitt." George W. Bush also developed his own outreach team for evangelical Christians in 2004 as major Christian Right organizations imploded. Harvey argues that party organizations traditionally specialize in winning over voters in geographic units, such as states and precincts, rather than social group units. Anna L. Harvey, *Votes Without Leverage: Women in American Electoral Politics, 1920–1970* (Cambridge: Cambridge University Press, 1998). Representative Robert Livingston wrote in a letter to Reagan that these groups have the ability to "marshal public opinion in support of [the president's] programs unaided by the media." Others

pointed out to Reagan that they were adept at generating news. Quoted in Katherine Krimmel, "Special Interest Partisanship: The Transformation of American Political Parties in Government" (paper presented at the annual meeting of the American Political Science Association in Seattle Washington, 2011), 31.

23. One exception seems to have taken place in 2004, when George W. Bush relied on his own reelection organization to mobilize Christian conservatives as the Christian Coalition floundered in disarray. Jon A. Shields, *The Democratic Virtues of the Christian Right* (Princeton, N.J.: Princeton University Press, 2009), 146).

24. The group "Win Without War" coordinated antiwar activities through existing groups of feminists, environmentalists, gay rights advocates, peace proponents, and Unitarians. Because members of the groups had fought side-by-side before and respected each others' work, which sometimes overlapped, they shared information and resources quickly. Nella Van Dyke and Holly J. McCammon, eds., *Strategic Alliances: Coalition Building and Social Movements* (Minneapolis: University of Minnesota Press, 2010).

25. While Christian Right groups have not threatened to support Democrats in a long time, they threatened not to turn out for the 2004 election if President Bush did not endorse a federal marriage amendment. And the AFL-CIO refused to endorse the Democratic ticket in 1972 when the party nominated George McGovern instead of Hubert Humphrey.

26. Franklin Roosevelt's party purge of southern conservatives in 1938 took place in a context in which Democrats would win the general election anyway

27. E. E. Schattschneider, *The Semisovereign People: A Realist's View of Democracy in America* (New York: Holt, Rinehart and Winston, 1960), 75.

28. Geoffrey C. Layman, and Thomas M. Carsey, "Party Polarization and "Conflict Extension" in the American Electorate," *American Journal of Political Science* 46, no. 4 (2002): 326.

29. Burnham argues for the growing weakness of parties as political organizations, but his account also views the parties as the coalition builders. Walter Dean Burnham, *Critical Elections and the Mainsprings of American Politics* (New York: Norton, 1970). Sundquist states that new issues create new voter cleavages and lead to realigning eras. But realignments are not "the rearrangement of the group components of parties—not the forming and reforming of coalitions of groups—but the reordering of individual attachments" through party behavior. James L. Sundquist, *Dynamics of the Party System: Alignment and Realignment of Political Parties in the United States* (Washington, D.C.: Brookings Institution, 1983), 41, 49. Carmines and Stimson espouse a candidate centered model of "issue evolution," emphasizing the role of politicians in changing partisan voter opinion. Prominent party leaders attempt to increase their vote margins by changing their stance on issues. When their vote margins increase, other politicians follow suit, and voters change their party identification with the politicians. Edward G. Carmines and James A. Stimson, *Issue Evolution: Race and the Transformation of American Politics* (Princeton, N.J.: Princeton University Press, 1989). Tichenor and Harris observe that "what is striking about this realignment scholarship in relation to the interest group literature is that organized interests are not usually viewed as agents of transformation" and are "typically understood as either an impediment to change or as entities acted upon by external forces." Daniel J. Tichenor and Richard A. Harris, "Organized Interests and American Political Development," *Political Science Quarterly* 117, no. 4 (2002): 603.

30. Stephanie L. Mudge and Anthony S. Chen, "Political Parties and the Sociological Imagination: Past, Present, and Future Directions," *Annual Review of Sociology* 40, no. 1 (2014): 305–30. One of the few social movement theorists to discuss group-party interactions, Mildred

Schwartz, identifies six strategies that organizations can use to change party trajectories, and shows that organizations employ similar strategies in response to similar organizational dilemmas. The "takeover" strategy she describes resembles the party transformations in this study, but she organizes her evidence around geographic settings, rather than groups or issues. She does not offer an in-depth look at the process by which a particular group transforms a party, instead offering brief sketches of how organizations respond to their dilemmas. Mildred A. Schwartz, *Party Movements in the United States and Canada: Strategies of Persistence* (Lanham, Md.: Rowman & Littlefield, 2006).

31. Anthony Downs, *An Economic Theory of Democracy* (New York: HarperCollins, 1997), 271–72.

32. John H. Aldrich, *Why Parties? The Origin and Transformation of Political Parties in America* (Chicago: University of Chicago Press, 1995).

33. Carmines and Stimson, *Issue Evolution.*

34. Kathleen Bawn, Martin Cohen, David Karol, Seth Masket, Hans Noel, and John Zaller, "A Theory of Political Parties: Groups, Policy Demands and Nominations in American Politics," *Perspectives on Politics* 10, no. 3 (2012): 571–97.

35. Daniel DiSalvo, *Engines of Change: Party Factions in American Politics, 1868–2010* (New York: Oxford University Press, 2012), 7; Geoffrey C. Layman, Thomas M. Carsey, John C. Green, Richard Herrera, and Rosalyn Cooperman, "Activists and Conflict Extension in American Party Politics," *American Political Science Review* 104, no. 2 (2010): 324–46.

36. Larry M. Bartels, *Presidential Primaries and the Dynamics of Public Choice* (Princeton, N.J.: Princeton University Press, 1988).

37. Robert H. Zieger, ed., *Minutes of the Executive Board of the Congress of Industrial Organizations, 1935–1955* (Frederick, Md.: University Publications of America, 1994), Meeting of October 29, 1943, microfilm (mf) 6.

38. Bawn et al., "A Theory of Parties."

39. Circumstances often prevent politicians with real commitments from implementing such agendas. No matter who was in the White House, southern MCs were able to prevent the passage of civil rights legislation until the wave election of 1964. And Republican presidents have been unable to muster the supermajorities necessary to amend the Constitution to allow school prayer or outlaw abortion.

40. Alexander Bolton, "Senator DeMint Relishes His Role as Kingmaker," *The Hill*, September 15, 2010. Available at http://thehill.com/homenews/senate/119115-sen-demint-relishes-role-as-kingmaker.

41. Manu Raju, "DeMint Assures Colleagues He Won't Back Primary Challengers," *Politico*, December 2, 2010. Blackwell says that the promise was somewhat easier to make given the large number of seats vacated by Democrats, but that the "heat" placed on him seems to have had some effect (interview with Morton Blackwell, April 27, 2011). Unless otherwise noted, all interviews conducted by the author.

42. David B. Truman, *The Governmental Process: Political Interests and Public Opinion* (New York: Knopf, 1951); Gina Reinhardt and Jennifer Victor, "Competing for the Platform: The Politics of Interest Group Influence on Political Party Platforms in the United States," prepared for the Annual Meetings of the American Political Science Association, New Orleans, 2012.

43. Gerald M. Pomper and Susan Lederman, *Elections in America: Control and Influence in Democratic Politics* (New York: Longman, 1980), 164.

44. Julia Azari and Stephen Engel, "Do the Words Matter? Party Platforms and Ideological

Change in Republican Politics," presented at the Annual Meeting of the Midwest Political Science Association in Chicago, April 13, 2007.

45. Cohen et al., *The Party Decides*, 572.

46. Wayne Steger, "The Party Decides—When It Isn't Divided or Undecided," prepared for the Annual Meeting of the American Political Science Association, 2015.

47. Schlozman, *When Movements Anchor Parties*, 3, 28. Unsuccessful would-be anchors "found fewer friends among partisan decision makers."

48. In 2013, House Republicans led by Senator Cruz supported a government shutdown. By the time the shutdown was concluded, public approval of the party had dropped by 10 percent to a new low of 28 percent. Since many of these Republicans were elected in safe Republican districts, some observers attribute the self-defeating strategy to the fear of potential Tea Party primary challenges. Senators Orrin Hatch and John McCain, among others, burnished their conservative credentials in the face of Tea Party challenges, and others have moved to the right to prevent such challenges from emerging in the first place. Among others, business groups such as the Chamber of Commerce have announced plans to support moderate primary candidates as a counterweight to Tea Party influence. As Lyndon Johnson reportedly lamented after the passage of the Civil Rights Act of 1964, "We have lost the South for a generation." Whether or not he said this, the point stands that politicians may sacrifice general election votes to assure their nomination or influence in the party.

49. Kenneth Joseph Arrow, *Social Choice and Individual Values* (New York: Wiley, 1951).

50. Truman, *The Governmental Process*, 169

51. Also see Schickler, *Racial Realignment*, 15–18.

52. Keith T. Poole and Howard Rosenthal, *Congress: A Political-Economic History of Roll Call Voting* (New York: Oxford University Press, 1997); D. Sunshine Hillygus and Todd G. Shields, *The Persuadable Voter: Wedge Issues in Presidential Campaigns* (Princeton, N.J.: Princeton University Press, 2008).

53. Matt Grossman and David Hopkins, *Asymmetric Politics: Ideological Republicans and Group Interest Democrats* (New York: Oxford University Press, 2016).

54. Frances Lee, *Beyond Ideology: Politics, Principles, and Partisanship in the U.S. Senate* (Chicago: University of Chicago Press, 2009), 82, 98.

Chapter 2

1. Kenneth Kersch, *Constructing Civil Liberties: Discontinuities in the Development of American Constitutional Law* (Cambridge: Cambridge University Press, 2004), 198–200; Beth Tompkins Bates, *Pullman Porters and the Rise of Protest Politics in Black America* (Chapel Hill: University of North Carolina Press, 2001), 108.

2. Kenneth Janken, *White: The Biography of Walter White, Mr. NAACP* (New York: New Press, 2003), 141.

3. Michael T. Heaney and Fabio Rojas, *Party in the Street: The Antiwar Movement and the Democratic Party After 9/11* (Cambridge: Cambridge University Press 2015), 6.

4. In 1952, pollster Elmo Roper said the NAACP position was "held in respect by at least 45 percent of Negroes," and argued they were capable of swaying the election. The NAACP was "far and away the most frequently mentioned organization" that held weight with African Americans. "Roper Reports on Importance of Negro Vote, NAACP Stand," June 22, 1952, NAACP II A452, Library of Congress, Washington, D.C.

5. The National Committee to Abolish the Poll Tax, for example, received significant

assistance from both the NAACP and the CIO. The National Urban League (NUL), formed one year after the NAACP, specialized in employment, not politics. The Congress of Racial Equality (CORE), founded in 1942, focused on direct action and civil disobedience rather than elections, nominations, and legal strategies. In 1957, black churches formed the Southern Christian Leadership Conference (SCLC) as a political arm. The SCLC, too, emphasized direct action over legislation and litigation; by the time it was formed, other groups had already laid the groundwork for a racially liberal Democratic Party. Steven Lawson, *Running for Freedom: Civil Rights and Black Politics in America Since 1941* (New York: McGraw-Hill, 1991), 9, 15, 63–64. A. Philip Randolph's March on Washington Movement (MOWM) successfully pressured presidents Roosevelt and Truman into signing an executive order in favor of civil rights. While these orders were pivotal events for party transformation, Randolph needed the help of the NAACP in Roosevelt's case and the CIO-NAACP alliance in Truman's case.

6. Eric Schickler and Devin Caughey, "Public Opinion, Organized Labor, and the Limits of New Deal Liberalism, 1936–1945," *Studies in American Political Development* 25, no, 2 (2011).

7. Dara Z. Strolovitch, *Affirmative Advocacy: Race, Class, and Gender in Interest Group Politics* (Chicago: University of Chicago Press, 2007), 121; Catherine M. Paden, *Civil Rights Advocacy on Behalf of the Poor* (Philadelphia: University of Pennsylvania Press, 2011), 10.

8. Eric Schickler, *Racial Realignment: The Transformation of American Liberalism, 1932–1965* (Princeton, N.J.: Princeton University Press, 2016).

9. These figures are calculated from Frank Hobbs and Nicole Stoops, *Demographic Trends in the 20th Century* (Washington, D.C.: U.S. Census Bureau, 2002).

10. Blacks enthusiastically supported Republican president Theodore Roosevelt in 1904 after he dined with Booker T. Washington, which was widely criticized by white Southerners as a harbinger of social equality. According to Washington, all but 5 of the 178 black newspapers supported Roosevelt's reelection in 1904. Robert J. Norrell, *Up from History: The Life of Booker T. Washington* (Cambridge, Mass.: Belknap of Harvard University Press, 2009), 246, 289. Later in his presidency, however, Roosevelt said that lynching was a response to rape. Catering to white Texans, he dishonorably discharged a contingent of experienced black soldiers who happened to be in a small Texas town during the murder of a white bartender. Tuskegee Institute president Booker T. Washington warned Roosevelt's successor, William Howard Taft, that appointing "lily white" Republicans to southern positions would destroy black Republican Party allegiance. Unfazed, Taft said he would not appoint any blacks if there were objections from southern whites (Norrell, *Up from History*, 384–86). Announcing that Reconstruction had failed, Taft said the government must practice restraint in appointments lest "the recurrence and increase of race feeling which such an appointment is likely to engender" counteract the "encouragement to the race." Ira Katznelson, *Fear Itself: The New Deal and the Origins of Our Time* (New York: Liveright, 2014), 134–35. The 1928 Republican nominee, Herbert Hoover, believed his Democratic opponent's Catholicism opened the South to Republican overtures (L. K. Williams to John Hamilton, undated, NAACP II A226). As mentioned earlier, he had even attempted to appoint a segregationist judge to the Supreme Court.

11. James Weldon Johnson, "Report of the Field Secretary on Interview with Senator Warren G. Harding," August 9, 1920, NAACP mf C 63–65.

12. Moorfield Storey to James Weldon Johnson, July 18, 1922, NAACP C75–77. In the House, the vote was 221/238 among Republicans and 8/103 among Democrats. No Democrats voted to end the Senate filibuster.

13. W. E. B. Du Bois, the *Crisis* 12 (October 1916) 268–69.

14. Nancy J. Weiss, *Farewell to the Party of Lincoln: Black Politics in the Age of FDR* (Princeton, N.J.: Princeton University Press, 1983), 9–11, 27. Walter White, who had been on leave from the NAACP to run Smith's campaign among African Americans, was disappointed and decided to return to the NAACP. A pro-Smith African American organization called the Colored League also worked for Smith's election on a budget of $125,000, and Smith-for-President colored clubs sprang up nationally.

15. Roger Biles, *The South and the New Deal* (Lexington: University Press of Kentucky, 1994), 127.

16. Senator James Byrnes told South Carolinians that "If Roosevelt is elected, I give you my word that South Carolina will be recognized as she has never been recognized by any Democratic President before." Leuchtenberg, *The White House Looks South: Franklin D. Roosevelt, Harry S. Truman, Lyndon B. Johnson* (Baton Rouge: Louisiana State University Press, 2005), 34–39.

17. David Karol, *Party Position Change in American Politics: Coalition Management* (Cambridge: Cambridge University Press, 2009).

18. Adviser Louis Howe said to remember "our southern brethren" and let the future take care of "our anxious colored brethren." David L. Lewis, *W. E. B. Du Bois* (New York: Holt, 1993), 329.

19. A handful of New Deal officials, including Interior Secretary Harold Ickes, worked to administer the laws in an unbiased manner, but had only partial success. More typical was NRA administrator Hugh Johnson, who refused to let a concerned government official look into New Deal discrimination in the South, and her entire unit was soon disbanded. Weiss, *Farewell to the Party of Lincoln*, 57.

20. Biles, *The South and the New Deal*, 111–14.

21. Katznelson, *Fear Itself*, 151.

22. George E. Mowry, *Another Look at the Twentieth-Century South* (Baton Rouge: Louisiana State University Press 1973), 70. Byrnes, who would become an important adviser to Roosevelt during his third term, had traditionally been a conciliatory figure, not a race baiter. He had never been prompted to issue such warnings during the Roosevelt administration until a majority of Northern Democrats voted for an antilynching bill.

23. Georgia Representative Edward Cox said that the Democratic Party was cowardly to betray their longstanding southern base with an antilynching law only after the party became more powerful nationally (Katznelson, *Fear Itself*, 180–81). Interestingly, the NAACP expressed more outrage at Republican MCs when the bills were defeated by a filibuster. Although Republicans voted for cloture, they had previously announced they would not. The NAACP interpreted this as evidence of credit-claiming, arguing that the public announcement led many Democrats not to vote for cloture (Roy Wilkins to John Hamilton, March 15, 1938, NAACP II-L-27; John Hamilton to Roy Wilkins, March 14, 1938, NAACP II-L-27; and Roy Wilkins to John Hamilton, March 15, 1938, NAACP II-L-27). Republican Party chairman John Hamilton wrote to the NAACP that the Republican minority was reluctant to vote for cloture because the filibuster was its only weapon left against President Roosevelt's proposals. He replied "It will not do now to say that a mere handful of Republican Senators—16 at the most—can be charged with any responsibility for the action of the Democratic majority of eighty" (John Hamilton to Roy Wilkins, March 14, 1938, NAACP II-L-27). Wilkins called the excuse "hollow" and blamed the Republicans more than the Democrats because the former had more at stake "from both a moral and political standpoint" (Roy Wilkins to John Hamilton, March 15, 1938, NAACP II-L-27).

24. Lewis, *W. E. B. Du Bois*, 329. White appears to have been impressed with Roosevelt at

the meeting. He said that the president showed "a more decent attitude towards the Negro than 90% of current contemporary Republicans" (Walter White to Henry C. Patterson, October 1, 1938, NAACP II-L-27).

25. Allan J. Lichtman, *White Protestant Nation: The Rise of the American Conservative Movement* (New York: Grove Press, 2008), 91. White also found blame to distribute to Republican senators, who caved in to a filibuster after two days.

26. McMahon, *Reconsidering Roosevelt on Race* (Chicago: University of Chicago Press, 2004). Roosevelt also supported Alben Barkley's bid to be Democratic Majority Leader over Mississippi's Pat Harrison. Although both had consistently supported the New Deal, Harrison's support was thought to be opportunistic rather than genuine.Leuchtenberg, *The White House Looks South*, 79.

27. Civil rights leaders said that whites were excluded so that the Communist Party could not wield influence, but of course, the Communist Party also included blacks (Janken, *White*, 255).

28. Sidney M. Milkis, *The President and the Parties: The Transformation of the American Party System Since the New Deal* (New York: Oxford University Press, 1993), 62. While black voters matched working-class white support for Roosevelt in 1936, it would not surpass it until the party embraced civil rights following the 1948 election.

29. James Farley Memorandum to Self, March 16, 1937, Box 40–42, Reel 3; James Farley Memorandum to Self, November 4, 1937, 40–42, Reel 3, both in James A. Farley Papers, Library of Congress, Washington, D.C (henceforth Farley Papers). After Guffey's successful use of the African American vote in Pennsylvania, Farley did provide jobs to 150 African Americans in ten northern cities (Schickler, *Racial Realignment*, 49).

30. Paul D. Moreno, *Black Americans and Organized Labor: A New History* (Baton Rouge: Louisiana State University Press, 2006), 160.

31. James L. Sundquist, *Dynamics of the Party System: Alignment and Realignment of Political Parties in the United States* (Washington, D.C.: Brookings Institution, 1983), 306.

32. Before a largely white audience in the Atlanta Exposition in 1895, Washington also declared to white capitalists that blacks would show loyalty "with a devotion no foreigner can approach" (both quoted in Kersch, *Constructing Civil Liberties*, 192).

33. Norrell, *Up from History*, 390, 405–7. There are some indications that Washington's viewpoint changed with changing attitudes among organized labor. In 1910, Washington became more optimistic about unions than he had been in the past after reading the results of a survey among labor leaders. In his twilight years, the survey results, along with his belief that discrimination was against union interests, led him to believe that unions could help blacks.

34. Norrell, *Up from History*, 287. Washington often downplayed the need for black political equality to keep physical threats at manageable levels, and still needed to flee the South during racially charged events. Francis Garrison said the Tuskegee Institute rested on a "powder magazine." In 1903, a principal of a black industrial school was killed in Louisiana as politicians like Mississippi gubernatorial candidate James Vardaman fanned the flames of racial resentment.

35. Norrell, *Up from History*, 229.

36. Garvey's brand of Black Nationalism urged blacks to start their own businesses, buy from other black businesses, and eventually undergo mass migration to Africa. Other civil rights groups worried about his separatism and the diversion of donations from organizations pursuing realistic goals. Publicly, they kept their doubts quiet to avoid antagonizing Garvey's followers.

37. Quoted in Kersch, *Constructing Civil Liberties*, 191.

38. Sitkoff, *A New Deal for Blacks. The Emergence of Civil Rights as a National Issue: The Depression Decade* (Oxford: Oxford University Press, 2008), 170.

39. Sterling D. Spero and Abram Lincoln Harris, *The Black Worker: The Negro and the Labor Movement* (New York: Atheneum, 1968), 133–34. When two Columbia researchers interviewed African American workers about their experiences, many reported that employers said they would have hired them, but their white workers would quit if they did. The findings were first published in 1931.

40. Walter White, "Solving America's Race Problem," *Nation* 128 (1929): 42–43.

41. Sitkoff, *A New Deal for Blacks*, 170. The AFL admitted A. Philip Randolph's BSCP, but only after Randolph had spent years cultivating a relationship, at times calling off strikes against the clear preferences of BSCP members.

42. Sophia Lee, *The Workplace Constitution: From the New Deal to the New Right* (Cambridge: Cambridge University Press, 2014), 14, 25.

43. Walter White to Senator James Couzens, April 11, 1934, NAACP I-C-257. Of course, some employers would also hire black replacement workers and dismiss them once the white strikers returned to work.

44. David Bernstein, *Only One Place of Redress* (Durham, N.C.: Duke University Press, 2001), 47–48. On the Teamsters, see "Panel Discussion: Economic Opportunity and Employment" (before the Thirtieth Annual Conference of the NAACP in Richmond, Virginia, June 28, 1939, NAACP mf Part 1 r10).

45. Black workers in the South were an important exception, where qualitative evidence conforms to Schickler and Caughey's (2011) early survey data. Executive Committee of the Tennessee State CIO PAC, Minutes of the Meeting, March 20, 1948, in Katherine F. Martin, ed., *Operation Dixie: The CIO Organizing Committee Papers, 1946–1953* (Sanford, N.C.: Microfilming Corporation of America, 1980). The voluminous correspondence of Lucy Mason, CIO director of public relations, includes only one mention of unreceptive blacks from her southern campaigns.Lucy Mason to editors, October 5, 1937; Lucy Mason to Miss Mary Jane Willett and Mr. William, March 31, 1939; Lucy Mason to Allan Haywood, February 24, 1941; Lucy Mason to Van Gelder, January 16, 1943; all in *Operation Dixie* mf 62). Also see E. L. Sandfeur to Lucy Mason, May 29, 1945, *Operation Dixie* mf 63. Of course, some CIO unions in the South failed to meet their expectations. Robert H. Zieger, *Southern Labor in Transition, 1940–1995* (Knoxville: University of Tennessee Press, 1997), 116–24).

46. August Meier and Elliott M. Rudwick, *Black Detroit and the Rise of the UAW* (New York: Oxford University Press, 1979), 26.

47. Janken, *White*, 244, 251. Even those less sensitive to the historic realities of labor unions had no idea if unions would succeed or control future hiring, in which case currying favor with management was less risky. On the other hand, NUL's Lester Granger (a CIO member) acknowledged in 1938 that an NAACP audience was much more receptive that year than it was five years earlier (Lester Granger, "The Negro in Labor Unions," Before the 29th Annual Conference of the NAACP, June 30, 1938, NAACP mf Part 1 r9). For another account of the NAACP avoiding labor support in the 1930s, see Goluboff, *The Lost Promise of Civil Rights* (Cambridge: Harvard University Press, 2007), 174–82.

48. Lucy Mason to W. W. Ball, May 27, 1940, *Operation Dixie* mf 62. Her statement of policy was corroborated by John L. Lewis in John L. Lewis to W. W. Ball, June 10, 1940, *Operation Dixie* mf 62.

49. Goluboff, *The Lost Promise of Civil Rights*, 174–82.

50. Even after years of education and workplace integration efforts in the UAW, a liberal CIO affiliate, blacks constituted only 2 percent of the well-compensated craft workers in 1960. Robert H. Zieger, *For Jobs and Freedom: Race and Labor in America Since 1865* (Lexington: University Press of Kentucky, 2007), 149). An investigation by the U.S. Commission on Civil Rights in 1961 found that Atlantic Steel's practices were even worse than a recent NAACP report indicated. No black workers received a pay grade above 8 on a scale of 1 to 26, and more than half earned a pay grade at 4 or below. Zieger, *Southern Labor in Transition*, 116–24.

51. Meier and Rudwick, *Black Detroit and the Rise of the UAW*, 16.

52. Bates, *Pullman Porters*, 48.

53. Zieger, *For Jobs and Freedom*, 121.

54. Bernstein, *Only One Place of Redress*, 92. Bernstein mistakenly dates the conference year as 1924. When Samuel Gompers urged African Americans to join AFL unions in 1918, the *Baltimore Herald* told African Americans to "Beware of Greeks Bearing Gifts," *Baltimore Herald*, September 1917, 126, NAACP C-142.

55. The author was John P. Davis, who later supported unions. The Black Man's Burden," *Nation* 128 (1929): 44.

56. Philip Sheldon Foner, *Organized Labor and the Black Worker* (New York: Praeger, 1974), 180. The BSCP needed to support civil rights and not merely "bread and butter" to win broader support from the black community (Bates, *Pullman Porters*, 85). Broad support may have factored into the Chicago *Defender's* change in tone in 1927; after that year, it ceased attacking the BSCP and eventually actively promoted union ideals (Bates, *Pullman Porters*, 81, 103).

57. The terms entered into a pro-quest search engine were union, labor, AFL, CIO, Green, strike, Wagner Act, capital, capitalism, socialism, and communism. The years were different for different publications based on availability. I generally chose 1922 and 1937 because anti-lynching laws were proposed in those two years, and I had originally planned to compare black newspapers to other newspapers on civil rights issues.

58. Only two of four editorials concerning unions in 1924 favored them. One editorial argued that wages are not raised by strikes, but productivity and profits. Another criticized black supporters of Progressive candidate Robert La Follette because of his support for discriminatory unions. The two supportive editorials praised Randolph's all-black BSCP and the right of its workers to a "living wage."

59. In 1937, twelve of fifteen *Pittsburgh Courier* editorials were pro-union.

60. T. Arnold Hill, NUL's national director of industrial relations, is quoted in Moreno, *Black Americans and Organized Labor*, 173.

61. For another interpretation of the Urban League's involvement in the Wagner Act, see Nancy Joan Weiss, *The National Urban League* (New York: Oxford University Press, 1974), 273. Also see a letter from the Urban League's executive secretary John T. Clark to the National Recovery Administration's executive secretary Donald Richburg in 1934, which reads "An additional evidence of the spread of union influence (which we would welcome if the Federation would broadly include Negro labor) is shown in a recent action of our Board of Alderman. They passed a law to permit only union waiters. . . . Does not such legislation prevent millions of unemployed, who are not affiliated nor care to affiliate with the present American Federation of Labor, from obtaining work. . . . We notice with alarm agents of the administration giving over more and more control on who shall work, to the American Federation of Labor, and with regret, that Negro labor finds it necessary to attempt to protect its right to work apparently against the

interests of the American Federation of Labor. . . . There are many evidences that the Negro's patience in the New Deal is being shaken—not because we do not have faith in its provisions, but because the Government, through its various agencies and representatives, seems to allow local "old deal" customs to continue only where Negroes are concerned" (Clark to Richburg, February 13, 1934, National Urban League Records 1-D-4, Library of Congress, Washington, D.C., henceforth NUL). The *Amsterdam News* also questioned whether the AFL provided any token of good faith in the same year (October 12, 1935, NUL 1-D-4).

62. T. Arnold Hill to William Green, November 30, 1935, NAACP I-D-4.

63. Foner, *Organized Labor and the Black Worker*, 217. Lester Granger, speaking to the NAACP in 1938, stated that "Given a fair and democratic union, and there is no question of the benefits received by Negroes under the Act. Given an undemocratic, anti-Negro union, however, the Act as passed constitutes a distinct threat to Negro job-holders or job-seekers. . . . Thus, a union which bars Negro membership is protected by the Wagner Act even as it goes into a shop where Negroes are employed and seeks to obtain a closed shop contract that would throw out of work every Negro employee. This is not an unlikely possibility conjured out of a timid imagination. . . . The New York Daily press reported a case of this kind in October, 1936." Lester Granger, "The Negro in Labor Unions," talk at the 29th Annual Conference of the NAACP, June 30, 1938, mf Part 1 r9 NAACP.

64. When the NAACP was founded, he characterized its leaders as a few insincere whites who tricked blacks into believing that "they can get what they ought to have in the way of right treatment by merely making demands, passing resolutions and cursing somebody" (Carolyn Wedin, *Inheritors of the Spirit: Mary White Ovington and the Founding of the NAACP* (New York: Wiley, 1998), 112–13.

65. In an obituary for Washington, Du Bois wrote that he "never adequately grasped the growing bond of politics and industry." Because of this, he was partially responsible for the entrenchment of segregation and Jim Crow (Norrell, *Up from History*, 421).

66. W. E. B. Du Bois, *Crisis* 37 (May 1930): 160.

67. Raymond Wolters, *Du Bois and His Rivals* (Columbia: University of Missouri Press, 2002), 213–14. Also see Lewis, *W. E. B. Du Bois* (265) for his study of the USSR.

68. More orthodox black socialists such as Abram Harris believed that Du Bois failed to appreciate the changes in ideology that would accompany fundamental economic transformations.

69. The fund was created by Charles Garland, a Wall Street heir who believed that business earned money by immoral means. Garland initially was going to refuse his inheritance, but socialist writer Upton Sinclair and American Civil Liberties Union (ACLU) president Roger Baldwin persuaded him to use it for philanthropy. Although Garland seemed to have been influenced most by Christian teachings about the poor, he funded the communist *Daily Worker* and the socialist *New York Call*, along with the ACLU and NAACP.

70. Among other founding members were muckrakers Ida Barnett and William Monroe Trotter, two relentless critics of Washington (Wedin, *Inheritors of the Spirit*, 49, 87).

71. IIbid., 62.

72. Ibid., 177. Another interesting founder was Oswald Garrison Villard, its principal financier. The owner of the *New York Evening Post* and the *Nation*, Villard had been a conservative "Goldbug" Democrat, but evolved with the party, later favoring Wilsonian progressivism and still later, the New Deal. Although Villard said publicly that the NAACP was "not to be a Washington movement, or a Du Bois movement," his preferences were well known. Theodore Roosevelt dishonorably discharged 167 black officers in Texas alleged by the townspeople to have killed a local

bartender, despite evidence that they were in their barracks. When Washington refused to publicly condemn Theodore Roosevelt, Villard and Washington's already-tense relations worsened (Norrell, *Up from History*, 387). When differences later emerged between Du Bois and Villard, Villard resigned.

73. Moorfield Storey to Mary W. Ovington, May 10, 1920, NAACP mf C75-77.

74. W. E. B. Du Bois, "What Is Wrong with the NAACP," speech to NAACP annual convention, May 18, 1932, NAACP I-B-8.

75. Lewis, *W. E. B. Du Bois*, 319. Du Bois overlooked more established black leaders such as Adam Clayton Powell and John Davis, who might challenge his agenda.

76. Harris and Houston also claimed that civil rights could not be achieved without interracial class solidarity. To obtain this, the NAACP needed to establish regional workers' and farmers' councils. Paul Frymer, *Black and Blue: African Americans, the Labor Movement, and the Decline of the Democratic Party* (Princeton, N.J.: Princeton University Press, 2008), 54.

77. They were especially appalled when an Interior Department official quoted Du Bois to push for resettling blacks into segregated communities. The NAACP Board of Directors eventually responded to Du Bois with the statement, "Enforced segregation by its very existence carries with it the implication of a superior and inferior group and invariably results in the imposition of a lower status on the group deemed inferior" (Lewis, *W. E. B. Du Bois*, 335, 342). Executive secretary White believed that segregation almost always meant inferior treatment. White was so light-skinned that he could pass for a white person in his investigations in the South. In 1931, his dying father was transferred to a dilapidated black hospital once the white hospital realized that he was black. Barbara Joyce Ross, *J. E. Spingarn and the Rise of the NAACP, 1911–1939* (New York: Atheneum, 1972), 195.

78. Janken, *White*, 182–84.

79. In the election of 1948, after which Du Bois had been brought back, White was once again able to dismiss Du Bois for campaigning for Henry Wallace despite White's relatively overt support for Truman. The board held that White's articles were his own evaluation, and Du Bois's support for Wallace violated NAACP policy against partisan activity. The double standard was transparent and the board did not explain why the two instances were different (Janken, *White*, 317).

80. Beth Tompkins Bates, "A New Crowd Challenges the Agenda of the Old Guard in the NAACP, 1933–1941," *American Historical Review* 102, no. 2 (1997): 352. Within the association, he prevented the NAACP from hiring radicals like John Davis, as recommended in the Harris report. In place of the worker's councils, the NAACP merely asked the branches to conduct workers' education classes at their own expense, without asking them to promote strikes or workers' agitation (Ross, *J. E. Spingarn*, 239). All Harris's proposals would have cost $12,000 per year and were easily dismissed as impractical. Yet, employing Davis to coordinate workers would have cost $2,500, and even the $12,000 sum was not unthinkable if the organization made as much effort on raising this money from the Garland Fund as it had made the legal effort against school segregation (Ross, 226–27).

81. Ibid., 230.

82. Janken, *White*, 195.

83. Wolters, *Du Bois and His Rivals*, 210. Abram Harris also complained "you can't rely upon the . . . Walter Whites for any new programs" (Lewis, *W. E. B. Du Bois*, 247).

84. William B. Hixson, *Moorefield Storey and the Abolitionist Tradition* (New York: Oxford University Press, 1972), 157.

85. "Address to the Country, 23rd Annual Conference of the NAACP, Washington DC," May 17–32, 1932, NAACP mf Part 1 r3.

86. Foner, *Organized Labor and the Black Worker*, 208–10; Bates, *Pullman Porters*, 109; Meier and Rudwick, *Black Detroit and the Rise of the UAW*, 24.

87. Walter White to Senator James Couzens, April 11, 1934, NAACP C257.

88. Walter White to Harry Hopkins, April 26, 1934, NAACP I-C-257. Assistant Secretary Roy Wilkins said that the closed shop is the white union shop, and even wrote in a 1934 issue of *Crisis* that he suspected the AFL was using the National Industrial Recovery Act to exclude African Americans from employment. Bernstein, *Only One Place of Redress*, 95; Roy Wilkins, *Crisis* 41 (February 1934): 40. In another telling example, the NAACP supported the employer in a Tampa labor dispute. White concluded, "Depriving these hundreds of Negroes of jobs by unions under a closed shop agreement is as effective as the taking of these jobs by force and violence." "Memo from the Secretary on interviews at Tampa, Florida, with respect to the Labor situation of the Tampa Shipbuilding and Engineering Company," July 20, 1939, *Operation Dixie* mf 64.

89. Walter White to Bill Hastie, March 1934, NAACP I-C-257. The amendment was not passed and Senator Wagner simply told civil rights groups that unions coming before the NRLB would have more credibility if they had nondiscrimination policies. Roy Wilkins, *Crisis* 42 (1935). Regarding 1940 support for the closed shop union, see Walter White to Alfred Baker Lewis, April 12, 1940, NAACP II-A-128. There is an NAACP application for a grant from the Falk Foundation in 1935, in which White suggested that the NAACP could accomplish its goals through contacts it made in Congress through its efforts on behalf of the Wagner bill as well as other bills (Application to the Maurice and Laura Falk Foundation, Re: Appropriation for gathering and utilization, through a Congressional investigation, of material on discrimination against the Negro under the "New Deal," April 9, 1935, NAACP I-C-278). I have not found evidence of this support, merely evidence of lobbying for the antidiscrimination amendment.

90. Thomas J. Sugrue, *Sweet Land of Liberty: The Forgotten Struggle for Civil Rights in the North* (New York: Random House, 2008), 36.

91. *Crisis* 43 (1936): 42.

92. Foner, *Organized Labor and the Black Worker*, 217.

93. Rudwick and Meier, *Black Detroit and the Rise of the UAW*, 57. The NAACP said that blacks should closely study a labor union's activities and the labor movement more generally before joining one (Resolutions adopted by the twenty-eighth Annual Conference of the NAACP, in Detroit, Michigan June 29–July 4, 1937, NAACP mf Part 1 r9). Wilkins wrote to a member advocating a more militant approach that a "national group . . . must of necessity be a compromise between the views of different sections." Roy Wilkins to A. C. MacNeal, April 13, 1936, NAACP I-G-53.

94. Alan Draper, "The New Southern Labor History Revisited: the Success of the Mine, Mill, and Smelter Workers Union in Birmingham, 1934–38," *Journal of Southern History* 62 (1996): 87–108.

95. Foner, *Black Americans and Organized Labor*, 216.

96. Ross, *J. E. Spingarn*, 151. In 1932, its recommendations to both party platform committees briefly moved beyond race issues. Although most recommendations concerned the traditional civil rights agenda, the final recommended plank supported "all sane methods towards the redistribution of present wealth through the systematic taxation of large incomes and the future conduct of industry for public good and not for private profit; this, also, to include sickness, old age, and unemployment insurance." A year later, White supported public works bills and the

American Labor Association asked White to endorse New York senator Wagner (American Labor Association to Walter White, May 4, 1933, NAACP I-C-257). There were some exceptions. One civil rights activist in the CIO acknowledged that "the NAACP and the NUL are deeply concerned over displacement of Negroes in many jobs . . . It was somewhat aggravated by NRA, when a fixed minimum wage no longer made it pay to use cheaper Negro help" (Lucy Mason to Jonathan Daniels, September 11, 1937, *Operation Dixie* mf 62). For studies confirming this concern, see William A. Keyes, "The Minimum Wage and the Davis-Bacon Act: Employment Effects on Minorities and Youth," *Journal of Labor Research* (1982): 399, 401; Gunnar Myrdal, Richard Sterner, and Arnold M. Rose, *An American Dilemma: The Negro Problem and Modern Democracy* (New York: Harper & Brothers, 1944), 397–98; and Ralph J. Bunche, *The Political Status of the Negro in the Age of FDR* (Chicago: University of Chicago Press, 1973), 610. The NAACP also testified against Social Security as written, given that it did not include traditionally African American occupations such as farm workers (Testimony of Charles Houston, representing the NAACP, February 9, 1935, NAACP I-C-257). That being said, the NAACP, soon afterward, worked toward ending discrimination (extending the benefits to exempted occupations) rather than ending Social Security.

97. Simon Topping, " 'Supporting Our Friends and Defeating Our Enemies': Militancy and Nonpartisanship in the NAACP, 1936–1948," *Journal of African American History* 89, no. 1 (2004): 20–22. Most NAACP leaders privately favored Democrats and progressive causes, but not as members of the NAACP. Wilkins, for instance, recounts that he repeatedly tried to persuade his wife to become a Democrat before the 1928 election. Roy Wilkins and Tom Mathews, *Standing Fast: The Autobiography of Roy Wilkins* (New York: Viking, 1982) 80.

98. Ross, *J. E. Spingarn*, 14.

99. Roy Wilkins to NAACP branch and Youth Council leaders, September 28, 1966 (quoted in Paden, *Civil Rights Advocacy on Behalf of the Poor*, 23). He continued, "If it goes up, the NAACP is a going concern. . . . If it goes down, the NAACP is dying on its feet. You know that is not a fair way to judge, but that is how it is today. The newspapers, the editorial writers, the columnists, the radio and TV commentators will judge the NAACP by the total membership. You know you did a good job in your city and state on several projects. You know you have backed the national program. . . . But they go by memberships. So—you must go by memberships."

100. Bates, *Pullman Porters*, 358; H. Viscount Nelson, "The Philadelphia NAACP: Race Versus Class Consciousness During the Thirties," *Journal of African American Studies* 5 (March 1975).

101. Walter White to Arthur Spingarn, October 5, 1939; White to William Rosenwald, October 10, 1939; White to Rosenwald, October 10, 1939; White to Rosenwald, November 22, 1939; all in NAACP I-80.

102. Memorandum from Roy Wilkins to Walter White, March 24, 1939, NAACP mf I-80.

103. Roy Wilkins to Walter White, March 11, 1939, NAACP mf I-80.

104. Janken, *White*, 259.

105. Bates, *Pullman Porters*, 369.

106. As Kersch interprets the events, "to persist in opposing a *fait accompli* of . . . governance by social collectives or groups now, to many African Americans, seemed futile." Ken I. Kersch, *Constructing Civil Liberties: Discontinuities in the Development of American Constitutional Law* (London: Cambridge University Press, 2004), 195. As mentioned earlier, this consideration is only a partial explanation for the change in black attitudes. Southern blacks showed great interest

in the CIO before it was clear that any union, let alone the CIO, would successfully unionize the South.

107. Meier and Rudwick, *Black Detroit and the Rise of the UAW,* 67.

108. Walter White to James McClendon, April 11, 1941, NAACP mf 13a r3.

109. Telegram from Walter White to James McClendon, April 5, 1941, NAACP mf 13a r3.

110. His own actions had little effect on the African American workers at Ford, who were already persuaded by the local NAACP. Nonetheless, they had high symbolic value.

111. David Lewis-Coleman, "African Americans and the Politics of Race Among Detroit's Auto Workers 1941–1971" (PhD Dissertation, University of Iowa, 2001), 40.

112. Walter White to Harry E. Davis, April 17, 1941; NAACP mf 13a r3. One African American UAW member, present in the union from the beginning, said that "hard as it might have been for the Negro auto worker to maintain his worker's economic equilibrium in the union, it would be much harder for him to be sure of a decent job if he should persist in staying out (Meier and Rudwick, *Black Detroit and the Rise of the UAW,* 77). The *Pittsburgh Courier* wrote that Detroit black leaders "who lean toward the CIO point out that the day of open shops has passed and that the Negro must line up with organized labor" (93).

113. Walter White to Jim Jayne, April 15, 1941, NAACP mf 13a r3.

114. Steve Fraser, *Labor Will Rule: Sidney Hillman and the Rise of American Labor* (New York: Free Press, 1991), 512.

115. Robert H. Zieger, *The CIO, 1935–1955* (Chapel Hill: University of North Carolina Press, 1995), 183. Its educational activities had a demonstrable impact on its workers' beliefs; in a survey of twenty-five Ohio cities, an advertising firm found that CIO workers were far more likely to take CIO positions than nonunionized wage earners (Green-Brodie, "Report to the Executives of the CIO," April 13, 1948, Philip Murray Papers Box 133, Folder 5, American Catholic History Research Center and University Archives, Catholic University, Washington D.C., henceforth Philip Murray Papers).

116. James Caldwell Foster, *The Union Politic* (Columbia: University of Missouri Press, 1975), 131.

117. Foster, *The Union Politic,* 46–49; Fraser, *Labor Will Rule,* 530–31. Hillman was working privately for months to find a Democratic vice presidential candidate acceptable to all party factions, given that Henry Wallace would not satisfy the South and segregationist James Byrnes would not satisfy the North.

118. He told National Labor Relations Board (NLRB) member James Reynolds that Taft-Hartley was necessary, but Congress would override his veto. According to Reynolds, Truman said "the Taft Hartley [Act] . . . is about that important compared to this," pointing to Eastern Europe on a map. "If I veto it, I'm going to hold labor support . . . [and] I'll be re-elected and the Marshall Plan will go forward" (Zieger, *The CIO,* 276).

119. Roy Wilkins to James Carey, June 14, 1944, CIO Office of the Secretary Treasurer Files 160. Also see Walter White to Phillip Murray, July 25, 1948; and James Carey to Walter White, August 13, 1946, both in CIO Office of the Secretary Treasurer Files 27, Walter Reuther Library, Wayne State University, Detroit Michigan (henceforth CIO Office of the Secretary-Treasurer Records).

120. "Special Meeting of the Board of Directors of the NAACP," July 31, 1944, NAACP mf 1 r11 (f471). Spingarn and White agreed that the NAACP should criticize both party platforms.

121. Janken, *White,* 316–17.

122. Ross, *J. E. Spingarn,* 230.

123. Wolters, *Du Bois and His Rivals*, 228; Levering, *W. E. B. Du Bois*, 335.

124. Wedin, *Inheritors of the Spirit*, 271.

125. William H. Hastie, Memorandum to the Committee to Study Discrimination in Labor Unions, February 19, 1940, NAACP II-A-128; Handwritten minutes, Committee to Study Discrimination in Labor Unions, June 9, 1940, NAACP II-A-128; Memorandum to Mr. Marshall from Mr. White, March 11, 1940; NAACP mf Part 13b r23.

126. Walter White to the Committee on Administration, March 15, 1940, NAACP II-A-443.

127. Memorandum to Dean Hastie, March 14, 1940, NAACP II-A-243. NAACP leaders also agreed not to reveal to Congress any unions that discriminate by name, in order to avoid antagonizing them (Walter White to Matthew Dunn, May 1940, NAACP II-A-443).

128. Memorandum to Mr. White from George B. Murphy, Jr., February 24, 1940, NAACP II-A-128. For the admittedly pragmatic issues that concerned NAACP leaders about the printer's union, see Memorandum to Mr. Murphy from Roy Wilkins, undated, NAACP I-C-80.

129. Goluboff, *The Lost Promise of Civil Rights*.

130. Memorandum to Roy Wilkins from Clarence Mitchell, NAACP IX-211.

131. Clarence Mitchell to James Longson, February 12, 1953, CIO Office of the Secretary Treasurer Files 160, Clarence Mitchell Folder.

132. Gilbert Jonas, *Freedom's Sword: The NAACP and the Struggle Against Racism in America, 1909–1969* (New York: Routledge, 2004), 237.

133. Frymer, *Black and Blue*, 59.

134. In addition to Du Bois, the most obvious example was the removal of *Nation* publisher Oswald Garrison Villard, the most important early financier of the NAACP, from the board of trustees for his hostility to labor unions. Several NAACP leaders said he was "out of step" and dismissed him. In a discussion of labor unions, Villard said there were many worthwhile political causes, and "if we should take time out to go into all of them the Association's work would suffer." The following month, Labor supporter William Hastie said that "we could not justify keeping on our Board someone who opposed the things we are working toward ("Minutes of the Meeting of the Board of Directors, January 9, 1946, NAACP mf 1 r3). Janken (2003) attributes the dismissal of Villard to his reservations about aiding unions, although the member calling for his dismissal mentions a letter to the *New York Times* coauthor by Villard. This letter opposed the New York State FEPC, arguing that prejudice would not be ended by legal penalties and the federal model worked well without such penalties. On the one hand, the minutes describing the dismissal did not specifically mention Villard's reservation about unions, and Villard was later reinstated after giving a stirring speech in which he supported a state FEPC after the federal FEPC was ended (Minutes of the Meeting of the Board of Directors, March 11, 1946, NAACP mf 1 r3). On the other hand, the timing of the dismissal just one month after his statement about organized labor suggests that it may have been one of the factors contributing to Villard's being "out of step" with the NAACP's goals.

135. CARD Minutes, February 11, 1947, CIO Office of the Secretary Treasurer Files 193, Civil Rights Committee Folder.

136. Labor secretary Herbert Hill told black workers with grievances that the first steps in promoting fair practices were to join a union and become active members. Denton L. Watson, *Lion in the Lobby: Clarence Mitchell, Jr.'s Struggle for the Passage of Civil Rights Laws* (New York: Morrow, 1990), 98. NAACP leaders spoke enthusiastically at labor conventions and honored union leaders such as Philip Murray, Walter Reuther, and George Meany at their own. As late as

1957, Hill wrote in the NAACP's annual report that "A close day-to-day working relationship between the NAACP and the organized labor movement was an important aspect of the Association's labor program" (Jonas, *Freedom's Sword*, 255).

137. Robert Zieger, *For Jobs and Freedom: Race and Labor in America Since 1865* (Lexington: University Press of Kentucky, 2010).

138. Walter White to William Green, October 6, 1947, NAACP mf Part 13C r 2. The NAACP was also more committed to labor laws than ever before. In 1947, White believed that he needed labor support for new cloture rules, and bargained for it with the NAACP's opposition to Taft-Hartley (White to Poppy Cannon White, Series I, Box 12, Folder 113, Walter Francis White and Poppy Cannon Papers, Beinecke Rare Book and Manuscript Library, Yale University. See also Assistant Special Counsel Marian Wynn Perry to Labor Secretary Clarence Mitchell, January 1947, NAACP I-X-211).

139. Frymer, *Black and Blue*, 71

140. "NAACP Greeting to CIO Hits Taft-Hartley Law," October 16, 1947, NAACP mf Part 13a r4.

141. George Meany to Roy Wilkins, July 10, 1958, and June 3, 1964, both in NAACP mf 13 supplementary reel 2.

142. In his own Senate roll calls, Taft consistently supported antilynching laws, desegregation of the armed forces, and abolition of the poll tax. He also sponsored federal aid to education and housing with an eye toward relieving African American poverty in the South. James T. Patterson, *Mr. Republican: A Biography of Robert A. Taft* (New York: Houghton Mifflin, 1972), 322–24; Robert Taft to Edward F. Hoban November 5, 1945, and Robert Taft to Edward Freking January 18, 1946, both Clarence Wunderlin, ed., *The Papers of Robert A. Taft 1945–1948*, vol. 2 (Kent, Ohio: Kent State University Press, 2003). Randolph had consistently called on Taft when trying to desegregate the armed forces. Robert Taft to A. Philip Randolph, February 5, 1948, in Clarence Wunderlin, ed., *The Papers of Robert A. Taft 1949–1953*, vol. 3, 385.

143. Patterson, *Mr. Republican*, 448.

144. Wunderlin, *The Papers of Robert A. Taft* 3, 38.

145. Walter White to Jack Kroll, June 30, 1950, NAACP II A246 1950.

146. Janken, *White*, 306.

147. Schickler, *Racial Realignment*, 94.

148. Eugene Cheeks to Roy Wilkins, February 25, 1950, NAACP II-A-246. Wilkins wrote that many members felt the same way (James E. McCann to Roy Wilkins, June 25, 1958, mf 13 Supplemental r14, 5; Roy Wilkins to James L. McDevitt, December 16, 1958 NAACP 13 Supplemental, r14, 76).

149. Madison Jones to Eugene Cheeks, April 6, 1950, NAACP II-A-246.

150. Risa Goluboff, " 'We Live's in a Free House Such as It Is': Class and the Creation of Modern Civil Rights," *University of Pennsylvania Law Review* 1977 (2003): 1979.

151. After 1949, the NAACP reversed policy and supported federal aid to housing and education only when they were not applied in a discriminatory manner. They were sometimes supported by the UAW and CIO, but opposed by most other liberal groups. Dona C. Hamilton and Charles V. Hamilton, *The Dual Agenda: Race and Social Welfare Policies of Civil Rights Organizations* (New York: Columbia University Press, 1997), chap. 5.

152. Bates, *Pullman Porters*, 372.

153. Memorandum from Herbert Hill to Walter White, April 20, 1953, NAACP II-A-347.

154. CARD Minutes, May 12, 1953, CIO Office of the Secretary Treasurer Files 193.

155. Gary Donaldson, *Truman Defeats Dewey* (Lexington: University Press of Kentucky, 1999), 107. Earlier, he tried to preempt the MOWM with a meeting with Roosevelt, which led only to Roosevelt falsely announcing that civil rights leaders had agreed to minor concessions. White was then forced to work with the movement due to his own fumbling. Once Randolph established the MOWM as a permanent organization, White tried to isolate him in the defense program (Janken, *White*, 253, 259).

156. Gloster B. Current to State Presidents and Secretaries, and Executive Secretaries of NAACP Branches, February 19, 1947, NAACP II-A347. Also see Wilkins, *Standing Fast*, 189–90.

157. John Brophy to Philip Connelly, November 26, 1946, *Operation Dixie* mf 26.

158. Watson, *Lion in the Lobby*, 166.

159. Ibid., 297.

160. Report of the Director, September 7, 1949, CIO Office of the Secretary Treasurer Files 79, CARD 1949; CARD Minutes, January 14, 1950, CIO Office of the Secretary Treasurer Files 193, Civil Rights Meeting Folder. The CIO was generally useful in providing the NAACP access to elected officials. Unions were instrumental in arranging for the NAACP and BSCP president A. Philip Randolph to attend meetings with members of the Roosevelt administration.

161. Minutes of the CARD, January 26, 1953, CIO Office of the Secretary Treasurer Files 193, Civil Rights Meeting Folder.

162. George Weaver to Robert Birchmann, June 12 1954, NAACP II A347. It raised another $25,000 from the CIO, the Steelworkers, and other union sources in 1953 (Walter White to James Carey, April 28, 1953, NAACP II A347; Walter White to George Meany, April 17, 1953, NAACP II A347). The CIO also filed an amicus brief in *Brown*.

163. Business groups like the National Association of Manufacturers had too few members who were too widely dispersed. David B. Truman, *The Governmental Process: Political Interests and Public Opinion* (New York: Knopf, 1951).

164. No organization rivaled the manpower of organized labor—not even African American fraternities and churches (NAACP A-454).

165. When the NAACP lobbied against discrimination in federal housing in 1954, few businesses joined the battle. One of the exceptions, the National Association of Real Estate Brokers, supported the NAACP's position and asked President Eisenhower to instruct housing agencies to revise their housing policies. But it did not provide funding for the NAACP or aid in the lobbying effort in Congress, as unions did (Watson, *Lion in the Lobby*, 250–56).

166. Goluboff, *The Lost Promise of Civil Rights*, 223.

167. The NUL trajectory provides a useful example of a civil rights organization funded by business. In the end, it had less success than the NAACP even in employment discrimination, even though employment was its niche issue. In 1934, it set up "Workers' Councils" to train blacks to establish and join unions and fight against discriminatory unions. Eventually, 70 councils were set up nationwide. However, many affiliates refused to cooperate because of the tensions the councils produced with donors. The NUL later testified to the PCCR that NUL efforts to persuade employers were inadequate and that the antidiscrimination laws espoused by the NAACP were necessary. Its witness told the committee that "we have fallen flat on our faces more often than we have succeeded" and recent antidiscrimination proposals in Congress helped the league negotiate with employers to voluntarily desegregate. See Lester Granger's testimony to the President's Committee on Civil Rights, April 17, 1947, CIO Office of the Secretary Treasurer Files 42.

Chapter 3

1. Among some of the important sources of information for this book were Alan Draper, *Conflict of Interests: Organized Labor and the Civil Rights Movement in the South, 1954–1968* (Ithaca, N.Y.: ILR Press, 1994); Michael Goldfield, *The Color of Politics: Race and the Mainsprings of American Politics* (New York: New Press, 1997); Michael K. Honey, *Southern Labor and Black Civil Rights: Organizing Memphis Workers* (Urbana: University of Illinois Press, 1993); Robert Korstad, *Civil Rights Unionism: Tobacco Workers and the Struggle for Democracy in the Mid-Twentieth-Century South* (Chapel Hill: University of North Carolina Press, 2003); Robert Korstad and Nelson Lichtenstein, "Opportunities Found and Lost: Labor, Radicals and the Early Civil Rights Movement," *Journal of American History* 75 (1988); David Lewis-Coleman, *Race Against Liberalism: Black Workers and the UAW in Detroit* (Urbana: University of Illinois Press, 2008); Nelson Lichtenstein, *Walter Reuther: The Most Dangerous Man in Detroit* (Urbana: University of Illinois Press, 1997); Nancy MacLean, "Achieving the Problem of the Civil Rights Act: Herbert Hill and the NAACP's Fight for Jobs and Justice," *Labor: Studies in Working-Class History of the Americas* (Summer 2006); Robert J. Norrell, "Caste in Steel: Jim Crow Careers in Birmingham, Alabama," *Journal of American History* 73 (December 1986); and August Meier and Elliott M. Rudwick, *Black Detroit and the Rise of the UAW* (New York: Oxford University Press, 1979).

2. This chapter has strived to capture its overall trajectory without becoming mired in extensive historical debates on the nature of the CIO. Two fundamental changes in the CIO that took place after its collaboration with the NAACP are especially noteworthy: its communist purge and its merger with the CIO. Neither prevented the NAACP and CIO from working with each other during the critical period in which civil rights was becoming integrated into the Democratic Party. When the CIO purged more than a million members during the postwar Red Scare, it lost many of its most racially progressive leaders, including unions that had taken the most steps to prevent hate strikes. Robert H. Zieger, *The CIO, 1935–1955* (Chapel Hill: University of North Carolina Press, 1995), 253–55. The national organization even sided with racists to defeat communist factions in some locals. This failed to strain the alliance; in fact, the NAACP applauded the communist purge and conducted one of its own. See Zieger, *The CIO*, 282; Paul Frymer, "Race's Reality: The NAACP Confronts Racism and Inequality in the Labor Movement, 1940–65," in Joseph Lowndes, Julie Novkov, and Dorian Warren, eds., *Race and American Political Development* (New York: Routledge, 2008), 190. The CIO's merger with the AFL in 1955 also produced less change than one might expect given the AFL's history of discrimination. The new organization continued to support civil rights and other liberal positions in the Democratic Party, though in a less confrontational manner. The AFL had been moving toward the CIO's ideological position and interest in politics as the merger approached, and their platforms nearly converged. Daniel Cornfield and Holly McCammon, "Approaching Merger: The Converging Public Policy Agendas of the AFL and CIO, 1938–1955," in Nella Van Dyke and Holly J. McCammon, eds., *Strategic Alliances: Coalition Building and Social Movements* (Minneapolis: University of Minnesota Press, 2010).

3. Zieger, *The CIO*, 16, 315. Southern public relations director Lucy Randolph Mason was advised to contrast the CIO with other unions in her presentations. One correspondent wrote, "Your mission should be to gather together the liberal groups—churches, university and colleges, welfare organizations—and impress these and other representative groups with . . . the real mission of the CIO . . . that it is not merely another labor movement but is a real epoch marking industrial and democratic upheaval seeking better economic conditions and also democracy in industry" (William Jeff Lauck to Lucy Mason, June 18, 1937, *Operation Dixie* mf 62).

4. The first CIO president, John L. Lewis, thought the CIO should remain politically independent and wait for parties to bid for CIO favor, but this position isolated him and helped lead to his resignation in 1941.

5. "CIO to Back [Kerr] Scott; Rail Unions Neutral," July 20, 1946, *Operation Dixie* mf 67.

6. E. L. Sandefur, "Report of Activities North Carolina PAC 1948–1949," July 1, 1949, *Operation Dixie* mf 67. It is important to acknowledge the regional variation in the AFL, as well as change over time. The Minneapolis AFL had a decisive influence in Hubert Humphrey's efforts in favor of civil rights, as well as the creation of a local FEPC. However, many in the CIO viewed the AFL's local autonomy as a way to nurture discrimination without implicating itself ("Memo from the Secretary on interviews at Tampa, Florida, with respect to the Labor situation of the Tampa Shipbuilding and Engineering Company," July 20, 1939, *Operation Dixie* mf 64).

7. Zieger, *The CIO*, 16, 315.

8. Meeting of October 29, 1943, *Minutes of the Executive Board* mf 6.

9. Steve Fraser, *Labor Will Rule: Sidney Hillman and the Rise of American Labor* (New York: Free Press, 1991), 514.

10. Meeting of October 29, 1943, *Minutes of the Executive Board* mf 6. As it turned out, Willkie was not the nominee and whatever support he gained from labor did not transfer to Thomas Dewey.

11. While Hillman was still active in the American Labor Party and the Labor Non-Partisan League, he largely arranged for them to take direction from Roosevelt, consolidating various left-wing splinter factions behind New Deal Democrats and even endorsing a conservative Democrat for governor of New York.

12. Fraser, *Labor Will Rule*, 503–4.

13. Sean Farhang and Ira Katznelson, "The Southern Imposition: Congress and Labor in the New Deal and Fair Deal," *Studies in American Political Development* 19, no. 1 (2005).

14. Gerald Friedman, "The Political Economy of Early Southern Unionism: Race, Politics, and Labor in the South, 1880–1953," *Journal of Economic History* 60, no. 2 (2000): 384–413.

15. Tracy Roof, *American Labor, Congress, and the Welfare State, 1935–2010* (Baltimore: Johns Hopkins University Press, 2011), 28.

16. Kathleen Bawn, "Constructing 'Us': Ideology, Coalition Politics, and False Consciousness," *American Journal of Political Science* 43, no. 2 (1999): 303.

17. Even in 1947, the PCCR said that "typical 'civil rights' cases involve such varied matters" including "racial, labor, pacifist, and alien rights" ("Federal Criminal Jurisdiction Over Violations of Civil Rights," January 15, 1947, CIO Secretary Treasurer Papers 41, Records of the President's Committee on Civil Rights, Harry S. Truman Library and Museum, Independence Missouri, henceforth PCCR).

18. Walter White to Sindey Hillman, April 1, 1940, NAACP mf 13a r4. Mason concurred that "the South is Fascist—its domination of the Negro has made it easy to repeat the pattern for organized labor. . . . There is a new reason for passing the Anti-lynching Bill—it will be a protection to organizers and union members" (Lucy Mason to Molly, September 6, 1937, *Operation Dixie* mf 62). Union organizers, both African American and white, had been lynched during efforts to unionize the South, and NAACP campaigns against lynching had succeeded in reducing lynching during the 1940s.

19. Although few matters were brought to trial, a single conversation between the office and a local police official would sometimes solve the problem. Lucy Mason to Tom C. Clark, May 19 1944; Toxey Hall to Lucy Mason, May 17, 1944; Lucy Mason to Allan Haywood, June 4, 1941; all

in *Operation Dixie* mf 62. Also see Lucy Mason to Van Bittner, December 9, 1948, *Operation Dixie* mf 63.

20. Draper, *Conflict of Interests*, 86–93.

21. See Lucy Mason to Victor Rotnem, January 16, 1943, *Operation Dixie* mf 62.

22. See George Weaver's testimony to the PCCR, April 14, 1947, CIO Office of the Secretary-Treasurer Records 42.

23. Proposed letter describing the plan for National Roosevelt Clubs, undated, Philip Murray Papers Box 131, Folder 5; CIO Department of Education and Research, "When the People Vote-they Win!," *Economic Outlook* 7, no. 6 (June 1946); Statement on Political Policy, 1948, John Brophy Papers Box 12, Folder 6, American Catholic History Research Center and University Archives, Catholic University, Washington, D.C. (henceforth John Brophy Papers).

24. Roof, *American Labor, Congress, and the Welfare State*, 33.

25. In Mississippi, twenty-six counties had an African American majority, and many of the most antilabor legislators came from those counties. Lucy Mason to P Murray, October 30 1944, *Operation Dixie* mf 63. The *Michigan Chronicle*'s George Crockett, reflecting on the increased Southern black turnout in 1944, wrote that "Properly channeled, this new vote can go a long way towards the elimination of some of the most reactionary southern congressmen. Indeed no progressive movement can be developed in the South without the support of the Negro vote'" George Crockett, "Labor Looks Ahead," *Michigan Chronicle*, January 26, 1946.

26. Gerald N. Rosenberg, *The Hollow Hope: Can Courts Bring about Social Change?* (Chicago: University of Chicago Press, 1991), 61.

27. Fraser, *Labor Will Rule*, 515–16.

28. "A Political Program for Liberals," November 1, 1948, in Jack T. Ericson, ed., *Americans for Democratic Action Papers, 1932–1965* (Sanford, N.C.: Microfilming Corporation of America, 1979), mf 106 (henceforth ADA mf); Clifton Brock, *Americans for Democratic Action* (Washington, D.C.: Public Affairs Press, 1962), 50, 73, 164–65; and James Caldwell Foster, *The Union Politic* (Columbia: University of Missouri Press, 1975), 131.

29. Jack Kroll, "Memorandum to President Philip Murray Regarding Long Range PAC Objectives," 1949, Philip Murray Papers Box 133, Folder 12; Foster, *The Union Politic*, 135.

30. The concept of an "anchoring coalition" is developed in Daniel Schlozman, *When Movements Anchor Parties: Electoral Alignments in American History* (Princeton, N.J.: Princeton University Press, 2015).

31. Ibid., 151.

32. Frank L. Weyher, "Rival Unions, the Politics of Race, and Interracial Equality: The CIO vs. the AFL, 1935–1950," (Ph.D. dissertation, University of California, Los Angeles, 2003).

33. Eric Schickler, *Racial Realignment: The Transformation of American Liberalism, 1932–1965* (Princeton, N.J.: Princeton University Press, 2016), 38. E. D. Rivers, segregationist Lister Hill, Mississippi senator Theodore Bilbo (a notoriously vocal racist), were among the Southern redistributionists enthusiastic about the New Deal. Frederickson depicts the South as a whole as enthusiastic for the New Deal. See Karl Frederickson, *The Dixiecrat Revolt and the End of the Solid South, 1932–1968* (Chapel Hill: University of North Carolina Press, 2000), 18, 26. At the 1948 Mississippi Democratic convention, a student named George Maddox said, "You have never objected to flood control programs, subsidies for farmers and education, and TVA or any of the other things the government has brought in to your profit." He called states rights hypocrisy, and was booed (Frederickson, *The Dixiecrat Revolt*, 144).

34. Only three southern Democrats consistently opposed New Deal economics from the

start—Carter Glass, Harry Byrd, and Josiah Bailey.Roger Biles, *The South and the New Deal* (Lexington: University of Kentucky, 1994), 137.

35. Leuchtenberg, *The White House Looks South*, 187.

36. Sidney M. Milkis, *The President and the Parties: The Transformation of the American Party System Since the New Deal* (New York: Oxford University Press, 1993), 89–91; Earl Black and Merle Black, *The Rise of Southern Republicans* (Cambridge, Mass.: Belknap Press of Harvard University Press, 2000), 80, 141, 160. According to their classifications of MCs, the Civil Rights Act of 1964 and Voting Rights Act of 1965 resulted in a large increase in "nominal" Democrats, a large decrease in moderate Democrats, and a somewhat smaller decrease in Democrats adhering to national party stances.

37. Zieger, *The CIO*, 83.

38. Maurice Zeitlin and Frank L. Weyher, "Black and White, Unite and Fight: Interracial Working Class Solidarity and Racial Employment Equality," *American Journal of Sociology* 107 (September 2001): 435.

39. In Memphis, for example, blacks constituted a majority of the 27,000 CIO members in 1944. Lucy Mason to Eleanor Roosevelt, March 10, 1944, *Operation Dixie* mf 62.

40. Carey Haigler to Lucy Mason, May 22, 1945, *Operation Dixie* mf 63.

41. See Mason's comments in Minutes of Regional Conference of CIO and International Union Directors October 12, 1942, *Operation Dixie* mf 64.

42. Noel Beddow to Philip Murray, July 12, 1943, Philip Murray Papers Box 42, Folder 15.

43. Antilabor politicians and newspapers could use union discrimination as an argument to oppose unions, as Senator Robert Taft would with the Taft-Hartley Act. Report of George Weaver to Committee Members, April 26, 1943, CIO Office of the Secretary Treasurer Records 192).

44. "Mr. Shapiro" stated at a regional CIO conference, "You have not mentioned the white workers who think and say they will not come into the union with 'niggers'—I have heard that time and time again. That is a problem of the entire south" (Minutes of Regional Conference of CIO and International Union Directors, October 12, 1942, *Operation Dixie* mf 64).

45. Barbara Griffith, *The Crisis of American Labor: Operation Dixie and the Defeat of the CIO* (Philadelphia: Temple University Press, 1988), 68, 72–82.

46. Zeitlin and Weyher, "Black and White, Unite and Fight," 442.

47. R. E. Farr to Philip Murray, May 19, 1950, Box 36, Folder 17; see Ernest Wooten to Philip Murray, June 2, 1950, Philip Murray Papers Box 36, File 18; Francis C. Shane to Philip Murray, May 23, 1950, Philip Murray Papers Box 36, File 17.

48. William Botkin to George Brown, April 5, 1944, *Operation Dixie* mf 62.

49. Robert H. Zieger, *For Jobs and Freedom: Race and Labor in America since 1865* (Lexington: University of Kentucky Press, 2007), 136.

50. Weyher, *Rival Unions, the Politics of Race, and Interracial Equality*.

51. When Southern public relations director Lucy Randolph Mason attempted to persuade white workers to welcome blacks into the union, she mentioned not only the greater likelihood of succeeding in securing higher wages, but their value as political allies. Mason declared that "A square deal on part of white workers for Negro workers means that both will be interested in the same qualified candidates for public office and will vote together . . . Negroes' votes will back white workers' votes if Negroes know they can trust white people to look out for economic interests of all workers." Lucy Mason, "Reasons White Workers Should Welcome Negroes into Unions," May 23, 1945, *Operation Dixie* mf 63. Also see Lucy Mason, "The CIO and the South," March 1944, *Operation Dixie* mf 64.

52. CARD Minutes, August 16, 1946, CIO Office of the Secretary Treasurer Records 192.

53. CARD Minutes, February 11, 1947, CIO Office of the Secretary Treasurer Records 192. Schlozman argues that Operation Dixie failed because the CIO, as a responsible Democratic Party "anchor," had purged the leftist unions that would have fundamentally challenged the power structures in the South and assisted the organizing drives. But CIO leaders decided to keep politics separate from organizing in the South well before the communist purge. No doubt they wanted Southerners to adopt their political goals, but merely organizing "bread and butter" unions was a difficult enough task for the time being. The CIO was prioritizing its southern membership goals over its political goals, not prioritizing its relationship with the Democratic Party over its southern membership goals (Lucy Mason to Jacob Billingkopf, May 20, 1942, *Operation Dixie* mf 62). On the dangers of public advocacy of civil rights, also see Lucy Mason, March 24 1942, *Operation Dixie* mf 62.

54. Roof, *American Labor, Congress, and the Welfare State*, 119.

55. Weyher, *Rival Unions, the Politics of Race, and Interracial Equality*.

56. Schickler, *Racial Realignment*, 36–42, 79.

57. Nelson Lichtenstein, *The Most Dangerous Man in Detroit: Walter Reuther and the Fate of American Labor* (New York: Basic, 1995), 50–59.

58. Meiers and Rudwick, *Black Detroit and the Rise of the UAW*, 44. One director of the CIO-affiliated United Electrical, Machine, and Radio Workers of America said that communists were among the most experienced and reliable labor organizers in the early CIO (Foster, *The Union Politic*, 80).

59. Zieger, *The CIO*, 28.

60. For example, see CARD Minutes, May 25, 1943, CIO Office of the Secretary Treasurer Records 192.

61. Pat Angelo, *Philip Murray—Union Man: A Life Story* (Bloomington, Ind.: Xlibris, 2003), 32, 46, 71, 182–83.

62. Foster, *The Union Politic*, 91.

63. Detroit socialists earlier attempted to isolate Reuther when he worked with the Farmer Labor Party, thought by older socialists to be a communist front.

64. Fraser, *Labor Will Rule*, 16, 434, 449.

65. Frances Fox Piven and Richard Cloward, *Poor People's Movements: Why They Succeed, How They Fail* (New York: Vintage, 1978), 161.

66. Paula F. Pfeffer, *A. Philip Randolph, Pioneer of the Civil Rights Movement* (Baton Rouge: Louisiana State University Press, 1996), 23–24.

67. "The CIO in the South," September 1941, *Operation Dixie* mf 64, 4; Lucy Mason, Radio Script for WGPC, Albany Georgia, June 22, 1948, *Operation Dixie* mf 64, 5; Lucy Mason, Spring 1939, *Operation Dixie* mf 64.

68. Paul Frymer, *Black and Blue: African Americans, the Labor Movement, and the Decline of the Democratic Party* (Princeton, N.J.: Princeton University Press, 2008), 54, 55–56. Both the AFL and the CIO blamed the NAACP when union members supported one over the other. See William Green to Roy Wilkins, October 22, 1943 and Walter White to William Smith, December 23, 1943, both in NAACP mf 13A r15.

69. George Weaver to Walter White, April 14, 1953, NAACP II-A-347. See also William Smith to Walter White, April 6, 1949, NAACP II-A-347.

70. John Kirk, *Redefining the Color Line: Black Activism in Little Rock, Arkansas, 1940–1970* (Gainesville: University Press of Florida, 2002), 31.

71. Patricia Sullivan, *Lift Every Voice: The NAACP and the Making of the Civil Rights Movement* (New York: New Press, 2009), 328; Henry Lee Moon, "Suffrage 52–53," NAACP II A452.

72. Among the groups were the Georgia Association of Citizens Democratic Clubs, Mississippi Progressive Voters League, Florida Progressive Voters League, and Jefferson County Progressive Democratic Council in Birmingham. Steven Lawson, *Black Ballots: Voting Rights in the South, 1944–1969* (New York: Columbia University Press, 1976), 125–26, 129. Lawson argues that while union officials were active in voter registration efforts, the rank-and-file was not (127).

73. Steven F. Lawson, *Running for Freedom: Civil Rights and Black Politics in America since 1941* (Philadelphia: Temple University Press, 1991), 57–58. NAACP efforts often fell short in rural areas. Communists were far more active in some areas, such as Winston-Salem. Honey, *Southern Labor and Black Civil Rights*; Rick Halpern, "Organized Labour, Black Workers and the 20th Century South: The Emerging Revision," *Social History* 19, no. 3 (October 1994), 361. For the extent of communist contribution, see Alex Lichtenstein, " 'Scientific Unionism' and the 'Negro Question': Communists and the Transport Workers Union in Miami, 1944–1949," in Robert Zieger, ed., *Southern Labor in Transition*, 1940–1995 (Knoxville: University Press of Tennessee, 1997), 59–60; August Meier and Elliott M. Rudwick, "Communist Unions and the Black Community: The Case of the Transport Workers Union, 1934–1944," *Labor History* 23 (1982): 196–97; and Korstad and Lichtenstein, "Opportunities Lost and Found," 791.

74. Remarks of Thurgood Marshall Before CIO Convention, Atlantic City, December 3, 1952, NAACP II-A347.

75. Zieger, *The CIO*, 157.

76. President's Committee for Civil Rights, September 12, 1947, CIO Office of the Secretary Treasurer Records 42, 906.

77. Arthur Goldberg to all regional CIO Directors, April 24, 1950, CIO Office of the Secretary Treasurer Records 193.

78. Minutes of the Meeting on Civil Rights, February 11, 1947, CIO Office of the Secretary Treasurer Records 192. Director George Weaver said "if you can go in and help them without a lot of publicity, you have made lifetime friends. . . . When it becomes a matter of public knowledge, you might be able to overcome the problem but you have made a lasting enemy. He will never forgive you." Some members objected that making an example out of some unions would spur others to action and use the publicity to show that CARD is accomplishing its task. Also see James Leary's comments in the CARD Minutes, December 16, 1947, CIO Office of the Secretary Treasurer Records 192.

79. Report of the Panel on Publicity and Education Techniques, CIO Office of the Secretary Treasurer Records 79, Committee to Abolish Racial Discrimination, 1947–48 Folder.

80. CARD Minutes, March 13, 1945, CIO Office of the Secretary Treasurer Records 192.

81. CARD Minutes, February 11, 1947, CIO Office of the Secretary Treasurer Records 192.

82. Meier and Rudwick, *Black Detroit and the Rise of the UAW*, 196, 217.

83. Korstad and Lichtenstein, "Opportunities Found and Lost," 797.

84. Lucy Mason to Jacob Billingkopf, May 20, 1942, *Operation Dixie* mf 62. On the dangers of public advocacy of civil rights, also see Lucy Mason, March 24, 1942, *Operation Dixie* mf 62.

85. Lucy Mason to W. W. Ball, May 27, 1940, *Operation Dixie* mf 62. Her statement of policy was corroborated by John L. Lewis in John L. Lewis to W. W. Ball, June 10, 1940, *Operation Dixie* mf 62.

86. Zieger, *The CIO*, 157. One CARD member reported that verbal ultimatums alone seem to have little impact on uncooperative unions: "I have seen international officers come in, lay down the law, and I have seen the international representatives agree wholeheartedly with him,

and then when they go away they say 'Hell, that's just part of their job—we don't have to pay any attention to that'" (CARD Minutes, December 16, 1947, CIO Office of the Secretary Treasurer Records 192). Also see James Carey's statements in CARD Minutes, March 13, 1945, CIO Office of the Secretary Treasurer Records 192.

87. In Jacksonville, a CIO affiliate instituted desegregated meetings after two years of education and the "opposition by white workers to mixed meetings" was still bitter (Charles Smolikoff to Lucy Mason, May 31, 1945, *Operation Dixie* mf 63). In another workplace, a Texas Packinghouse Workers Union negotiated with the company to remove signs for segregated facilities, and a "near-riot started among the workers" ("How Three CIO Leaders Answered This Question," April 4, 1946, *Operation Dixie* mf 64). In a subsequent election, however, the white supremacist faction of the union was defeated. In addition to fighting white racism, CARD taught blacks to "forget their historic animus to all whites and to forget extreme Negro nationalism" (Charles Smolikoff to Lucy Mason, May 31, 1945, *Operation Dixie* mf 63). Also see George Weaver's comments in Meeting of October 29, 1943, *Minutes of the Executive Board* mf 6).

88. Remarks of Thurgood Marshall Before CIO Convention, Atlantic City, December 3, 1952, NAACP II-A347.

89. Zeitlin and Weyher, "Black and White, Unite and Fight," 440.

90. Lucy Mason to William Watkins, November 5, 1946, *Operation Dixie* mf 64.

91. Director's Report, August 16, 1944, CIO Office of the Secretary Treasurer Records 196.

92. Report of PAC 1951, August 14, 1951, Jack Kroll Papers Box 7, Library of Congress, Washington, D.C. (henceforth Jack Kroll Papers), 10.

93. "PAC Organizational Program for 1952," Jack Kroll Papers Box 7, CIO PAC 1950–1953.

94. Paul Christopher to Jack Kroll, January 20, 1948, *Operation Dixie* mf 67.

95. Philip Murray Papers Box 132, Folder 5, Folder 4.

96. Jacob Clayman to George Weaver, June 30, 1950, CIO Office of the Secretary Treasurer Records 191, Civil Rights Conference Folder; also see George Weaver to C. B. Blankenship, July 31, 1950, CIO Office of the Secretary Treasurer Records 191.

97. George Weaver to Roy Wilkins, August 8, 1950, CIO Office of the Secretary Treasurer Records 191. Wilkins said that NAACP policy prevented him from supporting any statement but other civil rights leaders might do so as individuals (Wilkins to Weaver, August 30, 1950, CIO Office of the Secretary Treasurer Files 191).

98. The organizer wrote to the NAACP, "We find it rather difficult to do any effective work in race relations here in Hamilton, as long as the one and only negro newspaper comes out continuously against the CIO." Berkeley Watterson to Roy Wilkins, November 25, 1946, NAACP II-A-347.

99. Frymer, *Black and Blue*.

100. Robert L. Carter to branch presidents, August 31, 1964, NAACP mf supplement to Part 13, r11.

101. Editorial, *Twin City Observer*, May 5, 1960, 4.

102. Robert L. Carter to branch presidents, August 31, 1964, mf supplement to Part 13, r 11.

103. Schickler, *Racial Realignment*, 231.

Chapter 4

1. Some polls with different wording resulted in higher levels of support, but public opinion was ambivalent at best. Howard Schuman, Charlotte Steeh, Lawrence Bobo, and Maria Krysan,

Racial Attitudes in America: Trends and Interpretations (Cambridge, Mass.: Harvard University Press, 1998), 17.

2. Anthony Chen, *The Fifth Freedom: Jobs, Politics, and Civil Rights in the United States, 1941–1972* (Princeton, N.J.: Princeton University Press, 2009), 55–60; Schuman et al., *Racial Attitudes in America*, 207. Even Schumann et al. concede that attitude change is only a partial explanation of policy change, and that behavioral change (sometimes brought about by policy change) changes attitudes.

3. Edward G. Carmines and James A. Stimson, *Issue Evolution: Race and the Transformation of American Politics* (Princeton, N.J.: Princeton University Press, 1989), 36.

4. Brian Feinstein and Eric Schickler, "Platforms and Partners: The Civil Rights Realignment Reconsidered," *Studies in American Political Development* 22 (2008). Northern Democrats were more likely to vote for discharge petitions beginning in 1941 and more likely to make speeches on its behalf in 1945. By the 81st Congress (1949–1951), they were more likely to sponsor bills. I find the first major shift in presidential nominations and platforms in 1948, representing the party's national stance.

5. David Karol, *Party Position Change in American Politics: Coalition Management* (Cambridge: Cambridge University Press, 2009).

6. Anthony S. Chen, Robert W. Mickey, and Robert P. Van Houweling, "Explaining the Contemporary Alignment of Race and Party: Evidence from California's 1946 Ballot Initiative on Fair Employment," *Studies in American Political Development* 22 (2008): 204–28; Chen, *The Fifth Freedom*.

7. These figures are calculated from Frank Hobbs and Nicole Stoops, *Demographic Trends in the 20th Century* (Washington, D.C.: U.S. Census Bureau, 2002); also see Carmines and Stimson, *Issue Evolution*, 33.

8. NAACP II-A-226.

9. Carmines and Stimson, *Issue Evolution*, 7.

10. Ralph Bunche, "Report on the Needs of the Negro (for the Republican Program Committee)," July 1, 1939, NAACP II-L-27.

11. NAACP secretary White commented in 1947 that "Wendell Willkie in 1940 came closer to breaking the support given the Democrats by Negro voters than any other Republican since Theodore Roosevelt." After the 1940 election, Willkie had introduced him to Hollywood producers in his effort to persuade them to use less stereotypical depictions of African Americans. Kenneth Janken, *White: The Biography of Walter White, Mr. NAACP* (New York: New Press, 2003), 267–68.

12. Ralph Bunche, "Report on the Needs of the Negro (for the Republican Program Committee)," July 1, 1939, NAACP II-L-27. Weiss's account in *Farewell to the Party of Lincoln* largely concurs. Nancy J. Weiss, *Farewell to the Party of Lincoln: Black Politics in the Age of FDR* (Princeton, N.J.: Princeton University Press, 1983).

13. Georgia governor Eugene Talmadge assembled a group of Democrats to oppose Roosevelt's policies in 1938. At one of their gatherings, Senator Josiah Bailey declared that "Our Party is being taken away from us by John Lewis, Harold Ickes, Robert Vann, White of the Society for the Advancement of the Negroes, Madam Perkins, Harry Hopkins, Cochran and Cohen. . . . It is a singular thing that we have permitted men who were not Democrats to take our Party captive" (William Leuchtenberg, *The White House Looks South: Franklin D. Roosevelt, Harry S. Truman, Lyndon B. Johnson* (Baton Rouge: Louisiana State University Press, 2005),126–28).

14. Christopher Manning, *William L. Dawson and the Limits of Black Electoral Leadership*

(Dekalb, Illinois: Northern Illinois University Press, 2009), 97. Although Dawson had previously urged the removal of conservative southerners from the party, the pull of the Democratic Party toward the existing balance between North and South channeled his reconstructive sympathies into maintaining the status quo. However, Dawson did oppose the nomination of Byrnes as a vice president, and supported the controversial Wallace.

15. Republicans in the 80th Congress failed to honor any of the civil rights pledges of the 1944 platform, but Republicans had not controlled Congress in more than a decade when the NAACP analyzed the 1944 election.

16. "Special Meeting of the Board of Directors of the NAACP," July 31, 1944, NAACP mf 1 r11 (f471).

17. Ibid. Spingarn and White agreed that the NAACP should criticize both party platforms.

18. White opposed a public announcement of this priority in 1948 (Walter White to Richard Allan, February 27, 1948, NAACP mf 13 r 13). On the change in priorities, see CARD Minutes, January 14, 1950, CIO Office of the Secretary Treasurer Records 193, Civil Rights Meeting Folder. The NAACP and other civil rights groups convinced Truman's advisers to focus on the FEPC and drop other matters in 1950. On the NAACP's opposition to national action on the poll tax, see Conference of Negro Organization Minutes, September 4, 1953, NAACP II-A-452, 2.

19. Karol, *Party Position Change in American Politics.*

20. Denton L. Watson, *Lion in the Lobby: Clarence Mitchell, Jr.'s Struggle for the Passage of Civil Rights Laws* (New York: Morrow, 1990), 98. , 137.

21. Feinstein and Schickler, "The Civil Rights Realignment Reconsidered," 19; William Berman, *The Politics of Civil Rights in the Truman Administration* (Columbus: Ohio State University Press, 1970), 59.

22. Clarence Wunderlin, ed., *The Papers of Robert A. Taft 1945–1948*, vol. 2 (Kent, Ohio: Kent State University Press, 2003), 46–47. Of course, the Republicans could have used any number of rhetorical flourishes or constitutional rationales to paper over any such contradictions. For example, the Fourteenth Amendment might have been reinterpreted to justify federal civil rights policies while the Tenth Amendment left other economic matters to the states. Louis Kesselman, *The Social Politics of FEPC: A Study in Reform Pressure Movements* (Chapel Hill: University of North Carolina Press, 1948), 170.

23. Paul Sifton to George Weaver, January 30, 1947, CIO Office of the Secretary Treasurer Records 206, National Council for a Permanent FEPC Folder (1947).

24. Kevin McMahon, *Reconsidering Roosevelt on Race* (Chicago: University of Chicago Press, 2004), 101.

25. While it is possible that Roosevelt hoped to avoid unpleasant conversation by passing the responsibility to Hillman, contemporaneous written sources offer no support for this theory. Robert H. Ferrell, *Choosing Truman: The Democratic Convention of 1944* (Columbia: University of Missouri Press, 1994), 39–47.

26. Interview with Clark Clifford by Jerry Hess, May 10, 1971, Harry S. Truman Presidential Library and Museum, Independence Missouri (henceforth Truman Library).

27. Most of this memorandum was written by James Rowe, then working for the Hoover Commission, but Clifford synthesized other advice, adding several pages to the Rowe memorandum.

28. Memorandum from Clark Clifford to Harry S. Truman, November 19, 1947, Political File, Clark M. Clifford Papers (henceforth Clifford Papers), Truman Library. A Farm Credit

Administration official complained at the same time that, "Of course, they made their greatest progress under us and should be grateful; but you know, and I know, how easily they are swayed." Joseph Lawrence to Howard McGrath, May 18, 1948, Student Research File 19, J. Howard McGrath Papers, Truman Library.

29. Memorandum from Clark Clifford to Harry S. Truman, November 19, 1947, Political File, Clifford Papers.

30. William L. Batt, Jr., to Gael Sullivan, April 20, 1948, Political File, Clifford Papers.

31. Memorandum from Oscar Ewing and David Kingsley to Clark Clifford, January 30, 1948, George Elsey Papers, Folder 2, Truman Library.

32. David Niles to Phileo Nash, "A Minimum Civil Rights Program For the Eightieth Congress," January 8, 1948, Student Research File 19, Phileo Nash Papers, Truman Library.

33. Interview of Phileo Nash by Jerry Hess, October 18, 1966, Truman Library.

34. Leuchtenberg, *The White House Looks South*, 182, 185, 190.

35. Interview with Clark Clifford by Jerry Hess, April 13, 1971, Truman Library.

36. Gary Donaldson, *Truman Defeats Dewey* (Lexington: University Press of Kentucky, 1999), 121, 161.

37. James L. Sundquist, *Dynamics of the Party System: Alignment and Realignment of Political Parties in the United States* (Washington, D.C.: Brookings Institution, 1983), 306–7.

38. CIO state activity had a statistically significant impact on state party platforms in the 1940s; a strong CIO presence had a stronger effect on state Democratic parties than a large African American population (Feinstein and Schickler, "Platforms and Partners"). Feinstein and Schickler attribute much of the change at the state level to "meso level actors," who are statewide officeholders and office-seekers. During the 1940s, many meso-level actors were not vote maximizers seeking reelection as Downs imagines candidates, but amateur activists working for political causes. In this regard, they still resemble Cohen et al.'s intense policy demanders even though they hold office. Marty Cohen, David Karol, Hans Noel, and John Zaller, *The Party Decides: Presidential Nominations Before and After Reform* (Chicago: University of Chicago Press, 2008).

39. Jack Kroll, "Political Review," undated 1940, Jack Kroll Papers 4. Likewise, the CIO PAC public statement on the 1948 elections read, "A coalition of do-nothing Republicans and bigoted Dixiecrats has steadfastly adhered to the philosophy of the National Association of Manufacturers" (Meeting of October 29 1943, *Minutes of the Executive Board* mf 11). In another telling quote, UAW president Reuther wrote to White that the 1949 filibuster of a civil rights bill was an "unholy alliance between the Dixiecrats and reactionary Northern Republicans" that "underscores the need to bring about fundamental political realignments in American politics" (Walter Reuther to Walter White, March 30, 1949, NAACP VIII 83). I came across many statements such as this in my research.

40. In the South, seven PAC-endorsed candidates prevailed and only one survived a primary challenge (only two others survived a PAC challenge outside the South). Steve Fraser, *Labor Will Rule: Sidney Hillman and the Rise of American Labor* (New York: Free Press, 1991), 514.

41. James Caldwell Foster, *The Union Politic* (Columbia: University of Missouri Press, 1975), 28. In 1948, 64 percent of the 215 House candidates endorsed by the CIO PAC won, as did 81 percent of the 21 endorsed senators and 82 percent of the 17 endorsed governors (Jack Kroll, Report on 1948, Jack Kroll Papers 4).

42. Jack Kroll to E. L. Sandefur, July 13, 1949, *Operation Dixie* mf 67.

43. Lucy Mason to Jack Jenkins, July 14, 1949, *Operation Dixie* mf 63. Also see Alan Draper, *Conflict of Interests: Organized Labor and the Civil Rights Movement in the South, 1954–1968*

(Ithaca, N.Y.: ILR Press, 1994), 86–93. Draper documents examples of the response from the rank and file. Guernsey accused Citizen's Councils of using race to disguise an antilabor agenda. Many local union presidents said they were members and it had no such agenda (75–76).

44. Eric Schickler, *Racial Realignment: The Transformation of American Liberalism, 1932–1965* (Princeton, N.J.: Princeton University Press, 2016), 88.

45. Statement on Political Policy, 1948, John Brophy Papers Box 13, Folder 6.

46. Directors Report, June 29, 1948, CIO Office of the Secretary Treasurer Files 196.

47. Meeting of August 30, 1948, *Minutes of the Executive Board* mf 11.

48. Nash stated "Now, some of the President's advisers, I'm sure, thought it was time to ease off. I don't think that they were wrong, in general, they were just wrong, when reference to a convention where some people undoubtedly had concluded that Mr. Truman was going down to defeat anyhow and, therefore, they might as well take care of themselves" (interview of Phileo Nash by Jerry Hess, October 18, 1966, Truman Library).

49. James Loeb to Franklin Roosevelt, Jr., April 27, 1948, ADA mf 31.

50. James Loeb to Frank McCulloch, April 24, 1948, ADA mf 31.

51. James Loeb to Mr. and Mrs. Robert Richter, undated 1948, ADA mf 17; James Loeb to J.C. Schutte, July 27, 1948, ADA mf 17.

52. There are numerous letters making this point, including some form letters, between the convention and the general election (ADA mf 17).

53. CARD Minutes, November 19, 1948, CIO Office of the Secretary Treasurer Records 193, Civil Rights Committee Folder. Although Carey claimed that the presidents supported him throughout his efforts, historical accounts since then do not support this claim.

54. Of the 1,200 delegates, 120 were ADA members. Speech by Jack Kroll to Convention of United Gas, Coke, and Chemical Workers at Milwaukee, July 22, 1948, Jack Kroll Papers Box 4, January–July. President Truman later thanked the CIO for its maneuvering (CARD Minutes, November 19, 1948, CIO Office of the Secretary Treasurer Records 193, Civil Rights Committee Folder).

55. James Loeb to Joseph Sharts, July 27, 1948, ADA mf 17.

56. Interview with James Loeb by Jerry Hess, June 26, 1970, Truman Library.

57. Interview with Clark Clifford by Jerry Hess, July 26, 1971, Truman Library.

58. Leuchtenberg, *The White House Looks South*, 194.

59. Interview with Oscar Ewing by J. R. Fuchs, May 2, 1969, Truman Library. Phileo Nash remembered that the "President was going to have kind a hard time getting the nomination . . . in other words, if you are looking at blocs of voters, and you are interested in their sympathies, the pro-civil righters had been taken care of with a report and a strong message" (interview of Phileo Nash by Jerry Hess, October 18, 1966, Truman Library).

60. Leuchtenberg, *The White House Looks South*, 194.

61. Interview with Clark Clifford by Jerry Hess, July 26, 1971, Truman Library.

62. Interview with James Loeb by Jerry Hess, June 26, 1970, Truman Library.

63. Interview with John Barriere by Jerry Hess, December 20, 1966, Truman Library.

64. James Loeb to Alfred Baker Lewis, July 28, 1948, ADA mf 17.

65. Donaldson, *Truman Defeats Dewey*, 162.

66. Interview with Andrew Biemiller by James Fuchs, July 29, 1977, Truman Library.

67. Jack Kroll Speech to Convention of United Gas, Coke, and Chemical Workers at Milwaukee, July 22, 1948, Jack Kroll Papers 4, January–July, 3. Also see Lucy Mason to P. Murray, October 30, 1944, *Operation Dixie* mf 63.

68. Committee to Abolish Discrimination Meeting Transcript, April 4, 1949, CIO Office of the Secretary Treasurer Files 191, CIO Committee on Civil Rights Folder.

69. James Loeb to David Engvall, undated 1948, ADA mf 31; James Loeb to Babbette Deutsch, July 28, 1948, ADA mf 17.

70. H. L. Mitchell to James Loeb, July 20, 1948, ADA mf 31.

71. Patricia Sullivan, *Lift Every Voice: The NAACP and the Making of the Civil Rights Movement* (New York: New Press, 2009), 328.

72. African American support for Truman was over 70 percent (Figure 2), but white working class support for Truman was nearly 80 percent. David A. Bositis, "Blacks and the 2004 Democratic National Convention," Joint Center for Political and Economic Studies, Table 1, Presidential Vote and Party Identification of Black Americans, 1936–2000, 9; Abramson et al., *Change and Continuity in the 2008 Elections*, 174–75.

73. Paul Abramson, "Class Voting in the 1976 Election," *Journal of Politics* 40 (1978): 1068; Berman, *The Politics of Civil Rights in the Truman Administration*, 231; "CIO PAC Election Results," undated, Jack Kroll Papers 7, 6.

74. Milkis presents the executive order as Truman's own initiative, not hemmed in by party activists. Sidney M. Milkis, *The President and the Parties: The Transformation of the American Party System Since the New Deal* (New York: Oxford University Press, 1993), 158.

75. Scott C. James, "A Theory of Presidential Commitment and Opportunism: Swing States, Pivotal Groups and Civil Rights Under Truman and Clinton" (paper presented at the annual meeting of the American Political Science Association, 1997).

76. John Barriere, DNC research assistant, remembered that "after the adoption of the Humphrey-Biemiller amendment to the platform at the convention . . . you had no choice but to pursue a strong civil rights position and hope that this would enable you to bring out a big minority vote in the key urban industrial states and enable you to carry them; and that there was no point at that junction of trying to placate the South, that is, for better or worse you had taken the fork to try to get the Negro vote and that you just had to take your chances with the Southerners, you couldn't double track at that point. It seems to me, that once that amendment had been adopted the issue teas settled" (interview with John Barierre by Jerry Hess, December 20, 1966, Truman Library).

77. Milkis, *The President and the Parties.*

78. Daniel Schlozman, *When Movements Anchor Parties: Electoral Alignments in American History* (Princeton, N.J.: Princeton University Press, 2015).

79. Meeting of August 30, 1948, *Minutes of the Executive Board* mf 6.

80. Pat Angelo, *Philip Murray—Union Man: A Life Story* (Bloomington, Ind.: Xlibris, 2003), 32, 46, 71, 182–83.

81. Schickler, *Racial Realignment*, 218.

82. The most important party bosses were arguably New York's Flynn, who pressured the Pennsylvania delegation to support the plank, and David L. Lawrence, who controlled the Pennsylvania delegation. Flynn's small collection of written records is held at the Franklin Roosevelt Library in Hyde Park, New York. Almost no correspondence exists between him and other party bosses, or Humphrey and Biemiller. The University of Pittsburgh and the Pennsylvania State archives contain some written records from Lawrence, but only after he became governor in 1959. Illinois party boss Jacob Arvey's records are kept at the Truman Library. This collection consists of only 175 documents, just two of which date to Truman's years as president. Frank Hague of New Jersey, who also agreed to the civil rights plank, did not leave any substantial written records.

83. Several of these party bosses softened their willingness to antagonize the South over time. Bosses Arvey, Carmine De Sapio, and Lawrence later opposed efforts of an ambitious party chairman, Paul Butler, to liberalize the national party on civil rights. For a time, Butler was a conciliatory figure, but he seems to have changed course after the reaction of Southerners to the *Brown* decision, beginning with Little Rock. In late 1958, Butler said on national television that the South should not remain in the party just to retain chairmanships. Not only were southern leaders furious, but Pennsylvania boss Lawrence sent copies of Butler's 1954 pledge to National Committee members and called for his ouster. His opponents did not have enough votes to remove him before the 1960 convention, but Butler announced he would step down, knowing he would not win the next round. Butler's tenure showed that a party employee was willing to marginalize a party faction to advance another party faction, but this was more than a decade after the electoral implications of the Great Migration became clear. It was ten years after pressure groups were willing to marginalize the South at the 1948 convention, and even then, it cost him his job. George C. Roberts, *Paul M. Butler, Hoosier Politician and National Political Leader* (Lanham, Md.: University Press of America, 1987), 54, 94, 97, 160.

84. Timothy Thurber, *The Politics of Equality: Hubert H. Humphrey and the African American Freedom Struggle* (New York: Columbia University Press, 1999), 19, 43.

85. Jennifer A. Delton, *Making Minnesota Liberal: Civil Rights and the Transformation of the Democratic Party* (Minneapolis: University of Minnesota Press, 2002), 121.

86. Cohen et al., *The Party Decides*, 121.

87. Thurber, *The Politics of Equality*, 97.

88. Foster, *The Union Politic*, 32–33.

89. Hubert Humphrey to Phillip Murray, March 30, 1949, Phillip Murray Papers Box 143, Folder 14; Foster, *The Union Politic*, 134.

90. Clifton Brock, *Americans for Democratic Action* (Washington, D.C.: Public Affairs Press, 1962), 73–74, 164–65.

91. The ADA could have chosen to become a meeting ground for labor unions rather than a liberal advocacy group, but if it were limited to such a purpose, the other liberal interests in the organization would be overwhelmed. Discussed by James Loeb, Louis Schaeffer, and Morris Ernst in the minutes of the National Board Meeting, September 20, 1947, ADA mf 45.

92. "A Strategy for Liberals," undated, ADA mf 106.

Chapter 5

1. Steven Gillon, *Politics and Vision: The ADA and American Liberalism, 1947–1985* (Oxford: Oxford University Press, 1987), 133.

2. Nick Bryant, *The Bystander: John F. Kennedy and the Struggle for Black Equality* (New York: Basic, 2006), 181.

3. Edward G. Carmines and James A. Stimson, *Issue Evolution: Race and the Transformation of American Politics* (Princeton, N.J.: Princeton University Press, 1989), 35. Also see Marty Cohen, David Karol, Hans Noel, and John Zaller, *The Party Decides: Presidential Nominations Before and After Reform* (Chicago: University of Chicago Press, 2008), 89; Ira Katznelson, *Fear Itself: The New Deal and the Origins of Our Time* (New York: Liveright, 2014), 400.

4. Eric Schickler, "New Deal Liberalism and Racial Liberalism in the Mass Public, 1937–1968," *Perspectives on Politics* 11, no. 1 (2013): 33.

5. Arthur Schlesinger to William Rivkin, January 29, 1952, Stevenson Papers Box 73, Seeley Mudd Manuscript Library, Princeton University, Princeton, New Jersey (henceforth Stevenson

264   Notes to Pages 88–89

Papers); Walter Reuther to Adlai Stevenson, July 29, 1952, Stevenson Papers Box 68; Alfred Baker Lewis to Harry S. Truman, January 28, 1952, Harry S. Truman Papers Box 299. There is a lengthy correspondence between Eleanor Roosevelt and Adlai Stevenson (Stevenson Papers Box 68).

6. Arthur Schlesinger to Adlai Stevenson, March 25, 1952, Stevenson Papers Box 73.

7. Violet Gunther to Robert Trentlyon, February 18, 1952, ADA mf 21. Its annual convention in May did not endorse a candidate because loyalty was split between Stevenson, Kefauver, and Harriman (Reginald Zalles to Robert Thomas, October 22, 1952, ADA mf 21).

8. At the time, it was the Independent Voters of Illinois, which later became the Illinois ADA. Stevenson had forcefully denied he was a candidate. Porter McKeever, *Adlai Stevenson: His Life and Legacy* (New York: Quill, 1991), 180.

9. Denton L. Watson, *Lion in the Lobby: Clarence Mitchell, Jr.'s Struggle for the Passage of Civil Rights Laws* (New York: Morrow, 1990), 213–15.

10. Quoted in Carmines and Stimson, *Issue Evolution* (36) and McKeever, *Adlai Stevenson* (222).

11. Mississippi representative Frank Smith called the Richmond speech "the best summary of over-all Southern problems ever made by a national political figure," but "most of the knowledge of this speech in the South was confined to the headlines 'Stevenson Tells South he is still in Favor of Civil Rights.'" Frank Smith to Stephen Mitchell, September 25, 1952, Stevenson Papers Box 58.

12. Abraham Holtzman, "Party Responsibility and Loyalty," *Journal of Politics* 22, no. 3 (1960): 487. Stevenson's forgiveness alienated some liberals. Several hundred delegates gathered at 3 a.m. on the last day of the convention to oppose him. Humphrey persuaded them that Stevenson was a liberal and opposing his nomination would hurt them if the South could take credit for his inevitable victory. DA lobbyist Rauh and Chicago boss Arvey, both of whom supported the 1948 civil rights plank, supported party unity and applauded Humphrey for "pumping sense into large numbers of heads." Timothy Thurber, *The Politics of Equality: Hubert H. Humphrey and the African American Freedom Struggle* (New York: Columbia University Press, 1999), 82, 270 n34.

13. Many of the Dixiecrats who had opposed Truman continued opposing the national nominee in 1952. In the end, South Carolina governor Byrnes opposed Stevenson. He declared in a public address that "Four years ago the people of South Carolina at long last realized that the Democratic Party had deserted the principles upon which it was founded. There is no reason why a man who voted against Truman four years ago should not now vote against Truman's candidate, Adlai Stevenson" (Leuchtenberg, *The White House Looks South*, 221). Two prominent Virginia Dixiecrats, Harry Byrd and Howard Smith, also opposed Stevenson. "Key Facts on North Carolina," May 1, 1953, Truman President's Personal File Box 49, Truman Library.

14. Robert Caro, *Master of the Senate: The Years of Lyndon Johnson* (New York: Knopf, 2002), 464.

15. McKeever, *Adlai Stevenson*, 475.

16. Edgar Brown to Adlai Stevenson, January 3, 1953, Stevenson Papers Box 14. Brown reported after the election that "the bolters gave us a terrific race. It was the toughest political fight I have ever engaged in and we only kept the State in line by about 15,000 votes."

17. Caro, *Master of the Senate*, 822.

18. Paul Abramson, "Class Voting and the 1976 Presidential Election," *Journal of Politics* 40, no. 4 (November 1978): 1068.

19. Of course, many issues of the campaign other than race influenced southern voters, including Eisenhower's support for state control of Tidelands oil.

20. Of course, it stressed its own success in registering voters in these states as a reason for the Democratic surge among blacks. Henry Lee Moon, "Suffrage, 1952–53," NAACP II A 452.

21. Arthur Schlesinger to Adlai Stevenson, December 13, 1955, Stevenson Papers Box 73.

22. Stan Karson to Bill Blair, December 12, 1955, Stevenson Papers Box 12.

23. Arthur Schlesinger to Adlai Stevenson, June 11, 1956, Stevenson Papers Box 73; also see L. K. Garrison to William McCormick Blair, June 12, 1956, Stevenson Papers Box 36.

24. A southern journalist working for the campaign reported that southern politicians' "advice boils down to an urgent plea to avoid the race issue if you can, and play it down if you can't." A party bolt "will bring racists to power in many of the Southern states and may keep them there for years to come" (Memorandum for Governor Stevenson from Harry Ashmore, March 30, 1956, Stevenson Papers Box 168). Even Eleanor Roosevelt warned Stevenson that "There is a Negro situation here [in Florida] which I think a little later on you will have to think about seriously but at the moment I think the less you say here the better" (Eleanor Roosevelt to Adlai Stevenson, February 11, 1956, Stevenson Papers Box 68). Agnes Meyer, whose husband owned the *Washington Post*, canvassed Virginia Democratic leaders and reported that white voters will return to the fold. Despite her stellar record in civil rights, she advised Stevenson not to make any statements on "the desegregation mess" (Agnes Meyer to Adlai Stevenson, January 25, 1956, Stevenson Papers Box 56).

25. Adlai Stevenson to Harry Ashmore, December 23, 1954, Stevenson Papers Box 6; McKeever, *Adlai Stevenson*, 366–67.

26. Memorandum from Harry Ashmore, March 30, 1956, Stevenson Papers Box 168.

27. Adlai Stevenson to Hubert Humphrey, July 7, 1955, Stevenson Papers Box 41.

28. Adlai Stevenson to L. K. Garrison, July 20, 1955, Stevenson Papers Box 36.

29. L. K. Garrison to Arthur Schlesinger, August 12, 1955, Stevenson Papers Box 73; Memorandum for Archibald Alexander from L. K. Garrison, May 2, 1956, Stevenson Papers Box 354. Later, Chicago civil rights leader Frank Horne supplemented the list and reviewed the racial policies of the campaign headquarters (L. K. Garrison to Adlai Stevenson, April 30, 1956, Stevenson Papers Box 36).

30. L. K. Garrison to Adlai Stevenson, April 23, 1956, Stevenson Papers Box 36.

31. John Horne, "Thoughts on Integration," February 17, 1956, Stevenson Papers Box 294.

32. "Senator Kefauver's Inconsistency on Civil Rights," April 10, 1956, Stevenson Papers Box 268.

33. Stephen Mitchell to Adlai Stevenson, March 20, 1956, Stevenson Papers Box 48; Edgar Brown to Adlai Stevenson, February 11, 1956, Stevenson Papers Box 14.

34. McKeever, *Adlai Stevenson*, 374.

35. Memorandum for Adlai Stevenson, April 26, 1956, Stevenson Papers Box 354.

36. Harry Ashmore, *Civil Rights and Wrongs: A Memoir of Race and Politics 1944–1994* (New York: Pantheon, 1994), 118–20.

37. L. K. Garrison to William McCormick Blair, Jr., April 30, 1956, Stevenson Papers Box 36.

38. Edgar Brown to Adlai Stevenson, June 6, 1956, Stevenson Papers Box 14.

39. The Rayburn statement read, "We reject all proposals for the use of force to interfere with the orderly determination of these matters by the courts" and recognized "the Supreme Court of the United States as one of the three Constitutional and coordinate branches of the Federal Government, superior to and separate from any political party, the decisions of which are part of the law of the land." The platform also contained a statement reaffirming the party's longstanding belief in "the sound principles of local government" (McKeever, *Adlai Stevenson*, 384).

40. Mississippi's governor grumbled, "I am afraid the statement you made endorsing the Supreme Court decision is going to hurt you all through the South . . . If you follow the advice of Harry Truman . . . and Huberty Humphreys [*sic*], you need not expect any support in the South. . . . They are very unpopular throughout the South; as a matter of fact, they are more or less despised" (Hugh White to Adlai Stevenson, August 8, 1956, Stevenson Papers Box 89). In South Carolina, the governor echoed his concerns, writing, "What your speech did was to make it well nigh impossible to hold South Carolina in line. . . . You don't realize how fired up our people here are over this integration problem, and how hard it is for loyal Democrats to justify our enthusiasm for you in the face of the outlined situation. . . . Frankly, we could lose the state" (Edgar Brown to Adlai Stevenson, October 5, 1956, Stevenson Papers Box 14).

41. Roy Wilkins to Adlai Stevenson, October 23, 1956, Stevenson Papers Box 89; Ralph Bunche to Adlai Stevenson, July 31 and November 4, 1952, both in Stevenson Papers Box 15.

42. Harry Ashmore to Adlai Stevenson, August 2, 1956, Stevenson Papers Box 6. South Carolina governor Edgar Brown expected the same "defectors," but noted that the Republicans "sold the President down the river on his states rights and farm program promises" and the 1952 defectors are now "left high and dry" (Edgar Brown to Adlai Stevenson, February 11, 1956, Stevenson Papers Box 14). Texas governor Allan Shivers, who returned to the Democratic Party after bolting to the Republican Party in 1952, continued to oppose Stevenson.

43. Stevenson won comfortable margins in cities like New York, Chicago, Philadelphia, and Detroit. "Preliminary Analysis of 1956 National Elections," November 19, 1956, Jack Kroll Papers Box 6.

44. Robert Mann, *The Walls of Jericho: Lyndon Johnson, Hubert Humphrey, Richard Russell, and the Struggle for Civil Rights* (New York: Houghton-Mifflin, 1997), 264. Russell campaigned for Johnson in the fall in Texas after Lady Bird Johnson was assaulted at a Dallas rally. The ticket won in Texas by a small margin (288).

45. Leuchtenberg, *The White House Looks South*, 259–65.

46. The quote is from an interview with Strom Thurmond. Ann Mclaurin and John A. Goldsmith, "Colleagues: Richard B. Russell and His Apprentice, Lyndon B. Johnson," *Journal of Southern History* 61, no. 2 (1995): 65.

47. Leuchtenberg, *The White House Looks South*, 259–65.

48. David A. Nichols, *A Matter of Justice: Eisenhower and the Beginning of the Civil Rights Revolution* (New York: Simon & Schuster, 2008). Part 3 of Eisenhower's proposal gave the attorney general the authority to file suits for school desegregation and other constitutional rights. Johnson told Eisenhower he would defeat the bill unless Part 3 was removed. Johnson and his southern allies also passed an amendment requiring (white) juries in civil suits against discrimination.

49. Leuchtenberg, *The White House Looks South*, 279.

50. Interview with John M. Bailey by Charles T. Morrissey, April 10, 1964, John F. Kennedy Presidential Library (henceforth JFK) Oral History Program, Boston.

51. Carl Brauer, *John F. Kennedy and the Second Reconstruction* (New York: Columbia University Press, 1977), 19.

52. Interview with Orval Faubus by Larry Hackman, June 29, 1967, JFK Oral History Program.

53. Burner, David and Thomas West, *The Torch Is Passed: The Kennedy Brothers and American Liberalism* (New York: Atheneum, 1984), 94.

54. B. H. Peace, "Why Does the South Love Kennedy So?" *Grenville News*, JFK Pre-Presidential Files, South Carolina (A-C), JFK. Undated, but mailed to Kennedy October 1, 1958.

55. Even Johnson was suspect after playing a strong role in passing the Civil Rights Act of 1957. Robert C. Arnold (Chairman of University of Georgia) to John Hynes, September 29, 1959, JFK Pre-Presidential Files, Georgia: Political A-B; C. W. McKay, Jr., to Theodore Sorensen, March 10, 1960, JFK Pre-Presidential Files, Alabama: Political McKay; Edward Reid to H. Coleman Long, April 27, 1959, JFK Pre-Presidential Files, Alabama: Edward Reid file; Stuart Brown to William Battle, March 21, 1960, JFK Pre-Presidential Files, Virginia: Stuart Brown; Stuart Brown to Steven Smith, March 21, 1960, JFK Pre-Presidential Files, Virginia: Stuart Brown.

56. Jack Helms to John Hynes, January 6, 1960, JFK Pre-Presidential Files, Georgia Political H-J. Also see John K. de Loach to John Hynes, September 14, 1959, JFK Pre-Presidential Files, South Carolina: Political D-L; Asa Green to John Hynes, October 20, 1959, JFK Pre-Presidential Files, Alabama: Political D-G; Judge James Hugh McFaddin to John F. Kennedy, January 30 1959, JFK Pre-Presidential Files, South Carolina: Political M-P; CA Jacobs to John Hynes, September 10, 1959, JFK Pre-Presidential Files, VA: J-L.

57. Frank Barber to John Hynes, September 24, 1959, JFK Pre-Presidential Files, Mississippi: Political A-C. Alabama governor John Patterson later remembered that Southerners hoped "we would have a place where we could get an audience for the problems that we had." Sean Savage, *JFK, LBJ, and the Democratic Party* (New York: SUNY Press, 2004), 19.

58. Interview with Ruth M. Batson by Sheldon Stern, January 24, 1979, JFK Library Oral History Program.

59. Brauer, *John F. Kennedy and the Second Reconstruction*, 22. The statement in favor of upholding the law was enough to alienate South Carolina legislator Lloyd Bell, who wrote that before he approved of the use of troops, South Carolinians were prepared to support him in 1960.

60. Roy Wilkins to John F. Kennedy, May 29, 1960, Sorensen Subject Files Box 9, JFK Library.

61. Interview with Marjorie Lawson by Ronald Grele, October 25, 1965, JFK Library Oral History Program.

62. Quoted in John F. Kennedy to Herbert Tucker, January 24, 1959, Sorensen Subject Files Box 9.

63. John F. Kennedy to Lewis Weinstein, October 30, 1958, Sorensen Subject Files Box 9. Kennedy won 73.6 percent of the black vote in Massachusetts in November.Mark Stern, "John F. Kennedy and Civil Rights: From Congress to the Presidency," *Presidential Studies Quarterly* 19, no. 4 (1989).

64. Mann, *Walls of Jericho*, 271

65. Bryant, *The Bystander*, 135; Interview with Robert Troutman by David Powers, February 2, 1964, JFK Library Oral History Program.

66. Robert Dallek, *An Unfinished Life: John F. Kennedy, 1917–1963* (Boston: Back Bay Books, 2004), 268.

67. Interview with Harris Wofford by Larry Hackman, May 22, 1968, JFK Library Oral History Program.

68. Interview with John Feild (a member of the minorities division of the DNC) by John Stewart, January 16, 1967, JFK Library Oral History Program. Lawson, hired to work on a civil rights section for the campaign, recalled that she never knew if Kennedy made private commitments to Southern politicians, and "had difficult times trying to convince people that he had no deal with people like Patterson" (interview with Marjorie Lawson by Ronald Grele, October 25, 1965, JFK Library Oral History Program).

69. Nelson Lichtenstein, *Walter Reuther: The Most Dangerous Man in Detroit* (Urbana: University of Illinois Press, 1997), 355.

70. The prospectus said he needed to win Maryland, West Virginia, and Oklahoma, which leaned toward him ("Prospectus for 1960," undated, Sorensen Papers, Box 22).

71. Nelson Lichtenstein, *The Most Dangerous Man in Detroit: Walter Reuther and the Fate of American Labor* (New York: Basic, 1995), 355. Kenneth O'Donnell, Kennedy's campaign schedule director, was one of the aides making the promise.

72. Gillon, *Politics and Vision*, 133.

73. Brauer, *John F. Kennedy and the Second Reconstruction*, 52. The word "Constitutional" replaced the original word "Civil" to avoid alienating Southerners too much.

74. Interview with Harris Wofford by Berl Bernhard, November 29, 1965, JFK Library Oral History Program.

75. Interview with Orval Faubus by Larry Hackman, June 29, 1967, JFK Library Oral History Program.

76. Leuchtenberg, *The White House Looks South*, 286–91, 504 n60. Mississippi supported an independent Democrat.

77. Brauer, *John F. Kennedy and the Second Reconstruction*, 46.

78. After news of the call became public, Robert F. Kennedy was livid and declared, "You bomb-throwers have lost the whole campaign." Upon learning the details of King's imprisonment, however, he called the judge and arranged for King's release (Mann, *The Walls of Jericho*, 284).

79. Nixon's campaign did not intervene. The Democrats distributed two million copies of a pamphlet contrasting Nixon and Kennedy's reaction to King's sentence, quoting Nixon with a "No Comment" (Harris Wofford Memorandum to President-Elect Kennedy on Civil Rights, December 10, 1960, Robert F. Kennedy Papers (henceforth RFK) Box 62, JFK).

80. Meetings documented and quote obtained from Eric Schickler, *Racial Realignment: The Transformation of American Liberalism, 1932–1965* (Princeton, N.J.: Princeton University Press, 2016), 232.

81. Cheryl Lynn Greenberg, *Troubling the Waters: Black-Jewish Relations in the American Century* (Princeton, N.J.: Princeton University Press, 2006), 133.

82. Thurber, *The Politics of Equality*, 83.

83. Watson, *Lion in the Lobby*, 211.

84. Walter White, July 24, 1952, NAACP II A452; "Comparison of Two Platforms on Civil Rights," August 21, 1952, NAACP IX 71. Sparkman's nomination as Stevenson's running mate was arguably the most significant concession to the South in post-Truman nominations. Although Sparkman was consistently liberal on economic issues, he opposed civil rights measures up to and including the Civil Rights Act of 1964. In 1948, he told voters that he was "not a Truman Democrat" (Leuchtenberg, *The White House Looks South*, 188). Truman, Stevenson, Rayburn, and DNC chair Frank McKinney agreed on Sparkman as the vice presidential candidate in a small room behind the speaker's platform. They thought that Sparkman's liberalism on issues other than civil rights would help the ticket in the South, while keeping liberal opposition to a minimum (McKeever, *Adlai Stevenson*, 201–2). ADA director James Loeb called him "the national spokesman for the anti-civil rights people" (James Loeb to John Thomason, December 18, 1948, ADA mf 17) and the CIO qualified its endorsement of Stevenson with disapproval for Sparkman (Donald Montgomery to Paul Sifton, August 12 1952, Paul Sifton Papers Box 30). Harlem MC Adam Clayton Powell said that Sparkman would lead to "sheer political death" for

the Democrats (Thurber, *The Politics of Equality*, 270 n34). Reuther wrote that "My personal contact with key Negro leaders within the UAW-CIO, who are with us and who want to do the most effective job possible, confirms the impressions that I received from other sources" that Sparkman created serious doubts in the black community (Memorandum to Wilson Wyatt, August 26, 1952, Stevenson Papers Box 66). After receiving the vice presidential nomination, Sparkman told Southern voters that the Republican platform was stronger on civil rights and that Republicans were responsible for recent civil rights legislation in Congress. When asked if the platform unintentionally left out the FEPC, he answered that an FEPC amendment was offered in both the drafting committee and the full resolutions committee, and voted down (Arthur Schlesinger to Governor Stevenson on "John Sparkman in US News and World Report," undated; Stevenson Papers Box 75, Folder 14).

Sparkman was no Hubert Humphrey, but he was no James Byrnes, either. He was eager to repair relations with civil rights groups during the general election, especially when the *Baltimore Afro-American* rated his civil rights record below Republican vice presidential contender Nixon's. In response to the rating, he met with NAACP lobbyist Clarence Mitchell and suggested strategies for reforming the filibuster rules (Watson, *Lion in the Lobby*, 213–16). The ADA condemned his stance on civil rights, but said that he was better than any other potential running mate from the South (Reginald Zalles to Helen Rotch, August 12, 1952, ADA mf 21). Georgia senator Richard Russell was under consideration, and was conservative on more issues than Sparkman (Francis Biddle to Herbert Leman, July 4, 1952, ADA mf 21). Some, including Humphrey and Schlesinger, believed Sparkman could help change southern politics. His economic liberalism and his willingness to meet with liberals to discuss civil rights suggested that he might be persuaded to support civil rights down the line, and he would be in a better position to rally southern MCs (Thurber, *The Politics of Equality*, 84). While Walter White condemned the choice, he did not do so without adding that Republican vice presidential candidate Nixon was also an opponent of civil rights (Walter White to Arthur Summerfield, October 31, 1952, NAACP II-A-510; Archibald Carey to Roy Wilkins, November 6, 1952, NAACP II-A-510). The NAACP acknowledged the difference but claimed that they expected more from Nixon because he was not from a southern state.

85. James Byrnes to South Carolina State Democratic Convention, Stevenson Papers Box 16.

86. Tracy Roof, *American Labor, Congress, and the Welfare State, 1935–2010* (Baltimore: Johns Hopkins University Press, 2011), 115.

87. Roy Wilkins to Branch Officers, August 29, 1956, NAACP A245.

88. Mann, *The Walls of Jericho*, 273. Theodore Sorensen remembers that Robert F. Kennedy thought the platform promised "too many unwarranted hopes" and "specifics that could not be fulfilled." Brauer, *John F. Kennedy and the Second Reconstruction*, 36.

89. Stern, "John F. Kennedy and Civil Rights," 810.

90. August Meier and John Bracey, "The NAACP as a Reform Movement, 1909–1965: 'To Reach the Conscience of America,'" *Journal of Southern History* 59 (1993): 3–30.

Chapter 6

1. Lydia Bean, *Politics of Evangelical Identity: Local Churches and Partisan Divides in the United States and Canada* (Princeton: Princeton University Press, 2014).

2. Axel R. Schäfer, *Countercultural Conservatives: American Evangelicalism from the Postwar Revival to the New Christian Right* (Madison: University of Wisconsin Press, 2011), 3.

3. For example, Bean, *Politics of Evangelical Identity*, and Allan J. Lichtman, *White Protestant Nation: The Rise of the American Conservative Movement* (New York: Grove Press, 2008).

4. Bethany Moreton, *To Serve God and Wal-Mart: The Making of Christian Free Enterprise* (Cambridge, Mass.: Harvard University Press, 2010).

5. Darren Dochuk, *From Bible Belt to Sun Belt Plain Folk Religion, Grassroots Politics, and the Raise of Evangelical Conservatism* (New York: Norton, 2011).

6. Kevin *Kruse, One Nation Under God: How Corporate America Invented Christian America (New York: Basic, 2015).*

7. Bean, *Politics of Evangelical Identity,* 225.

8. Lichtman, *White Protestant Nation,* 127; and Geoffrey Layman, *The Great Divide: Religious and Cultural Conflict in American Party Politics* (New York: Columbia University Press, 2001), 188–93.

9. Presidential elections have been competitive among Catholics only since that time as well. It is unclear that the growth in Catholic identification with the Republican Party took place because of cultural issues—irregular church members were just as likely to become Republicans as regular church members (Layman, *The Great Divide,* 171).

10. Marty Cohen, "Moral Victories: Cultural Conservatism and the Creation of a New Republican Congressional Majority," Ph.D. dissertation, University of California, Los Angeles, 2005. The change in congressional politics arguably reflects the success of a second wave of cultural conservatives, introduced in the next chapter.

11. Lichtman, *White Protestant Nation,* 103.

12. The memo convinced Joseph Coors to play a more active role in politics and provide funding for the Heritage Foundation. Lee Edwards, *The Power of Ideas: The Heritage Foundation at 25 Years* (Ottawa, Ill.: Jameson Books, 1997), 9.

13. Rich Williamson to Ed Meese, December 30, 1979, Reagan Campaign Papers Box 107, Ronald Reagan Presidential Library (henceforth RR), Simi Valley California.

14. "House Republican Conference Program," Reagan Campaign Papers Box 106, RR.

15. Kira Sabonmatsu, *Democrats/Republicans and the Politics of Women's Place* (Ann Arbor: University of Michigan Press, 2004).

118. President Gerald Ford had originally proposed states' rights on abortion, but when Ronald Reagan proposed to challenge the state rights position before the platform committee, the platform commended groups working to pass an antiabortion amendment.

16. Jo Freeman, "Feminist Activities at the 1988 Republican Convention," *PS: Political Science and Politics* 22, 1 (March 1989): 40.

17. Daniel K. Williams, "The GOP's Abortion Strategy: Why Pro-Choice Republicans Became Pro-Life in the 1970s," *Journal of Policy History* (Fall): 6–7.

18. Dan Gilgoff, *The Jesus Machine: How James Dobson, Focus on the Family, and Evangelical America Are Winning the Culture War* (New York: St. Martin's, 2007), 75.

19. Daniel K. Williams, *God's Own Party* (New York: Oxford University Press, 2010), 97.

20. David Karol, *Party Position Change in American Politics: Coalition Management* (Cambridge: Cambridge University Press, 2009), 63–64.

21. Lisa Young, *Feminists and Party Politics* (Ann Arbor: University of Michigan Press, 2000), 82; Sabonmatsu, *Democrats/Republicans and the Politics of Women's Place,* 181; and Williams, "The GOP's Abortion Strategy."

22. Karol, *Party Position Change in American Politics,* 61.

23. Nancy Gibbs and Michael Duffy, "The Other Born-Again President," *Time,* January 2, 2007.

24. "Strategy-Vail," Personal/Political Campaign Correspondence, 1968–1976, Robert Dole

Archives and Special Collections Box 27, Folder 2 of 4, Robert J. Dole Institute of Politics, University of Kansas, Lawrence Kansas (henceforth Dole Institute).

25. Interview with Howard Phillips, March 18, 2011.

26. Daniel Kenneth Williams, "From the Pews to the Polls: The Formation of a Southern Christian Right," Ph.D. dissertation, Brown University, 2005, 139–40.

27. Interview with Mark Hatfield by Cal Skaggs, October 26, 1995, William Martin Religious Right Research Collection, Woodson Research Center, Fondren Library, Rice University (henceforth Martin Religious Right Research Collection).

28. Quoted in Michael Murphy, "Conservative Pioneer Became an Outcast," *Arizona Republic*, March 31, 1998.

29. Interview with George Shissias and Rusty DePass, March 19, 2013.

30. Ronald Reagan to Clark Reed, June 28, 1976, Dole Personal Political Subject Files (Republican) Box 399, Dole Institute.

31. Michele McKeegan, *Abortion Politics: Mutiny in the Ranks of the Right* (New York: Free Press, 1992), 8; interview with Don Devine, June 14, 2011.

32. Interview with David Keene, June 3, 2011.

33. Interview with Don Devine, June 14, 2011.

34. Marshall Ganz, *Why David Sometimes Wins: Leadership, Organization, and Strategy in the California Farm Worker Movement* (New York: Oxford University Press, 2009), 104, 134.

35. Often, they argued that the authors of the Bible were humans who imperfectly captured religious truths, leaving room for a selective reading and interpretation of the Bible. John C. Green, Corwin E. Smidt, Lyman A. Kellstedt, Margaret M. Poloma, and James L. Guth, *The Bully Pulpit: The Politics of Protestant Clergy* (Lawrence: University Press of Kansas, 1998), 9.

36. A recent summary reflects a century-old debate. Paul Pressler writes, "Liberals believe scripture is inspired in spots and that they are inspired to spot the spots. I think it is dangerous to attempt to edit God. What objective standard exists for doing the editing if a person believes that only portions of the Bible are inspired?" Paul Pressler, *A Hill on Which to Die: One Southern Baptist's Journey* (Nashville, Tenn.: B&H Publishing, 2002), 151.

37. Williams, *God's Own Party*, 15. Some conservative churches adhered to "Premillenial Dispensationalism," teaching that the world would become increasingly corrupt until Jesus returned for his one-thousand-year reign. The local and international events of the 1930s and 1940s added evidence that the end of an era was at hand, especially the prophesized creation of Israel. When Christ returns, he would save the souls of the converted. Why focus on anything other than conversion? Many mainline Protestants also absorbed biblical ideas of the end of times from popular culture, even if their pastors never brought it up. One survey showed that 48% of the modernist Presbyterian Church (USA) laity believed it (Green et al., *The Bully Pulpit*, 48).

38. Lucy Mason to Mr. McMullen, January 18 1946, *Operation Dixie* mf 63, 2.

39. Green et al., *The Bully Pulpit*, 59–61. Another commented, "I strongly believe that with the Power of the Spirit of God flowing over our land, and the people humbling themselves before God, the social problems would soon dissolve and disappear."

40. Williams, "From the Pews to the Polls," 55. In the largest Protestant sect, the SBC, J. Frank Norris was expelled in the 1930s as much for being politically outspoken as for being vocally anti-Catholic. Historian Oran Smith said, "Southern Baptists in the 1950s veered away from controversy. Ministers knew what to talk about and what not to talk about in their

sermons. . . . Most hid their heads in the sand and spoke the language of the people in the church, even if they didn't believe it" (interview with Oran Smith, March 19, 2013). Also see Oran Smith, *The Rise of Baptist Republicanism* (New York: New York University Press, 2000), 32–33, 46–47.

41. Quoted in Williams, "From the Pews to the Polls," 341. Falwell's announcement was arguably a cover for opposing clerical support of civil rights, but he was echoing a tradition much older than the civil rights movement. In the 1960s, the theologically conservative *Christianity Today* warned ministers involved in civil rights that their calling was spiritual, not political, and their tax exempt status depended on remaining aloof from politics. Williams, *God's Own Party*, 75.

42. Schäfer, *Countercultural Conservatives*, 3.

43. A recent study finds that to this day, theological conservatives are less likely to bring up political issues in sermons than theological liberals M. Woolfolk, "Sermons Aren't Explicitly Political: Political Cue-Giving in Sermons by US Christian Clergy," unpublished working paper, May 9, 2013.

44. Interview with anonymous subject, May 21, 2013.

45. Gilgoff, *The Jesus Machine*, 37; also see Bean, *The Politics of Evangelical Identity*, 85. In Green et al.'s survey, theologically conservative churches reported that moral and spiritual problems were the greatest problems in the nation, by far. Very few listed the environment, defense, or social welfare, although they were as interested in "hunger and poverty" as mainline churches. About half as many mainline churches ranked moral and spiritual problems first (Green et al., *The Bully Pulpit*, 72, 81–83). A conservative Presbyterian told the surveyors, "I make a distinction between political and moral items even though some moral items are also political. I would approve a sermon on an issue like abortion, which I consider moral . . . I would strongly disapprove of a sermon on the arms race, South Africa . . . The pulpit is for the exposition of the Bible, not other agendas."

46. After the *Schempp* decision was announced in 1963, the NAE and the ACCC responded with opposition.

47. Andrew R. Lewis, *The Southern Baptist Church-State "Culture War": The Internal Politics of Denominational Advocacy* (Washington, DC: American University, 2011).40; Williams, "From the Pews to the Polls," 174–77, 187. Catholics were critical of the *Engel* decision immediately.

48. Williams, "From the Pews to the Polls," 55.

49. "The CIO in the South," September 1941, *Operation Dixie* mf 64, 4. The Northern Methodists had a slightly stronger statement of support for unions. Daniel Schlozman discusses "anchoring groups" in *When Movements Anchor Parties: Electoral Alignments in American History* (Princeton, N.J.: Princeton University Press, 2015).

50. Lucy Mason, Radio Script for WGPC, Albany Georgia, June 22, 1948, *Operation Dixie* mf 64, 5.

51. "The CIO in the South," September 1941, *Operation Dixie* Reel 64, 4; Lucy Mason, Radio Script for WGPC, Albany Georgia, June 22, 1948, *Operation Dixie* Reel 64, 5; Lucy Mason, Spring 1939, *Operation Dixie* Reel 64.

52. Rick Perlstein, *Before the Storm: Barry Goldwater and the Unmaking of the American Consensus* (New York: Hill and Wang, 2001), 125. Graham told a CIO field director that "religion and organized labor have much in common, and that each needs to understand and respect each other" (Lucy Mason to Billy Graham, undated, *Operation Dixie* mf 64).

53. For Graham's relationship with Nixon, see Williams, *God's Own Party*, 90–96, 103.

54. Neil J. Young, *We Gather Together: The Religious Right and the Problem of Interfaith Politics* (Oxford: Oxford University Press, 2015).

55. Williams, "From the Pews to the Polls," 68–71. The NAE formed the National Religious Broadcasters (NRB) specifically to fight for air time. The Federal Council of Churches convinced all but one of the major radio networks to eliminate paid religious programming and substitute free "public service time" with their guidance. The NAE also fought for a place for socially conservative religious broadcasts, as the liberal Federal Council of Churches attempted to crowd them out.

56. Williams, "From the Pews to the Polls," 85.

57. Duane Oldfield, *The Right and the Righteous: The Christian Right Confronts the Republican Party* (Lanham, Md.: Rowman and Littlefield, 1996), 91; Williams, *God's Own Party*, 38–39, 74, 92. Although McIntire was highly interested in theological doctrine, he was also staunchly anticommunist and devoted to free enterprise. He claimed to be nonpartisan, but opposed Truman's health plan and blamed the communist takeover of China on Truman's State Department. Later, McIntire served on the board of Young Americans for Freedom (YAF), organized at *National Review* (*NR*) editor William F. Buckley's estate to engage young Americans in the battle against communism abroad and "big government" at home. McIntire became increasingly marginal within fundamentalist circles by the late 1960s. In 1969, the ACCC voted not to renew McIntire's seat on the executive committee because he supported Georgia's segregationist governor, Lester Maddox (Williams, *God's Own Party*, 92). Another politically active fundamentalist was Bob Jones, Jr., president of South Carolina's Bob Jones University (BJU), a nondenominational fundamentalist school. Jones opposed the liberal CIO's politically charged Southern drive (Lucy Mason to Raven McDavid, October 8, 1946, *Operation Dixie* mf 63). Like McIntire, Jones blamed the expansion of communism on the state department and the United Nations, and opposed Truman's health care proposals. A 1952 straw poll at BJU showed 80 percent of the students supporting Eisenhower, even though his Democratic opponent, Stevenson, won statewide (Williams, *God's Own Party*, 37, 74). Later, Jones would oppose the civil rights and economic policies of the Johnson administration; he supported 1964 Republican candidate Goldwater, even though he was "not conservative enough." Jones's father, the university's founder, had been a supporter of William Jennings Bryan and Prohibition, and later campaigned for Republican Herbert Hoover against Catholic presidential candidate Al Smith.

58. At first, both Holiness and Pentecostal gatherings were open to all races, but by the 1920s, black and white Pentecostal churches held separate services. Pentecostal churches were also known for providing women a greater role in church services. Another distinct feature of many Pentecostal churches was pacifism, though this seemed to dissipate after World War II.

59. Holiness church congregants often left their own churches for the emotional style of the Pentecostals, just as Methodists once left their churches for the Holiness churches. Pentecostal churches flourished in the South; in South Carolina alone, Methodists lost one third of their members to Pentecostal churches between 1908 and 1912.

60. R. G. Robins, *Pentecostalism in America* (Santa Barbara, Calif.: Praeger, 2010), 47.

61. Randall J. Stephens, *The Fire Spreads: Holiness and Pentecostalism in the American South* (Cambridge, Mass.: Harvard University Press, 2008), 2, 6, 9, 223, and 227; Robins, *Pentacostalism in America*, 32, 47, 78, 97.

62. Young, *We Gather Together*, 184.

63. Dirk Smillie, *Falwell Inc.: Inside a Religious, Political, Educational, and Business Empire* (New York: St. Martin's, 2008), 106.

64. Transcript of a phone conversation between Doug Wead and Karl Rove, September 23, 1998, provided by Doug Wead.

65. Young, *We Gather Together*.

66. Bob Jones to Ronald Reagan, December 30, 1983, Morton Blackwell Box 16, RR; Williams, *God's Own Party*, 209.

67. Matthew C. Moen, *Christian Right and Congress* (Tuscaloosa: University of Alabama Press, 1992), 72.

68. Bush later apologized to New York's Cardinal O'Connor for not differentiating himself from BJU. (David Kuo, *Tempting Faith: An Inside Story of Political Seduction* (New York: Simon & Schuster, 2006), 130.

69. Over time, abortion rights have defined cultural politics more than any other issue in public opinion surveys (Larry Bartels, "What's the Matter with What's the Mater with Kansas," Quarterly Journal of Political Science 2006, 1; D. Sunshine Hillygus and Todd G. Shields, *The Persuadable Voter: Wedge Issues in Presidential Campaigns* (Princeton: Princeton University Press, 2008).

70. Frank Schaeffer, *Crazy for God: How I Grew Up As One of the Elect, Helped Found The Religious Right, and Lived to Take All (Or Almost All) of It Back* (Cambridge, Mass.: Da Capo Press, 2008), 266.

71. Williams, *God's Own Party*, 92, 116–118.

72. Independent Baptist churches, however, were more likely to oppose abortion, civil rights, and economic liberalism during the period discussed. Williams, *God's Own Party*, 92, 116–18.

73. National Election Studies data is too noisy to interpret until 1988. Only after that point were Baptists consistently less likely to identify as liberals and more likely to identify as conservatives. The SBC rank and file was slightly more prolife than the average American. Between 1972 and 1980, they were as unlikely to favor a complete abortion ban as most others, but about 10 percent less likely to support a prochoice position and 10 percent more likely to favor abortion only under restricted conditions. Smith, *The Rise of Baptist Republicanism*, 160.

74. Williams, "From the Pews to the Polls," 289.

75. Interview with Eric Woolson, May 24, 2013. Conservative radio show host Jan Mickelson also believes that Catholic and Protestant identities shape political contests in Iowa (interview on May 21, 2013). A plurality of evangelicals in the Iowa caucuses still voted for Santorum.

76. Green et al., *The Bully Pulpit*, 53–55, 91.

77. Williams, "From the Pews to the Polls," 55; interview with Oran Smith, March 19, 2013; Smith, *The Rise of Baptist Republicanism*, 32–33, 46–47.

78. Ibid., 82–83.

79. Ibid., 157. Smith includes 1972–1992 in his study.

80. David T. Morgan, *The New Crusades, the New Holy Land: Conflict in the Southern Baptist Convention, 1969–1991* (Tuscaloosa: University of Alabama Press, 1996), 6.

81. Smith, *The Rise of Baptist Republicanism*, 32–33

82. Barry Hankins, *Uneasy in Babylon: Southern Baptist Conservatives and American Culture* (Tuscaloosa: University of Alabama Press, 2002), 4. Many theologically conservative churches were also independent churches that did not identify with any particular denomination. The advantages to this approach are obvious to any pastor that can gather an adequate following. Kevin Baird runs an independent church outside of Charleston, South Carolina. Once a Nazarene pastor, he decided to run an independent church based on a religious experience. Since 1989, his congregation has been more pastorally driven than driven by a board of directors or parent organization. In the wake of Hurricane Katrina, he could mobilize volunteers immediately without needing permission from a church hierarchy. Denominational churches sometimes

incorporate features of independent churches to sustain member interest (interview with Kevin Baird, March 21, 2013).

83. James C. Hefley, *The Truth in Crisis*, vol. 1, *The Controversy in the Southern Baptist Convention* (Garland, Tex.: Hannibal, 1986), 58.

84. Hankins, *Uneasy in Babylon*, 27

85. John Marley, *Pat Robertson: An American Life* (Lanham, Md.: Rowman and Littlefield, 2007), 34. Pentecostal broadcaster Pat Robertson wrote to rival Jim Bakker that his network "refused to accept your affiliate in Savannah, Georgia, because we did not feel it was ethical, and within weeks our kindness was repaid by your attempt to take away our Orlando affiliate and your entry into the Hartford market . . . This is a totally uncalled for waste of the money of God's people merely for the purpose of gratifying your personal ego and unbelievable competitive spirit."

86. Smillie, *Falwell, Inc.*, 70.

87. Lichtman, *White Protestant Nation*, 74–75, 129.

88. Schäfer, *Countercultural Conservatives*, 48.

89. Lichtman, *White Protestant Nation*, 161, 206.

90. Stephen Johnson and Joseph Tamney, eds., *The Political Role of Religion in the United States* (Boulder, Colo.: Westview, 1986), 133. Religious leaders, like most group leaders, differ systematically from followers and members, usually holding more extreme views. In 1991, however, most theologically conservative clergy reported being more liberal on economic issues than their congregations, and only one third reported being more conservative on cultural issues (Green et al., *The Bully Pulpit*, 113).

91. Schäfer, *Countercultural Conservatives*, 4.7, 78.

92. D. Sunshine Hillygus and Todd G. Shields, *The Persuadable Voter: Wedge Issues in Presidential Campaigns* (Princeton: Princeton University Press, 2008).

93. William F. Buckley (WFB) to Pat Manion, February 1, 1965, William F. Buckley Papers I 35, Yale University Manuscripts and Archives, New Haven, Conn. (henceforth WFB Papers). Buckley explained that although *NR* featured many Catholic authors, it was a secular publication and could not write with "specifically Catholic presuppositions."

Chapter 7

1. A smaller shift occurred among Catholics, but without regard for church attendance, suggesting that their shift was due more to a change in class. Geoffrey Layman, *The Great Divide: Religious and Cultural Conflict in American Party Politics* (New York: Columbia University Press, 2001), 188–93.

2. Lydia Bean, *Politics of Evangelical Identity: Local Churches and Partisan Divides in the United States and Canada* (Princeton, N.J.: Princeton University Press, 2014), 165. Of course, there is some dispute over the extent to which religious officials can influence their congregations or networks. On the one hand, Djupe and Gilbert conclude that committed members of two major church congregations misgauged their pastors' views, and the pastors' main impact was to bring congregants closer to congregational norms. In other words, congregations change their members' political behavior, not pastors (Paul A. Djupe and Christopher P. Gilbert, *The Political Influence of Churches* [New York: Cambridge University Press, 2009]). Jelen even finds that a congregation's theological conservatism influences one's cultural conservatism better than one's own theological conservatism! But a growing scholarly literature finds evidence that religious institutions do shape political behavior (Ted G. Jelen, *The Political Mobilization of Religious Beliefs* [Westport, Conn.: Praeger, 1991]; ibid., "Political Christianity: A Contextual Analysis,"

American Journal of Political Science [1992]: 692–714; and ibid., *The Political World of the Clergy* [Westport, Conn.: Praeger Publishers, 1993]). Bjarnason and Welch's survey of Catholic priests and parishioners finds that parishioners with more frequent contact with their priests are more likely to oppose the death penalty, controlling for other beliefs and church activity (Thoroddur Bjarnason and Michael R. Welch, "Father Knows Best: Parishes, Priests, and American Catholic Parishioners' Attitudes Toward Capital Punishment," *Journal for the Scientific Study of Religion* 43, no. 1 [2004]: 103–18). One more recent experiment finds that church sermons have a statistically significant impact on voter views when they are implicit, but not when they are explicit (Miya Woolfalk, "Sermons Aren't Explicitly Political but Clergy Are: Political Cue-Giving in Sermons by US Christian Clergy," Unpublished paper available at http://miyawoolfalk. com/pages /mw-research [2012]). Bean writes that "the most explicitly partisan cues happened in unofficial, backstage, church settings: small group conversations, chatting over Sunday lunch, informal gatherings with church friends." Trusted pastors played an important signaling role to congregations. Bean, *Politics of Evangelical Identity*, 79.

3. Matt Grossman and David Hopkins, *Asymmetric Politics: Ideological Republicans and Group Interest Democrats* (New York: Oxford University Press, 2016), 89.

4. Layman, *The Great Divide*, 50.

5. Hans Noel, "The Coalition Merchants: How Ideologues Shape Parties in American Politics." Ph.D. dissertation, University of California at Los Angeles, 2006.

6. Grossman and Hopkins, *Asymmetric Politics*, 72.

7. Interview with Paul Weyrich by unknown interviewer, unknown date, Martin Religious Right Research Collection. Rockefeller had worked tirelessly to block the advance of the Goldwater faction and flaunted his disregard for traditional values by rapidly divorcing his wife to marry a recently divorced employee. One of their leaders, Heritage Foundation cofounder Paul Weyrich, later recalled, "That move . . . contributed to the development of the new right . . . than any other single move . . . Nelson Rockefeller was symbolically the devil incarnate for the conservatives in the country. . . . It said 'you people don't mean anything. We're going to take the party in a different direction'. . . . We can no longer influence this party from the inside. We will have to try to influence it from the outside."

8. Lee Edwards, *The Conservative Revolution: The Movement that Remade America* (New York: Free Press, 1999), 183–84.

9. Most CFNM members were familiar with Kevin Phillips's *The Emerging Republican Majority* (New York: Arlington House, 1969) which argued that blue collar ethnic voters had become disgruntled with liberalism and were ripe for a new party. Phillips argued that George Wallace's third-party performance in 1968 was proof that such voters were looking for alternatives to the Democratic Party, and Republicans could become the majority party by augmenting their coalition with voters attracted to Wallace.

10. "Fission on the Right: Richard Viguerie's Bid for Power 1977," *The Nation*, January 29, 1977, 105.

11. Before the 1976 election, *National Review* publisher William Rusher formed the CFNM to synthesize various conservative groups into a new majority party. A CFNM study asserted that "to have survived as party capable of winning elections, the Republican party would have to have violated the interests of large scale corporate structures, structures within which the names Rockefeller, Scranton, Lodge, Percy and Romney are so prominent . . . A major party will only collapse if a dominant function of the party prevents it from accepting new interest groups" (untitled manuscript, 1975–1976, William Rusher Papers 142, "Committee for a New Majority").

The study concluded that any third party, including any CFNM effort, needed to shift its emphasis beyond its founders' agenda. To avoid the fate of the Free Soil Party, CFNM needed to unite
its economic and foreign policy conservatives with cultural conservatives. The nucleus of CFNM
and its supporters consisted of economic conservatives such as the ACU members and *NR* readers. The National Republican Party of the 1820s and the Free Soil Party of the 1840s sought to
become major parties but failed because they catered too heavily toward the groups initiating the
party. Howard Phillips also attempted to learn the lessons of past realignments, listing the 1828
Democratic Party as an example to follow. In 1974, he wrote that "How to bring together parents
against busing, workers fed up with high taxes, right-to-lifers, advocates of capital punishments,
opponents of gun control, foes of pornography . . . is the same kind of organizational challenge
which confronted 1820s 'conservatives.'" Howard Phillips, "Jacksonian Democracy Offers Precedent for the 'New Majority,'" *Human Events*, October 5, 1974, 1. Most CFNM members were
familiar with Kevin Phillips's *The Emerging Republican Majority*, which argued that blue collar
ethnic voters had become disgruntled with liberalism. Phillips argued that George Wallace's
third-party performance in 1968 was proof such voters were looking for alternatives to the Democratic Party. Attempting to understand a potential new constituency, CFNM profiled them as
less concerned with "unrestrained free market economics [and] more concerned with retaining
social structures that maintain social cohesion. . . . Social conservatives have a basic animosity
against social control by the upper classes in general, which includes the economic conservatives. . . . Their talk is rougher and many racist statements they make in their bars and homes
reflect the rhetoric of a frustrated and unrepresented voting block that is not more capable of a
more articulate vocalization." The essay classified ethnic Democrats as another group ready to
join a new party. This included Greeks who wanted Greek taught in school and the Irish in South
Boston who resisted busing. The author cautioned against employing America's Judeo-Christian
heritage openly, as it would create worries against some of the ethnic groups (untitled manuscript, 1975–1976, William Rusher Papers 142, 12).

   12. Daniel Joy, the legal counsel to conservative Senator James Buckley, concurred that the
New Right was most willing to compromise on economic issues. "Fission on the Right: Richard
Viguerie's Bid for Power 1977"; also see Axel R. Schäfer, *Countercultural Conservatives: American
Evangelicalism from the Postwar Revival to the New Christian Right* (Madison: University of Wis-
consin Press), 158.

   13. Blackwell recalls, "It was clear we needed to bring in a lot of new people. At one of those
meetings, I said . . . theologically conservative Christians were the largest tract of virgin timber
on the political landscape. And we, in these meetings that Richard had, one of the things we
focused on was how the theologically conservative Christians could be awakened politically"
(interview with Morton Blackwell, April 27, 2011). Ed Dobson confirms Blackwell's account in
an interview with David Van Taylor, November 30, 1995, Martin Religious Right Research Collection. In 1976, Viguerie told *Sojourners*, a progressive Christian magazine, "The next real major
area of growth for the conservative ideology and philosophy is among evangelical people. I
would be surprised if in the next year you did not see a massive effort to involve them, utilizing
direct mail and other techniques." Daniel Kenneth Williams, "From the Pews to the Polls: The
Formation of a Southern Christian Right," Ph.D. dissertation, Brown University, 2005, 330).
Mickey Edwards, a founding member of the Heritage Foundation, recalls that most attendees at
Viguerie's meeting agreed that a majority of Americans were conservative in their beliefs, but
liberals somehow kept on winning elections. Opinion polls showed that 60 percent of Americans
identified as conservatives ("Fission on the Right"). A Heritage Foundation visit to Youngstown,

Ohio, confirmed their belief that American workers were fundamentally conservative. The way to reach these Americans was through the churches (interview with Mickey Edwards on March 15, 2011). Watergate burglar Charles Colson, author of *Born Again*, disagreed with the strategy of politicizing the churches, but corroborates Blackwell's account (interview with Charles Colson by unknown author, unknown date, Martin Religious Right Research Collection).

14. It is noteworthy that frequent church attendees were more likely to switch parties than other white southerners (Layman, *The Great Divide*, 188–93).

15. Neil J. Young, *We Gather Together: The Religious Right and the Problem of Interfaith Politics* (London: Oxford University Press, 2015), chap. 7.

16. Reichley, *Religion and American Public Life* (Washington, D.C.: Brookings Institution Press, 2010), 315.

17. Moreton argues that Christian corporations such as Wal-Mart assuaged some of the economic insecurities in a rapidly changing, global economy. Bethany Moreton, *To Serve God and Wal-Mart: The Making of Christian Free Enterprise* (Cambridge, Mass.: Harvard University Press, 2010). Also see Axel R. Schäfer, *Countercultural Conservatives: American Evangelicalism from the Postwar Revival to the New Christian Right* (Madison: University of Wisconsin Press 2011), 27–30. In some cases, political conservatism led to the growth of conservative sects rather than the other way around. One study shows that 20 percent of his sample joined or changed denominations as a result of their experience in the pro-life movement. (Ziad W. Munson, *Morality and Society Series: Making of Pro-Life Activists: How Social Movement Mobilization Works* [Chicago, Ill.: University of Chicago Press, 2009], 183).

18. Reichley, *Religion and American Public Life*, 315.

19. Doug Wead, "The Republican Party and the Evangelicals," undated, provided by Doug Wead.

20. In 1978 Pat Robertson told the *Washington Post* that the evangelical community was a "sleeping giant." John Marley, *Pat Robertson: An American Life* (Lanham, Md.: Rowman and Littlefield, 2007), 63.

21. Billy Graham rose from a field representative of "Youth for Christ" to a national broadcaster when he made an anticommunist speech in Los Angeles. Publisher William Randolph Hearst took great interest in the speech, and instructed his twenty-two papers to carry full-page stories on Youth for Christ. Hearst ordered his editors to "puff Graham," propelling his national career. William Martin, *With God on Our Side: The Rise of the Religious Right in America* (New York: Broadway, 2005), 27–29.

22. Interview with Doug Wead, June 21, 2013.

23. Dirk Smillie, *Falwell Inc.: Inside a Religious, Political, Educational, and Business Empire* (New York: St. Martin's, 2008), 84.

24. Young, *We Gather Together*, 162.

25. Interview with Paul Weyrich by unknown interviewer, unknown date, Martin Religious Right Research Collection.

26. Martin, *With God on Our Side*, 173. Also see Robert Freedman, "The Religious Right and the Carter Administration," *The Historical Journal* 48 (2005), and Daniel K. Williams, *God's Own Party* (New York: Oxford University Press, 2010), 85–88. Former ACU president Mickey Edwards claimed this did not motivate the public or parents, but it mobilized Protestant leaders (interview with Mickey Edwards, March 15, 2011). The MM's first president, Bob Billings, qualified that the issue activated religious conservatives, but they had also been concerned about the

moral direction of the country for years (interview with Bill Billings by unnamed interviewer, October 3, 1995, Martin Religious Right Research Collection).

27. Michael Cromartie, *No Longer Exiles: The Religious New Right in American Politics* (Washington, D.C.: Ethics and Public Policy Center, 1993), 26.

28. Freedman, *The Religious Right and the Carter Administration*, 223, 240; Martin, *With God on Our Side*, 173; Williams, "From the Pews to the Polls," 317.

29. Michael Hartney, "Turning Out Teachers: The Causes and Consequences of Teacher Political Activism," Ph.D. Dissertation, University of Notre Dame, 2014.

30. Christopher Baylor, "Ahead of the Class: Feminists and Unions in the Democratic Party Coalition" (working paper).

31. Richard Viguerie, *America's Right Turn: How Conservatives Used New and Alternative Media to Take over America* (New York: Taylor Trade, 2004), 132. The New Right wrongly concluded Robertson was not interested in politics, partly because his own public statements were inconsistent. For example, Robertson left the conservative "Religious Roundtable" in 1980 because it distracted him from preaching the Gospel, but months later formed his own political organization, the "Freedom Council." James Robison offered to lend money and support a political organization, but not run it himself (Marley, *Pat Robertson*, 64–65).

32. Interview with Paul Weyrich by unknown interviewer, Martin Religious Right Research Collection. McAteer's pastor, Adrian Rogers, later became SBC president and steered it toward conservative political positions and biblical inerrancy in theology. McAteer introduced Weyrich to most of the evangelical leaders he worked with. He agreed to head an ecumenical cultural conservative group named the "Religious Roundtable" in a meeting with Phillips, Viguerie, Rogers, and Schlafly.

33. The source asked to remain anonymous, but was interviewed on August 13, 2013.

34. Smillie, *Falwell, Inc.*, 85–86.

35. Interview with MM vice president Ronald Godwin by Randy Miller and Cline Hall, June 30, 2010, Digital Commons, Liberty University; interview with Doug Wead, June 21, 2013.

36. A 1984 Gallup poll showed he had lower ratings among evangelical Christians than any other Christian leader besides Oral Roberts. Polls in 1985 showed that 29 percent of Reagan voters viewed him favorably and 44 percent unfavorably (Doug Wead to Lee Atwater, "Falwell Fallout," January 27, 1986, provided by Wead). George H. W. Bush's 1988 campaign for president estimated that Falwell had a 3:1 "leanaway" nationally (Doug Wead, "Evangelical Targets," December 28, 1985, provided by Wead). Between 1982 and 1985, the percent of Virginia voters who said they were less likely to vote for someone Falwell endorsed grew from 28 to 51 percent. Dudley Clendinen, "Virginia Polls and Politicians Indicate Falwell is Slipping in his Home State," *New York Times*, November 24, 1985.

37. Corwin E. Smidt and James M. Penning, eds., *Sojourners in the Wilderness: The Christian Right in Comparative Perspective* (Lanham, Md.: Rowman and Littlefield, 1997), 28.

38. Interview with Morton Blackwell, April 27, 2011.

39. Interview with MM vice president Ronald Godwin by Randy Miller and Cline Hall, June 30, 2010, Digital Commons, Liberty University.

40. Cromartie, *No Longer Exiles*, 94–95.

41. William Clyde Wilcox, *God's Warriors: The Christian Right in Twentieth-century America* (Baltimore: Johns Hopkins University Press, 1992), 116.

42. Committee for the Study of the American Electorate study cited in Daniel Galvin,

Presidential Party Building: Dwight D. Eisenhower to George W. Bush (Princeton, N.J.: Princeton University Press, 2010), 135

43. Williams, *God's Own Party*, 179–82. Falwell was notably absent, perhaps viewing Robertson as a competitor.

44. Interview with Doug Wead by Brad Lichtenstein, March 18 1996, Martin Religious Right Research Collection.

45. Duane Oldfield, *The Right and the Righteous: The Christian Right Confronts the Republican Party* (Lanham, Md.: Rowman and Littlefield, 1996), 101–2.

46. Martin, *With God on Our Side*, 205.

47. Viguerie claims that Reagan could not have won without direct mailing, as he raised twenty-five to fifty dollar donations from 250,000 people. Direct mail accounted for 75 percent of Reagan's campaign funding in 1980 (Viguerie, *America's Right Turn*, 135).

48. Oral Roberts, Robert Schuller, and Rex Humbard led the ratings for most of the 1980s. This is not to say any particular broadcaster was better off with an apolitical program, any more than MSNBC would be better off adopting a conservative slant because Fox News has higher ratings. Some broadcasters maximize profits by appealing to a niche market, like the fusion of theological and political conservatism.

49. Unable to find values in reason, they turned to emotions and experience to find meaning, and "found themselves separated from reason and without any human or moral values." Searching into "non-reason to find optimism without reason . . . [there are] no categories upon which to distinguish between reality and illusion." Francis Schaeffer, *How Should We Then Live?: The Rise And Decline Of Western Thought And Culture* (Wheaton, Ill.: Good News Publishers, 1976), 168, 202, 206, 225.

50. Williams, *God's Own Party*, 140–41.

51. Martin, *With God on Our Side*, 194.

52. Young, *We Gather Together,* 160–65.

53. Bean, *The Politics of Evangelical Identity*, 63–67.

54. Schäfer, *Countercultural Conservatives*, 139–42. Conservatives also recruited left evangelicals from the Jesus movement by emphasizing the individualism of the marketplace (113–19). Of course, some evangelicals pushed back against the Third Wave (Young, *We Gather Together*, 182–84).

55. Oran Smith, *The Rise of Baptist Republicanism* (New York: New York University Press, 2000), 46–53. Ralph Elliot, SBC seminary professor, shocked some conservatives into action with a widely distributed book advancing a modernist interpretation of the Bible. The SBC also issued a whole-hearted apology for its racist history, and some pastors became involved in civil rights and peace movements. Conservatives responded to what they perceived to be the rising tide of moderates by creating a new seminary, publishing their own newsletter, and forming the Baptist Faith and Message Fellowship. Hankins argues that as the South modernized and adopted the cultural norms of other parts of the country, the conservative cadre felt more threatened and therefore became more active in politics. Barry Hankins, *Uneasy in Babylon: Southern Baptist Conservatives and American Culture* (Tuscaloosa: University of Alabama Press, 2002).

56. Rick Perlstein, *Before the Storm: Barry Goldwater and the Unmaking of the American Consensus* (New York: Nation Books, 2009), 125; Smith, *The Rise of Baptist Republicanism*, 37–38; and James C. Hefley, *The Truth in Crisis*, vol. 1, *The Controversy in the Southern Baptist Convention* (Garland, Tex.: Hannibal, 1986), 52.

57. Paul Pressler, *A Hill on Which to Die: One Southern Baptist's Journey* (Nashville, Tenn.: B. & H. Publishing, 2002), 95

58. David T. Morgan, *The New Crusades, the New Holy Land: Conflict in the Southern Baptist Convention, 1969–1991* (Tuscaloosa: University of Alabama Press, 1996), 36.

59. Hefley, *The Truth in Crisis*, 16, 42. Some were very close; Adrian Rogers and his successor, for example, won just over 51 percent of the vote in 1979 and 1980. But as time passed, the conservative candidate margins of victory increased. Moderates wrongly dismissed the 1979 election as an aberration, and were confident that they would regain control of the SBC, as they had in the past after temporary moves to the right (76). A proposal from the moderates to have appointment powers shared by the president and two vice presidents was defeated (Morgan, *The New Crusades*, 57).

60. Hefley, *The Truth in Crisis*, 38

61. In the 1990s, the SBC required churches not to marry or ordain homosexuals, although the number of churches expelled for violating this rule is very small. The Baptist Faith and Message Statement of 1998 called for a wife to "submit graciously to the servant leadership of her husband," and serve as his helper. Hankins, *Uneasy in Babylon*, 9, 196.

62. Williams, *God's Own Party*, 157–58, 192. Religious historian Oran Smith argues that the publicized takeover made it more difficult for pastors and congregants to avoid controversy, as they had so often in the past. He said, "Controversy was one of the worst things that could happen. . . . It was considered to be ill-mannered and a distraction from the purpose of the group. . . . Even abortion didn't alarm anybody because there wasn't much of a knowledge as to how widespread it was. But as the Christian Right movement developed, it kind of blew a lid off this silence, this moderation, and forced everyone to line up on one side or the other" (interview with Oran Smith, March 19, 2013). Pastor Bill Monroe, head of the South Carolina MM, disagrees: "If the takeover made Southern Baptists more active, I never saw it," he claims. Monroe mostly expanded MM membership by recruiting churchgoers. The pastors active after the takeover were also active before the takeover. Culturally conservative resolutions did provide protection to pastors who wanted to tell congregants the official position of the SBC on abortion and other issues, without fear of repercussions from their church's board of trustees (interview with Bill Monroe, June 24, 2013).

63. John C. Green, Corwin E. Smidt, Lyman A. Kellstedt, Margaret M. Poloma, and James L. Guth, *The Bully Pulpit: The Politics of Protestant Clergy* (Lawrence: University Press of Kansas, 1998), 145, 149. Religious identities were so bound up with political identities that both conservatives and their opponents hired political consultants without hesitation, sometimes in academic or theological disputes (Smith, *The Rise of Baptist Republicanism*, 58). Only rarely did political entanglement become too excessive. Both President Reagan and Republican nominee George H. W. Bush had to cancel their appearances to the SBC in June 1988. Moderates were alleging the convention was becoming too politicized, and Bush was scheduled to speak on the day a new president was being selected. The president was considered too controversial because, as the media recently revealed, he had hired an astrologer (Doug Wead to Ceci Cole, June 9, 1988, provided by Wead).

64. Meyer never liked the term fusionism, because one does not fuse these fundamental truths together. Rather, they were both true in the same way that "the sun rises" and "sunlight leads to sunburn" are both true.

65. Some view it as the set of ideas bringing about Reagan's election and the growing conservatism of the Republican Party. An anonymous head of an FOF branch told me in an

interview that fusionism defined the three-legged stool in the Reagan coalition. In a follow-up interview, he acknowledged that it was developed in response to communism and encroachments on economic freedom, and it was not designed with cultural issues in mind.

66. Interview with Grover Norquist, July 24, 2010.

67. Interview with Mickey Edwards, March 15, 2011.

68. Interview with an anonymous subject, March 2, 2011.

69. Interview with the author; the subject asked to remain anonymous.

70. William Rusher to WFB, March 1, 1966, WFB Papers.

71. Interview with David Keene, June 3, 2011.

72. Michele McKeegan, *Abortion Politics: Mutiny in the Ranks of the Right* (New York: Free Press, 1992), 8.

73. WFB to James McFadden, April 4, 1973, WFB II 66.

74. Young, *We Gather Together*, 179.

75. Williams, "From the Pews to the Polls," 224.

76. Williams, *God's Own Party*, 155–56.

77. Francis Schaeffer, *Pollution and the Death of Man* (Wheaton, Ill.: Crossway).

78. "Terracide," *Christianity Today* 15 (April 23, 1971); James M. Houston, "The Environmental Movement: Five Causes of Concern," *Christianity Today* 16 (September 15, 1972); Martin LaBar, "A Message To Polluters From the Bible," *Christianity Today* 18 (July 26, 1974; Peter Wilkes, "No Return to Eden: The Debate over Nuclear Power," *Christianity Today* 24 (April 4, 1980); Loren Wilkinson, "Global Housekeeping: Lords or Servants?" *Christianity Today* 24 (June 27, 1980); and George Sweeting, "Entering the Twilight Age: The Energy Problem Comes Full Circle, Exposing Our Sin and Greed," *Christianity Today* 24 (June 27, 1980).

79. Williams, *God's Own Party*, 139.

80. Barry Hankins, *Francis Schaeffer and the Shaping Of Evangelical America* (Grand Rapids, Mich.: Eerdmans, 2008), 202.

81. D. Ingleborg Nimrod to Jerry Falwell, Undated (between 1980 and 1983), Falwell Family Papers Series 1, Box 3–2, Liberty University.

82. Francis A. Schaeffer, *Plan for Action: An Action Alternative Handbook for Whatever Happened to the Human Race?* (New York: F. H. Revell and Company, 1980), 68.

83. Even Falwell, who invoked it to justify the ecumenical outreach of the MM, was never able to extend his political arm much beyond Southern Baptists. Michael Sean Winters, *God's Right Hand: How Jerry Falwell Made God a Republican and Baptized the American Right* ([New York: HarperCollins, 2012), 99, 118–19.

84. Young, *We Gather Together*, 147–53.

85. McKeegan, *Abortion Politics*, 23–25. After *Roe v. Wade* was decided, the National Conference of Catholic Bishops adopted a thirteen-page plan for prolife activities, including an effort in every parish and congressional district. The plan called for a "systematic organization and allocation of the Church's resources of people, institutions and finances," and cooperative ties with other opponents of abortion. The Conference's Family Life Division created the National Right to Life Committee, which had eleven million members in 1979. Boston Archbishop Cardinal Medeiros urged Catholics to vote against any prochoice candidates in 1980. Of course, Catholics were involved in many political causes other than abortion, including world hunger and refugee acceptance, and the National Conference of Catholic Bishops criticized the media for overcovering their position on abortion relative to other issues. Katherine Krimmel, "Special Interest Partisanship: The Transformation of American Political Parties in Government" (paper

presented at the annual meeting of the American Political Science Association in Seattle Washington, 2011), 25.

86. Weyrich declared, "We will not support candidates who are not sound on the abortion issue, and a Carter-like stance (i.e., I am opposed to it but won't do anything about it) won't wash with this committee." Daniel Schlozman, "The Making of Partisan Majorities: Parties, Anchoring Groups, and Electoral Change," Ph.D. dissertation, Harvard University 2011, 220.

87. Williams, "From the Pews to the Polls," 330.

88. Quoted in Williams, "From the Pews to the Polls," 347.

89. Jeffrey K. Hadden, Anson Shupe, James Hawdon, and Kenneth Martin, "Why Jerry Falwell Killed the Moral Majority," in *The God Pumpers: Religion in the Electronic Age* (Bowling Green: Bowling Green State University Popular Press, 1987): 101–15.

90. Young, *We Gather Together*, Chapter 6.

91. Presbyterian J. I. Packer, a harsh critic of Roman Catholic theology, said he approved *Together* because it "declares war on anti-Christian statism and specifies social values that must be fought for . . . It identifies common enemies and pleads that the counterattack be cooperative." One layman commented that "the document pretends to have found common ground between Roman Catholics and Evangelicals when in actuality it appears that all that has been found is that both oppose abortion and pornography . . . The most powerful alliance for influencing of the general society with the message of Christ is not a political alliance, it is the alliance of the message of the Gospel ministered through a changed life." Smith, *The Rise of Baptist Republicanism*, 180.

92. Oldfield, *The Right and the Righteous,* 25–31.

93. Young, *We Gather Together*, 178–82.

94. "Minutes at the home of Carl Henry," Falwell Family Papers Series 1, Box 3–2, Liberty University.

95. Young, *We Gather Together*, 182–84.

96. Schäfer, *Countercultural Conservatives*, 89–93.

97. Young, *We Gather Together*, 225.

98. Michael D. Lindsay, *Faith in the Halls of Power: How Evangelicals Joined the American Elite* (New York: Oxford University Press, 2008), 68.

99. Craig A. Rimmerman, Kenneth D. Wald, and Clyde Wilcox, eds., *The Politics of Gay Rights* (Chicago: University of Chicago Press, 2000), 123. Business groups such as the Chamber of Commerce and National Federation of Independent Businesses rarely involved themselves in abortion or gay rights, and mostly sought to avoid controversy.

100. Interview with Morton Blackwell, April 27, 2011. In 1982, Weyrich organized a one-day conference between evangelicals and "neoconservatives," who had almost no personal contact between each other (Paul Weyrich to Morton Blackwell, June 11, 1982, Morton Blackwell Box 2, OA 1976, RR). Eventually, the meetings became too large for the meeting room, and different kinds of conservatives met at different times and places.

101. Interview with Edward Hudgins (former Heritage Foundation analyst), August 6, 2010.

102. Interview with Paul Weyrich, Martin Religious Right Research Collection.

103. Williams, *God's Own Party*, 181. New Right leaders knew the chances of passing the amendment were small, but hoped to identify supporters and opponents of their agenda on record for the next election (Martin, *With God on Our Side*, 233).

104. Williams, *God's Own Party*, 201–2. SBC president Draper still wanted assurance that the amendment would prevent government employees from writing the prayers. Faith Whittlesey to M. B. Oglesby, February 13, 1984, Carolyn Sundseth Papers Box 3, RR.

Chapter 8

1. Billings later admitted he was bluffing to gain the administration's attention, and his supporters would not have voted for Jackson (interview with Bill Billings by unknown interviewer, October 3, 1995, Martin Religious Right Research Collection).

2. David Karol, *Party Position Change in American Politics: Coalition Management* (Cambridge: Cambridge University Press, 2009).

3. Donald Crichtlow, *Phyllis Schlafly and Grassroots Conservatism* (Princeton, N.J.: Princeton University Press, 2005), 241, 381 n 67.

4. Barry Goldwater, *Goldwater* (New York: Doubleday, 1988), 29.

5. M. Stanton Evans to Ronald Reagan, undated 1975, William Rusher Papers 134 (Committee for a New Majority), Library of Congress, Washington, D.C. (henceforth William Rusher Papers).

6. Crichtlow, *Phyllis Schlafly and Grassroots Conservatism*, 191, 205.

7. Julie Threlkeld, "The Gay Rights Issue in American Politics 1980: Not a Kiss of Death to Politicians; Maybe a Political Plus," National Gay and Lesbian Task Force Records 188, Cornell University.

8. Nick Kotz, "King Midas of the New Right," *Atlantic*, November 1978.

9. Bill Brock did not answer any of my efforts to obtain an interview.

10. Council for a National Policy, Council Update, April 1, 1985, William Rusher Papers 185. The Republican Party sponsored "roving registrars" in many states that registered new people to vote, though not especially targeting cultural conservatives (interview with Mickey Edwards on March 15, 2011).

11. V. O. Key observed that "Southern Republican leaders are usually pictured as vultures awaiting the day when the party wins the nation and they can distribute patronage in the South. Meantime, they exert themselves only to keep the party weak in the South in order that there will be fewer faithful to reward." Quoted in Earl Black and Merle Black, *The Rise of Southern Republicans* (Cambridge, Mass.: Belknap Press of Harvard University Press, 2000), 58. In Arizona, Rep. John Conlan recalls that Republican politicians were upset that he was recruiting hundreds of idealistic new party members in the late 1960s. He said the older politicians "were in politics primarily to become rich in this new dynamic economy of Arizona, if you could control zoning . . . you can take raw acreage that you bought at a dollar . . . an acre, and convert it into industrial or commercial or home developments for this new spreading metropolis that was growing out of Phoenix and Tuscon" (interview with John Conlan, Martin Religious Right Research Collection).

12. Interview with David Keene, June 3, 2011.

13. Interview with Faith Whittlesey, September 21, 1995, Martin Religious Right Research Collection. Other New Right leaders did not specifically bring up social standing, but nonetheless agreed that Republican politicians had a gut-level aversion to the new wave of cultural conservatives. Howard Philips said that establishment Republicans were not "ideologically motivated." "No strong issue or principle" drove their political involvement, and "when they found people who were very strongly motivated by policies and principles, it made them feel a little bit uncomfortable" (interview with Howard Philips on March 18, 2011). STOP ERA leader Phyllis Schlafly attributed establishment Republican resistance to a power struggle in which existing politicians and party leaders feared that culturally conservative, lower-class voters would not follow the lead of party leaders (interview with Phyllis Schlafly on February 14, 2011).

14. William Clyde Wilcox, *God's Warriors: The Christian Right in Twentieth-Century America* (Baltimore: Johns Hopkins University Press, 1992), 175–77.

15. Kitty Kelly, *The Family: The Real Story of the Bush Dynasty* (New York: Bantam, 2005), 430.

16. Daniel Kenneth Williams, "From the Pews to the Polls: The Formation of a Southern Christian Right," Ph.D. dissertation, Brown University, 2005, 420–21.

17. "South Carolina Political Brief," October 9, 1980, RR Box 525 Campaign Papers.

18. Paul L. Martin, "The Conservatives' Drive for a Stronger Voice," *U.S. News and World Report*, July 11, 1977, 47. Viguerie told *U.S. News and World Report* in 1979 that "I just think conservatives have made a mistake in the past by putting all their eggs in the Republican basket. After all, there are more conservatives today in the country who consider themselves members of the Democratic Party." Quoted in "Raising Millions of Dollars for Conservatives—The Way It's Done," *U.S. News and World Report*, February 26, 1979.

19. In Massachusetts, Avi Nelson weakened Massachusetts senator Edward Brooke, who won the Republican nomination, but lost in the general election to Paul Tsongas. Howard Philips also ran in the Democratic Primary, hoping to rally conservative Democrats against Brooke. Schlafly campaigned for a prolife Democrat against "Rockefeller Republican" senator Charles Percy. The New Right fought to replace Baptist minister John Buchanan, an Alabama Republican who had voted to create the Department of Education, with a more conservative Republican. Though Buchanan prevailed in 1978, he was defeated in 1980 when Christians registered five thousand new voters in his district. Buchanan later headed People for the American Way to combat influence of culturally conservative groups. Michele McKeegan, *Abortion Politics: Mutiny in the Ranks of the Right* (New York: Free Press, 1992), 35.

20. Daniel K. Williams, *God's Own Party* (New York: Oxford University Press, 2010), 168.

21. David Wyles, "Hance Defeats Bush," in *W: The Official Film Guide*, http://www.wthefilm .com/guide/pages/27-Hance-Defeats-Bush.html (accessed October 24, 2016).

22. William Rusher to William Brock, December 21, 1978, WFB III: 38. Also see William Rusher, "Raising Conservative Bucks," *National Review*, October 8, 1978, 1531, and Richard Viguerie, *America's Right Turn: How Conservatives Used New and Alternative Media to Take Over America* (New York: Taylor Trade, 2004), 133.

23. William Brock to William Rusher, December 19, 1978, WFB III-38.

24. One study finds that he received far more endorsements from party officials than Bush, Connally, or Illinois Representative John Anderson. Marty Cohen, David Karol, Hans Noel, and John Zaller, *The Party Decides: Presidential Nominations Before and After Reform* (Chicago: University of Chicago Press, 2008), 301. Another finds that even moderates and Bush delegates at the 1980 convention believed that Reagan was the most electable candidate. Walter Stone and Alan Abramowitz, "Winning Isn't Everything, But It's More Than We Thought: Presidential Party Activists in 1980," *American Political Science Review* 77 (1983): 945–56.

25. John Conlan to Ed Meese, May 15, 1980, RR Campaign Papers Box 114.

26. Third Century Publishers distributed theologically conservative books and attempted to prepare conservatives for running for public office. John Conlan to William Casey, April 24 1980, RR Campaign Papers Box 307.

27. John Conlan, untitled memorandum, June 24, 1980, RR Campaign Papers Box 343.

28. Darren Dochuk, *From Bible Belt to Sun Belt: Plain Folk Religion, Grassroots Politics, and the Raise of Evangelical Conservatism* (New York: Norton, 2011), 308.

29. Doug Wead to Ron Kaufman, September 25, 1985, provided by Wead.

30. Pete Hannford to Ed Meese, December 20, 1979, RR Campaign Papers Box 44.

31. Daryl Borgquist to Tony Dolan, "Meeting with Craig King on Key Issues in the South," September 15, 1980, RR Campaign Papers Box 867.

32. Deaver said "I honestly can't tell you in my mind, anyway, or I don't think even in Reagan's mind, an attempt to go out and try to target that kind of a vote. . . . There were organizations of Catholics for Reagan, Labor for Reagan, Pipe-Fitters for Reagan, all that kind-a stuff, and it all got into the mix, so that if we were going to Steubenville, Ohio and it was a . . . Catholic organization or area, we might meet with the representatives of that organization, and Reagan would talk with them about some of these things. But, it was another segment. And I don't think it was much different than what had gone on in politics . . . before that anyway" (interview with Michael Deaver by unknown interviewer, October 7, 1995, Martin Religious Right Research Collection).

33. John Conlan to Bill Timmons, October 22, 1980; Bill Timmons to John Conlan, October 28, 1980, both in RR Campaign Papers Box 256.

34. Elizabeth Dole to Bill Timmons, August 16, 1980, RR Campaign Files Box 256.

35. William Martin, *With God on Our Side: The Rise of the Religious Right in America* (New York: Broadway, 2005), 209.

36. Max Hugel to William Chasey, August 19, 1980, RR Campaign Papers Box 307. According to Don Devine, Hugel, a businessman who had steered Reagan's campaign in New Hampshire, was "very concerned about the negative aspects of being associated with the Christian right" (interview with Don Devine, July 25, 2012).

37. Elizabeth Dole to Bill Timmons, August 16, 1980, RR Campaign Files Box 256.

38. See their letters of recommendation in RR Campaign Files Box 343.

39. See Stan Anderson's comments on Bob Billings to Max Hugel, September 26, 1980, RR Campaign Files Box 307. Billings visited Illinois, Pennsylvania, New Jersey, Ohio, Virginia, Mississippi, Tennessee, and Louisiana.

40. Stan Anderson's comments are written on a copy of "Reagan Visit Worries Staffers," *The Daily Advance*, October 3, 1980; Lorelei Kinder to Stan Anderson, October 9, 1980, RR Campaign Files Box 307.

41. Eleanor Callahan to Max Hugel, September 17, 1980, RR Campaign Papers Box 312; untitled, undated, Box 228, RR Campaign Papers, Voter Groups folder.

42. Ronald Reagan, "Christian Chain Letter," undated, RR Campaign Files Box 248.

43. Sara Diamond, *Roads to Dominion* (New York: Guilford Press, 1995), 209.

44. Kira Sabonmatsu, *Democrats/Republicans and the Politics of Women's Place* (Ann Arbor: University of Michigan Press, 2004), 99.

45. Geoffrey Layman, *The Great Divide: Religious and Cultural Conflict in American Party Politics* (New York: Columbia University Press, 2001), 47.

46. Catherine E. Rymph, *Republican Women: Feminism and Conservatism from Suffrage Through the Rise of the New Right* (Chapel Hill: University of North Carolina Press, 2006), 228.

47. Williams, "From the Pews to the Polls," 371. The presidents of the National Right to Life and Eagle Forum were also pleased. Jo Freeman, "Feminist Activities at the 1988 Republican Convention," *PS: Political Science and Politics* 22, 1 (March 1989): 42–43.

48. John Marley, *Pat Robertson: An American Life* (Lanham, Md.: Rowman and Littlefield, 2007), 79.

49. There is another side to both stories. Reagan's defenders in the movement claim that

because of the assassination attempt on the president, the Secret Service thought appearing in person would be too great of a security risk (interview of Carolyn Sundseth by Bennett Singer, January 28, 1996, Martin Religious Right Research Collection). Reagan may have had an interest in avoiding too close an association with any one preacher in the competitive market of religious broadcasting. Promoting Robertson's new enterprise may have slighted other Pentecostal broadcasters.

50. Martin, *With God on Our Side*, 209.

51. Duane Oldfield, *The Right and the Righteous: The Christian Right Confronts the Republican Party* (Lanham, Md.: Rowman and Littlefield, 1996), 116. Connally also lacked support among established Republican politicians and obtained only 13 percent of the endorsements. Despite spending eleven million dollars, he obtained only one delegate at the 1980 convention (Cohen et al., *The Party Decides*, 195). Both cultural conservatives and party insiders were looking for more than a conservative southern Democrat.

52. Martin, *With God on Our Side*, 209.

53. Robison's show was temporarily cancelled when he labeled the assassination of San Francisco gay rights leaders the "judgment of God." Reagan walked on the platform while Robison was speaking. Robison ranted against "radicals and perverts . . . coming out of the closet." He concluded that not voting is a sin and "It's time for God's people to come out of the closet" (Martin, *With God on Our Side*, 216–17; Oldfield, *The Right and the Righteous*, 117).

54. Rymph, *Republican Women*, 229.

55. Crichtlow, *Phyllis Schlafly and Grassroots Conservatism*, 274.

56. Mary Katznelson and Carol McClurg, eds., *The Women's Movements of the United States and Western Europe* (Philadelphia: Temple University Press, 1987), 230.

57. Matthew C. Moen, *Christian Right and Congress* (Tuscaloosa: University of Alabama Press, 1992), 43.

58. Michael Sean Winters, *God's Right Hand: How Jerry Falwell Made God a Republican and Baptized the American Right* (New York: HarperCollins, 2012), 242.

59. Interview with David Keene, June 3, 2011.

60. Edwards, *The Strategic President*, chapter 2.

61. Williams, *God's Own Party*, 200.

62. Gary Jarmin to School Prayer Leaders, August 9, 1983, Dee Jespen Box 1, RR.

63. Interview with Carolyn Sundseth by Bennett Singer, January 28, 1996, Martin Religious Right Research Collection.

64. Moen, *The Christian Right and Congress*, 133. Aid to the contras, of course, was important to cultural conservatives' anticommunist agenda as well as other kinds of conservatives. Pat Robertson had raised millions of dollars to aid them and several authoritarian, but noncommunist, Central American governments. Williams, *God's Own Party*, 214.

65. Memorandum for Edwin Harper, October 13, 1982, Stephen Galebach Box 1, RR.

66. The "braiding" metaphor is borrowed from Sean Farhang and Ira Katznelson, "The Southern Imposition: Congress and Labor in the New Deal and Fair Deal," *Studies in American Political Development* 19, no. 1 (2005).

Chapter 9

1. See interviews with Jerry Falwell, Bobbie Kilberg, Ralph Reed, and Guy Rodgers, all in Martin Religious Right Research Collection. Also see Daniel K. Williams, *God's Own Party* (New York: Oxford University Press, 2010), 199. One study finds that most state MM chapters were

inactive based on the organization's newsletter. Jeffrey K. Hadden, Anson Shupe, James Hawdon, and Kenneth Martin, "Why Jerry Falwell Killed the Moral Majority," in Marshall W. Fishwork and Roy B. Browne, eds., *The God Pumpers: Religion in the Electronic Age* (Bowling Green, Ky.: Bowling Green State University Popular Press, 1987), 103. An exception was the Illinois MM, which helped defeat the ERA and even affect legislation in other locations. Aaron K. Davis, "The Illusion of Power: The Illinois State Chapter of the Moral Majority, 1980–1988," MA thesis, Western Illinois University, 2010.

2. Justin Watson, *The Christian Coalition: Dreams of Restoration, Demands for Recognition* (New York: Palgrave Macmillan, 1999), 63, 73.

3. Henry E. Brady, Richard Johnston, "What's the Primary Message: Horse Race or Issue Journalism?," in Garry Orren and Nelson Polsby, eds., *Media and Momentum: The New Hampshire Primary and Nomination Politics* (London: Chatham House, 1987), 127–86; Larry M. Bartels, *Presidential Primaries and the Dynamics of Public Choice* (Princeton, N.J.: Princeton University Press, 1988); Patrick J. Kenney and Tom W. Rice, "The Psychology of Political Momentum," *Political Research Quarterly* 47 (1994): 923–38.

4. Dan Gilgoff, *The Jesus Machine: How James Dobson, Focus on the Family, and Evangelical America Are Winning the Culture War* (New York: St. Martin's, 2007), 88.

5. Matthew C. Moen, *Christian Right and Congress* (Tuscaloosa: University of Alabama Press, 1992), 154–56.

6. For example, see Steve Bruce, *The Rise and Fall of the New Christian Right: Conservative Protestant Politics in America, 1978–1988* (Oxford: Clarendon, 1988).

7. Robertson said that his goal was to have "ten trained activists in every district. I was playing for the long haul, and I knew the answer was to move into the precincts, get to know the people and understand their needs and desires, and build an organization." William Martin, *With God on Our Side: The Rise of the Religious Right in America* (New York: Broadway, 2005), 259.

8. Doug Wead, "Religion and Presidential Politics in Iowa," May 7, 1986, provided by Wead.

9. Doug Wead to Lee Atwater, Craig Fuller, Ron Kaufman, and Pete Teeley, November 18, 1985, provided by Wead.

10. A survey of Robertson donors in 1987 revealed that 30 percent of his donors had only become politically active in the past ten years, compared with 7 to 12 percent of the other 1988 Republican contenders. Sara Diamond, *Spiritual Warfare: The Politics of the Christian Right* (Boston: South End Press, 1989), 81. Surveys of campaign contributions show that Robertson contributors were far more likely than other Republican candidates to have donated based on a personal request from a stranger, and more than 70 percent viewed religious television programming weekly. William Clyde Wilcox, *God's Warriors: The Christian Right in Twentieth-Century America* (Baltimore: Johns Hopkins University Press, 1992), 172–78.

11. Interview with Doug Wead, June 21, 2013. Robertson dropped out before the California primary in June, but stayed until May 11. Two other competitors, Robert Dole and Jack Kemp, dropped out before the end of March, recognizing Bush's unstoppable momentum, and Bush had enough delegates to win the nomination on April 26. Although Robertson stayed in the race long after most competitors, he did drop out before he had the chance to campaign among the wealthy evangelical donors in California.

12. Diamond, *Roads to Dominion*, 13.

13. Interview with Lynn Proudfoot, May 23, 2013.

14. Corwin E. Smidt and James M. Penning, eds., *Sojourners in the Wilderness: The Christian Right in Comparative Perspective* (Lanham, Md.: Rowman and Littlefield, 1997), 54.

15. Bruce Nesmith and Jeremy Mayer, "Everything Comes Up Rosy," in Mark J. Rozell and Clyde Wilcox, eds., *God at the Grass Roots* (New York: Rowman and Littlefield, 1997).

16. Neil J. Young, *We Gather Together: The Religious Right and the Problem of Interfaith Politics* (New York: Oxford University Press, 2015), 247.

17. Martin, *With God on Our Side*, 366.

18. Gary Miller and Norman Schofield, "Activists and Partisan Realignment in the United States," *American Political Science Review* 97 (2003): 245–60. Also see Kathleen Bawn, "Constructing "Us': Ideology, Coalition Politics, and False Consciousness," *American Journal of Political Science* 43, no. 2 (1999): 303–34.

19. Geoffrey C. Layman, Thomas M. Carsey, John Green, Richard Herrera, and Rosalyn Cooperman, "Activists and Conflict Extension in American Party Politics," *American Political Science Review* 104 (2010): 2.

20. Wilcox, *God's Warriors*, 197–98.

21. Interview with Ralph Reed, October 23, 1995, Martin Religious Right Collection.

22. Daniel Kenneth Williams, "From the Pews to the Polls: The Formation of a Southern Christian Right," Ph.D. dissertation, Brown University, 2005, 455.

23. Interview with an anonymous source, March 21, 2013. Interviews with Tony Beam (Director of the Christian Worldview Center, March 18, 2013) and Janice McCord (former South Carolina CC Field Director, April 29, 2013) corroborate this account. Drew McKissick disagrees, claiming that theological conservatives had always tended to be economic conservatives (interview on March 20, 2013). As employees of the CC who had worked on Robertson's campaign, McCord's experience with CC members seemed more relevant. All agree that cultural conservatives tend to be economic conservatives today.

24. Interview with Ralph Reed by unknown interviewer, October 23, 1995, Martin Religious Right Research Collection; interview with Michael Horowitz, April 25, 2011.

25. In a 1990 survey of donors to the Christian Coalition, 55 percent ranked abortion the most important issue, followed by education at 13.5 percent (Young, *We Gather Together*, 247).

26. Smidt and Penning, *Sojourners in the Wilderness*, 25.

27. John Marley, *Pat Robertson: An American Life* (Lanham, Md.: Rowman and Littlefield, 2007), 206.

28. Smidt and Penning, *Sojourners in the Wilderness*, 26. One anonymous CC president explained that they tried to persuade members to support viable candidates even when they were not ideological purists; corroborated by interview with Janice McCord,South Carolina Republican executive committeewoman and field director for the South Carolina Christian Coalition), March 21, 2013.

29. Since 1976, the largest changes in press attention from before to after the Iowa caucuses were solid cultural conservatives. Pat Robertson (1988) and Mike Huckabee (2008) experienced a 21 percent increase, and Pat Buchanan (1996) a 17 percent increase. David P. Redlawsk, Caroline J. Tolbert, and Todd Donovan, *Why Iowa? How Caucuses and Sequential Elections Improve the Presidential Nominating Process* (Chicago: University of Chicago Press, 2011) 81, 152–53).

30. John H. Aldrich, *Before the Convention: Strategies and Choices in Presidential Nomination Campaigns* (Chicago: University of Chicago Press, 1980); Nelson W. Polsby, *Consequences of Party Reform* (Oxford: Oxford University Press, 1983).

31. Interview with Eric Woolson, May 24, 2013. This is not to say that the "retail politics" can substitute for paid campaigns. Even Huckabee needed money for phone calls (live and recorded), mail, and advertising. Redlawsk, Tolbert, and Donovan, *Why Iowa?, 26.*

32. Interview with Eric Woolson, May 24, 2013.

33. Interview with Greg Heartsil, May 22, 2013.

34. Bob Dole's campaign hired Steve Scheffler in 1996 and John McCain hired Marlys Popma in 2008. Both had been visible state party activists in the previous two decades.

35. Redlawsk, Tolbert, and Donovan, *Why Iowa*, 116.

36. Kerry Howley, "The Road to the White House is Paved with Pizza," *New York Times*, March 11, 2011.

37. Redlawsk, Tolbert, and Donovan, *Why Iowa*, 151.

38. Interview with Eric Woolson, May 24, 2013.

39. Interview with Julie Roe, May 23, 2013.

40. Subsequent Republican candidates, including Rick Santorum and Michelle Bachmann, attempted to capture the homeschooler vote in 2012, but unlike Huckabee, they had not accomplished anything concrete for homeschoolers. Home School Legal Defense Association founder Michael Farris declined to endorse anyone in 2012 and the homeschooler vote was dispersed among several candidates.

41. Interview with an anonymous member of the Faith and Freedom Coalition, May 23, 2013.

42. Barry Kosmin and Egon Mayer, "American Religious Identification Survey" (published by the Graduate Center of the City University of New York, December 19, 2001); Doug Wead, "Religion and Presidential Politics in Iowa," May 5, 1987, provided by Wead.

43. Michael Sean Winters, *God's Right Hand: How Jerry Falwell Made God a Republican and Baptized the American Right* (New York: HarperCollins, 2012), 117.

44. Interview with an anonymous subject, May 21, 2013.

45. Interview with Lynn Proudfoot, May 23, 2013.

46. Thomas Edsall, "Evangelicals Take on GOP Regulars," *Washington Post*, May 29, 1986; also see Martin, *With God on Our Side*, 265.

47. Interview with Steve Roberts, August 8, 2013. Roberts invited them to his law office and suggested that they walk across the street to the *Des Moines Register* to publish the dispute. His challengers backed away, fearing his informant might leak their private statements to the press. Roberts lost his party position in 2008, with a high turnout among evangelical Christians.

48. Maralee Schwartz, "Fundamentalists Elected," *Washington Post*, April 9, 1986.

49. Interview with Steve Roberts, August 8, 2013.

50. Drew Ivers to George Wittgraf, October 8, 1988, and Drew Ivers to Robertson Campaign, November 4, 1988, provided by Ivers.

51. Drew Ivers to George Wittgraf, October 8, 1988, and Drew Ivers to Robertson Campaign, November 4, 1988, provided by Ivers.

52. Interview with an anonymous subject, May 21, 2013.

53. Richard Berke, "In Many States, Abortion Feuds Splits GOP," *New York Times*, June 20, 1996.

54. Craig Robinson, "Getting to Know Christian Fong," *Iowa Republican*, July 7, 2009.

55. Interview with Steve Roberts, August 8, 2013.

56. Interview with Joy Corning, May 29, 2013. Former New Jersey governor Christine Todd Whitman (June 7, 2013) and Eric Woolson (May 24, 2013) used almost the exact same words as Joy Corning in a separate interview.

57. Barbara Norrander, *Super Tuesday: Regional Politics & Presidential Primaries* (Lexington: University Press of Kentucky, 1992), 98.

58. Georgia held its primary earlier in 1992. Louisiana held its caucuses earlier in 1996.

59. "Absolutely," he said. "They know that if nothing else, it gives a greater outsized role in who the nominee will be. . . . It's less important for us to be at the convention sitting in the seats than to have control or influence over the nomination" (interview with Drew McKissick, March 20, 2013).

60. The cultural conservative candidacies of Reagan (1980), Buchanan (1996), and Buchanan (1992) also received a boost, though not as big, with 17, 11, and 9 percent, respectively. Redlawsk, Tolbert, and Donovan, *Why Iowa*, 148.

61. BJU loyalists have often been elected to the county council, city council, school board, and state senate. Alan Ehrenhalt, *The United States of Ambition: Politicians, Power, and the Pursuit of Office* (New York: Times Books, 1991), 97–99; interview with Oran Smith, March 19, 2013.

62. Interview with George Shissias and Rusty DePass, March 19, 2013.

63. Interview with Janice McCord, April 29, 2013.

64. Interview with anonymous subject, March 21, 2013.

65. Interview with Drew McKissick, March 20, 2013. The CC was influential in electing state party chair Henry McMaster and Governor David Beasley. Beasley won only 43 percent of mainline Protestants, but over 60 percent of evangelical Christians, and won in traditionally Democratic counties (James Guth, "The Christian Right Wins One," in Mark J. Rozaell and Clyde Wilcox, eds., *God at the Grassroots* (Lanham, Md.: Rowman and Littlefield, 1995), 137–39.

66. Oran Smith, *The Rise of Baptist Republicanism* (New York: New York University Press, 2000), 128–29. The Palmetto Family Council, a South Carolina affiliate of FOF, conducted a three-month campaign to increase turnout among evangelical Christians in 2000, but found that most churchgoers were already registered. The CC had done its work all too well (interview with Oran Smith, March 19, 2013).

67. Smith, *The Rise of Baptist Republicanism*, 137.

68. Interview with an anonymous subject, March 21, 2013.

69. Smith, *The Rise of Baptist Republicanism*, 127. Shissias was able to contribute to Beasley's defeat after his first term, but most observers attribute that to the video poker industry rather than internal Republican Party divisions. Beasley did not face any significant primary challenges.

Chapter 10

1. Alan Cooperman, "Openly Religious, to a Point: Bush Leaves the Specifics of His Faith to Speculation," *Washington Post*, September 16, 2004.

2. Interview with Doug Wead, June 21, 2013.

3. Interview with Carl Anderson by unknown interview, November 21, 1995, Martin Religious Right Research Collection.

4. Michael Sean Winters, *God's Right Hand: How Jerry Falwell Made God a Republican and Baptized the American Right* (New York: HarperCollins, 2012), 299.

5. William Clyde Wilcox, *God's Warriors: The Christian Right in Twentieth-century America* (Baltimore: Johns Hopkins University Press, 1992), 154–57. Among Pentecostals, Robertson beat Bush only 45 to 40 percent.

6. Barbara Norrander, *Super Tuesday: Regional Politics & Presidential Primaries* (Lexington: University Press of Kentucky, 1992), 47.

7. Doug Wead to Ron Kaufman, September 25, 1985, provided by Doug Wead. Apart from Pat Robertson, Jim Bakker was possibly the most widely viewed Assemblies of God televangelist.

8. Bo Denysyk, "Coalition Development Preliminary Campaign Plan," May 1987, Box 27, Robert Dole Archives.

9. "Evangelicals for Dole," January 12, 1988, Box 28, Robert Dole Archives.

10. Tanya Melich, *The Republican War Against Women: An Insider's Report from behind the Lines* (New York: Bantam, 1996), 119–22.

11. It sounded as if he had not accepted Jesus's admonition that one must be born again to be admitted to the kingdom of Heaven; he might have at least framed baptism as a rebirth. Even 1984 Democratic nominee Mondale elaborated on his father's ministry rather than provide a one-word answer. Doug Wead to George W. Bush, April 23, 1998, provided by Wead.

12. Doug Wead to Ron Kaufman, October 29, 1985, provided by Wead.

13. John J. Brady, *Bad Boy: The Life and Politics of Lee Atwater* (Reading, Mass.: Addison-Wesley, 1997), 120, 135, 141. Sally Atwater said she does not have a copy of this strategy. On April 22, 2016, the Bush Library indicated that it has the strategy but has not yet made it public, nor is it sure when it will be.

14. Oran Smith, *The Rise of Baptist Republicanism* (New York: New York University Press, 2000), 125.

15. Interview with Doug Wead by Brad Lichtenstein, March 18, 1996; interview with Carolyn Sundseth by Bennett Singer, January 28, 1996, both in Martin Religious Right Research Collection.

16. Interview with Bobbie Kilberg by unknown interviewer, November 20, 1995, Martin Religious Right Research Collection.

17. Atwater and other senior advisers thought Wead's memos exaggerated their influence, but nonetheless relayed them to the vice president (interview with Doug Wead, June 21, 2013).

18. Michigan allocated support for the Republican nomination through a state convention in 1988 consisting of delegates elected at the precinct level in 1986. Bush's Midwest Regional Director, Mary Matalin, gerrymandered Michigan's districts to favor Bush. Robertson's supporters unsuccessfully challenged the plan in court and held separate rump conventions, expecting them to be honored at the national convention. In an effort at reconciliation, Bush campaign leaders offered Robertson's delegates valued seats at the convention, to the chagrin of actual party delegates. William Martin, *With God on Our Side: The Rise of the Religious Right in America* (New York: Broadway, 2005), 285, 291. In Michigan, Robertson won, but the press announced that Bush won for the first two weeks, just as the press announced the wrong Iowa victor in 2012. The Bush campaign had a computerized system that assimilated the results from all of the precincts. Members of the press decided to obtain statewide information using the hour-by-hour reports published by the Bush campaign's computer, which announced that Bush won the state. The campaign knew better (Interview with Doug Wead, June 21, 2013). Wead's estimates of Robertson's delegate count were magnitudes larger than that of any other campaign official, and turned out to be accurate. Ron Kaufman and Lee Atwater, two senior campaign advisors, had estimated that Robertson would recruit about five hundred precinct captains. Wead estimated five thousand, and Bush confronted him with Atwater's figure. Bush said, "I've talked to every county Chairman up there, and they don't know of a single person who's supporting Robertson. I can't figure it out." Wead replied, "I can't figure it out either, Mr. Vice President, but apparently they live in two separate worlds, and were not talking to each other. But they're out there." Martin, *With God on Our Side*, 263.

19. Most of that had been spent, but Robertson had more cash-on-hand than Bush by Super Tuesday as well. Norrander, *Super Tuesday*, 67.

20. Marlin Fitzwater to Doug Wead, June 9, 1986, provided by Doug Wead. When Robertson delivered his Michigan filings at the last minute, Atwater called Wead several times and said "you gotta get back here. We gotta talk." Martin, *With God on Our Side*, 267.

21. Interview with Bobbie Kilberg by unknown interviewer, November 20, 1995, Martin Religious Right Research Collection.

22. Martin, *With God on Our Side*, 263–64. Additionally, professing a born-again experience might alienate nonevangelicals

23. Doug Wead to George W. Bush, April 23, 1998, provided by Wead.

24. Doug Wead, "Evangelical Targets," December 28, 1985, provided by Wead.

25. Doug Wead to Ron Kaufman, October 21, 1985, provided by Wead.

26. Doug Wead to Ron Kaufman, August 25, 1985, provided by Wead. Zeoli, a friend of Wead's, endorsed Bush despite receiving a $194,000 grant from CBN. Doug Wead to Ron Kaufman, May 13, 1986, Office of the Chief of Staff, Vice Presidential Files, George H. W. Bush Presidential Library, College Station, Texas (henceforth Bush Library).

27. Doug Wead to Ceci Cole, June 9, 1988, and June 13, 1988, provided by Wead.

28. E. Ray Moore to Lee Atwater, April 9, 1988, provided by Doug Wead.

29. Out of the leading Pentecostals, he suggested Jim Bakker, whose "Heritage Village" received more visitors than any theme park besides Disneyworld and Disneyland. Doug Wead to Ron Kaufman, October 21 1985, provided by Doug Wead.

30. Doug Wead, "The Vice President and the Evangelicals A Strategy," December 18, 1985, provided by Wead.

31. Doug Wead to Ron Kaufman, May 13, 1986, Office of the Chief of Staff, Vice Presidential Files, Bush Library.

32. Doug Wead, "Evangelical Targets," December 28, 1985, provided by Wead. As it turned out, both Bakker and Swaggart were implicated in serious scandals in 1988, but this arguably hurt other religious broadcasters more than Bush. Robertson's campaign alleged that Bush leaked evidence on them to the press. An associate of Jim Bakker, Richard Dortch, resented Swaggart's attacks on Bakker and confessed to being the source, illustrating the cutthroat nature of religious broadcasting (Martin, *With God on Our Side*, 289).

33. See Vice Presidential Box 13, Folder 9, Bush Library. Bush replied that he found himself "far closer to Dr. Falwell than to his most liberal critics." Bush is quoted in George Bush to Mrs. Douglas Bryant, March 6, 1986.

34. Doug Wead, "Evangelical Targets," December 28, 1985, provided by Wead.

35. Winters, *God's Right Hand*, 299. Despite the care Bush had taken to diversify his support, religious rivalries threatened to undo Bush's evangelical strategy. Falwell announced that he had "delivered" the vice president, suggesting that Bush was not a cultural conservative until Falwell persuaded him otherwise. By making it appear as Bush favored one particular ministry, Falwell undercut Bush's strategy to use him to win over others. Doug Wead to Lee Atwater, January 7, 1986, provided by Wead.

36. Interview with Doug Wead, June 21, 2013.

37. The mailer stressed the impact of bad economic policies on families, although it briefly mentioned fatherless families, pornography, and the "permissive society." The author of the mailer said, "I don't think we can 'out-Falwell' anyone" and Bush "would feel uncomfortable if we tried." Timothy Roper to Craig Fuller, June 17, 1986, provided by Wead.

38. Doug Wead to Craig Fuller, Lee Atwater, Marlin Fitzwater, Ron Kaufman, Peter Teeley, and Bill Philips, "Evangelical Update," January 22, 1986, provided by Wead.

39. Doug Wead, "The Republican Party and the Evangelicals," undated, provided by Wead. Although Iowa is important in presidential nominations, Atwater had visited the state ahead of time and thought it was unwinnable. Even though Bush's local supporters invoked the fear of an evangelical takeover, many moderates who supported Bush in 1980 no longer supported him in 1988. Robertson had beat him to the state's cultural conservative activists and Bush was left without a base of support (Interview with then Christian bookstore owner Lynn Proudfoot, May 23, 2013). He finished in second place (behind Bob Dole) after travelling around the state in a bus. Bush's embarrassing loss in the state was attributed partly to his association with President Reagan, under whom Iowa farmers fared poorly. Jack W. Germond and Jules Witcover, *Whose Broad Stripes and Bright Stars?: The Trivial Pursuit of the Presidency, 1988* (New York: Warner, 1989), 101–2.

40. According to Wead, they would say, "I notice you had tables out in the vestibule last Sunday for Robertson. I'd like to put a table out there for Bush." Most pastors would respond "Nope, this is a church, not a political organization. We're not going to do that. We can't do it for everybody, so we're not going to do it for anybody." It "involved a lot of finances, building relationships, a lot of work. But that turned out to be one of our most effective projects" (Martin, *With God on Our Side*, 279, 289).

41. Interview with Doug Wead, January 21, 2013.

42. Doug Wead to George W. Bush, April 23, 1998, provided by Doug Wead.

43. Doug Wead to George W. Bush, Pete Teeley, and David Q. Bates, April 8, 1988, provided by Doug Wead.

44. Daniel Kenneth Williams, "From the Pews to the Polls: The Formation of a Southern Christian Right," Ph.D. dissertation, Brown University, 2005, 423.

45. Martin, *With God on Our Side*, 293–94. Bush did make a high-profile appearance at the Christian Booksellers Convention in July, the last chance to meet and energize a large congregation of high-ranking evangelicals before the general election (Doug Wead to Cici Cole, June 9, 1988, provided by Wead).

46. Melich, *The Republican War Against Women*, 231.

47. Lisa Young, *Feminists and Party Politics* (Ann Arbor: University of Michigan Press, 2000), 109. Earlier, Bush staffer Lindsay Johnson announced that Bush supported an antiabortion amendment providing exceptions for rape, incest, and the life of the mother. When antiabortion activists resisted, Johnson responded "Since it's not a clean-cut issue, it doesn't pick up anybody . . . so we won't discuss it within any coalition . . . We want a broad base and we don't want to lose anybody." Donald Crichtlow, *Phyllis Schlafly and Grassroots Conservatism* (Princeton, N.J.: Princeton University Press, 2005), 292.

48. Christina Wolbrecht, *The Politics of Women's Rights: Parties, Positions, and Change.* (Princeton, N.J.: Princeton University Press, 2000), 55–60.

49. Melich, *The Republican War Against Women*, 145.

50. George C. Edwards, *The Strategic President: Persuasion and Opportunity in Presidential Leadership* (Princeton, N.J.: Princeton University Press, 2009), 153.

51. "Oh, he has to go" to NRB. "We were very, very, mistaken to have turned him down in 1977. It would be a bad signal not to go this time." Missouri governor John Ashcroft agreed that the NRB was becoming too powerful, but said that if Bush "wants to get re-elected he ought to go." Doug Wead to John Sununu, January 11, 1989, P2/P5 Box 8 (2321), Bush Library). Reagan had spoken to NRB both as a candidate and as president.

52. David Demarest, "Briefing for the President," January 23, 1989, P2/P5 Box 17 (5002), Bush Library.

53. His first appointment to the Supreme Court, David Souter, was ratified by the Democratic Senate with the absence of a record. While Souter later voted with the liberal wing, the president was assured by chief of staff John Sununu that Souter was a conservative. Sununu had met with Souter privately and was convinced by his statements and body language that he would vote to overturn *Roe v. Wade*. John Sununu, *The Quiet Man: The Indispensable Presidency of George H. W. Bush* (Northhampton, Mass.: Broadside, 2015). The National Right to Life Committee supported Souter after hearing that. David Kuo, *Tempting Faith: An Inside Story of Political Seduction* (New York: Simon & Schuster, 2006), 34). Sununu told a group of conservatives that "This is a home run—and the ball is still ascending. In fact, it's just about to leave earth orbit." Robertson wrote to Sununu that "The Souter appointment was brilliant. I noticed your previous comment that 'when you are old and gray people will say that this was your finest act.'" See Pat McGuigan to John Sununu, undated, Box P2/P5 16,281–16550 (Document 16,375); Pat Robertson to John Sununu, July 23, 1990, Subject File, Federal Government (OA/ID 17636); also see James Dobson to George Bush, November 23, 1992, Box Alpha File D, James Dobson File, all in Bush Library. Bush's second appointment, Clarence Thomas, would generally oppose abortion rights and gay rights, sometimes arguing that the majority opinion should have gone further to overturn wrongly decided precedents. Blackwell remembered that "George Bush was absolutely determined that Clarence Thomas was going to be confirmed by the United States Senate, and if there had been a similar determination where the whole White House operation was committed to the confirmation of Judge Robert Bork, he would have been confirmed. But it was of a lesser priority, uh, then; the Reagan administration put a lesser priority on confirmation of Bork than did the Bush administration for the confirmation of Clarence Thomas" (interview with Morton Blackwell by unknown interviewer, July 22, 1995, Martin Religious Right Research Collection). Bush's solicitor general also endured protests from more than two hundred Justice Department lawyers when he argued that *Roe v. Wade* should be overturned (Melich, *The Republican War Against Women*, 274).

54. Memorandum from Doug Wead to David Demarest, July 19, 1989; James Dobson to John Sununu, July 7, 1989, both in Box Alpha File D, James Dobson File, Bush Library.

55. Bush called on Frohnmayer to "take leadership," but consistently opposed content control for government-funded art. Congress passed a law requiring that grants be made in accordance with "general standards of decency" in response to the controversy, but Frohnmayer refused to interpret the law broadly.

56. Jack W. Germond and Jules Witcover, *Mad as Hell: Revolt at the Ballot Box, 1992* (New York: Warner, 1993), 232.

57. Meeting of August 30, 1948, *Minutes of the Executive Board* mf 11.

58. Interview with Morton Blackwell by by unknown interviewer, July 22, 1995, Martin Religious Right Research Collection.

59. Crichtlow, *Phyllis Schlafly and Grassroots Conservatism*, 2. Gary Bauer, Beverly LaHaye, and Morton Blackwell served on the "RNC for Life" committee and actively encouraged abortion opponents to serve as delegates and platform committee members.

60. Duane Oldfield, *The Right and the Righteous: The Christian Right Confronts the Republican Party* (Lanham, Md.: Rowman and Littlefield, 1996), 198.

61. Jo Freeman, "Feminism vs. Family Values: Women at the 1992 Democratic and

Republican Conventions," *PS: Political Science and Politics* 26, no. 1 (March 1993): 22. One of the few prochoice speakers, Massachusetts governor Bill Weld, was booed for supporting abortion rights.

62. Germond and Witcover, *Mad as Hell*, 411; cf. Bruce Nesmith, *The New Republican Coalition* (New York: Peter Lang, 1994), 142. Nesmith quotes Don Devine in 1992 as saying "When you're 26 points behind, the first thing you've got to do is firm up your base."

63. Wolbrecht, *The Politics of Women's Rights*, 64.

64. Oldfield, *The Right and the Righteous*, 195. Oldfield bases this on an interview with NAE's Robert Dugan.

65. Ibid., 201.

66. Interview with Ralph Reed by More, October 23, 1995, Martin Religious Right Research Collection.

67. Nesmith, *The New Republican Coalition*, 143.

68. Interview with Doug Wead, June 21, 2013.

69. See Chapter 8, as well as Mark J. Rozell and Clyde Wilcox, eds., *God at the Grass Roots* (New York: Rowman and Littlefield, 1997), and John Green, Mark Rozell, and Clyde Wilcox, eds., *Prayers in the Precincts: The Christian Right in the 1998 Elections* (Washington, D.C.: Georgetown University Press, 2000).

70. Oldfield, *The Right and the Righteous*, 220.

71. Doug Wead to George W. Bush, January 5, 1998, provided by Doug Wead.

72. Interview with Faith and Freedom Coalition legislative liaison Lynn Proudfoot, who had worked on Buchanan's campaign, May 13, 2013.

73. Dan Gilgoff, *The Jesus Machine: How James Dobson, Focus on the Family, and Evangelical America Are Winning the Culture War* (New York: St. Martin's, 2007), 109.

74. Marty Cohen, "Moral Victories: Cultural Conservatism and the Creation of a New Republican Congressional Majority," Ph.D. dissertation, University of California, Los Angeles, 2005.

75. Interview with Ralph Reed, March 18, 2013.

76. Justin Watson, *The Christian Coalition: Dreams of Restoration, Demands for Recognition* (New York: Palgrave Macmillan, 1999), 82–83.

77. Smith, *The Rise of Baptist Republicanism*, 130; Gilgoff, *The Jesus Machine*, 102.

78. E. E. Schattschneider, *Party Government* (New York: Holt, Rinehart and Winston, 1942), 86.

79. When his communications director, Eric Woolson, traveled through Iowa with Gary Hart and Huckabee, the candidates were happy to meet with a group of six to twenty people at a time. Bush used mass mailers, phone calls, and paid advertising to rally crowds of five hundred people or more. Candidates like Huckabee and Santorum often traveled with their staff in a single car while Bush had a plane that fit a staff of eighteen people (interview with Eric Woolson, May 24, 2013).

80. Doug Wead to Billy Zeoli, January 11, 1998, provided by Wead.

81. Doug Wead to George W. Bush, April 23, 1998, provided by Wead.

82. Doug Wead to George W. Bush, January 27, 1999, provided by Wead.

83. Doug Wead to George W. Bush, September 26, 1998, provided by Wead.

84. Doug Wead to George W. Bush, "Education Hits a Nerve," undated, provided by Wead.

85. Ralph Reed, who attended, said Bush had already won over the people in attendance, but spoke in person to sustain their enthusiasm and active participation in the campaign (interview with Ralph Reed, March 18, 2013).

86. Transcript of a phone call from George W. Bush to Doug Wead, June 8, 1998. Bush had considered him for his ultimate appointment as attorney general as early as June of 1998.

87. Doug Wead to George W. Bush, December 11, 1998, provided by Wead.

88. Marty Cohen, David Karol, Hans Noel, and John Zaller, *The Party Decides: Presidential Nominations Before and After Reform* (Chicago: University of Chicago Press, 2008), 241–43. His criticisms appeared to reflect genuine political leanings, since he voted against an amendment to outlaw gay marriage in 2004.

89. Interview with Ralph Reed, March 18, 2013.

90. Clyde Wilcox and Carin Robinson, *Onward Christian Soldiers? The Religious Right in American Politics* (Boulder, Colo.: Westview, 2011), 111.

91. Interview with Janice McCord, April 29, 2013.

92. McCain was asked if he wanted Democrats to switch parties to vote for him. McCain replied that he welcomed Democrats, communists, vegetarians, and a number of other groups to support him. Reed said it "made it starkly clear that McCain was relying on Democrats to win the nomination" (interview with Ralph Reed, March 18, 2013).

93. Transcript of a phone call between George W. Bush and Doug Wead, September 23, 1998, provided by Wead.

94. Transcript of a phone call between George W. Bush and Doug Wead, undated, provided by Wead.

95. Daniel K. Williams, *God's Own Party* (New York: Oxford University Press, 2010), 257. The FOF was willing to lay off several staffers in their successful fight to repeal gay marriage in California in 2008. Cara Degette, "More Layoffs at Focus on the Family," *Colorado Independent*, November 17, 2008.

96. Gilgoff, *The Jesus Machine*, xii.

97. Williams, *God's Own Party*, 258–61.

98. Gilgoff, *The Jesus Machine*, 164. An anonymous participant in Arlington Group meetings said that the Arlington Group did not contact Bush about the Federal Marriage Amendment. He claimed instead that John Boehner persuaded Bush (interview with an anonymous subject, May 30, 2013). Newspaper accounts indicate that Boehner had such conversations with Bush only after he had changed course.

99. Williams, *God's Own Party*, 252.

100. Interview with Carolyn Sundseth by Bennett Singer, January 28, 1996, Martin Religious Right Research Collection.

101. Gregg Jackson and Steve Deace, *We Won't Get Fooled Again: Where the Christian Right Went Wrong and How to Make America Right Again* (Bridgeport, Conn.: JAJ Publishing, 2011).

102. Interview with Oran Smith, March 19, 2013.

103. Williams, *God's Own Party*, 251. Gary Bauer, Pat Robertson, and James Dobson were reportedly unimpressed (Cohen et al., *The Party Decides*, 242).

104. The Log Cabin Republicans, with whom Romney refused to meet, also sponsored advertisements with this message. Jim Rutenberg, "Log Cabin Republicans Release Anti-Romney Ad," *The Caucus: The Politics and Government Blog of the New York Times*, October 4, 2007).

105. Quoted in Cohen et al., *The Party Decides*, 334. Huckabee also lost support from some cultural conservatives by supporting tax increases in his home state. A member of the Arlington group said that "some evangelicals have held back because [Huckabee] is a challenge to some in the foreign policy ranks and even some fiscal conservative groups are opposed to him" (quoted in Cohen et al., *The Party Decides*, 334). Others thought Romney offered the best balance of

conservatism and electability. Family Research Council president Tony Perkins released a video called Citizen Link that focused on each candidate's weaknesses except for Romney. According to former CNP president Richard Baldwin, this "left the impression that Romney was the last guy standing and should be the guy." Schlafly and Weyrich also jumped on the Romney band-wagon, though Weyrich later said he was wrong to do so.Jackson and Deace, *We Won't Get Fooled Again*, 40–43.

106. John O'Connor, "Is South Carolina Win McCain's Gateway to the South," *Florida Times-Union,* January 20, 2008; interview with Ralph Reed, March 13, 2013. Huckabee said that McCain encouraged Fred Thompson to stay in the race just to drain votes away from him. McCain and Thompson have both denied this allegation. Jim Geraghty, "Fred Thompson: Like Heck I Stayed in the Race to Hurt Huckabee," *National Review*, January 13, 2012.

107. John Heilemann and Mark Halperin, *Game Change: Obama and the Clintons, McCain and Plain, and the Race of a Lifetime* (New York: Harper Perennial, 2010), 353–58.

108. Interview with an anonymous subject, May 21, 2013.

109. Jackson and Deace, *We Won't Get Fooled Again*, 40–43.

110. Dirk Smillie, *Falwell Inc.: Inside a Religious, Political, Educational, and Business Empire* (New York: St. Martin's, 2008), 206–7. Giuliani's aggressive foreign policy stance toward the Middle East may have been an attempt to compensate for his cultural liberalism. While he se-cured Robertson's endorsement, Robertson was well past his peak in influence, and the Family Research Council said the endorsement would further erode his influence. David Kirkpatrick and Michael Cooper, "In a Surprise, Pat Robertson Backs Giuliani," *New York Times*, November 8, 2007.

111. Cohen et al., *The Party Decides*, 340–41.

112. Interview with an anonymous subject, May 21, 2013.

113. Among those present were Gary Bauer, James Dobson, Richard Viguerie, and Paul Pressler (who had switched his vote from Rick Perry). Bob Allen, "Pressler Denies Santorum Endorsement Was Rigged," *Christian Century,* January 18, 2012; and Rick Santorum, "Over 30 National Conservative Leaders Endorse Santorum," January 20, 2012, available at http://www.presidency.ucsb.edu/ws/?pid=99224.

114. Wead told journalists that Santorum supporters were disproportionately represented and he was the only Paul supporter. The original organizer hardly spoke without Family Research Council president Perkins whispering in his ear, he claimed. After the meeting adjourned, at-tendees received text messages saying that Santorum appreciated their support; apparently, San-torum's campaign had been provided with the contact information (interview with Doug Wead, June 21, 2013).

115. Michael Klarman, *From the Closet to the Altar* (New York: Oxford University Press, 2013), 155.

Chapter 11

1. The Task Force, initially the National Gay Task Force, became the National Gay and Les-bian Task Force in 1985 and the National LGBTQ Task Force in 2014. Since the archival records take the name National Gay and Lesbian Task Force, I will use its shorthand in this book.

2. Daniel Letwin, *The Challenge of Interracial Unionism: Alabama Coal Miners, 1878–1921* (Chapel Hill: University of North Carolina Press, 1998). Karin A. Shapiro, *A New South Rebellion: The Battle Against Convict Labor in the Tennessee Coalfields, 1871–1896* (Chapel Hill: University of North Carolina Press, 1998); Matthew Hild, *Greenbackers, Knights of Labor, and Populists:*

Farmer-Labor Insurgency in the Late-Nineteenth-Century South (Athens: University of Georgia Press, 2010).

3. Scott C. James, *Presidents, Parties, and the State: A Party System Perspective on Democratic Regulatory Choice, 1884–1936* (Cambridge: Cambridge University Press, 2006).

4. Michael Kazin, *A Godly Hero: The Life of William Jennings Bryan* (Norwell, Mass.: Anchor, 2007), 115, 283–84.

5. Robert B. Mitchell, *Skirmisher: The Life, Times, and Political Career of James B. Weaver* (Roseville, Minn.: Edinborough Press, 2009), 141. The Southern Alliance was renamed National Farmers' Alliance and Industrial Union.

6. The KOL membership shrank as black membership grew. "Nigger and Knight have become synonymous terms," complained one member in North Carolina. Gretchen Ritter, *Goldbugs and Greenbacks: The Antimonopoly Tradition and the Politics of Finance in America, 1865–1896* (Cambridge: Cambridge University Press, 1999), 211.

7. Hild, *Greenbackers, Knights of Labor, and Populist*, 74.

8. Mitchell, *Skirmisher*, 130.

9. Daniel Schlozman, *When Movements Anchor Parties: Electoral Alignments in American History* (Princeton, N.J.: Princeton University Press, 2015), 145. Gompers had attended a seminal meeting of populists in 1891. American Railway Union Founder Eugene Debs supported the Democratic ticket.

10. Ruth Bordin, *Frances Willard: A Biography* (Chapel Hill: University of North Carolina Press Books, 2014), 180–81.

11. Mitchell, *Skirmisher*, 160, 167–73.

12. Schlozman, *When Movements Anchor Parties*, 113–15.

13. Ibid., 114–15.

14. Charles Postel, *The Populist Vision* (Oxford: Oxford University Press, 2007), 273.

15. Schlozman, *When Movements Anchor Parties*, 114.

16. Kazin, *A Godly Hero*, 68–69, 77; M. Elizabeth Sanders, *Roots of Reform: Farmers, Workers, and the American State, 1877–1917* (Chicago: University of Chicago Press, 1999), 434.

17. Postel, *The Populist Vision*, 223. Even Debs's American Railway Union opposed admitting blacks to his union in order to work better with the Farmers' Alliance.

18. Kazin, *A Godly Hero*, 69.

19. Michael Kazin, *The Populist Persuasion: An American History* (Ithaca, N.Y.: Cornell University Press, 1998), 35, 43. One labor editor from Pittsburgh, for example, wrote that the "The republic cannot afford to have such ignorant animals within its borders," referring to Slavs, Chinese, and Hungarian "black sheep" that could be manipulated into breaking strikes.

20. Ritter, *Goldbugs and Greenbacks*, 249.

21. Kazin, *A Godly Hero*, 106.

22. Most studies looking at change over time rely on aggregate county data, and differ on whether Populists became Democrats, Republicans, or Socialists from 1900 onward. One study of over 400 individual populist votes in California shows that a plurality became Democrats, even among those who began as Republicans. Michael Magliari, "What Happened to the Populist Vote? A California Case Study," *Pacific Historical Review* 64, 3 (August 1995). Delivering their votes as a unified bloc, as the CIO did, may have been a better tactic.

23. Though Bryan continued to insist on free silver in the 1900 platform as a condition of accepting the nomination, he seldom campaigned on the issue, instead attacking the trusts and the Spanish-American War. In 1908, Bryan attacked the power of corporations in

America, but the Republican Party diverged less on actual policy (Kazin, *A Godly Hero*, 100, 106, 154–68).

24. Gerald H. Gaither, *Blacks and the Populist Movement: Ballots and Bigotry in the New South* (Tuscaloosa: University Alabama Press, 2005), 111.

25. Mitchell, *Skirmisher*, 166.

26. Schlozman, *When Movements Anchor Parties*, 112.

27. Kazin argues that they generally appealed to blacks on economic issues while telling white voters that they opposed racial reform. Kazin, *The Populist Persuasion*, 40.

28. Postel, *The Populist Vision*, 177.

29. Gaither, *Blacks and the Populist Movement*, 21, 25.

30. Ibid., 2.

31. Hild, *Greenbackers, Knights of Labor, and Populists*, 79.

32. Postel, *The Populist Vision*, 178.

33. Ibid., 179–80

34. Gaither, *Blacks and the Populist Movement*, 24.

35. Ibid., 78.

36. Ibid., 97, 102, 131.

37. Hild, *Greenbackers, Knights of Labor, and Populists*, 118, 167.

38. They continued to oppose poll taxes, which also prevented poor whites from voting. Postel, *The Populist Vision*, 201.

39. Greg Cantrell and Scott Barton, "Texas Populists and the Failure of Biracial Politics," *Journal of Southern History* 55, no. 4 (November 1989).

40. Gaither, *Blacks and the Populist Movement*, 93.

41. Ritter, *Goldbugs and Greenbacks*, 225.

42. Schlozman, *When Movements Anchor Parties*, 118–19. The 1898 Wilmington Race Riot Commission called him the precipitator of the riot through his writings in the *News and Observer*.

43. Jennifer Delton, *Making Minnesota Liberal* (Minneapolis: University of Minnesota Press, 2002). Ultimately, the Farmer-Labor Party merged with the Democratic Party in 1944, dropping some of the visions of its more radical founders.

44. Tina Fetner, *How the Religious Right Shaped Lesbian and Gay Activism* (Minneapolis: University of Minnesota Press, 2008).

45. In the 111th Congress, thirteen states had senators from different parties. Democratic senators from these states receive an average of 88 percent from HRC, compared with 10 percent for Republicans from the same states. David Karol, "Party Position Change and the Politics of Gay Rights in the U.S. Congress," paper at APSA 2011 Annual Meeting, 7.

46. Such health centers emerged in Washington, D.C., Los Angeles, and San Francisco, among others (interview with Jeffrey Levy, August 15, 2014; interview with Lance Ringel, July 18, 2014).

47. Craig A. Rimmerman, *From Identity to Politics: The Lesbian and Gay Movements in the United States* (Philadelphia: Temple University Press, 2002), 173. During the second Bush administration, NGLTF's executive director criticized groups for working with the administration, even for AIDS funding in Africa. Gays and lesbians needed to be part of a larger campaign that included welfare benefits, abortion rights, affirmative action, and environmental issues. Shawn Zaller, "Marching on But Apart," *National Journal* 34, no. 2 (January 12, 2002).

48. Interview with Lance Ringel, July 18, 2014; Coexecutive Directors to Board of Directors,

June 1978, NGLTF Box 2, Division of Rare and Manuscript Collections, Cornell University Library, Ithaca New York (henceforth NGLTF).

49. Foreman and Heidepriem to Board of Directors of the Triangle Institute, February 2, 1988, HRC Box 6, Division of Rare and Manuscript Collections, Cornell University Library, Ithaca New York (henceforth HRC).

50. "McGovern Denies Gay Rights Statement," undated, *The Fountain*, NGLTF 171.

51. Karol, "Party Position Change and the Politics of Gay Rights in the US Congress," 4; Jean O'Leary, "From Agitator to Insider," in John D'Emilio, William B. Turner, and Urvashi Vaid, eds., *Creating Change: Sexuality, Public Policy, and Civil Rights* (New York: St. Martin's, 2000), 88–92.

52. Dudley Clendinen and Adam Nagourney, *Out for Good: The Struggle to Build a Gay Rights Movement in America* (New York: Simon and Schuster, 2001), 272.

53. Interview with Ginny Apuzzo, July 15, 2014.

54. Jo Daly, quoted in Clendinen and Nagourney, *Out for Good*, 278.

55. Paul Smith (Iowa delegate), "Response to NGLTF Platform Recommendations," undated 1976, NGLTF 171.

56. Clendinen and Nagourney, *Out for Good*, 276–77.

57. The president's surgeon general no longer participated in screening immigrants for sexual orientation. Charles Brydon to Margaret Standish (Playboy Foundation), November 14, 1979, NGLTF 188.

58. Midge Costanza was ultimately dismissed for criticizing Carter from the left, which was upsetting to gay rights as well as feminist groups. J. Brooks Flippen, *Jimmy Carter, the Politics of Family, and the Rise of the Religious Right* (Athens: University of Georgia Press, 2011, 133.

59. Midge Costanza to the President, February 21, 1978; Richard Pettigrew to the president, February 22, 1978. Eizenstat said, "We must not be hamstrung by taking an unpopular stand, i.e. support of gay rights. It will cost us votes in the Senate and muddy the waters . . . In the House, this language might be difficult to pass—if any language is included, it should be very low key" (Stu Eizenstat and Steve Simmons, Feb 25, 1978). Both in Carter Presidential Papers-Staff Offices, Box 74, Jimmy Carter Presidential Library.

60. Flippen, *Jimmy Carter*, 144, 181.

61. Ibid., 140; Self, *All in the Family: The Realignment of American Democracy Since the 1960s* (New York, N.Y.: Hill and Wang, 2012), 321. Carter eventually said, "we must not limit our vision of what a good family is just to what a family was in the past" (Flippen, 220), but his appointed conference organizer said the conference would not be a "referendum on homosexuality" (Self, *All in the Family*, 333–35).

62. Flippen, *Jimmy Carter,* 147. The commission recognized gay rights after contentious debates.Carol Foreman and Nikki Heidepriem to Board of Directors of the Triangle Institute, February 2, 1988, HRC Box 6.

63. *Gay Community News*, November 10, 1979, NGLTF 79. The organization said the platform would "give gay activists leverage to open doors and get help from party sources," but "most importantly, it would be an important step in forging a majority coalition in the country in support for human rights for gay people" ("Gayvote," July 11 1980, NGLTF 171).

64. O'Leary, "From Agitator to Insider," 86, 94.

65. GRNL Board of Directors General Report Packet, February 21, 1981, HRC Box 6.

66. Kurt Vorndran, "Voter Registration Handbook," 1984, NGLTF Box 141.

67. Susan Green to Jim Featherstonnauge, March 4, 1982, HRC Box 5.

68. NGLTF to members, October 9, 1978, NGLTF Box 171. A New York ERA interest group admitted that the ERA would accomplish no legal victories for gay rights but "will demonstrate popular support for a more humanistic government."

69. Untitled notes for Gay Male Resource Book outline, undated 1977, NGLTF Box 2.

70. The executive director also met with the ACLU's director and persuaded him to send letters to every member of Congress."NGTF Wins Congress Support from ACLU and NOW," undated 1974, NGLTF Box 167).

71. Charles Brydon to Margaret Standish, September 30, 1980, NGLTF Box 168.

72. Rimmerman, *From Identity to Politics*, 173; Press Release on Organized Labor, March 24, 1982, HRC Box 5.

73. Kitty Krupat and Patrick McCreery, *Out at Work: Building a Gay-Labor Alliance* (Minneapolis: University of Minnesota Press, 2001), 24, 28.

74. Interview with Ginny Apuzzo, July 25, 2014.

75. Minutes of the Board of Directors Meeting, September 22, 2000, NEA Box 94, NEA Records, Estelle and Melvin Gelman Library, George Washington University (henceforth NEA); NGLTF, "The National Education Association," 1981, 52, NGLTF Box 167.

76. Although the first group of openly gay teachers were not taken seriously, NEA first recognized a gay caucus in 1972 to advocate for legislation pertinent to gays and drew up materials to educate the community about gay teachers and students (NEA Gay Teachers Caucus, undated, NEA Box 167 folder 8; NGLTF, "National Education Association," 1981, 53, NGLTF 167; John Mathews, "Gay Teachers at Convention Seek Rights," July 3, 1973, *Sunday Star*). Among other signs of its support, its 1979–80 handbook added sexual orientation to race, national origin, religion, sex, age, handicap, and economic status as sources of discrimination that Americans should eliminate. In 1988, it began developing plans to improve the effectiveness of teachers in working with gay and lesbian students, learning from programs in big cities that offered counseling for them (Minutes of the Annual Meeting of the NEA Representative Assembly, July 7, 1988, 262). By the early 1990s, the NEA called for affiliates to submit their contract language addressing civil rights and hiring practices related to sexual orientation, lamenting that most affiliates had no provisions on the subject ("Language on Sexual Orientation, NBI 1991–93," NEA Box 3080, folder 13).

77. Gareth Davies, *See Government Grow: Education Politics from Johnson to Reagan* (Lawrence: University Press of Kansas, 2007), 222–28.

78. FPA Meeting, October 2, 1981, NGLTF Box 147.

79. Interview with Leonard DeFiore, former superintendent of Catholic schools in Washington, D.C., March 24, 2011. In some cases, textbooks were considered insufficiently anticommunist by groups such as the John Birch Society, Billy James Hargis's Christian Crusade, and Young America's Foundation. The NEA worked to repeal the "Hatch Amendment" of 1978, which prevented schools from examining students psychologically without their consent. In 1985, the RA declared that teachers "must be legally protected from censorship because it is the right of every individual to live in an environment of freely available information, knowledge, and wisdom about sexuality." Other groups took over Parent Teacher Associations (PTA) and complained that teachers should not have the discretion to veer from an approved curriculum or answer questions about controversial issues (*The Reporter*, "Revivalism on the Far Right, July 20, 1961, NEA Box 2161 and *School Management*, "How to Cope with Attacks from the Fanatic Fringe," undated, NEA Box 2156, folder 7). Administrators responded by having set procedures for the adoption of curriculum and good relations with PTA.

80. Though it voted for a gay rights resolution in 1970, it was not proactive until the Briggs initiative of 1978 (Albert Shanker to Bruce Voeller, March 4, 1974, NGLTF Box 171). The AFT came around to this position in spite of its longtime president Albert Shanker, who opposed a gay rights resolution in New York City's flagship AFT union because it was too divisive. Karen Marie Harbeck, *Gay and Lesbian Educators: Personal Freedoms, Public Constraints* (Malden, Mass.: Amethyst, 1997), 243. Nonetheless, school teachers formed groups for gay teachers that successfully pressured the AFT to issue an unequivocal statement of opposition to the Briggs initiative Sara Smith, "Organizing for Social Justice: Rank-and-File Teachers' Activism and Social Unionism in California, 1948–1978," Ph.D. dissertation, University of California Santa Cruz, 2014, 364.

81. Interview with Jeffrey Levy, August 15, 2014 and Lance Ringel, July 18, 2014.

82. Clendinen and Nagourney, *Out for Good*, 477.

83. Rimmerman, *From Identity to Politics*, 173.

84. "Key issues for next meeting," April 28 Box 1984, NGLTF 3; NGLTF staff to NGLTF Board, November 1988, NGLTF Box 191.

85. "National Issues Agenda" draft, undated, NGLTF Box 3.

86. Carol Foreman and Nikki Heidepriem to Board of Directors of the Triangle Institute, February 2, 1988, HRC Box 6.

87. Marjorie Storch (Charlotte president of NOW) to Mary Jean Collins (vice president for political action), November 12, 1983, NOW Carton 100 Box 35.

88. Mary Jean Collins to the National Board, May 4, 1984, NOW Box 5.

89. Democratic Task Force Meeting Minutes, May 18, 1984, NWPC Box 286, Schlesinger Library, Radcliffe Institute for Advanced Studies (henceforth NWPC).

90. Presidential candidate Jerry Brown had also done so in 1980, but he was not a frontrunner.

91. "Mondale Adds Gay Consultant: Hart Gay Aide Departs," NGLTF Box 171.

92. Clendinen and Nagourney, *Out for Good*, 504.

93. Urvashi Vaid to NGLTF Board of Directors, March 17, 1992, NGLTF Box 3.

94. Obama also toured with a gospel singer who said God had delivered him from homosexuality. He denied he was choosing between two constituencies, pointing out that he was also accompanied by a gay pastor and hoped to promote a dialogue. However, the gay pastor spoke only briefly compared with the gospel singer. Kerry Eleveld, *Don't Tell Me to Wait: How the Fight for Gay Rights Changed America and Transformed Obama's Presidency* (New York: Basic, 2015), 8–14.

95. Elsewhere, Obama said that he opposed the proposition because marriage was already a matter of state law, while also saying he supported the right of states to make their own decision on such issues. He refused to say to a reporter that the California referendum bothered him. Eleveld, *Don't Tell Me to Wait*, xi, 29, 195.

96. David Axelrod, *Believer: My Forty Years in Politics* (New York: Penguin, 2015), 447. In 1996, Obama wrote on a gay newspaper's questionnaire that he supported marriage equality, but said he was undecided two years later, and opposed it during the 2008 election. Documentation of his earlier support did not surface until after he won the election. Privately, his campaign advisers thought he had supported it all along. Mark Halperin and John Heilemann, *Double Down: Game Change 2012* (New York: Penguin, 2013), 57.

97. Eleveld, *Don't Tell Me to Wait*, 55, 89, 102.

98. Ibid., 262.

99. Axelrod, *Believer*, 447.

100. Halperin and Heilemann claim that Obama had privately decided to make an announcement in support of gay marriage after widespread support for Freedom to Marry's platform, but no final decision was made about the time or venue. Halperin and Heilemann, *Doubling Down*, 298.

101. Eleveld, *Don't Tell Me to Wait*, 254–56.

Conclusion

1. William H. Riker, "Implications from the Disequilibrium of Majority Rule for the Study of Institutions," *American Political Science Review* 74, no. 2 (1980): 445.

2. Daniel Schlozman, *When Movements Anchor Parties: Electoral Alignments in American History* (Princeton: Princeton University Press, 2015), 151.

3. Interview with Christine Todd Whitman, June 7, 2013.

4. Interview with Drew McKissick, March 20, 2013. For another effort to defeat Tea Party Republicans, see Michael Bender and Kathleen Hunter, "Republican Civil War Erupts: Business Groups vs. Tea Party," *Bloomberg News*, October 18, 2013.

5. Some state-level chapters of said groups endorsed Sanders. The national AFL-CIO has stayed neutral.

6. Marty Cohen, David Karol, Hans Noel, and John Zaller, *The Party Decides: Presidential Nominations Before and After Reform* (Chicago: University of Chicago Press, 2008).

7. Nominal evangelical Christians strongly support Trump, but active churchgoers with constrained religious beliefs do not (https://www.barna.org/research/culture-media/research-release/americas-faith-segments-divided-presidential-race#); Geoffrey Layman, "Where Is Trump's Evangelical Base? Not in Church," The Monkey Cage at the *Washington Post*, March 29, 2016.

8. Seth Masket, "Is the GOP Deciding? The Evidence Post-South Carolina," *The Mischiefs of Faction* blog at Vox.com, February 23, 2016.

9. Eric Garcia, "Can Marco Rubio Appeal to Evangelicals." *Roll Call*, January 8, 2016.

10. "Is American Christianity Turning Charismatic?" Barna.org, January 7, 2008.

11. Sarah Pulliam Bailey, "Still the Best Candidate: Some Evangelicals Still Back Trump Despite Lewd Video," *Washington Post*, October 8, 2016.

12. Untitled Manuscript, 1975–1976, William Rusher Papers 142 ("Committee for a New Majority"), 12.

13. Kevin S. Price, "The Partisan Legacies of Preemptive Leadership: Assessing the Eisenhower Cohorts in the U.S. House," *Political Research Quarterly* 55 (2002): 609–31.

14. Hans Noel, "Why Can't the G.O.P. Stop Trump?" *New York Times*, March 1, 2016.

15. Phrase adopted from Marty Cohen, David Karol, Hans Noel, and John Zaller, "Beating Reform: The Resurgence of Parties in Presidential Nominations, 1980–2000" (prepared for presentation at the annual meeting of the American Political Science Association, 2001).

16. Schattschneider, *The Semisovereign People,* 54–57.

17. Walter Dean Burnham, *Critical Elections and the Mainsprings of American Politics* (New York: Norton, 1970), 133.

18. Marjorie Hershey, *Party Politics in America* (New York: Pearson-Longman, 2000), 305.

19. They lambasted ideological "hybrids" and sought a Democratic Party committed to the "programmatic liberalism" of the New Deal. The APSA even authored a one hundred-page pamphlet called *Toward a More Responsible Two-Party System*, arguing that the responsive parties

should reflect pure liberal and conservative ideologies despite the lack of support for such party reforms in opinion polls at the time. See Sam Rosenfeld, "The Idea of Responsible Partisanship" (Ph.D. dissertation, Harvard University, 1–13). The first chapter is available at http://scholar.harvard.edu/files/samrosenfeld/files/rosenfeld_-_dissertation_chapter_1.pdf.

20. Robert A. Dahl, *A Preface to Democratic Theory* (Chicago: University of Chicago Press, 2013), 92–102.

21. Mancur Olson, *The Logic of Collective Action* (Cambridge Mass.: Harvard University Press, 1965).

22. Kenneth J. Arrow, *Social Choice and Individual Values* (New Haven, Conn.: Yale University Press, 2012).

23. Doug Wead to Craig Fuller, Lee Atwater, Ron Kaufman, Peter Teeley, and Bill Philips, January 16, 1986, provided by Wead.

24. Law provided Wead with "names and addresses, national networks of information, fund raisers, resource people, suggestions of prominent Catholics of influence who we might cultivate for our Steering Committee, even ideas on strategy" (Doug Wead to Ron Kaufman, June 12, 1986, provided by Wead).

25. Neil J. Young, *We Gather Together: The Religious Right and the Problem of Interfaith Politics* (Oxford University Press, 2015), 227.

26. Larry M. Bartels, "What's the Matter with What's the Matter with Kansas?" *Quarterly Journal of Political Science* 1, no. 2 (2006): 201–26.

27. Douglas J. Ahler and David E. Broockman, "Does Polarization Imply Poor Representation? A New Perspective on the "Disconnect" Between Politicians and Voters" (working paper, 2015, available at https://people.stanford.edu/dbroock/sites/ default/files/ ahler_broockman _ideological_innocence.pdf).

28. Ian Shapiro, *Democracy's Place* (Ithaca, N.Y.: Cornell University Press, 1996, 48).

MANUSCRIPT SOURCES

Archival Sources

Boston, Massachusetts—John F. Kennedy Library
    Democratic National Committee Papers 1932–1964
    John F. Kennedy Papers
    Robert F. Kennedy Papers
    Theodore Sorensen Papers
Cambridge Massachusetts—Radcliffe Institute for Advanced Study
    Records of the National Organization for Women
    Records of the National Women's Political Caucus
College Station, Texas—George H. W. Bush Presidential Library
Detroit, Michigan—Walter Reuther Library
    CIO Office of the Secretary-Treasurer Records (JBC)
    UAW Presidents Office: Walter P. Reuther Records
Houston, Texas—Rice University
    William Martin Religious Right Research Collection
Independence, Missour—Harry S. Truman Library
    Clark Clifford Papers
    George Elsey Papers
    J. Howard McGrath Papers
    Phileo Nash Papers
    Stephen Spingarn Papers
    Harry S. Truman Papers
Ithaca, New York—Cornell University Library
    Records of the Human Rights Campaign Fund
    Records of the National Gay and Lesbian Task Force
Lawrence, Kansas—Robert J. Dole Institute of Politics
    Robert J. Dole Archives and Special Collections
New Haven, Connecticut—Yale University
    William F. Buckley (WFB) Papers
New Haven, Connecticut—Yale Collection of American Literature, Beinecke Rare Book and
    Manuscript Library.
    Walter Francis White and Poppy Cannon Papers

Princeton, New Jersey—Seeley G. Mudd Manuscript Library
    Adlai Stevenson Papers
Simi Valley, California—Ronald Reagan Presidential Library
Tempe, Arizona—Arizona Historical Society
    Barry M. Goldwater Papers
Washington, D.C.—Catholic University
    John Brophy Papers
    Philip Murray Papers
Washington, D.C.—Georgetown University
    Leon Keyserling Papers
    Robert F. Wagner Papers
Washington, D.C.—Estelle and Melvin Gelman Library
    Records of the National Education Association
Washington, D.C.—Library of Congress
    William E. Baroody Papers
    Bainbridge Colby Papers
    James A. Farley Papers
    Henry P. Fletcher Papers
    John D. Hamilton Papers
    Jack Kroll Papers
    NAACP Papers
    Edward V. Rickenbacker Papers
    Paul Sifton Papers
    William Rusher Papers
    Robert Taft Papers
    James W. Wadsworth Papers
    Roy Wilkins Papers

Microfilm Manuscript Collections

Ericson, Jack T. 1979. *Americans for Democratic Action Papers, 1932–1965*. Sanford, N.C.: Microfilming Corporation of America.

Martin, Katherine F., ed. 1980. *Operation Dixie: The CIO Organizing Committee Papers, 1946–1953*. Sanford, N.C.: Microfilming Corporation of America.

Zieger, Robert H., ed. 1994. *Minutes of the Executive Board of the Congress of Industrial Organizations, 1935–1955*. Frederick, Md.: University Publications of America.

133, 144, 169, 268, 269, 272; on abortion, 106; on civil rights, 268n79, 269n84
Noel, Hans, 5, 8, 12, 16, 26, 121, 228
nominations: overview of importance to party transformation, 13–17
Norquist, Grover, 133
nuclear weapons, 118, 135, 230

Obama, Barack, 205; on gay rights, 213–15, 303nn94–96, 304n100
O'Connor, Sandra Day, 107
O'Donnell, Christine, 14, 16
officeholders: as impediments to party change, 4, 7–15, 23, 121, 142
O'Leary, Jean, 207, 208
Olson, Mancur, 10, 229
Operation Dixie, 43, 56, 58, 59, 62, 255n53
Ovington, Mary White, 37, 38, 45

Paden, Catherine, 26
Palin, Sarah, 191, 225
Parker, Alton, 24, 31, 196
Parker, John, 24, 31
party bosses, 30, 75, 166, 193, 203, 262–63nn82–83; role in party change, 79, 83
party identification, 8, 11, 12, 73, 81, 92, 104; among blacks, 81; among Catholics, 270n9
party platforms: importance of, 15–16, 69–70
party primaries: compared and contrasted with conventions 13, 19, 156–57, 174, 178–79; role of median voters, 229–30; role of nonbinding primaries, 91, 95
Patterson, Paige, 131, 132, 188
Paul, Ron, 163, 166, 192
Pentecostal Christians, 103–4, 111–13, 116, 124, 128, 138, 159–60, 170, 176–77, 179, 186, 188, 273nn58–59; relationship with Holiness Churches, 112–13
Pepper, Claude, 29
Pew, John Howard, 117, 129, 133
Philips, Howard, 122, 127, 129, 284n13, 285n19
Phillips, Kevin, 276n9
Piven, Frances Fox, 61
political parties: defined, 3; and democracy, 23, 110, 228, 229, 231, 234, 235, 304–5n19;

and median voters, 5, 14, 70, 150, 185, 228–30
poll tax, 55, 56, 66, 72, 74, 237, 249, 259, 300
Pomper, Gerald, 15
Poole, Keith, 18
Populist Party, 7, 19, 22, 25, 62, 194–204, 215, 218, 221, 299n22, 300; racial divisions, 200–204, 300n27; as test of claims, 19–20, 22
Powell, Adam Clayton, 92, 244, 268n84
Powell Amendment, 90
Powell Memo, 104
President's Committee on Civil Rights (PCCR), 49, 56, 63, 78, 250n167
Pressler, Paul, 131, 132, 192, 193, 271n36
primary sources: use in political science, 17–21
Progressive Party, 17, 44, 57, 83
Prohibition, 104, 196, 198
prolife movement. *See* abortion
protectionism, 226–27
Protestants: decline in mainline membership, 124–25; mainline, 1, 104, 107, 108, 115, 118, 124, 160, 167, 168, 177, 188, 271nn35–37, 272, 291. *See also* evangelical Christians; fundamentalist Christians; individual denominations; theological conservatives
public opinion: as explanation of party change, 12, 42–43, 70, 205; and gay rights, 209, 214–15
pundits: role in ideology, 8–9

Quayle, Dan, 167, 170

Randolph, A. Philip, 30–31, 49–50, 60, 62, 238n5, 241n41, 242n58, 249n142, 250n155
Rauh, Joseph, 95–96
Rayburn, Sam, 91, 265n39
Reagan, Ronald, 20, 22, 104, 106–8, 114, 122–23, 127–28, 139, 142–55, 159, 169, 173, 175–77, 179, 181–83, 185–87, 189–93, 208, 220, 230, 234n22, 270n118, 281n63, 285n24, 286–87n49, 291, 294, 295; and antiabortion amendment, 153–54; lack of campaign outreach to cultural

ACKNOWLEDGEMENTS

I have been working on this book for more than seven years, and most of it passed by far too quickly. In that time, entire work weeks would be spent sifting through dusty old boxes and sleeping in Motel 6s, with little or no social contact save for the dedicated archivists and night shift receptionists. Despite the solitary nature of this line of work, this book could not have been done without the help of other people. I would like to thank, first and foremost, John Zaller for his guidance, from prospectus stage to book stage. Professor Zaller read over several versions of this manuscript and offered constructive feedback on both the substance and style for many years after I finished the first draft. Though he works primarily with quantitative methods, he was always open to other approaches to investigating American politics. Professor Zaller and his cohorts, including Kathy Bawn, Marty Cohen, David Karol, Seth Masket, and Hans Noel developed the line of research on parties that inspired this project.

Several other scholars warrant praise for the amount of time they spent reading early versions of my work. Among them, Scott James stands out for reading several drafts. Rachael Cobb and David Karol also provided important, timely, feedback. Eric Schickler and two anonymous reviewers working for *Studies in American Political Development* provided helpful feedback for my research on civil rights at a critical juncture. Kenneth Kersch, whose critique of Whig history informed this book, was also generous enough to read the whole manuscript, as well as my friend Kate Brick.

Rick Vallely and Peter Agree at the University of Pennsylvania Press supported this project enthusiastically from the very beginning. Two anonymous reviewers working on behalf of University of Pennsylvania Press offered excellent feedback and pushed me to clarify the claims being made. *First to the Party* is a much stronger book as a result of their scrutiny. Lily Palladino and Alison Anderson were exceptionally responsive and thorough editors.

As I said, I had to travel to numerous historical archives to complete this book. My requests for boxes of materials were extensive and the turnarounds between requests for boxes and their arrival to my work station were quick. I thank the efficient archivists at the Beinecke Rare Book and Manuscript Library at Yale University, Catholic University, Cornell University Library, the George Bush Presidential Library, Georgetown University, the Harry S. Truman Library, the John F. Kennedy Library, the Library of Congress, the Robert J. Dole Institute of Congress, the Ronald Reagan Presidential Library, the Schlesinger Library at Radcliffe College, and the Seeley G. Mudd Manuscript Library. Historians Beth Tompkins Bates and Kenneth Janken offered helpful advice as well as some documents relevant to civil rights research. Arlington Public Library offered a great service by obtaining microfilm via interlibrary loan. William Martin saved me a costly trip to the Woodson Research Center at Rice University by sending me transcripts of his informative interviews with cultural conservatives and their interlocutors. The Robert J. Dole Institute of Congress, Wellesley College, and the College of the Holy Cross provided generous funding for travelling to archives and interviewing subjects in other states. I will forever appreciate the YMCA at Oak Square for providing a desk in a sunny stairwell that I often used as a writing space.

Numerous activists freely gave their time as interview subjects, providing important data for recent years where archival evidence is not yet complete. Most of these subjects have busy lives and could have easily ignored my requests. I thank Ginny Apuzzo, Kevin Baird, Tony Beam, Morton Blackwell, David Boaz, Roberta Combs, Joy Corning, Cindy Costa, Steve Deace, Rusty DePasse, Don Devine, Leonard DiFiore, Mickey Edwards, Tim Goeglin, Greg Heartsil, Michael Horowitz, Ed Hudgins, Drew Ivers, Darrell Kearney, David Keene, Brian Kennedy, Erica Kraus, Jeff Levi, Joe Mack, Gary Marx, Janice McCord, Drew McKissick, Gene Meyer, Jan Mickelson, Bill Monroe, E. Ray Moore, Pat Murphy, David Nagle, Grover Norquist, Howard Phillips, Marlys Popma, Lynn Proudfoot, Lance Ringel, Ralph Reed, Steve Roberts, Julie Roe, Terry Scanlon, Phyllis Schlafly, Tamara Scott, George Shissias, Amy Sinclair, Karen Slifka, Oran Smith, Christine Todd-Whitman, Richard Viguerie, Doug Wead, and Eric Woolson. I owe special thanks to Doug Wead and Drew Ivers for sharing written records with me.

My parents have always been supportive of my choice of a career in academia and my graduate school education. Numerous other people offered all kinds of support—intellectual, financial, and emotional. Some offered support of the crash space and airport pickup as well. I will do my best to be comprehensive to those to whom I owe my sincere gratitude: Hovannes Abramyan, Nigel Ashford, Charles Backman, Libby Barringer, Kate Brick, Tom Burke, Edward Carmines, Daniel Di Salvo, Daniel Carpenter, Anthony Chen, Rachael Cobb, Jose Duarte, Justin and Emily Ekins, Hahrie Han, Michael Heaney, David Kelley, Jackie Kerr, Jonathan Kirzner, John Malsberger, James Marshall, Rob Mickey, Kira Newman, Analise McNeill, Or Meiri, Carmen Pavel, Ben Parizek, Amanda Philips, Joe Pompei, Daniel Richards, Fabio Rojas, Scott and Corlis Schneider, Theodore Schick, Daniel Schlozman, Ilya and Alison Somin, Rose Talbert, Michael Tesler, William Thomas, Jason Walker, Nate Wolff, and Carolyn Yeh.